The Spanish Civil War

The Spanish Civil War has long been approached by historians as a single, self-contained event and as a dichotomous conflict between Christianity and atheism, fascism and democracy, capitalism and socialism. *The Spanish Civil War: A Modern Tragedy*, the first book on the subject to combine an integrative analysis with primary source material, moves beyond this one-dimensional, reductionist view to examine it as a multifaceted, heterogeneous conflict, providing:

- an up-to-date analysis of both domestic and international aspects of the war
- an examination of the impact of gender and race on events
- the inclusion of key primary sources from contemporary media accounts, diplomatic records, political publications and popular propaganda
- the use of rare documents, published for the first time
- a guide to further reading and glossary
- a critical overview of the key historiographical issues regarding the Civil War and Revolution

George Esenwein teaches at the University of Florida. In addition to the many reviews and articles he has published on modern Spanish and European history, he is author of a monograph on Spanish anarchism, *Anarchist Ideology and the Working-class Movement in Spain, 1868–1898*, and co-author of a history of the Spanish Civil War, *Spain At War: The Spanish Civil War in Context, 1913–1939* (1995).

The Spanish Civil War

A Modern Tragedy

George R. Esenwein

Routledge
Taylor & Francis Group

NEW YORK AND LONDON

First published 2005 by Taylor & Francis Inc.
270 Madison Avenue, New York, NY 10016

Simultaneously published in the UK by Routledge
2 Park Square, Milton Park, Abingdon, Oxon OX14 4RN

Routledge is an imprint of the Taylor & Francis Group

Typeset in Galliard and Gill by Keystroke, Jacaranda Lodge,
Wolverhampton
Printed and bound in Great Britain by The Cromwell Press, Trowbridge,
Wiltshire

British Library Cataloguing in Publication Data
A catalogue record for this book is available from the British Library

Library of Congress Cataloging in Publication Data
A catalog record for this book has been requested

ISBN 0–415–20416–X (hbk)
ISBN 0–415–20417–8 (pbk)

To Marnie

Contents

Maps

Series editor's preface

The *Sources in History* series responds to the continued shift of emphasis in the teaching of history in schools and universities towards the use of primary sources and the testing of historical skills. By using documentary evidence, the series is intended to reflect the skills historians have to master when challenged by problems of evidence, interpretation and presentation.

A distinctive feature of *Sources in History* is the manner in which the content, style and significance of documents is analysed. The commentary and the source are not discrete, but rather merge to become part of a continuous and integrated narrative. After reading each volume a student should be well versed in the historiographical problems which sources present. In short, the series provides texts which will allow students to achieve facility in 'thinking historically' and place them in a stronger position to test their historical skills. Wherever possible, the intention has been to retain the integrity of a document and not simply to present a 'gobbet', which can be misleading. Documentary evidence thus forces the students to confront a series of questions which professional historians also have to grapple with. Such questions can be summarised as follows:

1   What type of source is the document?
    - Is it a written source or an oral or visual source?
    - What is its importance?
    - Did it have an effect on events or the decision-making process?

2   Who wrote the document?
    - A person, a group or a government?
    - If it was a person, what was his/her position?
    - What basic attitudes might have affected the nature of the information and language used?

3   When was the document written?
    - The date, and even the time, might be significant.
    - It may be necessary to understand when the document was written in order to understand the context.
    - Are there any special problems in understanding the document as contemporaries would have understood it?

4   Why was the document written?
  •   For what purpose(s) did the document come into existence and for whom was it intended?
  •   Was the document 'author-initiated' or was it commissioned for somebody? If the document was ordered by someone, the author could possibly have 'tailored' his/her piece.

5   What was written?
  •   This is the obvious question, but stating the obvious can be crucial.
  •   It is sometimes more revealing to ask the question: what was *not* written?
  •   What other references (to persons, events, other documents, etc.) need to be explained before the document can be fully understood?

Sources in History is intended to reflect the individual voice of the volume author with the aim of bringing the central themes of specific topics into sharper focus. Each volume consists of an authoritative introduction to the topic, chapters discuss the historical significance of the sources, and the final chapter provides an up-to-date synthesis of the historiographical debate. These books will become contributions to the historical debate in their own right.

George Esenwein's *The Spanish Civil War* offers a vibrant new assessment of one of the most complex civil wars of the twentieth century. In the 1930s and 1940s the war was perceived in broad ideological terms as part of a wider European struggle between democracy or communism on the one hand and fascism on the other. The war has come to be seen as specifically Spanish in its origins and its outcome and comprehensible only in terms of a deeper understanding of Spanish history and the longstanding tensions that existed between rural and urban experiences. By utilizing a wide variety of sources, Professor Esenwein's analysis throws new light on the questions these controversies have raised about interpretation. Postmodernists and cultural historians, for example, have questioned the assumptions underlying the traditional narrative approach. The author attempts to demonstrate how previous interpretations have either ignored or downplayed the contribution of women and less privileged elements in society. This important volume broadens our perspective on the war by including material on issues such as race and gender – topics which are no longer treated as footnotes to the history of the conflict. George Esenwein's volume offers a clear and accessible introduction to the Spanish Civil War and provides a mature and perceptive synthesis of recent scholarship.

David Welch
Canterbury 2005

Acknowledgements

In the course of writing this book I have incurred a number of intellectual and professional debts. For providing me with summer travel money, I would like to thank the College of Liberal Arts and Sciences at the University of Florida. Mrs Betty Corwine and Professor Robert McMahon were particularly helpful in securing me a grant from the Humanities Scholarship Enhancement Fund. The staff at various archives and libraries in Spain, Great Britain, and the United States greatly facilitated my research. I am especially grateful to the librarians and archivists at Brandeis University (Special Collections Division), the Tamiment Institute (New York University), the Hoover Institution (Stanford University), and the Centre d'Etudis Històrics Contemporánis, (Fundació Figures) in Barcelona, Spain.

Permission to quote from Arturo Barea's *The Forging of a Rebel* was granted by Granta Press, London. Material from *The Spanish Civil War: Revolution and Counter Revolution* by Burnett Bolloten is © 1991 by the University of North Carolina Press and used by permission of the publisher. *British Documents on Foreign Affairs* are reproduced courtesy of University Publications of America and Her Majesty's Stationery Office. Permission to quote from *The Spanish Anarchists* by José Peirats and *Spain and the World 1936–1939* edited by Vernon Richards was granted by Freedom Press, London. The extract from *The Civil War in Spain* by Robert Payne is © Robert Payne. Material from *Spain Betrayed* edited by Ronald Radosh, Mary R. Habeck, and Grigory Sevostianov is © Yale University Press and is reproduced by permission of Yale University Press. The author and publisher have made every effort to contact copyright holders of documents used in this volume. However, we would like to hear from any we were unable to reach.

For having read through a draft of the manuscript, I would like to thank Professor Stanley G. Payne. His careful reading saved me from making a number of misleading statements and factual errors. I am also grateful to the Series Editor, Dr David Welch, for his helpful advice and useful suggestions. At Routledge (Taylor & Francis) I greatly benefited from the astute observations of Vicky Peters. Besides being exceedingly patient with me she also provided encouragement when I most needed it. Philippa Grand of Routledge and Ruth Jeavons of Keystroke did a superb job overseeing the final stages of the project. Any errors of fact and interpretation that remain in the text are my own responsibility.

George Esenwein

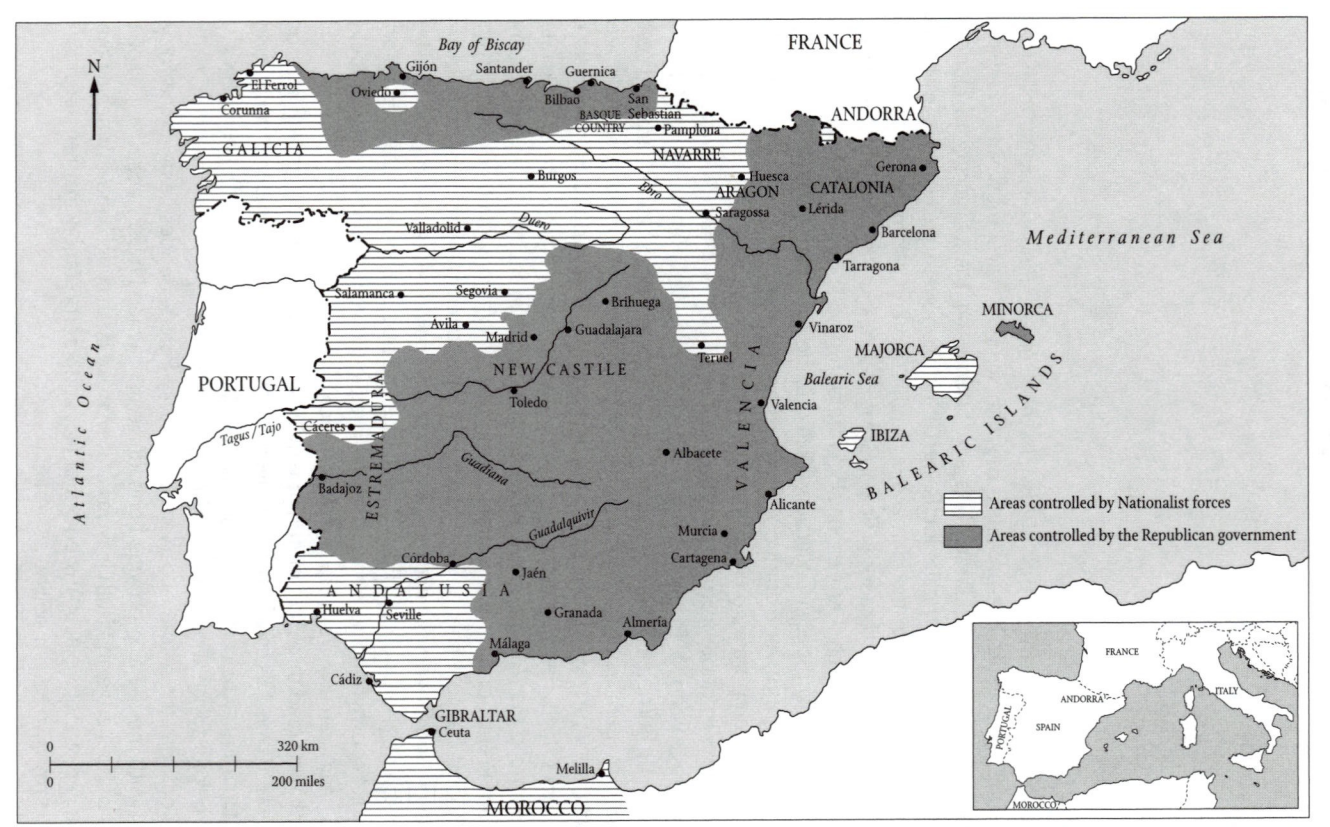

N

Bay of Biscay

Gijón
Santander
Guernica
El Ferrol
Oviedo
Bilbao
San Sebastian
Corunna
BASQUE
COUNTRY
Pamplona
GALICIA
Burgos
NAVARRE
Huesca
Gerona
ARAGON
CATALONIA
Valladolid
Duero
Saragossa
Lérida
Ebro
Barcelona
Salamanca
Segovia
Tarragona
Ávila
Brihuega
Mediterranean Sea
Madrid
Guadalajara
Vinaroz
NEW CASTILE
Teruel
MAJORCA
MINORCA
PORTUGAL
Toledo
VALENCIA
Balearic Sea
Cáceres
Valencia
IBIZA
ESTREMADURA
Tagus / Tajo
Guadiana
Albacete
BALEARIC ISLANDS
Badajoz
Alicante
Atlantic Ocean
Guadalquivir
Córdoba
Murcia
Jaén
Cartagena
ANDALUSIA
Huelva
Granada
Seville
Almería
Málaga
Cádiz
GIBRALTAR
Ceuta

Areas controlled by Nationalist forces
Areas controlled by the Republican government

0   320 km
0   200 miles

Melilla

MOROCCO

FRANCE
ANDORRA

FRANCE
ANDORRA
ITALY
PORTUGAL
SPAIN
MOROCCO

Map 1 August 1936 – The area of Spain controlled by Nationalist forces and Republican government

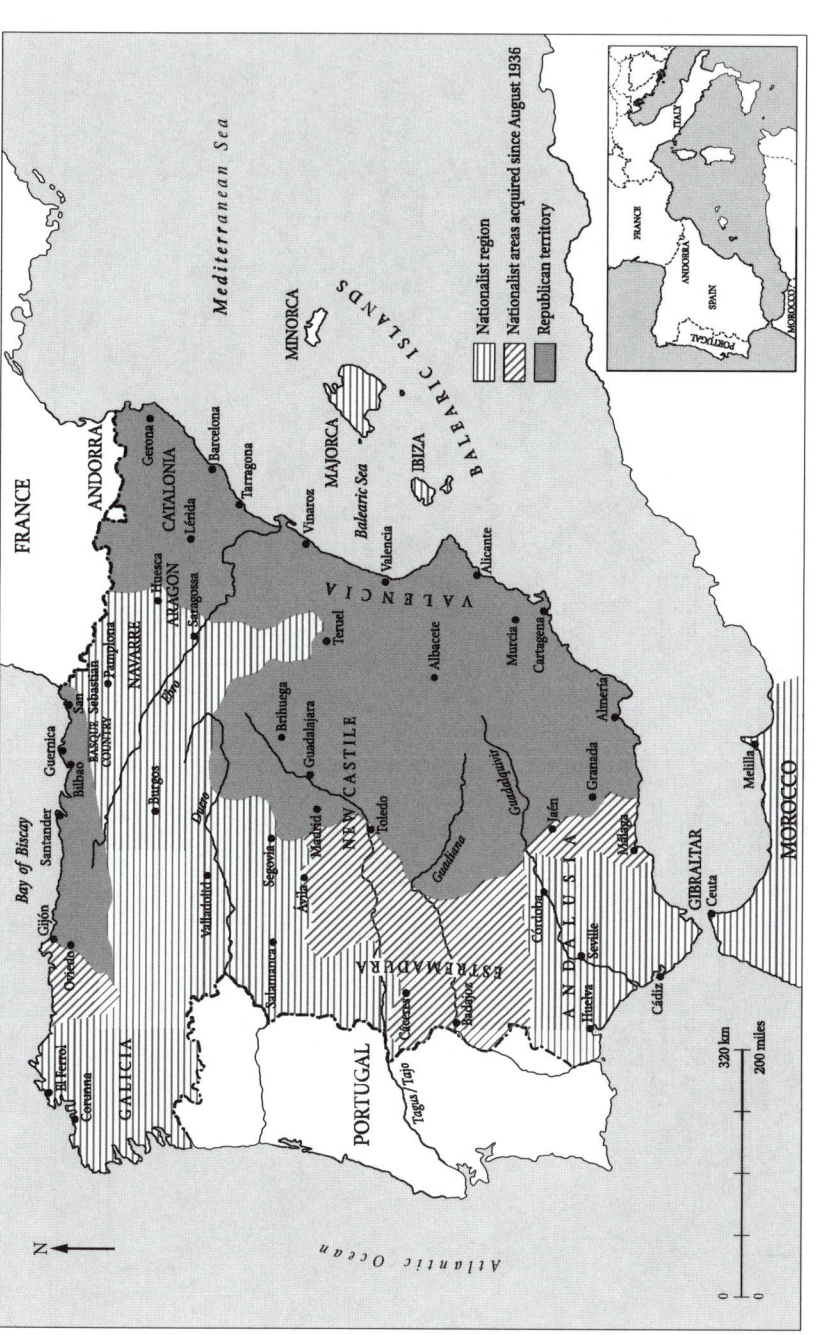

Map 2 February 1937 – Nationalist region with areas acquired since August 1936 and Republican territory

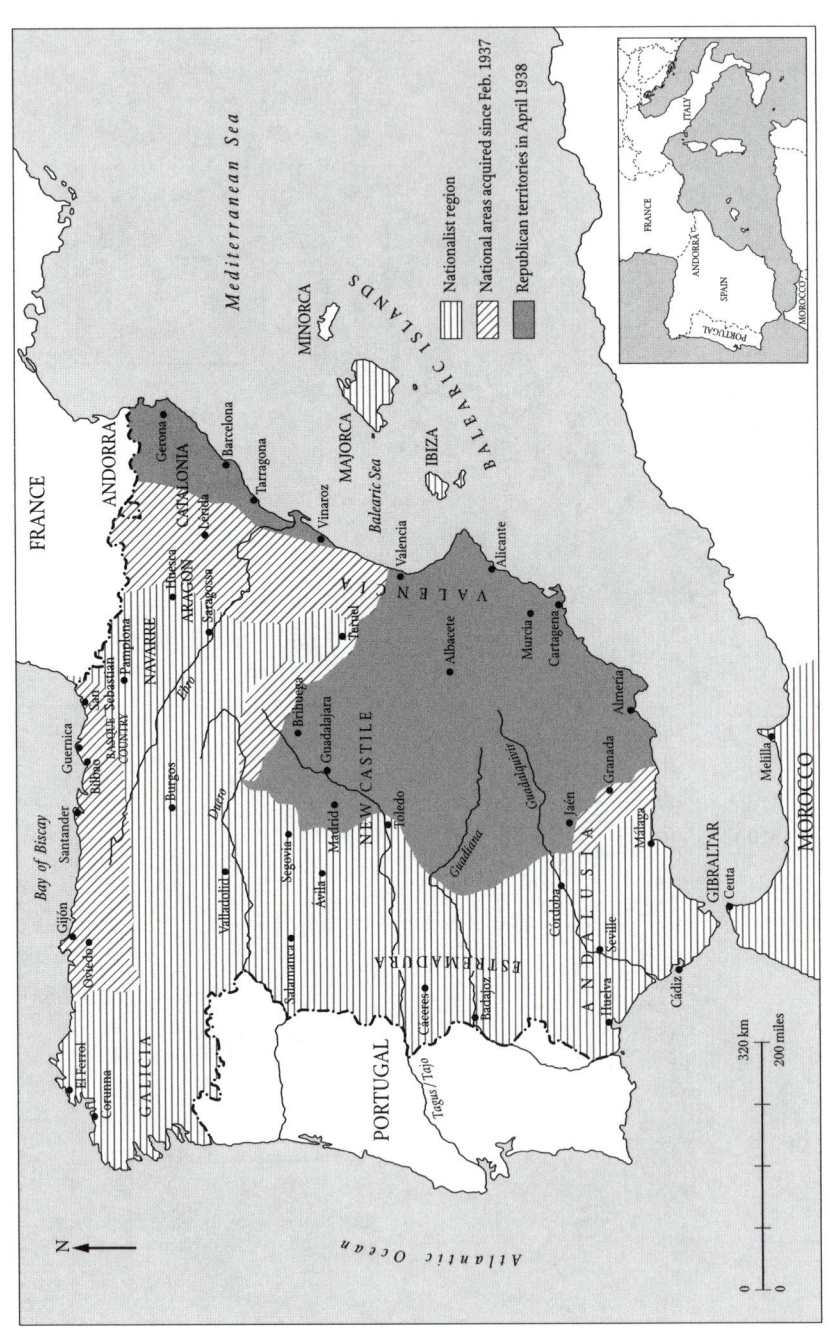

Map 3 April 1938 – Nationalist and Republican territories in April 1938

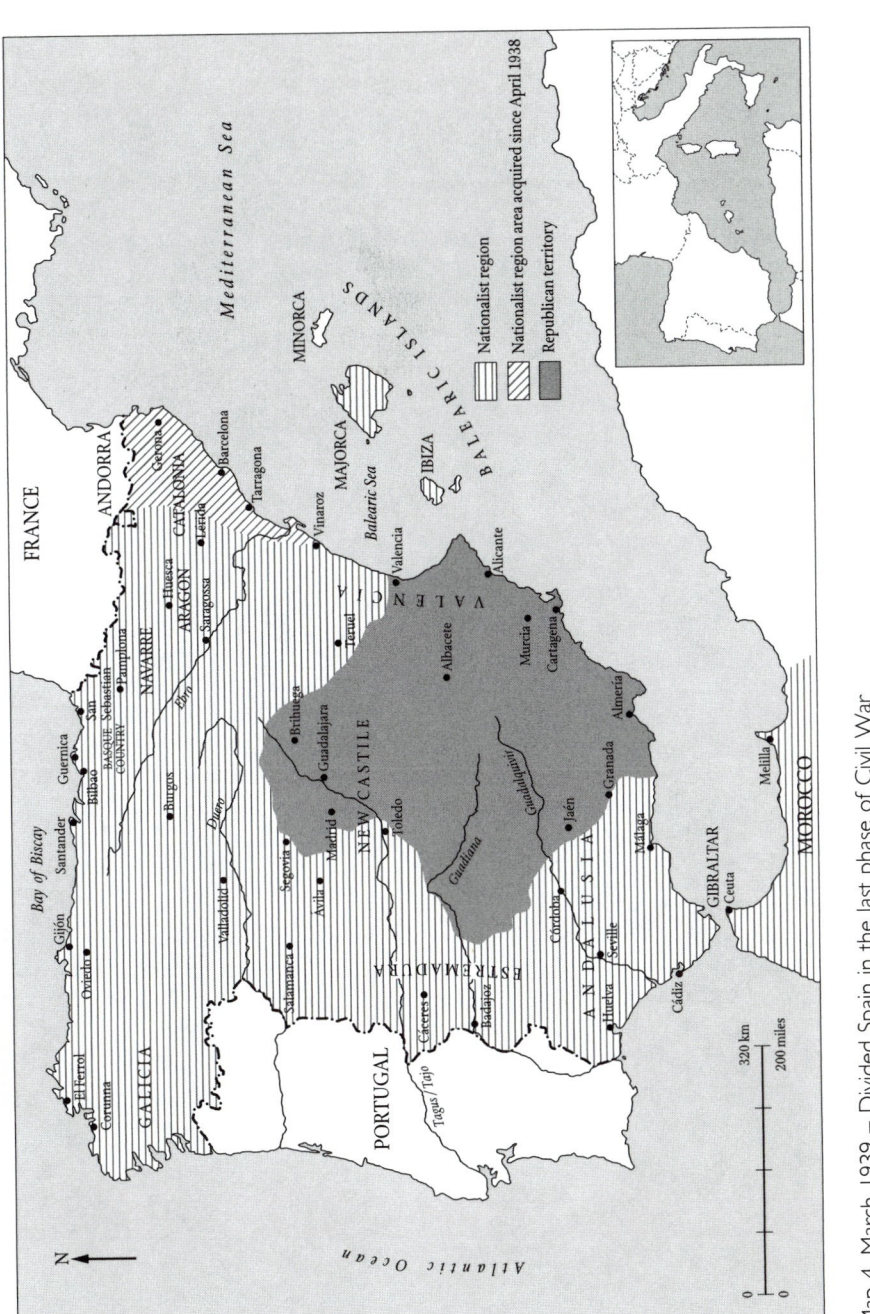

Map 4 March 1939 – Divided Spain in the last phase of Civil War

Introduction: Interpreting Spain's Civil War and Revolution

It is customary for scholars to offer reassessments of watershed events at regular intervals, not least because our historical perspective of them is constantly changing. This is especially true of events such as the Spanish Civil War (1936), which, because of its multiple political and ideological dimensions, has been the focus of numerous revisionist histories since it ended over sixty-five years ago. When it broke out in July 1936 most people outside of Spain paid scant attention to a conflict that seemed remote to world affairs. Nor did many know or even care about the origins or possible consequences of the conflict. Yet all this changed when Germany, Italy, and the Soviet Union got involved in the fighting and Spain's internal war was overnight transformed into an event of much wider significance. Because the Civil War was now being viewed as the stage on which the major ideological struggles of the day – particularly between fascism and communism – were being played out, many foreigners believed that they, too, had a stake in the outcome of the struggle. At the time, there was no end to the interpretations given it: for some it was a contest between Christianity and atheism, others saw it as a showdown between fascism and democracy, while still another group pictured it as a dialectical confrontation between capitalism and socialism. Given that both outside observers and participants alike were intent on depicting the war in such dichotomous terms, it was to be expected that early interpretations of the war tended to be reductionist and two-dimensional. More surprising, perhaps, was the fact that the ideological overtones of the conflict would persist long after the war had ended.

Historiographical trends

Above all, this persistence was due in varying degrees to the long shadows that the Second World War (1939–45), Franco's dictatorship (1939–75), and the Cold War (1948–89) cast over its historiography. The fact that the political passions and ideological struggles of Spain's war mirrored those of the Second World War, for example, has contributed to a view that has long been popular with Western liberal and Marxist historians, namely, that the two events should not be regarded as distinct historical episodes. Rather, it is assumed by this group that both formed part of the same general movement in Europe during the interwar period in which the defenders of democracy were locked in a life-and-death struggle with the supporters of fascism. On this assumption, the republicans in Spain were, just like the Western Allies during the Second World War, fighting to uphold the institutions of liberal democracy against the forces of international fascism.

The long-surviving authoritarian regime of Francisco Franco further reinforced the trend to explain the war in terms of its moral dualisms. By foreclosing any serious discussion and debates on politically sensitive topics, Franco's culturally repressive regime effectively prevented a critical school of historical scholarship on the Civil War from developing inside of Spain. Not surprisingly, the state-sponsored writings on the Civil War, which were usually poorly documented and patently tilted towards the right, did more to enshrine than to debunk the numerous myths and misconceptions surrounding the origins and significance of the war. As a result, several generations of Spaniards grew up learning only the 'official' version of the Civil War, one which presented it as a modern-day Christian crusade against the godless forces of international communism.

The polarized intellectual climate of the Cold War era had an impact on Civil War historiography in several different and, sometimes, unexpected ways. On the one hand, it served both to popularize and to validate histories that interpreted the Civil War as a Manichean struggle between 'good' and 'evil'. Inside of Spain, for example, the regime's assertion that the communists were solely responsible for having caused the Civil War resonated with the anti-communist views that were increasingly shaping the thinking of Western writers, particularly during the early years of the Cold War, 1948–60. Ironically, however, the anti-communist mind-set that was gripping the greater part of the Western intellectual world did not produce a corresponding shift in the orientation of Civil War history writing, which was dominated by liberals and leftists who were either sympathetic to or not particularly hostile towards the communists. This is illustrated by the fact that some of the most widely read and academically respected works published in this period – including Hugh Thomas's *The Spanish Civil War* (1961) and Gabriel Jackson's *The Spanish Republic and Civil War* (1965) – continued the pro-republican tradition of presenting the communists as allies in the 'Good Fight' against fascism.

Standing outside of both the Francoist and conventional Western academic traditions developing at this time was a small community of pro-Republican writers whose works were at odds with the standard interpretations of the Civil War outlined above. One group was comprised mostly of left-wing exiles whose writings on the war were aimed not at advancing scholarly research on the Civil War but rather at explaining the causes of Republican defeat. Besides rehashing the emotive inter-party polemics of the war years, these studies offered a scathing indictment of the communists, accusing them, among other things, of subverting the interests of the Republic in order to serve Soviet foreign policy objectives. Writing from a similar anti-communist perspective, but one that was distinguished by the author's exhaustive (and unparalleled) examination of the main primary and secondary sources that were then available to historians working outside of Spain, was the independent scholar Burnett Bolloten. One of the cornerstones of his ground-breaking study, *The Grand Camouflage* (1961), was the thesis that the July military rebellion unleashed a massive popular revolution that produced far-reaching consequences for the course of Republican affairs. But by assigning importance to this dimension of the war, Bolloten forcefully challenged the views of pro-republican historians such as Thomas and Jackson, whose studies either downplayed or completely ignored the impact of the revolutionary movement in the Republican camp. Another central aspect of Bolloten's work that was highly unpopular at the time was his trenchant analysis of the role of the communists. For documenting extensively (to his critics, obsessively) the various ways in which the communists crushed the revolution and cynically manipulated other parties on the left in order to achieve their hegemonic aims in the Republican camp, Bolloten was accused by both liberals and Marxists alike for adhering to a 'Cold War' explanatory model.[1]

In fact, Bolloten's brief against the communists – like those more famously found in the writings of George Orwell, Franz Borkenau, and Gerald Brenan – was neither conceived nor inspired by Cold War politics. Bolloten himself began writing his history in 1937–38 and the methodological and analytical contours of his published account of the war (finished in 1953) were shaped more by his accumulated knowledge of the enormous body of oral testimonies and primary sources he gathered during the immediate post-Civil War period than by the highly charged ideological debates and discussions that swirled around the Cold War.

Even though it was widely acknowledged at the time that the empirical foundations of, *The Grand Camouflage* substantially advanced Civil War scholarship, its communist-centred analysis of Republican politics argued against the historical paradigm that was being promoted by the vast majority of liberal and left-wing historians in Europe and the United States. As a result, Bolloten was seen more as a Cold War prosecutor than as a serious historian, and his writings on the Civil War were therefore consigned to relative obscurity for a number of years. Following the publication of a new and greatly expanded edition of his first book in 1979, this all changed. From then until the appearance of his *magnum opus*, *The Spanish Civil War: Revolution and Counter-revolution* (1989–91), Bolloten's reputation as a major figure in Civil War scholarship was firmly established. Above all, this was due to the prodigious scholarship that he ultimately brought to bear in support of his provocative reading of the war. However, the fact that Bolloten's historical works had at last acquired a certain respect and legitimacy among scholars did not mean that a 'universal consensus' had grown up around his interpretation of republican politics. As we shall see, his so-called thesis about the role of the communists during the Civil War has been at the centre of the historiographical debates preoccupying a new generation of scholars.

Civil War studies after Franco and the Cold War

The collapse of the Francoist system in the late 1970s and the demise of the Cold War in 1989–91 have served as major impetuses for a growth of revisionist studies on the Civil War. This explosion of interest in rewriting the history of the Civil War, mainly centred in Britain and Spain, has been accompanied by the emergence of a variety of approaches, all of which are aimed at casting fresh light on different aspects of the Civil War. For example, in the past ten years the majority of studies appearing on the war outside of Spain have been influenced by contemporary historiographical trends which emphasize the importance of social and cultural factors. Inside of Spain itself, the opening of local and national archives – most of which had been off-limits to the public throughout the Franco dictatorship – has yielded an extraordinary number of richly detailed regional histories of the Civil War. But while it is true that this latest wave of both micro- and theoretically oriented historical studies have significantly advanced our knowledge and understanding of this watershed event, a consensus view of the Civil War is still as far away as ever. In fact, it is largely because writing about the Civil War can now take place in an open arena that a newer generation of scholars have set themselves the task of completely revising our assumptions about the significance of the war. In this connection, it is important to bear in mind that, while the research undertaken by the revisionists is aimed primarily at shedding light on aspects of Spain's conflict that were formerly obscured by the polemics of previous generations, it has also had the (unintended) effect of reviving the debates and discussions that have long been associated with the Civil War.

In the past decade, a group of revisionist historians, based mainly in Great Britain and Spain, has sought to overturn the so-called 'Cold War' interpretive paradigm of the Civil War. In varying degrees these studies are aimed primarily at rescuing the reputation of the communists and their supporters who have tended to be portrayed in the literature that grew up during the Cold War era as the main villains of the war. This group of revisionists (whom I shall refer to as the 'Popular Front' school of historians) have insisted that the outcome of the Civil War owed more to the failure of Western democracies (principally Britain, France, and the United States) to enforce the policy of non-intervention adopted at the time by the international community than it did to communist intervention in Republican affairs. The 'Popular Front' revisionists further argue that, though guilty at times of sanguinary excesses, the communists nevertheless played a progressive role during the war. Above all, they argue that the Cold War historical paradigm which places the communists at the centre of political events in Republican Spain is untenable not least because it greatly exaggerates the extent to which the communists exercised control and influence over republican affairs.

The leading representative of the 'Popular Front' school, Helen Graham, goes further in this direction by contending that histories informed by the 'Cold War' paradigm have both unfairly and inaccurately maligned the communists for having repressed their political rivals in order to advance their own agenda. Far from their wanting to use the Republic as a Trojan horse for their own Machiavellian designs, Graham contends that their real aim was to work jointly with their republican allies to construct a coherent, centralized liberal state system that could be used as an effective vehicle for prosecuting the war effort. Viewed in this way, the communists can be regarded, if not as heroes, at least as the leading representatives of the progressive forces on the Republican side who were attempting at all costs to save a democratic government from the onslaught of international fascism.[2]

It is noteworthy that revisionist historians of this school tend to discount much of the evidence used to support the anti-communist judgements found in the so-called Cold War literature on the war. This is particularly true of memoirs and personal testimonies written by ex-communists – notably, Julián Gorkín and Walter Krivitsky – who, whether justly or not, became identified as Cold War warriors. Because the testimonies produced by this group are based largely on individual experiences and are frequently marred by personal prejudices, the revisionists maintain that they are of little or no use to the serious historian.

On the other hand, the recent unearthing of new documentary material relating to the communists' role in Spain has served only to undermine the Popular Front interpretation outlined above. Records relating to the Soviet's and communists' role in Spain during the Civil War that have been buried in the military, Communist Party, and state archives in Russia for nearly sixty years tend to confirm the view that the communists (1) played a dominant role in determining Republican affairs during the last year-and-a-half of the war, and (2) employed both subversive and coercive tactics to achieve their political goals. For example, the British writer Gerald Howson has recently published an exposé of the communists' role in supplying armaments to the Republic. His researches demonstrate not only that the Soviets provided far less aid than previously thought – rather than supply the Republicans with the latest and best military equipment, they sold them out-of-date guns and in insufficient numbers – but also that they systematically defrauded the Republicans by 'cooking the books' on the exchange rates. Above all, Howson's meticulous research into the arms questions seriously undermines the revisionist view that the Soviets ought to be viewed simply as representatives of the progressive forces on the Republican side who were attempting to prevent another European democratic government from succumbing to the forces of fascism.

Other recent publications that force us to focus our attention on the empirical foundations of the revisionist debate are the various collections of Soviet and Comintern documents that have been published by Yale University in its documentary series called 'Annals of Communism'. This is particularly true of the volume devoted to the Spanish Civil War, which is edited by the American historian Ronald Radosh.[3] Many of the internal (and formerly secret) documents relating to the Comintern's activities in Spain reproduced in this publication further substantiate most – if not all– of the claims made by historians who have long been critical of the communists' role in Republican affairs and who have insisted that, at their core, the Soviet Union's motives for helping the Republic were both sinister and self-serving.

The revisionists attempt to get round the accumulated body of evidence that has informed so-called 'Cold War' studies by positing an explanation of the dynamics of Republican politics that draws upon an entirely different group of historical sources.[4] Unlike the 'Cold War' school, the revisionist group are focused upon generating new interpretations of the Civil War based on an empirical base that speaks to the theoretical underpinnings of their historical analyses. In this way, they hope to construct an understanding of the Civil War that is not rooted in the ideological disputes of the past.

Although this new group of scholars would most likely argue that the value and validity of their revisionism lies in providing a more sophisticated or 'nuanced' view of the Civil War, the fact is that their more theoretically grounded interpretations are no less polemical and political than those of previous generations. An example of this can be found in their dismissive attitude towards studies that do not portray the communists as playing a constructive role in what they see as the larger, mostly 'neutral' political processes that were developing during the war – such as the state-building and national mobilization projects of the moderate Republican governments in the 1937–38 period. But by claiming that any analysis of republican politics that offers a critical assessment of the communists must be operating from a 'Cold War' perspective, members of the revisionist school demonstrate how difficult – if not impossible – it is for historians to transcend the dichotomous nature of Civil War historiography.

New directions in Civil War research

Not all attempts to revise our understanding of the Civil War have revolved around a political axis. A small but growing number of social historians contend that politics has for too long over-determined the direction of Civil War research and writing. Instead they are interested in producing studies that foreground the social, economic, and psychological aspects of the conflict that have been hitherto neglected or misunderstood.[5] Attention has recently been paid, for instance, to the social and economic tensions that existed between rural and urban settings. In the opinion of one historian viewing Spain's war from the bottom upwards, these conflicts were 'as consequential for the Republic's decline as the political disputes, class divisions, and international rivalries, which have been the traditional focus of much Spanish Civil War historiography'.[6] Moreover, oral historians such as Ronald Fraser have demonstrated that there are other dimensions of Spain's civil war, such as the personal experiences of individuals (both men and women), that have to be taken into account if we are too achieve a deeper understanding of the many subjective meanings associated with the Civil War.

Interpretations of the Civil War and revolution that have heretofore concentrated on the political (and military) dimensions of the conflict are also increasingly coming under attack from postmodern and cultural historians, who question the assumptions underlying the narrative approach to history. For them, this type of history greatly distorts the past on a number of levels. By focusing on men and other so-called hegemonic groups, it is argued, these 'old fashioned' histories either ignore or down-play the contributions of women and less privileged elements of society. Questions relating to gender, sexual orientation, power relations and other theoretical preoccupations that the postmodern group of historians take to be central to historical inquiry are thus not taken into account.[7] More trenchantly, it is asserted that traditional histories are flawed because they tend to attach too much importance to personalities and episodes that already form a part of a well-known (but contrived) storyline. As such, it is argued, they offer a one-dimensional summary of events that demands a far more subtle and in-depth explanation.

And, finally, whether current and future efforts to rewrite the history of the Civil War are influenced by these newer or by traditional approaches, it is necessary for historians to confront the fact that our knowledge and understanding of the losing side far exceeds that of the Nationalists, who, after all, won the war. Clearly a reversal of the historiographical trend to focus on the Republic will have to come about if we are ever to attain a balanced picture of how Spain was transformed during the years between 1936 and 1939.

Choice of texts/documents

While this book of documents seeks neither to engage nor resolve the ongoing historiographical debates on the Civil War, it is hoped that viewpoints presented here will throw some light on the questions these controversies have raised about our interpretations of the conflict. Another aim of the book is to broaden our perspective on the war by including material which focuses attention on issues such as race and gender, topics which are no longer being treated simply as footnotes to the history of the Civil War.

Given the staggering scale of the documentary evidence available on the Civil War, the challenge has been in selecting materials. In choosing the texts reproduced here, the author has been guided by several considerations. Bearing in mind the controversial nature of the subject matter, the documents that have been selected are not intended to advance a particular thesis or argument. Rather, the decision was to chose excerpts from a variety of political and non-political sources so that the reader can be presented with a multifaceted view of the war. With this in mind, items were chosen if they clearly and concisely summarized the viewpoints of both individuals and groups who participated in the war irrespective of the author's ideological or political leanings. Sources which offer revealing testimony or commentary to significant military, political, social, economic, and cultural developments during the war and revolution were also chosen without regard to the author's political or social background. It should be pointed out in this connection that this author recognizes that the documents found here do not offer a distortion-free image of events that occurred at the front lines and in the rearguard. Nor, as the discussion found below suggests, is it assumed that 'facts speak for themselves'. On the contrary, it has been presumed throughout that the various types of materials used to document the war and revolution cannot be taken as a definitive treatment of any topic.

Prescriptive writings

The documents themselves also fall into various analytical categories. Some are prescriptive writings or works that are self-consciously aimed at persuading the reader to adopt a particular point of view. This kind of writing is also directed at an audience that already shares or is potentially sympathetic to the ideological beliefs of the writer. Prescriptive literature is often characterized as 'propaganda' in so far as the author is more concerned with convincing the reader of the correctness of his or her viewpoint than with establishing empirical truths (though the latter is often asserted in the form of statistics and other allegedly objective criteria). Much of the prescriptive literature reproduced here is drawn from political pamphlets, public speeches that were reproduced in printed form, and journal and newspaper articles. In evaluating the texts or extracts taken from the printed media, the reader should also bear in mind that there are significant differences between the newspapers and journals of today and those which functioned during the Civil War. Generally speaking, the press (in all its forms) was devoted to the idea not of accurately and dispassionately covering events as they unfolded but of expressing a particular ideological viewpoint. It was also true that newspapers and periodicals were subject to censorship on both sides. In the early months of the war, the absence of formal government regulation meant that the press representing the various factions in the Republican camp was freed from restraint. After the anti-revolutionary forces gained control over the administrative functions of the state, however, press freedoms were increasingly circumscribed. This was particularly evident in the wake of the May Day Events of 1937, after which the political press on the left was, if not completely shut down, no longer allowed to challenge the policies of the central government. On the Nationalist side, the question of censorship was never openly debated. As early as 1936, Franco decreed the dissolution of all pro-Republican publications and saw to it that all forms of the printed media were converted into mouthpieces for the *Movimiento*. In this sense, the publications of the Nationalists presented a much more monochromatic view of events than their counterparts on the Republican side.

If the printed media offer varied and often conflicting perspectives of the war and revolution, the question arises as to whether they should be treated as documentary sources. The decision to do so here is based on two considerations. First and foremost is the fact that these publications testify to the various ways in which the different parties constructed their own version of the central realities of the war and revolution. Second, party-sponsored publications – usually in pamphlet form – were also used as vehicles for reproducing the texts of important speeches and policy statements, and, as such, they provide vital clues not only for measuring how a party was responding to current events but also for tracing over time the ebb and flow of the activities of the various factions.

Government documents

A variety of documentary sources have been selected for this volume. The reader should know, however, that the historical value of these 'official' sources has to be weighed alongside a number of factors. For example, foreign government documents were composed by intelligence agents, foreign service officers, who had access to only certain groups of people. They also experienced the war as foreign observers and not as representatives of native Spanish parties. It must also be borne in mind in this connection that most of the government sources used here were never intended to see the light of day and, like all such documents, their content was meant to be read and interpreted by a select group of officials, not the general public or the academic community. As such these documents offer a direct window on to the thinking of the community of foreign diplomats who were reporting on the Spanish situation. This is not to say, however, that the documents themselves can be taken at face value. Members of the diplomatic corps often reported on events from a perspective informed not just by their own experiences but by their personal contacts, (heavily censored) newspaper accounts, and other media that were far from being reliable sources. Thus, for example, the fact that some German dispatches relating to the Guernica bombing of 26 April 1937 suggest that German aircraft were not involved in the incident cannot be taken as definitive proof of the Nationalists' claim that the Republicans themselves were responsible for destroying the historic Basque town. On the contrary, much of the available evidence gathered at the time and subsequently shows that the Germans, along with the Italians, carried out the aerial bombing of Guernica on that fateful afternoon. (See below, Chapter 7.)

Eyewitness accounts

It is well known that eyewitness accounts present a problem to historians. On one level, the accuracy of first-hand testimonies can be compromised by several factors. Chief among these is the difficulty in recording faithfully all the information needed to reconstruct a full picture of the event or events being chronicled. Here memory is a key factor: what the author actually remembers and what actually happens can be very different things. Memory is also influenced by such things as the passage of time – when the vividness of the details of a particular recollection inevitably fades. Time also presents another problem associated with memory. The more time that elapses between the occurrence of an event and the moment it is committed to writing the more likely the 'memory' of the incident will be coloured by other sources. For example, the author's reading of newspaper accounts, secondary works, or other documents relating to his or her primary experience could easily be influenced by the knowledge acquired from these other viewpoints. In short, eye-witness testimonies must be read with a great deal of caution.

Preference was given to those texts which were written by participants or observers (both foreign and native) who were close to the events they were recording. The eyewitnesses themselves come from a variety of backgrounds: journalists, writers, political activists (including foreign volunteers), diplomats, adventurers, and travellers. In reading this class of documents, it is important to bear in mind that the reliability of these accounts varies from person to person. While some participants – George Orwell, for example – were capable of providing a relatively clear-eyed view of events, even these accounts are bound to contain factual errors and distortions due to language, cultural and other 'structural' barriers to the 'reality' they were trying to capture in their writings and oral testimonies.

Should we then discount eyewitness testimonies? For most historians the answer to this question is, no. As distorting as eyewitness reports can be, they nevertheless constitute an important and valuable resource for reconstructing events. It is through first-hand testimonies that others are offered direct access to events as they unfolded. In this sense, both the immediacy of the event as well as the general atmosphere in which it occurred can be conserved. In the hands (or eyes) of a particularly sharp-eyed observer, first-hand experiences often provide details that are essential for constructing a coherent and meaningful interpretation of an historical episode. Thus history would be much the poorer without eyewitness accounts.

Structure of the book

The following chapters offer a narrative of events – accompanied by a broad range of mostly primary sources – which covers both familiar and relatively uncharted territory. Chapter 1 presents a summary of the political and social developments of the Second Republic (1931–36) which formed the backdrop to the military rising of July 1936. The next chapter focuses on how each side responded to the challenge of fighting a civil war. In addition to profiling the relative strengths and weaknesses of the opposing sides, this section briefly reviews the outcomes of key military engagements during the first seven months of fighting. Chapter 3 considers the impact that the popular revolution and violence had on the course of the Civil War. This chapter is followed by a descriptive account of the political factions on both sides. The international ramifications of the Civil War, particularly the origins and consequences of foreign intervention in Spain's domestic struggle, are outlined in Chapter 5. Though the greater part of this study is structured around the political and military aspects of the Civil War, an effort has been made to recognize the role played by other factors. To this end, the extent to which the war was about race, gender relations, and religious conflicts is the subject of Chapter 6. The left-wing political drama that was being played out behind the lines throughout the war and which helped to determine the fate of the Republic is examined in Chapter 7. The next chapter explains how the Civil War was won and lost on the battlefield by focusing on the major military campaigns that were carried out in the last year and a half of the war. The book ends by reviewing the declining phases of the war, placing special emphasis on the fact that it was not just military defeats but also the pressures of domestic and international affairs which hastened the collapse of the Republic.

From Republic to Civil War | **1**

To understand Spain's two-and-a-half year Civil War it is necessary to bear in mind that it was not a single, self-contained event. Rather, it was composed of several overlapping and interrelated conflicts that operated on various levels. First and foremost, the Civil War represented the culmination of decades of political instability and domestic unrest. The war itself pitted the Spanish left – as represented by the greater part of the organized workers' movement, regionalists in Catalonia and the Basque country, and progressive segments of the bourgeoisie – against the forces of the right, who were led by the conservative elements of the military, the Catholic Church, and Spain's traditional social and economic elites. The grouping together of such disparate elements on both sides inevitably produced further arenas of conflict. For example, in Republican Spain all parties were unified in their opposition to the Nationalists but were irreconcilably divided among themselves over a number of fundamental issues. Chief among these was the question of whether the massive working-class revolution that was unleashed by the July military rebellion helped or hindered the Republicans' war effort. Political differences also existed in the Nationalist camp, though, in contrast to the Republican side, tensions aroused by factional disputes were kept under control by the military dictatorship that grew up around Francisco Franco.

Not long after it had begun, Spain's internal war transcended its national boundaries. From a diplomatic standpoint this was true because the Civil War was widely perceived as a potential threat to the fragile peace and stability of Europe as a whole. It was largely for this reason that most countries decided to adopt a hands-off policy towards Spain's domestic troubles. However, three of the signatories to a non-intervention pact concluded in August 1936 – Germany, Italy, and the Soviet Union – refused to abide by the terms of the agreement and instead chose to use the Civil War as a means of furthering their respective foreign policy agendas. In this way Spain became a proxy battleground for the leading fascist and communist powers of the day.

In addition to the diplomatic concerns it raised, the Civil War aroused the passions and pricked the public conscience of the international community, particularly among those who came to believe that they too had a stake in the outcome of the Civil War. Politically engaged citizens, intellectuals, writers, and artists saw the Civil War as a reflection of the wider ideological struggles that were increasingly dividing the world into mutually hostile blocs. While some interpreted it as a contest between Christianity and godless Bolshevism, others insisted that it was a life-and-death confrontation between democracy and fascism. In an attempt to place the Civil War in its proper historical context, many historians have tended to emphasize the international aspects of the conflict, insisting that the Spanish conflict is best understood as a dress rehearsal for the Second World War. But even though there are direct parallels between the two wars, it would be wrong to conclude – as some have done – that the causes and consequences of the Spanish Civil War were connected to those of the Second World War. A brief review of the historical period that formed the backdrop to Spain's war will help to explain why this is the case.

Second Republic, 1931–36

Ever since Queen Isabella II was deposed in 1868, Spain rarely enjoyed long periods of good government. From 1876 until 1923 a liberal monarchy ruled, though this was deeply flawed both by its anti-democratic character and by its inability to rise above the corruption that characterized politics at the local and national levels. Above all, however, it was the liberal system's failure to respond swiftly and effectively to the demands of rapid economic and social change at the turn of the century which undermined its ability to govern.

By the early 1920s, the dynastic ruling parties who monopolized political power under the Restoration were so thoroughly discredited that they were easily swept to the side by a military-led coup d'état. But unlike the military *pronunciamientos* of the nineteenth century, which were usually followed by popular unrest in the towns and countryside, this revolt brought about a period of relative stability under the dictatorship of Miguel Primo de Rivera (1923–30). In fact, Primo's intervention came at a time when many believed that the only way Spain could overcome its growing social, colonial, and economic problems was to establish an authoritarian government. In the event, from the beginning the dictatorship won the support not just of the middle classes but of the army, the monarchy and Spain's ruling social and economic elites. No less important to the early success of his rule was the fact that Primo managed to avert full-scale warfare with the country's revolutionary organizations by adopting a pragmatic approach to resolving the labour question. On the one hand, he used the machinery of the state to repress groups on the far ends of the political spectrum – the anarchosyndicalist CNT, for example. At the same time, he was solicitous towards right-wing (Sindicatos Libres) and moderate organizations such as the socialist PSOE and UGT, both of which saw collaboration with the one-party state system as a means of defending the interests of their own working-class constituents.

During the first phase of his rule, Primo's government patterned itself after fascist and authoritarian regimes elsewhere in Europe who were using the state as a vehicle for solving economic and social problems. Yet, despite the early successes of his state interventionist policies, Primo failed to develop the institutional basis that could sustain his rule. For example, the single party he created in 1926, the Patriotic Union

(Unión Patriótica), never succeeded in mobilizing a popular base of support for the regime. By 1926 his paternalistic dictatorship was generating a ground-swell of opposition among various sectors of society, including the middle classes, regionalists (particularly in Catalonia), and elements of the army. For many, republicanism became a political rallying point, and over the course of the next three years the movement attracted a sizeable following. After 1929 the mounting pressures of an ailing economy further undercut much of Primo's support not just among the aforementioned groups but also among ruling elites who refused to subsidize the state's efforts to ward off Spain's rapidly developing economic crisis. Abandoned by his former supporters, which by now included King Alfonso XIII and key sections of the army, Primo was forced to step down in January 1930. The collapse of his dictatorship led directly to the downfall of the Bourbon monarchy. In national elections held on 12 April 1931 the monarchist parties were defeated at the polls by their Republican and socialist opponents. To the cheers of millions of pro-democratic citizens, Spain's Second Republic was declared two days later.

For the first two years of its existence, the Second Republic was ruled by a coalition of socialist and middle-class Republican politicians who wanted to modernize Spain by transforming the social, political, and economic structures associated with the old regime. Government reformers took special aim at the military and the Catholic Church, two major institutions which had for many years enjoyed a privileged position in Spanish society. In addition, the government introduced progressive economic reforms and social legislation which directly threatened Spain's dominant economic classes: the land-owning and industrial elites.

In a country as steeped in traditions as Spain was, such a bold and sweeping agenda was bound to create problems. Not surprisingly, the efforts of civilian politicians to reform the army – particularly their plans to reduce the size of the over-bloated officer corps – stirred up resentment among the traditional ruling military castes, causing some to begin plotting against the Republic. No less hostile to liberal change was the Catholic Church, which greatly resented the government's attempts to secularize Spain. When the anti-clerical Republican prime minister Manuel Azaña triumphantly proclaimed in 1932 that 'Spain was no longer Catholic!' his words offended many Spaniards, but especially those who identified themselves and their country with the policies and practices of the Catholic Church.

In a two-year period the left-wing governments of the Second Republic had achieved an impressive reform record. In addition to expanding public education, greatly reducing the role of the Church in social affairs and restructuring the military, the government promulgated wide-ranging labour and political legislation, such as the Agrarian Reform Law (1932) and the statute of regional autonomy for Catalonia (1932). But at the same time the government was striving to revamp Spain's out-dated social, military, and economic structures, its popular support was being eroded. On the socialist left, one of the principal players in the government's ruling coalition, this was due to the fact that the rate of legislative reform failed to keep pace with the workers' rising expectations for change. In some cases, such as the government's failure to bring about a meaningful redistribution of land in the countryside, the growing frustration of the rural labourers had a radicalizing effect. The result was that, by mid-1933, the socialist–Republican political alliance began to crumble.

Both the credibility and stability of the government was further shaken by the persistent agitation of the far left. Between 1931 and late 1933 the anti-Republican stance of Spain's classic anti-statist revolutionaries, the anarchosyndicalists of the CNT-FAI, was summed up in their slogan: 'Our Revolution is made not in Parliament but in the streets'. To this end, they spearheaded a series of wildcat strikes and staged insurrections which they referred to as 'revolutionary gymnastics' that sought to overturn the 'bourgeois' Republic. While most of these never seriously threatened to bring down the capitalist system, they none the less greatly contributed to the destabilization of the regime. The revolutionary acts of the far left also rebounded negatively on the workers themselves as these often provoked swift and often brutal responses from both national (Asaltos and Guardia Civil) and local authorities. On the other hand, state 'repression' of this sort – such as during the infamous Casas Viejas rising in January 1933 when nearly a dozen peasants were summarily executed by state policemen – tended to reinforce the libertarians' revolutionary message by calling into question the government's commitment to the working classes.

Right-wing opposition to the Republic

Given its left-wing orientation, it is hardly surprising that the liberal Republic faced its greatest challenge from the Spanish right. As noted above, the government's anti-clerical orientation – enshrined in Article 26 of the Constitution – provoked a hostile reaction from Spain's large Catholic community, many of whom deeply resented the passing of secularizing legislation that, among other things, legalized divorce and greatly diminished the Church's role in education (Law on Religious Confessions and Congregations, 1933).[1] Opposition to the liberal government from defenders of religion and traditional social values crystallized in the formation of political parties such as the CEDA, a broad coalition of right-wing Catholic groups that came into being in February 1933. The CEDA's relationship to the Republic was highly ambiguous, as evidenced in its commitment to an opportunistic policy known as 'accidentalism', which placed loyalty to the Catholic Church above allegiance to any particular form of government. But while the CEDA demonstrated a willingness to work within the bounds of a legal framework, this was not true of groups on the far right known as 'catastrofistas'. The parties of the hard-line Carlists (Comunión Tradicionalista) and Alfonsine Monarchists (Renovación Española) sought to over-throw the liberal Republic and replace it with an authoritarian form of government. The fanatical supporters of the Carlist pretender to the Bourbon throne were true reactionaries in that they strove to establish a clerical monarchy organized along corporatist lines. Their commitment to the use of force was underscored by their ever-expanding para military organization, *requetés*, whose numbers had grown to over six thousand by 1935. Unlike the Carlists, whose influence was geographically centred in the Navarre region, the Alfonsine monarchists appealed to conservative

Spaniards throughout the peninsula. Their goal was to set up a military-style monarchy (much like the one that developed under Primo de Rivera) headed by the deposed Alfonso XIII. Another fiercely anti-Republican party that came into being around this time was the Spanish Falangist Party. Between 1933 and 1934 an assortment of pro-fascist groups began coalescing around the charismatic José Antonio Primo de Rivera, the eldest son of the former dictator, Miguel. This new party sought to finish the authoritarian state-building process begun by Miguel Primo de Rivera by creating a modernizing totalitarian state modelled on Mussolini's fascist Italy and Hitler's Nazi Germany. Though none of the aforementioned parties attracted a mass following before 1936, their activities had a corrosive effect on the authority of the legitimate government and collectively they contributed to the polarization of political life in Republican Spain.

In the general elections held in November 1933, the Spanish political pendulum swung to the right. At first the right-leaning government moved cautiously in its attempts to block the reforms and undo the progressive social measures begun under their predecessors. But, against the background of the rising tide of fascism in Europe, these actions were interpreted by the left as direct assaults on the institutional foundations of the Republic. The fact that some right-wing leaders adopted the rhetoric of fascism – the bombastic José María Gil Robles of the CEDA, for example – gave greater credence to the suspicion held by many on the left that the right-wing forces in parliament were following in the footsteps of the Nazis: they were using the legal channels of the Republic to destroy its democratic framework.

The left in opposition

Historically the Spanish working-class left had been divided into several mutually antagonist movements. One major current was represented by the anarchists, who traced their roots in Spain back to 1869. By the early decades of the twentieth century, anarchist associations, such as the nationally based National Confederation of Labor (CNT) and Iberian Anarchist Federation (FAI, created in 1927), had become important, not just because of their massive size but also because of their deeply entrenched presence within infrastructures of working-class society. During the Second Republic anarchist strength and influence in the labour movement was challenged by Marxist organizations such as the Spanish Socialist Party (PSOE), its trade union affiliate, the General Union of Workers (UGT). This rivalry – which was reflected in both ideological and organizational differences – persisted throughout the Second Republic and Civil War period, 1936–39.

The unity of the Spanish left was further undermined by the creation of several new socialist organizations. For example, the Spanish Communist Party or PCE (formed in 1921) and the Unified Marxist Workers' Party or POUM (created in 1935 as a result of the fusion of two independent Marxist groupings, BOC and ICE) were two significant Marxist parties that competed not only with the socialists and anarchists but also with each other. During the years of the Second Republic inter-union tensions and intra-party divisions shaped the course of left-wing politics in a number of ways. Above all, however, they prevented the left from presenting a united front against their common enemies on the right.

Despite the doctrinal and organizational differences that separated the various parties on the left, it was apparent to all after the November elections that the right was now in the ascendant. In an effort to prevent them from firmly establishing their political hegemony, activists such as the Marxist theorist Joaquín Maurín began searching for ways of bridging the divisions on the left. His idea of linking the ideologically disparate left-wing parties through an ecumenical workers' alliance (Alianza Obrera) gained popularity throughout the course of 1934, especially among the Catalan Marxist parties such as Maurín's BOC, non-sectarian sections of the CNT, and the socialist UGT. Its effectiveness was put to the test on 6 October 1934, when the peninsula was jolted by a series of revolutionary strikes and uprisings. The signal for the left's collective response was the entry of three CEDA ministers into Alejandro Lerroux's radical government's cabinet. Given the CEDA's pro-fascist tinge and equivocal stance towards the Republic, the left were convinced that a preemptive move against the government would rescue them from the fate suffered by workers in Austria and other fascist countries who had been, under similar political conditions, brutally repressed. However, with the lone exception of Asturias, the ill-timed and poorly co-ordinated revolutionary activities of labour groups throughout the peninsula were easily put down by the authorities. In Asturias, socialist, communist, and anarchist miners jointly established a revolutionary commune which managed to survive for nearly two weeks before it succumbed to the savage onslaught of military troops brought in from Africa.

The Popular Front: The promise of unity

In the aftermath of the failed Asturian rebellion, thousands of workers were imprisoned by a vindictive right-wing government, and the left in general was thrown into disarray. It was in these bleak circumstances that yet another strategy for unifying the Spanish left was born. In contrast to the notion of the Alianza Obrera, which was meant to be an exclusively working-class alliance, the Spanish Communist Party (PCE) began promoting the idea of building working-class strength through alliances with the anti-fascist parties of the bourgeoisie. The new strategy, which was formally adopted by the Communist International (Comintern) in the late summer of 1935, represented a complete about turn for the PCE in that it demanded that the party should replace its strategy of revolutionary 'maximalism' with an anti-revolutionary one that gave primacy to the struggle between the forces of democracy on the one side and the forces of fascism on the other. This major shift in policy did not mean that the communists themselves were abandoning their ultimate goal of revolution. Nor were the communists necessarily committing themselves in the long term to participating in a pluralistic political system that was based on capitalism. Rather, in recognition that proletarian parties such as the PCE in Spain or the PCF in France were too weak to effect political change by themselves, the communists felt it was tactically necessary for them to ally with the bourgeois parties on the left, who were to play a leadership role in establishing the Popular Front government.

It should not be forgotten in this connection that the primary *raison d'être* of the Popular Front strategy was to serve the diplomatic and strategic interests of the Soviet Union, the mainspring for international socialism. Ultimately, therefore, the policy of Popular Frontism was defined and directed not by the independent communist parties adhering to it but by Moscow and its international arm, the Comintern.

Parallel to these developments other Spanish left-wing groups, including the middle-class left republican parties, were also searching for ways to create a united front against the right. In fact, only six months after it had been announced by the Comintern, a Popular Front alliance was born in Spain, though it was not led by the relatively small PCE. Nor did it embody all the ideals with which the communists were identified. The former prime minister Manuel Azaña understood the Popular Front as an electoral strategy which could be used to rebuild the Republican–socialist coalition that had disintegrated in late 1933. His efforts to win the socialists over to this policy met with mixed results. While moderate socialists were eager to embrace Azaña's plans, the left wing of the socialist movement adamantly opposed it. To understand why the socialists themselves represented the greatest obstacle to forming a Popular Front alliance, we need to review briefly the power struggle that was developing between Francisco Largo Caballero (popularly known as Caballero) and Indalecio Prieto, the leaders of the two major opposing wings of the Spanish socialist movement.[2]

Though he had long been identified as a reformist (he held a government post in Miguel Primo de Rivera's right-wing dictatorship), Caballero underwent a political conversion in the months leading up to the July rebellion. By the spring of 1936 he was widely viewed as the 'Spanish Lenin', an uncompromising critic of the bourgeois Republic who would lead the working-class revolution that many on the left (and right) believed was imminent. Prieto, the head of the PSOE's centrist social democratic faction, fought hard against this current of 'revolutionism', arguing that the socialists had to avoid the error of 'electoral isolation' of 1933, which had resulted in a right-wing victory at the polls. He therefore urged socialists of all stripes to ally with the middle-class Republican parties.

The decision by both Largo and Prieto to adopt a Popular Front strategy in late 1935 served – at least temporarily – as a focal point for conciliation within the socialist movement. Though for quite different reasons, both agreed to join the electoral pact that had been cobbled together by Manuel Azaña. Whereas Prieto saw the Popular Front as a strategy for rebuilding the Republic along reformist lines, the revolutionary Caballero viewed the pact simply as a tactical necessity. In line with the orthodox communists of the PCE, he believed that a broad left-wing front was imperative at this juncture in order to check the growing might and menace of the pro-fascist forces in Spain. For this reason, he threw the weight of the UGT and its affiliates behind the Popular Front electoral coalition that was formally concluded in January 1936 and which comprised parties ranging from Republicans to socialists, communists, syndicalists and the independent Marxists of the recently formed POUM (Document 1.1).

Document 1.1 Contrasting Popular Front Strategies: Communism versus Republicanism

(a)

The united front government will be a government of the workers' organizations, a government of the people's front, a government consisting of representatives of the political organizations of other classes which stand on a common platform with that of the workers' organizations to fight against the capitalist offensive, fascism and war. It will not be a government of normal times, but a government of the period of *political crisis*. . . .

On the whole, the tactical line of the Seventh Congress corresponds to the *relation of class forces* in the present period, it corresponds to the present *level of the movement and strength of the Communist Parties*, as it is today, and will be in the immediate future. These are tactics calculated for a long time to come. Tactics, generally, may change, but the general line of the Communist International, *the course it is steering for the proletarian revolution, based on the welding of the forces of the working class, remains unchanged.*

Source: Manuilsky, D.Z. (1937) *The Work of the Seventh Congress of the Communist International*, New York.

(b)

These, then, were the parties which formed the 'Frente Popular.' Their essential characters were so diverse and so far contradictory that their common electoral programme was necessarily very simple. At the same time, it did not attempt to conceal various doctrinal schisms. The following were the main points:–

(1) *General Amnesty* for all politico-social offences subsequent to November 1933 – the date of the elections which had returned a right-wing majority to Cortes. The main body whose liberation was intended were the 30,000 people imprisoned as a result of the Asturian rising of October 1934. This section of the manifesto also advocated the reinstatement of all persons dismissed from office or employment for political reasons.

(2) *Protection of Liberty and Justice.* – Various proposals designed to ensure that the courts should not be used to attack the working class or the republic.

(3) *Agricultural Reform.* – The Republicans explicitly rejected the Socialists' demand for the nationalisation of the land, but approved of credits,

reduction of interest charges, elimination of middlemen's profits: technical development and agricultural education; reform of the land laws, and
increased security of tenure; repeal of the law returning landed property
to the nobility.

(6) *The Republic* was not to be an instrument of class warfare, but a régime
of democratic liberty animated by motives of public interest and social
progress. Nevertheless, privilege should not obstruct the raising of the
workers' moral and material conditions to the highest level consistent with
the general interests of production. The Republicans rejected the
Socialists' demand for control by the working class; but they agreed to
the re-establishment of social legislation, the reorganisation of labour
tribunals and the protection of wages. Social services were to be developed, private charity unified under State control.

The principles of local autonomy were to be restored in accordance with
the Constitution.

Foreign policy was to follow the principles of the League of Nations.

Source: British Documents on Foreign Affairs, Series F, Europe, vol. 27,
Document no. 63, 13 January 1937.

The results of the last free elections of the Second Republic (held in February 1936)
were extremely close. The Popular Front parties won by a razor-thin margin:
4,654,116 to the right's 4,503,524 (Document 1.2).[3] For the defeated, the triumph
of the Popular Front meant the right had lost their opportunity to conquer political
power. In practice this translated into abandoning the legalist strategy that the
'accidentalists' of the CEDA had been following up to now. In fact, the next few
months saw a massive defection from the CEDA (particularly from its youth movement, the JAP or Japosos) to the Falange and other extremist parties. Meanwhile,
the Popular Front coalition itself was at the point of unravelling. A government was
formed under the leadership of Azaña, but, unlike in 1931, the socialists refused
to join his administration. Like the right, the vast majority of the Spanish left had
lost faith in the constitutional process. This was evident in both the towns and
the countryside. Thousands of strikers in Madrid, Barcelona, and other major cities
increasingly took to the streets partly to demonstrate for better pay and working
conditions and partly to assert their power in the face of the ever-increasing numbers
of militant right-wing groups. In the countryside, radical unions – the socialist
Federation of Landworkers (FNTT), for example – encouraged peasants impatient
for land reform to take matters into their own hands. Between March and July, their
de facto occupations of large landed estates in Estremadura and elsewhere offered
a clear sign of the degree to which the workers' movement was no longer tied to
the policies of the liberal bourgeois government.

Document 1.2 February Election Results, 1936

The figures given below are taken from the Record of the Spanish Cortes, January–February, 1936, issue (*Boletin de Información Bibliografica y Parliamentaria, Num. 19*). The figures cover the period up to February 25, 1936, and do not include the elections in Cuenca and Granada, originally cancelled as illegal, or the result of the official recount. That is to say, the Popular Front and Government Parties are credited with less votes than shown in the final tabulation:

Electoral Census: 13,700,000

Rightist Parties:

Right Parties	3,423,450
Catalonian Lliga	487,920
Total	3,911,370

Parties Supporting the Government:

Left Center Parties	4,255,550
Center	363,620
Basque Nationalists	132,270
Total	4,751,440
Total votes polled	8,662,810

Number of Deputies Elected to Parliament and their Affiliations

Leftist Parties:

Socialists	89
Left Republicans	83
Union Republicans	34
Left Catalonians	22
Communists	14
Others	18
Various Center Parties	66
Total	326

Rightist Parties:

Spanish Confederation of Autonomous Right Parties (CEDA)	96
Catalonian Lliga	12
Monarchists	14
Nationalists	2
Others	23
Total	147
	473

Source: Spain's War of Independence (1937), Washington, DC.

The question of national identity

Further undercutting the unity of the Republic's state system was the growing pull of peripheral nationalisms. Ever since 1931, successive Republican governments had been wrestling with the problem of how to balance the demands of resurgent regionalist movements – particularly in Catalonia and the Basque country – with the needs of a centralized liberal state. During the first two years of left-wing rule (*bienio*), the government had attempted to answer this question by granting a large degree of autonomy to Catalonia, a region whose political backing had been instrumental in establishing the Republic. The Catalan statute passed in September 1932 relieved much of the pro-nationalist pressures that had been building in that region for some years. Yet, tensions there resurfaced when the general movement towards greater political devolution within the Republican state system was halted by the centre-right governments that ruled between 1933 and 1936. For the mostly conservative parties that were now in the ascendant, the idea of granting autonomy to Catalonia (or to any other region in Spain) was anathema, not least because they believed that region-alism threatened the unity and integrity of Spain's traditional institutions. When, in October 1934, it appeared as though the Catalan Statute might be repealed, the left-Republican President of the Generalitat, Lluis Companys, responded by proclaiming the establishment of a Catalan state within the Spanish Federal Republic. But from the outset of the October revolt it was apparent that Companys's claim for regional independence was premature. As we have already seen, the socialist-led October revolt was immediately put down by the government, and, in the following weeks, Catalan autonomy was drastically curtailed.[4] Repression tended to inflame rather than diminish regionalist feelings, and, as a result, it effectively destroyed the basis of a political consensus on the nationalist question that the Republic needed in order to maintain its overall stability.

Eve of military rebellion

Against the backdrop of widespread economic disruptions and almost daily bloody street confrontations that broke out between groups on the left and right during the spring of 1936, it was hardly surprising that rumors began spreading about an impending military coup. When Azaña's government felt that these threats could no longer be ignored, the premier sought to diffuse the situation by transferring several generals known for their anti-Republican beliefs as far away from the centres of power as possible: Francisco Franco was relieved of his post in Madrid as Chief of Staff and sent to the Canary Islands, General Goded was dispatched to the Balearics, and General Emilio Mola was assigned to Navarra (the heartland of Carlist territory). But Azaña's precautionary measures did little to disrupt the plotting among a core group of army officers who were convinced that a military coup was the only way of stopping Spain from being plunged into a state of chaos (Document 1.3).

Document 1.3 The Spring Crisis

Madrid was on tenterhooks. Twice a week we got word that the revolt was scheduled for that night or the next. We sat up many a night beside the telephone, waiting for the terrible news that the Madrid garrison, or some other garrison, had risen against the Republic. And every morning, after such a sleepless night, Ignacio would go to the War Ministry and beg his immediate superior, the War Minister and Premier since Azaña's election to the Presidency, Cesares Quiroga, to act. . . . Azaña had lost touch with the people. Remote, disinterested, he had already sunk into the lethargy that was later to overcome him completely. . . .

'The Republic is sufficiently protected,' Azaña told Ignacio coldly.

'But the generals who have been transferred to the islands, like Francisco Franco and Goded, still command troops. The only effect of transferring them is to make them think they are regarded as traitors and to force them to act quickly!'

'The Cabinet is in full control of the situation.' It was Azaña's last word on the matter.

Source: De la Mora, C. (1939) *In Place of Splendor*, New York.

The main protagonists behind this conspiracy belonged to the Unión Militar Española (UME), which was a *sub rosa* military organization that came into being in 1933–34. Its original mission was to protect the constitutional government from being overthrown by left-wing revolutionaries. Some of its members, though, saw the organization as an instrument that could be used to spearhead a right-wing coup. By March 1936 it claimed a membership of some 3,500 officers. Recognizing that if their plan to set up an authoritarian directory was ultimately to succeed it would be necessary for them to secure civilian support, the military leaders established ties with right-wing groups ranging from the Alfonsine monarchists to extremist para-military groups such as the Carlist *requetés* and the Falangist militia squads. At this point, however, only a handful of generals were willing to assume an active role in the conspiracy. Chief among them was General Mola, a former national police chief who was entrusted with organizing the plot to overthrow the Republic. General Sanjurjo, who had been banished to Portugal after leading an abortive coup (*san-jurada*) against the government in 1932, remained at the margins of the plotting until May, when he agreed to become the nominal head of the revolt. Perhaps the most highly regarded military figure in Spain, Francisco Franco, waited for the right moment before committing himself to the rebellion. In fact, at least until early July, Franco seems to have been still hoping that the government of Casares Quiroga (who had replaced Azaña as prime minister in May) would call in the army to put an end to the escalating violence and chaos.

One of the complicating factors associated with this anti-government conspiracy at this point in time was that it was not entirely a military affair. As has already been mentioned, the chief organizer of the plot, General Mola, early on recognized that the military alone could not carry out a successful coup. He, along with the others who joined the conspiracy, therefore turned to Spain's right-wing civilian groups which could be relied on to support a rebellion. By taking this step, it was clear that the military were not simply interested in re-establishing law and order to a country that was being convulsed by strikes and street demonstrations. For by enlisting the support of the Carlists and other extremist groups on the right, the officers were committing themselves to a plot that involved not only overthrowing the Republic but also developing the basis of an authoritarian regime that could be used to repress the left.

Meanwhile, throughout the spring of 1936, the dialogue between the left and right had broken down and, and the voices of political compromise and restraint were soon drowned out by a wave of violence. On 13 April a judge who had just sentenced a Falangist to thirty years in prison for killing a socialist newsboy was shot dead in the streets of Madrid. The next day some socialists retaliated by killing a lieutenant in the Civil Guard during a Republic Day parade. Two months later the Cortes was the scene of menacing exchanges between right-wing politicians and their left-wing counterparts. Both sides made it clear that they were prepared to resort to force in order to prevent their political enemies from achieving power (Document 1.4). A few weeks later the growing tensions between the two extremes came to a head. On Sunday night 12 July, a pro-Republican Assault guard officer, Lt José Castillo, was murdered on his way to work by three Falangists. The crime provoked an immediate response from the left. In the small hours of the 13th, an Assault Guard squad comprised of a Civil Guard captain named Fernando Condés and four young socialists, arrived at the house of the reactionary politician and member of parliament José Calvo Sotelo.[5] Moments after he had been abducted, one of the socialist militants shot the deputy in the back of the head. His body was then dumped at a nearby cemetery (Document 1.5). The conspirators plotting against the government reacted to the news by setting their plans in motion. Four days later the military rebellion began.

Document 1.4 War of Words

Sra Ibárruri, Communist, gave the long-awaited speech signalled several days ago by the marxists as one which would produce a major sensation in Parliament. Let us say it once and for all: Sra Ibárruri spoke in the chamber as if it were a public rally, with unproven primary arguments, and with all the cutting phrases . . . which at election times always win applause and cheers of passion and hate. The speaker paraded before the chamber what she usually says about the supposed repression in Asturias and several times demanded the punishment of the guilty. And she glorified the Asturian revolution, considering it the purest and most perfect of any that has ever been attempted by the proletarian masses of any country. The strange thing about all this is that a demagogic speech, glorifying the marxist revolution, which aimed at destroying the very foundations of a bourgeois society, should be applauded with great enthusiasm by the left-wing republican parties which figure in the Popular Front and which call themselves bourgeois. We have never seen a greater inclination towards suicide.

Source: Low, R. (1992) *La Pasionaria: The Spanish Firebrand*, London

Document 1.5 The Countdown Begins

(a)

In the early hours of the morning of July 13 a service truck bearing the number 17 drove out of the Pontejos Barracks, went down Diego de León Street and finally turned into Velázquez Street where it pulled up on the right hand side opposite 89 Velázquez Street. Here was the apartment of Señor Calvo Sotelo.

Captains Condés, José del Rey and Victoriano Cuenca thereupon descended, together with a number of Assault Guards.

Señor Sotelo got into the third compartment of the truck (the first being occupied by the driver), and he took the fourth seat. Assault Guard and a cavalry trooper sat beside him.

The truck reached the point where Ayala and Velázquez Streets cross, and here Victoriano Cuenca drew out a pistol and fired two shots at the back of Señor Sotelo's head so quickly that the other men in the truck had the impression that only one shot had been fired.

'Someone will surely denounce us.' Condés replied: 'Don't worry. Nothing will happen,' and José del Rey said: 'Whoever whispers a word about this is a dead man. We'll kill him in the same way that we killed that swine.'

Source: Radosh, R., Habeck, M. and Sevostianov, G. (eds) (2001) *Spain Betrayed: The Soviet Union in the Spanish Civil War*, New Haven, p. 241

(b)

That week was one of incredible tension. Calvo Sotelo's funeral was turned into a demonstration by the Right and ended in shooting between them and the Shock Police. In the Cortes, Gil Robles made a speech in Calvo Sotelo's memory, which was officially described as a declaration of war. Prieto asked Casares Quiroga to arm the workers, and the Minister refused. Detentions and assaults were on the increase in all districts of Madrid. Building trade workers of the U.G.T. went to work in the University City under police escort, for the C.N.T. continued to attack them. Expensive cars, with their luggage carefully covered so as to escape attention, left the town in considerable numbers on the roads to the north. People began to flee from Madrid and from Spain.

On the following day, Saturday, July the 18th, the Government openly announced that there had been insurrections in many of the provinces, although it continued 'to have the situation well in hand.' Rumors and news, inextricably mixed, chased each other: Morocco was in the hands of Franco; the Moors and the Foreign Legion were disembarking in Seville; in Barcelona the battle was raging; in the provinces a general strike had been declared; the Fleet was in the hands of the rebels – no, it was in the hands of the sailors who had thrown their officers overboard.

Under the avalanche of contradictory reports, the people reacted in their own way . . . The Right had taken to open insurrection. The Government was tottering.

Source: Barea, A. (1946) *The Forging of a Rebel*, London, pp. 500–3

Civil War and revolution

The group of generals and army officers who rose against the Republic on 17 July 1936 were confident that their military takeover would be swift and decisive. But, within days of the first rising in northern Spanish Morocco (Melilla), the coup had met with only partial success (Document 1.6). In pro-Republican cities, such as in Saragossa and Seville, the insurgents quickly gained the upper hand by moving with great speed to control military garrisons and other strategic facilities, thereby preventing working-class organizations from mounting an effective response (Document 1.7). Where the population was already predominantly anti-Republican, the rebels were greeted by enthusiastic crowds. In Pamplona, one of the centres of the rebellion in the north, the uprising was celebrated by the spirited but well-disciplined columns of Carlist *requetés* or civilian militias, who marched through the city singing religious hymns and shouting ¡Viva Cristo Rey! (Long live Christ our King!) to the cheers of thousands of onlookers. The rebels could also count on the support of other traditionally conservative towns and villages, such as Burgos, Salamanca and Avila, where there was hardly any opposition to the rising (Document 1.8).

Document 1.6 Declaration of War

July 18, 1936

I DECLARE:

Once again the Army, together with the other armed forces of the nation, has deemed it necessary to respond to the ardent desire of the grand majority of Spaniards, who with infinite bitterness saw disappear that which can unite us all in a common ideal: SPAIN.

It is a question of reestablishing ORDER within the REPUBLIC, not only in appearance or external signs, but also in its very essence, ceasing to be a country divided in two groups: those that enjoy power and violated even the laws they themselves made, and those whose rights were trampled. The manner in which the two groups conduct themselves will determine their relations with AUTHORITY, another feature vanished from our nation and which is indispensable for any human community, whether it be a democratic system or a Soviet one – the latter in which it will reach its maximum rigor. It is therefore necessary to act with justice, which takes no heed of class or social category – which is neither exalted nor persecuted. The reestablishment of this principle of AUTHORITY, forgotten in recent years, demands that punishment be exemplary in the severity with which it will be imposed and the celerity with which it is carried out without hesitation or vacillation.

Source: Díaz-Plaja, F. (1969) *Guerra en España en sus documentos,* Barcelona, pp. 229–30.

Document 1.7 The Generals Launch the Uprising

Don Antonio Bahamonde y Sánchez de Castro (Aide to Queipo de Ilano, who helped to establish rebel control of Seville)

July 18th

The rumours which had been circulating were confirmed. The garrison in Africa had revolted. The communications with the rest of Spain were interrupted.

The chiefs of the General Staff of the Division, in complicity with Queipo, took its Commander, General Villa-Abraille, prisoner. Queipo immediately assumed the command, and, with the aid of the chiefs of the garrison, quartered the troops for lack of confidence in them.

At 3 o'clock in the afternoon, the first skirmish took place; the Assault Guards, under the command of a lieutenant, placed a machine-gun in the Plaza Nueva. Captain Escribano, with a group of soldiers, warned them to remove it, and when the lieutenant refused, the soldiers fired. A number of discharges were exchanged, and some moments later the Guards surrendered.

The soldiers attacked the telephone building, which was defended by the Assault Guards, who surrendered after a short resistance. Some moments later, the soldiers took possession of the Town Hall, and the Municipal Guards, who were inside, surrendered without combat.

The insurgents, at 6 o'clock in the afternoon, were masters of the centre of the city and of the barracks of the Assault Guards, situated in the Alameda de Hércules. It was owing to the adhesion of these that the insurgents were able to take possession of Seville with such rapidity. The police, for the most part, adhered to the movement, giving their service to it from the very first day.

On that same day (the 18th) at 8 o'clock at night, Queipo spoke over the radio, saying that the movement had triumphed in all Spain. He exhorted the workers who resisted in the districts to surrender, and said, 'Those who do not report for work on Monday, will be discharged: the directors of the syndicates will be shot if they do not give the order to resume work. This movement is not against the Republic, but against the Government of the

Popular Front.' He ended with a 'Viva la República!' which was followed by the national hymn. Queipo continued for many nights to end his talk with this 'Viva la República!' and the transmitter, for a considerable period of time, played several times a day the 'Himno de Riego.'

Seville in a few days was under total domination. Queipo said over the radio, 'The movement has triumphed in all Spain; I solemnly promise that those who cease their resistance have nothing to fear; the Foreign Legion and the Regular troops which have come from Africa will level to the ground the villages which do not lay down their arms.' Every day he announced brilliant victories, and promised the triumphal entrance of the Nationalist troops into Madrid within a very brief time. He fixed upon different dates: first, it was July 25th, the festival of the Apostle Santiago, patron of Spain; then it was the day of the Virgin of the Kings, patroness of Seville; later, October 1st; and, finally, as a definite date, he guaranteed that Mola would speak from the Ministry of Government in Madrid before November 10th. He gave assurance that, as soon as the capital was taken, the end of the war would be a question of days.

Source: Payne, R. (1962) *The Civil War in Spain, 1936–1939*, New York: Putnam, 1962 pp. 27–30

Document 1.8 With the Rebels

(a)

What happened in Burgos, the capital of the rebel government, that eventful week-end when the civil war began, was doubtless typical of what went on in many other Spanish cities. An Englishwoman from Warwickshire, married to a photographer of Burgos, told me what had occurred in that city the night of July 18.

'Early on that evening,' she said, 'crowds were promenading up and down the Paseo, as usual, and couples were flirting in the balconies. Then suddenly Socialist guards with red arm bands appeared, and everybody fled terrified to their houses. For several hours the streets were entirely deserted except for the patrolling Red Guards. About two o'clock in the morning, soldiers from the garrison began parading the streets, and after beating drums read a pronunciamento announcing that the city was under martial law. Immediately people poured out of their homes, and soon the streets were filled with cheering crowds. The Reds simply vanished from sight. The Socialist civil governor was asked to give up the seals of office, and when he refused he was locked up. Other Socialist leaders were arrested. The enthusiasm continued throughout the next day, Sunday, when young girls, after attending Mass to pray for the success of the rebel armies, went about distributing cigarettes and chocolate to the Fascist youths guarding the bridges.'

One Sunday morning in August, I witnessed the tremendous ovation given to General Franco when he stepped out on the balcony of the Capitanía General at Burgos.

A great roar went up from the vast concourse of people assembled in the square in front of the government building. General Franco, wearing the red sash of a general in the Spanish army around his olive-green uniform, showed himself flanked on one side by General Mola and on the other by President Cabanellas. Loud cries of 'Viva España!' went up as the three rebel leaders embraced one another effusively and the crowd broke into the national anthem. They were cheering because they felt sure that this triumvirate was going to end anarchy in Spain and bring to the country the boon of orderly and stable government.

Source: Elliott, J. (1936) in *The Atlantic Monthly*, vol. 158, issue 5.

(b)

In Pamplona, July 19 showed a remarkable resurrection of the Carlist legend. Pamplona was throbbing with emotion, hoarse from cheering, her heart trembling with gratitude because the prophecies were coming true. Pamplona was red with red berets, and covered with Spanish flags which were waved impatiently by those who were eager to embark upon the conquest and tell the prodigious story to the rest of the country.

A short while after four o'clock, General Mola, the outstanding leader in these developments, was reviewing the first Traditionalist battalion.

Evening came, and the lorries loaded with Requetés were off to war, singing old tunes with new vigour. It was as though Navarre had opened her arteries to inundate Spain to her last drop of blood. More and more lorries went forth, forming an endless line along the road, accompanied by the sound of the motors and the youthful shouting, fragrant and freedom-loving, the voice of the warlike and conquering Navarre of old. And the voices vanished into the warm atmosphere of that hot July night.

Source: Arrarás, J. (1938) *Francisco Franco*, London, pp. 182 and 183.

But in Spain's capital (Madrid) and several other key cities (Barcelona, Bilbao, and Valencia) the military rebellion was crushed by leftist trade unions, improvised popular militias, and the military and police forces (Civil and Assault Guards) who remained loyal to the Republic (Document 1.9). Another major setback came when nearly two-thirds of Spain's naval fleet declared for the Republic (Document 1.10). This unanticipated development not only prevented Franco from transporting his highly trained Army of the Africa from Morocco to the mainland but, perhaps even more significantly, it also led to the internationalization of the conflict. Fearing that the rebellion might bog down without the support of their crack troops, Generals Franco and Mola urgently appealed to both Italy and Germany for aid. By the end of July, transport planes sent by Hitler and Mussolini were assisting the insurgents in the first major military airlift in modern warfare.

Document 1.9 Defending the Republic

(a)

Radio Broadcast, Madrid, 19 July 1936

Danger! To Arms!

Workers, anti-fascists, and labouring people!

Rise as one man! Prepare to defend the Republic, national freedom and the democratic liberties won by the people.

Everybody now knows from the communications of the government and of the People's Front how serious the situation is. The workers, together with the troops which have remained loyal to the Republic, are manfully and enthusiastically carrying on the struggle in Morocco and the Canary Islands. Under the slogan, 'Fascism shall not pass, the October butchers shall not pass!' . . .

All Spain has risen to the struggle. In Madrid the people have come out into the streets, lending strength to the government by their determination and fighting spirit, so that it may utterly exterminate the reactionary fascist rebels.

Young men and women, sound the alarm! Rise and join the battle!

Source: Ibárruri, D. (1938) *Speeches and Articles, 1936–1938*, London.

(b)

Lawrence Fernsworth

From the top of the Ramblas I struck across the Plaza de Cataluña, a broad and beautifully flowered park, with its statues and fountains banked in shrubbery, which here forms a spacious, roughly circular plaza flanked by cafés, banks, restaurants, the American consulate, the telephone building, which is a skyscraper ending in a dome, and the military casino, among others. The Plaza de Cataluña is a kind of central hub into which various avenues and paseos lead. At the upper side the Paseo de Gracia cuts up through the center of the newer and more open part of the town, just as from the lower side the Ramblas cut through the older and more congested quarters. In a way the Ramblas and the Paseo counterbalance each other.

A column several thousand strong had come down the Diagonal from Pedralbes bent on marching down the Paseo de Gracia to the Plaza de Cataluña. The object was to capture the government buildings and the city hall which lay off the Ramblas to the left, just behind the cathedral. Other rebel regiments were engaged in an attempt to take these from the loyal defenders. From that direction already came the cannonading of artillery.

By that time I realized that a real revolution was on.

The officers of the artillery column had professed to be favorable to the republic and had come out to defend it against the rebels. However, when the officers considered themselves sufficiently advanced and safe, they disarmed the Anarchists and continued onward to join their fellow rebels.

But when they arrived near the Ritz they were rushed by Shock Police and citizens. Many citizens went into the fray armed with staves or only with their bare hands. The officers scurried to shelter in a doorway. Little valiance was shown anywhere by officers. Cowardice and treachery were the outstanding characteristics of their movement.

I could not quite understand this spectacle of Shock Police and citizen militia cooperating with the army. Had the Shock Police gone over to the rebels? Such swift changes sometimes occurred. Or were these troops aiding the government?

But it was the same old story, as I learned later. The troops, whose officers pretended to be loyal, had gained access to the university and won the cooperation of the loyal forces to further their rebellion.

Although fighting was still going on, and would continue for the next two or three days, it became evident by late afternoon that the constituted government was the victor.

Source: Payne, R. (1962) *The Civil War in Spain, 1936–1939*, New York, Putnam, 1962, pp. 56, 58, 60, 61, and 62

Document 1.10 Failure of a Coup

At the opening of the war the Government ships were usually captained by ex-petty officers, who were unable to give orders without the approval of soviets of the ship's company. Thus the Sailors' Council of one destroyer, for example, deposed their commanding officer because she had rammed a mole on leaving Barcelona harbour.

All the officers had been killed on July 19th, but their cabins and mess-room had been carefully sealed to prevent looting. Other eye-witnesses of that first summer report seeing loyalist sailors, clad in no semblance of uniform, lounging about and smoking on neglected decks, and numerous complaints of their seamanship and gunnery were made by neutrals.

The refusal of the sailors to join their officers in revolt was one of Franco's greatest disappointments.

Source: 'The Naval Side of the Spanish Civil War' (1938), *The Fortnightly Review*, London.

Because their plans for achieving complete control of Spain had failed, the insurgent generals and their right-wing civilian allies were forced to conduct a war against the legitimate Republican government. The country was now split into two mutually hostile 'red' and 'white' zones. The Republicans controlled the major urban and industrial zones in the north (Bilbao), centre (Madrid), north-east (Barcelona), and east (Valencia) as well as Spain's considerable gold reserves, while their opponents, who referred to themselves as 'Nationalists' rather than as rebels, held approximately one-third of the peninsula, including vast stretches of sparsely populated territory and farmland in the central, southern and north-western sections of the country.

2 | Men and women in arms

For most historians, the military triumph of the Nationalists over the Republicans can be explained in terms of the advantages the former held throughout much of the conflict in the areas of (1) military organization and (2) the quality and quantity of troops and *matériel* supplied by foreign powers. While this view does not take into account other crucial factors, such as the degree of ideological and political cohesiveness on both sides, it goes a long way towards explaining the one-sided outcomes of the vast majority of battles that were fought during the war.

At the outset of the Civil War, the disparities of the two opposing military forces were not immediately apparent. On paper, at least, the size and relative strengths of the two sides were nearly evenly matched. The Republicans possessed an army that was approximately one-third larger than that of the insurgents, and the government retained control over Spain's tiny air force and navy. In addition, there were numerous civilians affiliated to left-wing organizations who rallied to the defence of the Republic. Indeed, it was thanks to the overwhelming surge of popular forces in Catalonia and elsewhere that the initial military rebellion was crushed in those regions. But the rebels quickly made up the ground they lost during the first weeks of fighting. Not only did they enjoy the enthusiastic support of tens of thousands of paramilitary forces drawn from the Falangist and the Carlist movements, but they were led by the formidable Army of the Africa, which, in terms of its combat abilities and military capacities, was far superior to the loyal units of the Peninsular Army who were defending the Republic (Document 2.1). There were further reasons why the rebels gained the upper hand in military affairs soon after the outbreak of hostilities. After the lines of fighting had been drawn, rebel forces (now calling themselves Nationalists) displayed a level of military training and competency that could not be matched by their opponents. This was in large measure due to the fact that, in contrast to the Republican army, the Nationalist army was composed of a relatively homogenous group of experienced senior, junior, and non-commissioned officers and infantrymen who were eventually placed under an efficiently run central command structure.

Document 2.1 Fighting for the Crusade

(a)

I have a slight personal knowledge of military affairs, and I saw that Franco had fighting for him men who were disciplined and who had an ideal. His African troops were not only well in hand, but they possessed a very high level of fighting ability. The volunteer militia units were, naturally, not so well trained, but their keenness was such that it was evident they would gain those other military qualities in the course of the campaign.

It was in this month of August that Spain's National army was being formed. Young men were marching to exercise, were standing at the rifle butts or were kneeling round a machine-gun, all over Nationalist Spain. Some of them in khaki with a khaki forage cap with green or scarlet tassel hanging over the forehead – these were men belonging to the classes of conscripts being called up, three in August and two later in December. These conscripts were just 200,000 in number, and they were to form the solid flesh of the skeleton Regular Army which was all that had been left after five years of republic.

Their discipline was severe, their training hard, and they turned out to be very fine soldiers.

Despite this, my favourites were always the volunteer battalions – the young men of the Requetes or the Falangists. The first, so gay and dashing with their scarlet *boinas*, or berets, rather like the tam-o'-shanter but without the tassel, worn hanging down over the right ear, their khaki shirts, wide open on the chest, their buff equipment, and their white socks neatly rolled round the ankle over their *espargatas*, or cord-soled shoes. The second, in their blue uniforms, looked so workman-like, and how they sang their Falangist hymn as they marched! There was much work in those early days, but also much singing, and 'Oriamendi' for the Requetes, the Falangist hymn, and the 'Novio de la Muerte' for the Spanish Legion, could be heard over the tramp of feet and the roar of the motor traffic on every road and in every town square of Nationalist Spain.

The Requetes must have put in the field, mainly in the north as I have already said, something like 100,000 men, nearly all of whom were used for active military purposes. The Falangists had perhaps double that number, but many of their units were used on lines of communication and for garrison purposes. Many also were kept in Majorca to protect that island from further menace and also to act themselves as a perpetual threat to Barcelona.

None of these troops were completely trained, and yet most of them had to be used in the front line as necessity dictated.

Source: Cardozo, H. G. (1937) *The March of a Nation: My Year of Spain's Civil War*, London, pp. 57–8.

(b)

Lieut.-Colonel Millán Astray came out of the tent, followed by a couple of officers. The crowd fell silent. The Commander stretched his bony frame, while his hands mangled a glove until it showed the hairs of the fur lining. The whole might of his stentorian voice filled the encampment, and the noises from the bivouacs of the other units died down. Eight thousand men tried to hear him, and they listened.

'*Caballeros legionarios!*'

'Gentlemen of the Legion . . . yes, gentlemen! Gentlemen of the *Tercio* of Spain, offspring of the Flanders *Tercios* of old. Gentlemen! Some people say that before coming here you were I know not what! but anything rather than gentlemen: some murderers, others thieves, and all with your lives finished – dead! And it is true what they say. But here, since you are here, you are gentlemen. You have risen from the dead – for don't forget that you have been dead, that your lives were finished. You have come here to live a new life for which you must pay with death. You have come here to die. It is to die that one joins the Legion.

'What are you? The Betrothed of Death. You are the gentlemen of the Legion. You have washed yourselves clean, for you have come here to die. There is no other life for you than in this Legion. But you must understand that you are Spanish gentlemen, all of you, knights like those other legionaries who, conquering America, begat you. In your veins there are some drops of the blood of Pizarro and Cortés. There are drops of the blood of those adventurers who conquered a world and who, like you, were gentlemen – the Betrothed of Death. Long live Death! . . . '

'*Viva la Muerte!*'

Source: Barea, A. (1946) *The Forging of a Rebel*, London, p. 293.

Another advantage that the Nationalists permanently gained over the Republican forces in the early stages of the war was the military assistance they received from Italy and Germany. It is well known that the joint commitment of these two renegade nations to supply the Nationalists with combat troops and military advisers as well as armaments (tanks, aircraft, artillery and munitions) greatly contributed to Franco's ability to gain the upper hand in nearly every theatre of conflict on land, sea, and air. In this connection, it is important to point out that, after it became apparent that the fascist powers were prepared to intervene as long as it took for a Nationalist victory, the Soviets committed themselves to the idea of assisting the Republic's war effort. However, their ability to do so was seriously undermined by several factors beyond their control. The diplomatic barriers they encountered were the most formidable in this regard. Even though an arms embargo had been imposed on the Spanish conflict, its uneven enforcement benefited the Nationalists more than the Republicans. This was due in part to the fact that, given the centrality of their position in the emerging diplomatic order of Europe, no country was prepared to challenge

Germany's and Italy's flagrant violations of this policy. On the other hand, the Soviet Union, which was only beginning to emerge from the diplomatic limbo to which it had been consigned since 1917, stood to lose more than either Germany or Italy by incurring the wrath of the international community. As a result, Soviet efforts to render aid and assistance to the Republic were far more circumscribed than those of the fascist powers.

While the Nationalists did not receive substantially more military assistance from their allies than the Republicans did from the Soviet Union or other foreign suppliers, the most serious disparity between the war materials being imported by both sides was in their overall quality. Early on in the war, the republicans could rely on regular Soviet shipments, and the aircraft and weaponry the Russians sold them tended to be superior to that being sent by the Germans and the Italians. For example, the Russian fighter planes (Tupolev SB and Polikarpov I–16) that arrived during the Battle of Madrid (November 1936 to January 1937) were, according to the historian Gerald Howson, 'in advance of anything in service in other air forces at the time'.[1] Over time, however, the quality of the Russian war materials declined, whereas the supplies Franco was receiving from his fascist allies – particularly the aircraft, rifles, and artillery weapons – outmatched anything that the Republicans were receiving from the Russians or other foreign sources.

Opposing sides: Republican zone

Given that the July Rebellion had shaken the foundations of Spain's military structures to their core, the most pressing question facing the Republicans at the outset of the conflict was how to mount an effective response to the pro-rebel forces. During the first weeks of the war, the struggle against the insurgents had been successfully waged by both civilian and loyal Republican army and police units, who were, for the most part, willing to co-operate with one another. Yet these initial victories relied more on the élan and sheer numbers of the anti-insurgent forces than on the organized power of the pro-Republicans. Once it became clear that the rebellion was developing into a more protracted struggle, the republicans were forced to develop a war strategy that could effectively integrate the civilian militias that had spontaneously sprung up in July alongside the loyal Republican military units. To achieve this goal, however, the Republicans faced a number of enormous obstacles. The early months of fighting saw the Republican forces in disarray. With each trade union organization fielding its own columns (militias) and determining their own military objectives, there was little or no co-ordination of the war effort. For the anarchosyndicalists, the initial goal was to advance their overall revolutionary agenda by conquering regions where a significant number of their followers were being executed and/or suppressed by the triumphant Nationalists. To this end, they paid little heed to the operations of other republican units, particularly as these tended to be directed by rival political organizations such as the POUM or the communists of the PCE (Document 2.2).

Document 2.2 Building a People's Army

(a)

What were the defects of the militias of the Romantic Period? Certainly not lack of heroics or personal combativity. General Lister, in an article in the organ of the Fifth Regiment had pointed out that a senior Commander, on suggesting to a body of troops that they take up a certain tactical position, was met with point-blank refusal. 'You are wearing stars and even if you hadn't got them we should take no more notice of you'. This happened to Lister, whom no man could suspect of belonging to the old military cases, whose revolutionary zeal was beyond question. The political parties too often disposed of their troops according to imagined party necessity, or for reasons of prestige, or distrust of other parties.

But there were other defects inside the units. Excessive rank-and-filism, leading to rejection of reasonable commands, or such long discussion of them that decision was taken too late, impaired their efficiency. Often irreconcilable factions developed in the course of the debate. More subtly than this, the rank-and-filism of the militias often weakened confidence in the very principle of command, collective or personal.

Political debates themselves, expressing divergent tendencies within one form of belief, often robbed the militia of unanimity.

We are getting near the problem, but I must make another demand on the reader's imagination.

Each battalion had its own Intendencia, or supply service, its own transport section, as well as its own general staff. This was a necessity in the early days, because the government was unable to provide it.

By packing a department with a staff of its own political faith, a party might switch the precious ammunition, machine guns, rifles, etc., toward its own column out there on the crackling Sierras.

Source: Bates, R. (20 October 1937), 'Castilian Drama: An Army Is Born', *The New Republic*, 286–87.

(b)

Toronto Daily Star, 5 August 1936 by Pierre Van Paassen

Durruti, a syndicalist metal-worker, is the man who led the victorious bayonet-charge of the People's Militia on the stronghold of the Fascist rebels at San Rafaele yesterday. I met him today. He is a tall, swarthy fellow with a clean-shaven face, Moorish features, the son of a poor peasant, which is noticeable by his cracking, almost guttural dialect.

'We must take Saragossa, and after that we must turn south to face Franco, who will be coming up from Seville with his foreign legionnaires and

Moroccans. In two, three weeks time we will probably be fighting the decisive battles.'

'Two, three weeks?' I asked crestfallen.

'Yes, a month perhaps, this civil war will last at least all through the month of August. The masses are in arms. The army does not count any longer. There are two camps: civilians who fight for freedom and civilians who are rebels and Fascists. All the workers in Spain know that if fascism triumphs, it will be famine and slavery. But the Fascists also know what is in store for them when they are beaten. That is why the struggle is implacable and relentless. For us it is a question of crushing fascism, wiping it out and sweeping it away so that it can never rear its head again in Spain. We are determined to finish with fascism once and for all. Yes, and in spite of the government,' he added grimly.

Source: Paz, A. (1977) *Durruti: The People Armed*, Montreal.

(c)

A middle-aged CNT peasant, Fernando ARAGON, in the village of Angüés, only a few kilometres behind the line on the Huesca front, wryly observed them. The anarchist *Roja y Negra* column was on one side of the village, the POUM militia on the other.

When the former went into action, the latter sat back with their hands in their pockets, laughing. When the POUM was in combat the anarchists, I have to admit, did the same. That's no way to fight a war, let alone win it. They should have got together to fight the common enemy . . .

Source: Fraser, R. (1979) *Blood of Spain: An Oral History of the Spanish Civil War*, New York, p. 135.

Over time, however, the anarchists, as well as other revolutionary militias, recognized that their mounting losses against the Nationalists were not sustainable (Document 2.3). However, their efforts to reorganize the libertarian militias along more conventional lines inevitably aroused the anger of the purists, who believed that the militarization of the militias flagrantly violated the central tenets of their anti-authoritarian creed (Document 2.4).

Document 2.3 Anarchist Military Organization

(a)

Army Reorganization:

Militarization, But Not the Old Style

The Secretary of C.N.T. Explains How Reorganization is Carried Out

'Our comrades,' said comrade Vazquez, 'should not feel upset simply because they don't like a word. We have already been "militarized" from the first moment when we had to accept for our war operations the united command and the discipline demanded by every joint operation.'

'And, besides, this militarization – even if the other parties of the anti-Fascist front do want quite the opposite – will not go beyond establishing the necessary harmony in the joint work of the military technician, who works out the operative plans, and those who defend the country with arms in their hands. We will never tolerate the revival of the old militarist privileges.'

'Otherwise there will be no changes of a basic nature. Military command in the new brigades will remain in the same hands as before. Comrades who have come to trust those that bore the responsibility for the military operations will not be compelled by senseless changes to submit themselves to people whose ideological views they do not share.

'The political commissars for our brigades will be named by the C.N.T. organization, and it is to the latter that they will be responsible at every moment, even during the preliminary period of compulsory training in the schools specially established for that purpose.'

No Mixed Brigades

'As to the question whether the new brigades are going to be mixed in their make-up, that is, whether they will be made up of the new soldiers of the regular army, Marxists and C.N.T. battalions of the old militia, Vazquez said that a proposal was made to that effect. The C.N.T., however, made its own proposal that the brigades which are made up of the C.N.T.-F.A.I. comrades should be controlled by those organizations.

'Get rid, comrades, of the mistaken notion,' said the Secretary, in conclusion, 'that it is a despotic sort of militarization that we are concerned with now. From the first days we set ourselves the task of establishing a firm discipline and now, for the interests of everyone, we intend to give it a definite direction.'

Source: Spanish Revolution: A Bulletin Published by the United Libertarian Organizations, New York, vol. 1. no. 15 (9 April), 1937, CNT–FAI.

(b)

The tacit consent to militarization on the part of our Spanish comrades was a violent break with their Anarchist past. But grave as this was, it must also be considered in the light of their utter military inexperience, theirs but ours as well. While it is true that after July 19 tens of thousands of old and young men volunteered to go to the front – they went with flying colors and the determination to conquer Franco in a short time – they had no previous military training or experience. If it was inconsistent on the part of the

CNT–FAI to consent to militarization, it was also inconsistent for us to change our attitude toward war, which some of us had held all our lives. We had always condemned war as serving capitalism and no other purpose; but when we realized that our heroic comrades in Barcelona had to continue the anti-Fascist struggle, we immediately rallied to their support, which was undoubtedly a departure from our previous stand on war. Once we realized that it would be impossible to meet hordes of Fascists armed to the very teeth, we could not escape the next step, which was militarization. Like so many of the actions of the CNT–FAI undoubtedly contrary to our philosophy, they were not of their making or choosing. They were imposed upon them by the development of the struggle which, if not brought to a successful end, would exterminate the CNT–FAI, destroy their constructive achievements, and set back Anarchist thought and ideas not only in Spain but in the rest of the world.

Source: Goldman, E. (1983) *Vision on Fire*, New Paltz, pp. 230–1.

Document 2.4 Libertarian Opposition to Military Conventions

We know that for us it will be totally impossible to submit to tyranny and ill treatment, because it would take something less than a full man to stand meekly by, rifle in hand, swallowing insults; we are in possession, nevertheless, of disquieting news of militarized comrades having – like being handed slabs of lead – to take orders from people in many cases inept and in every case hostile.

We used to believe that we were fighting for redemption and salvation, and here we see ourselves slipping back into the same thing that we are fighting against: tyranny, the power of castes, and the most brutal and penetrating authoritarianism.

But the hour is grave. We have been caught – we know not why, and if we did know, we would say nothing now – we have been caught, I repeat, in a trap and we must get out of it, we must escape from it as best we can, for there are traps bristling all over.

The militarists, all the militarists – and there are fanatical ones in our own camp – have us surrounded. Yesterday we were masters; today they are. The popular army, which has nothing popular about it except that the people form it, and this has always been the case, does not belong to the people but to the Government and it is the Government that commands, it is the Government that gives orders. The people are allowed only to obey, as they are required to do always.

Source: A Day Mournful and Overcast . . . , (1937) London, reprinted 1993.

Another revolutionary military strategy pursued in the early months of the war was that of the anti-Stalinist POUM, the organization made famous by George Orwell's autobiographical tribute to the Spanish Civil War, *Homage to Catalonia*. This small but potent Marxist party argued for the creation of a revolutionary fighting force in the image of Leon Trotsky's Red Army (Document 2.5).

Document 2.5 The POUM's Idea of a Red Army

In the cause, we find ourselves in complete agreement with the 'professed aims' both of the recent governmental reforms in Catalonia and the new military measure looking towards a unified command and a more effective army: but this army must be the Red Army of the workers. Revolutionaries are not mercenaries; they are the autonomous heroes of the proletarian revolution. Without damaging the perfect right of everyone to express his political opinion and social ideas, it is necessary to keep the strictest discipline in the military sense and to carry out to the letter all orders coming from the unified command. From every combatant must be exacted unshakable revolutionary conscience and self-denial. But if it is necessary to abolish the Antifascist Militia Committee in order to avoid the dangers of dual power after its mission is accomplished, it is not necessary to recreate the army of the state, the tool of government, capable one day of being used against the people and against the cause for which we are struggling and daily offering our lives.

We object to the present measures which create an army other than the Red Army. The combatants of the revolution must not be the headless automatons who so efficiently click their heels and do and die for Hitler and Mussolini. They must be the red army of the workers, fighting under a coordinated military command more capable of winning the war than the independent action of every political party's command. The unified command and the tightening of discipline are necessary but after the model of Trotsky's army.

Source: The Spanish Revolution, Weekly Bulletin of The Workers' Party of Marxist Unification of Spain, vol. I, no. 2 (Barcelona), 28 October 1936.

Opposing both of these military models were the liberal left parties of the republican, socialist, and official communist movements. Of these it was the communists of the PCE (and later the PSUC) who developed the most coherent military plan, one that combined elements of the revolutionary strategies cited above (where the army retained a definite political character) with the traditional model of organizing a military force. This was called the Popular Army (*Ejército Popular*), which was in principle an over-arching structure representing the interests of all republican groups but which in practice was one that increasingly reflected the will and authority of the communists and their allies. Like the other anti-revolutionary groups in the anti-fascist camp, the PCE violently objected to the fragmentation of power, which was, during the first months of the war, scattered among the various left-wing trade unions and political organizations that controlled their own military columns or popular militias. Though these civilian-led forces had filled the breach created by the near-collapse of the Republican army, it soon became apparent that they were no match for the better trained and better equipped Insurgent troops. It was against the background of repeated Republican defeats that the PCE took the initiative in calling for the creation of a 'Popular' or 'People's' army which possessed a centralized command that could enforce 'Discipline, Hierarchy, and Organization' in the formation of depoliticized military units.

At the same time that they were insisting upon the 'militarization' of the militias – that is, the merging of the civilian militias into military units – the communists made it clear that they were not aiming merely to resurrect the old framework of the republican army. Instead they were seeking to construct the basis of an army of a new type, namely, a 'Popular' or 'People's' army that embodied the political ideals of popular frontism. Thus, according to communist propaganda, the new Popular Army being forged by the republicans was to be welded together by the most progressive elements of the 'democratic parties who accepted the strictest discipline and carried out the orders of the High Command'.[2]

There were both military and political reasons why the communists were promoting these views. From a strategic standpoint, they strongly believed that reorganization of the army along conventional lines was the only effective way of defending the Republic against the professional units of the rebel army. Furthermore, they knew that a policy of 'militarization' would be politically advantageous for them, not least because the implementation of this measure meant divesting rival political organizations the power they wielded through their own militias (Document 2.6).

Document 2.6 POUM Reasons for Adopting Militarization Measures

To meet the needs of the first days of struggle, the anti-fascist militia were created as a revolutionary workers' movement to fight against the decayed and reactionary forces of feudal and capitalist Spain. None of the revolutionaries who enlisted in the militias would have consented to join the Spanish army, nor are they now in agreement to form part of it. If none of the combatants had any objection to being in the militias, which they consider as a revolutionary force, they would certainly have made every resistance against being enrolled into the very army against which they were fighting. It would not have been possible to organise the peoples' army by means of military organization. The Militias were born of the spontaneous organisation of the moment, and when accusing them of lacking the necessary discipline it is well to remember that at a time when they possessed none of the material which is in their hands today they promised that fascism should not pass and faithfully kept that promise. Fascism was defeated when it came face to face on the battlefield with these fighters for the revolution and their great courage.

Of course we are in favour of discipline, but it must be revolutionary discipline which is the only guarantee we have that the Army of the Revolution will not be turned into a mercenary force, capable one day of betraying the interests of its own class and the revolution.

Source: The Spanish Revolution, Weekly Bulletin of The Workers' Party of Marxist Unification of Spain, vol. I, no. 7 (Barcelona), 2 December 1936.

The communists' own prototype of the Popular Army, the celebrated Fifth Regiment, came into being during the first weeks of fighting. Drawing upon the organizational framework provided by the Workers' and Peasants' Anti-Fascist Militia (MAOC) – communist-led defence committees that had been set up before the war – the Fifth Regiment became a magnet for a wide variety of Republican groups. Although initially based upon recruits from the Communist-Socialist Youth Movement (JSU) and other communist organizations, its ranks were soon swelled by socialists, Republicans, and other anti-revolutionary members of the Popular Front coalition who were attracted to the regiment's iron discipline, military efficiency, and moderate political line. Thanks in part to the dynamic leadership of communists such as the Italian Vittorio Vidali (known in Spain as Carlos or Comandante Contreras) and Enrique Líster, who became commander in chief of the regiment in September 1936, the Fifth Regiment rapidly evolved into a formidable fighting unit. In December the communists launched the next phase of their military strategy by progressively dissolving the Fifth Regiment so that its battalions could be gradually fused into the 'mixed brigades' of the emerging Popular Army. In this way the communists were able to occupy commanding positions in four of the six original brigade units.

Given its popularity as well as its demonstrated military capabilities (it played a pivotal role during the November siege of Madrid), it is not surprising that the Fifth Regiment became one of the basic building-blocks of the Popular Army that was being formed under the direction of the central government based in Valencia. In fact, ever since September, when he assumed direct command of the republic's armed forces as minister of war, Largo Caballero had been following a blueprint for organizing a Popular Army that corresponded closely to the one being promoted by the communists. A feature common to both the Fifth Regiment and the new army was the commissariat system, a network of political delegates or commissars through which the government (or party) could exert its influence over military officers and troops. As in the Russian Civil War (1917–21), when they were introduced into Trotsky's Red Army, the political-military commissars in the Popular Army performed a dual role. On one level they acted as liaisons with the 'military specialists' or former Republican (and therefore politically suspect) officers and thereby ensured their loyalty. They were also used to maintain 'revolutionary discipline', which was accomplished by regularly indoctrinating the troops with the proper political perspective as defined by the communists. In the latter case, the commissariat system provided the communists (particularly Soviet advisers) with a means of penetrating the various military apparatuses of the army (Document 2.7).

Document 2.7 The Role of Commissars in the People's Army

(a)

Spain
The Conference of Political Army Commissars in Albacete

The Conference of Political Army Commissars in Albacete, the first conference of its kind to be held since the creation of this institution, means a great step in the direction of improving the whole of the political work within the army. The experiences in connection with this work, which was examined with the collaboration of all the division commissars and inspectors, gives clear proof of the growth of authority of the commissars among the armed forces of the Republic. This authority and this prestige of the commissars in the army are due above all, to the great work which they have performed in organising the regular army, to their courageous self-sacrifice and the services they have performed in all units of the People's Army.

The commissar is becoming more aware every day of his responsibility for the course of the war. He already feels himself to be no longer a simple collaborator but a leader assisting the military commander, a political leader of all the forces which form his unit.

In examining the propaganda activity of the commissariat, the conference recognised that in spite of the good work being performed in this connection, it will be necessary to intensify propaganda in the armed forces and above all, in the camp of the enemy. There already now exist brigade newspapers, many battalion newspapers and also wall newspapers. The propaganda must, however, be more methodical and much more adapted to the requirements of the troops. The conference clearly stated that the system of propaganda must be adapted to the actual requirements of the soldiers, and general propaganda which is of less interest must be discarded.

Source: Mije, Antonio, in *International Press Correspondence*, English edition, vol. 17, no. 20, 8 May 1937, p. 477.

(b)

The following is an extract from the Book of the 15th International Brigade.

Brigade Commissariat of War

Political Commissars, or 'Commissar Delegates of War' – as they are officially termed in the Spanish Republican Army – arose out of the same historical necessity that gave birth to the first Political Commissars on record – the Commissars of the French Revolution.

Faced with the task of defending their newly-won freedom against the armed combination of reactionary powers of Europe, beset with treachery on all sides, forced to rely on military leadership whose loyalty was often doubtful, the members of the Paris Convention hit upon the expedient of sending to the Army units their own delegates – tried and trusted adherents of the Revolution. The experiment justified itself; these Commissars guided the army, established discipline, built up morale, spread education among the men and carried the revolution into the enemy camp.

The creation of Political Commissars in Spain closely parallels the French historical example.

The Commissars are an integral part of the Army. Primarily their role is to inspire their unit with the highest spirit of discipline and loyalty to the Republican cause and establish a feeling of mutual confidence and good comradeship between Commanders and men.

Source: Landis, A. (1967) *The Abraham Lincoln Brigade*, New York, pp. 28–9.

There were other factors that strengthened the communists' efforts to implement their plans to construct a Popular Army over which they could exercise political control. Certainly the most important of these was the power and prestige they acquired from Soviet aid. There can be no doubt that, without the material contributions of the Soviet Union, the only major country that was willing to assist the Republicans, Popular Front resistance would have collapsed long before 1939. In the early phase of the war, for instance, Soviet aeroplanes and tanks, which had arrived in October, were decisive factors in preventing the Nationalists from completely overrunning republican forces in Madrid. As indispensable as it was, though, Soviet aid arrived with certain strings attached and this inevitably had a profound impact on Republican military affairs.

Opposing sides: Nationalists

Unlike their Republican counterparts, the Nationalists were not irrevocably divided over military strategy and goals. From the beginning, the Nationalists were commanded by the defecting segments of Spain's military. Not only junior and senior army officers, but also rank-and-file soldiers who believed that the Republic was no longer viable were prepared to overthrow the legitimate government and replace it with a new one defined along anti-democratic lines. No one from this group disputed the need to maintain a hierarchical chain of command, and thus all respected the supremacy of the military leaders who had assumed *de facto* control over Nationalist forces.

From civilian quarters, too, there was a general acceptance of the authority of the military leaders, although, during the first weeks of the war, military supervision over the Falange and Carlist militias (*requetés*) was uneven. This was especially true in regions where these groups had a mass following. Thus, in the Navarre, the heartland of the Carlist movement, the *requetés* co-operated with General Mola's troops during the initial uprising, but, given their enormous popularity and combat strength, they maintained a certain degree of independence from his command.

The army also turned to these civilian organizations to assist them in establishing order in the rearguard. In addition to enforcing the strict and severe order introduced by the military authorities, Falangist and Carlist militias also played a major role in implementing the policy of terror that the military relied on to consolidate their control of occupied territory.

In contrast to the Republican side, the question of whether the Nationalist army would be able to sustain its commanding role once the coup failed and civil war broke out was never in serious doubt. Several factors militated against the aforementioned civilian forces from challenging their hegemony. First and foremost was the fact that the forces of opposition lacked effective leadership. The Carlists were led by the blinkered Manuel Fal Conde, who wanted to use the military revolt as a springboard for establishing a corporate, clerical state under the Carlist pretender to the throne, Alfonso Carlos. But his efforts to retain a certain independence for the *requetés* – such as his plans to establish a Carlist military academy in Toledo – revealed how little he grasped of the developing political reality on the Nationalist side. Because such a move challenged the army's control over military affairs, Franco reined in on Fal Conde by having him banished from Spain for the remainder of the war.

Falangist pretensions to play a leadership role were also fatally undermined by the fact that, from the outset of the rebellion, their movement had been virtually decapitated. Most of the old-guard figures (*camisas viejas*) perished during the opening stages of the war: the charismatic José Antonio Primo de Rivera was executed by a Republican firing squad in November 1936, and Onésimo Redondo, another highly regarded Falangist leader, was killed in the early days of fighting. Efforts to replace those who had fallen proved fruitless. Not longer after José Antonio's execution it became apparent that his successor, a former mechanic named Manuel Hedilla, lacked the political experience and personal skills needed to lead a movement that had grown exponentially since July 1936. Moreover, his stubborn insistence on maintaining an independent role for the Falange threw him into conflict with Franco and his supporters. When, in April 1937, Hedilla refused to subordinate the Falange to Franco's control, he was summarily removed from his post. He was tried on 29 May for plotting to kill the Caudillo. Though he was sentenced to death, Hedilla's life was spared and he spent the next few years in prison.

The Provisional Junta's decision at the end of September 1936 to name Franciso Franco as the supreme commander of Nationalist forces (Generalissimo) and head of state (Caudillo), reinforced the army's control over military operations. Over the course of the next few months, Franco constructed a power-base for himself that effectively prevented any rival individuals or organizations from challenging his control over the Nationalists' war effort.

Foreign participants

Though the Republicans received little aid from abroad, the involvement of thousands of foreign volunteers coming from some fifty nations who fought against the

Nationalists represented another complicating feature of their military strategy. While the Republican government was at first opposed to the idea of foreigners fighting on its side, the decision of the Soviet Union to send aid to the Republic in October, 1936 paved the way for the creation of a communist-controlled volunteer army known as the International Brigades. Perhaps more so than any other military force that fought during the Civil War, the International Brigades achieved a celebrity status that has lasted up to the present. The reasons for this are not difficult to determine. First and foremost, the vast majority of volunteers included idealistic men and women who were prepared to sacrifice their lives for a political cause. To most the war in Spain was about taking a stand against the menace of European fascism in the hopes of averting another world war. They also collectively represented the forces of modern society who were seeking to achieve a greater social, economic, and political equality for all at a time when, in part because of the Great Depression and the rise of anti-democratic movements across the globe, these goals seemed increasingly remote. Unemployed workers, exiles from anti-leftist regimes in Europe, Jewish activists, African-Americans, politically conscious poets, artists, and writers, of both sexes, all saw in Spain the opportunity to realize their 'utopian' ideals, and their attempts to do so both then and ever since have attracted the attention of the international media (Document 2.8).

Document 2.8 Volunteers for Liberty

(a)

Between October, 1936, and February, 1937, thousands of anti-fascists of all countries hurried to Spain. About 15,000 men of all ages and professions. They came from every country of Europe and America, from democratic countries and fascist countries. They represented every tendency of the working-class movement and the democratic movement, even the most moderate. Veterans of the great war of 1914–18 rubbed shoulders with young anti-fascist fighters. They came to Spain to put their military ability and their experience of the anti-fascist struggle at the disposal of the Spanish people and its Government of the People's Front.

Their aims? Only one: to help the Spanish people to win the war. Every one of them understood quite well that the fate of all progressive and civilised mankind was at stake in Spain.

Source: Marty, A. in *International Press Correspondence*, English edition, vol. 17, no. 24, p. 585.

(b)

We Americans did not come to Spain because we have any romantic childish notions about war, nor were we impelled by fanfare and large cheering

parades. We left America quietly, without publicity, with the serious minded-
ness as to the work before us; compelled by the need to fight against the
criminal invasion of Spanish soil, which represented a threat to human liberty
everywhere.

Source: Landis, A. (1967) *The Abraham Lincoln Brigade*, New York, p. 3.

While the legend of the IBs has been constructed around their self-sacrificing
contributions to the Republican cause as well as to the progressive beliefs and values
alluded to here, there is also a darker side to their history. Both their Republican
and right-wing anti-communist critics have portrayed them not as heroes of a democratic struggle but as the pawns of the Soviet Union or as soldiers of fortune. This
negative image is partly based on the assumption that, owing to the strict military
and dogmatic ideological discipline enforced within the Brigade units, anyone who
was affiliated with them was incapable of expressing his or her own volition. In fact,
it was true that all volunteers serving in IB units – irrespective of their own personal
political and social beliefs – found themselves powerless to resist the pressures to
conform to communist policies to which they were continuously subjected.

Documents relating to the internal affairs of the IBs that have come to light only
recently suggest that the image of the politically and socially enlightened Brigade
volunteer is also in need of revision. According to these, relations among the various
foreign contingents enrolled in the Brigades were not always friendly. Furthermore,
there is evidence that ethnic stereotyping was not uncommon, and that some
Brigade units treated rival national groups, and even the Spaniards themselves, as
though they were their inferiors (Document 2.9).

Document 2.9 International Brigades: Dissenting Viewpoints

(a)

It is time that the part played by the International Brigades in Spain should
be known.

To the world they have been presented as having saved Republican Spain
from many a defeat, as anti-fascist, heroic Legionaries, and, above all, as the
creation of the Communist Party and the 3rd International. Obviously, the
3rd International itself undertook the task of spreading the impression, making
use of its established propaganda machine for the purpose.

We should note that, at first, these Brigades, organised hurriedly, with the
aid of sincere and self-sacrificing anti-fascists; coming from all parts of the
world, and of various political tendencies, behaved magnificently in Madrid,
where many a good man and true amongst them fell. In Aragon as well, international bodies were organised, particularly Italian and German, who took
part in the fight along with the Spanish forces. But though they were reckoned
as International, they were not of the International Brigade nor under their

control, being composed of Socialists and anarchists who had no wish to be included among those units which had gradually passed under the control of the Communists.

Once arrived in Spanish territory, the volunteers were completely isolated and put at the disposal of the Communist leaders. The documents which had been given to them were useless for getting out of the country. The Communists in charge of them, as well as the Cheka, took good care to arrest and accuse of spying all those who wanted to turn back or fight with other units. Special barracks, under the sole control of the Communists, were used for this purpose, in Figueras, Barcelona, Valencia, Albacete, etc. The Albacete barracks acquired special notoriety, on account of the foul behaviour of the Communists there against real militant revolutionaries.

Apart from these details, which show the privileged handling of the International Brigade by the Communist Party, there must be mentioned another loathsome and terrible aspect of its behaviour. We refer to the political persecution carried out against those who were of non-communist sympathies. Both as regards the International Brigades and Spaniards who were commanded by Communists, there was murdering, torturing and ill treatment of hundreds of militant revolutionaries, who came to Spain at the call of the ghastly struggle let loose by Fascism.

Source: 'The International Brigades in Spain', (1 May 1939), *Spain & the World*, reprinted London, 1990, p. 263.

(b)

The great majority of officers, non-commissioned officers and volunteers in the International Brigades, are militants or political men who know how to see, judge, and understand. Whether they be Communist or Socialist, Republican or antifascist with no defined political party, today all are consumed by the idea that the International Brigades are considered to be a foreign body, a band of intruders – I will not say by the Spanish people as a whole, but by the vast majority of political leaders, soldiers, civil servants, and political parties in Republican Spain.

Tracing the reasons for this state of mind among Spanish comrades of whatever rank or organization is beyond the purview of this note. What is true is that, at least superficially, numerous facts justify the opinion gradually spreading through the ranks of the internationals. Among these facts, I will cite the following:

- First, it is the prevailing opinion among high officers in the Spanish army, more or less irrespective of political affiliation, that the International Brigades are nothing but a foreign legion, an army of mercenaries fighting for money, who therefore have only one right: the right to obey. Do not say I exaggerate. The fact is known, it is patently clear. It is possible to debate only whether this opinion of the International Brigades is more or less widespread. Certainly the militants in the International Brigades are quite aware of this situation; they cannot help perceiving this treatment as an insult to their antifascist convictions and to the millions of comrades who came with them and have since fallen in defence of Republican Spain.

- The unequal treatment of the Spanish and the International Brigades further justifies the opinion emerging among the international militants, who have been treated like a foreign legion ready to be sacrificed, to which no attention need be paid. This difference in treatment is striking in matters of arms and tactical deployment.

Source: Radosh, R. Habek, M. and Sevostianov, G. (eds) (2001) *Spain Betrayed: the Soviet Union in the Spanish Civil War*, New Haven, p. 241.

Whether the international volunteers who fought for the Republic are portrayed as heroes or not, there can be little doubt about the importance of their military contributions to the war effort. The number of foreigners who fought on the Republican side as members of the International Brigades has been estimated to be between 31,000 and 32,000, though it is likely that no more than 15,000 were ever actively engaged in military operations at one time (Document 2.10). No less important were the contributions of the select group of Soviet and Comintern advisers who were sent to Spain, not as volunteers but to offer their technical expertise in military matters. Because they believed that the communists offered the only successful strategy for winning the war, both Soviet and Comintern officials – notably, Vittorio Vidali, Yan Berzin, Grigory Shtern, Luigi Longo, and Palmiro Togliatti – set themselves the task of controlling all aspects of the Republic's military operations. To this end, the some seven hundred military advisers, NKVD agents, and seasoned *apparatchiks* who were sent to Spain during the war simultaneously sought to achieve communist hegemony in the political and economic affairs of the Republic.

Document 2.10 International Brigades: A Statistical Profile

About the numerical composition of the internationalists.

By nationality		*Up to 30 April 1938*		*Available personnel on 31/3/38*	
		Sent home	*Dead and missing*	*Internationalists in various units*	
Germans	2,180	189	308	Base	1,259
Americans	2,274	337	276	Train. battn.	1,467
Austrians	846	79	138	Almansa and others	1,104

Balkans	2,056	54	96	Representatives	145
Baltic states	862	17	179	15th Division	17
Belgians	1,701	330	185	35th Division	215
Canadians	510	51	71	45th Division	388
Czechs	1,046	142	133	DESA	727
Scandinavians	662	92	91	Artillery	873
French	8,778	2,301	942	Battn. air defence	82
Dutch	586	82	42	11th Brigade	1,134
Hungarians	510	40	56	12th Brigade	826
English	1,806	460	124	13th Brigade	1,293
Italians	2,908	3,335	526	14th Brigade	1,568
Poles	3,034	240	466	15th Brigade	982
Portuguese	132	–	–	129th Brigade	992
Swiss	406	46	78	Hospital staff	559
Others	1,072	267	864	Hospitalised	2,361
Total:	31,369	5,062	4,575	Total:	15,992

Conclusion:

Total arrivals	31,969 [*sic*]
Present on 31.III.38	15,992
Difference	15,377
Of them badly wounded	5,062
Dead	4,575
Difference	5,740

Source: Radosh, R., Habek, M. and Sevostianov, G. (eds) (2001) *Spain Betrayed: The Soviet Union in the Spanish Civil War*, New Haven, p. 468.

Because they were used as shock troops in nearly every major military engagement between 1937 and the time of their withdrawal in late 1938, the IBs saw some of the fiercest fighting of the war. This was particularly evident at the battles of Jarama (February 1937), Brunete (July 1937), and Teruel (December 1937 to February 1938), where the IBs suffered heavy losses. It is also true that, despite the many horrifying experiences they faced in combat, many members of the IBs distinguished themselves by exhibiting an unusually high degree of dignity and valour on the battlefield.

In contrast to the men and women who enlisted in the International Brigades, foreign volunteers who went to fight for the Nationalist side have not received much publicity. This is partly due to the fact that the Nationalists themselves did not want to generate any diplomatic waves by drawing attention to the foreigners who were fighting on their behalf. For similar reasons, the Germans and other foreign elements tended to downplay the full extent of their military contributions (Document 2.11). It was also true that, unlike the Republicans, the Nationalists were either unwilling or unable to capitalize on the propaganda value of having foreigners join what was, according to their own rhetoric, a national crusade. In the event, several thousand anti-communist volunteers hailing from Portugal, France, Romania, Russia, Britain and Ireland joined Franco's crusade against 'red' Spain. The vast majority of these volunteers were organized into military units (*banderas*) that served in the Foreign Legion, though most did not see action throughout the war. Moreover, owing in part to language and cultural barriers and in part to the uneven quality of their fighting abilities, most of the foreigners, like the some seven hundred members of Eoin O'Duffy's Irish Brigade, saw themselves and were widely seen by the Nationalists as outsiders (Document 2.12).

Document 2.11 Concealing German Involvement

From the conversations with General Franco and his brother, Nicolás Aurelio, the following is noteworthy:

General Franco showed great understanding for the fact that we are not yet recognizing the Burgos Government. He understood perfectly that it was much easier for us to furnish aid to the extent done heretofore as long as the possibilities of support were not hampered by international complications.

Source: Documents on German Foreign Policy, vol. III, Series D, no. 96, p. 106.

Document 2.12 Foreigners Fighting for Franco

(a)

The Irish Brigade was composed of some seven hundred young men mostly in their early twenties, but some hundred were mere boys and were shipped back from Spain on the urgent demands of parents and relatives. The officers and about half of the rank-and-file were ex-members of the 'Blueshirts,' a semi-fascist organization set up by Cumann na nGaedhael, led by ex-President Cosgrave of the Irish Free State after his defeat at the 1932 elections by the Fianna Fail Party led by De Valera. General Eoin O'Duffy became leader of the Blueshirts (until he fell out with Cosgrave) after he had been pensioned from his job as Commissioner of Civic Guards by President De Valera. The Blueshirts imitated the Black-shirts of Mussolini and the Storm Troopers of Hitler both in policy and tactics.

And so it went on. The absurdity of Moors fighting for Christianity became apparent to all. No matter how crudely it was expressed the conviction grew that O'Duffy's statement that we were fighting to defend Christianity was only a lie used to lure Irish lads into fighting for Franco against the democratic Spanish Republic. But we were in a terrible state of mental confusion. Our officers and the Blueshirt section of the bandera, ably supported by priests we had been taught to respect, tried to persuade us to disbelieve our own eyesight: Regular Nazi officers sent by a regime that persecutes Catholics in Germany, and Moors hired by the Spanish reactionary monarchists and aristocrats fighting to 'defend Christianity!'

Source: MacKee, S. (1938) *I Was a Franco Soldier*, London, pp. 6 and 19–20.

(b)

It must be emphasised that contrary to the general belief we were by no means pressganged into this enterprise. There was no coercion, but unlike the International Brigade, the 'Last of the Idealists', who were encountered later and won our respect, our participation had little or nothing to do with political ideology. Our model was the *Landsknecht*, the colourful, swaggering mercenary from a romantic tradition of what in Britain would have been regarded as *Boy's Own* paper stuff. A civil war in Russia would have caused much less interest, let alone sufficient enthusiasm to participate in it. Our only concern was that this caper should not exceed our regular date of discharge from the Wehrmacht, and nobody was ever motivated by the expectation of financial gains.

Source: Toynbee, P. (ed.) (1976) *The Distant Drum: Reflections on the Spanish Civil War*, London, p. 97.

While it is true that Franco did not look to foreigners to supply the manpower he needed to wage war, his army, navy, and, above all, airforce relied on the military experience and technical knowledge provided by outsiders. This was particularly true after 1937, when it became apparent that the Nationalists were able to achieve air superiority thanks to the fact that they were receiving from both the Germans and Italians more aircraft of a greater quality than Russia was making available to the Republican side. But however dependent he became on this assistance and despite the friction that arose between himself and his allies, Franco refused to allow either the Germans or Italians to exert undue influence over his military operations (Document 2.13).

Document 2.13 The Limits of Fascist Intervention

Franco, on the other hand, rightly took the stand that another military reverse for the Italians, who were also responsible for the temporary set-back at Bermeo, was intolerable for political reasons and that therefore they could be assigned a decisive attack only after they had proved their ability through easier tasks.

With their present corps of officers and non-commissioned officers the Spaniards are not in a position to lead and successfully conclude attacks independently and without foreign aid. The experiences with the two brigades of *Flechas Negras* and *Flechas Azules* have proved that the Italians likewise are not capable of doing this. Both brigades were organized 6 months ago with Italian officers, non-commissioned officers, and specialists (20 percent) and with Spanish men (80 percent) and were trained and commanded by the Italians. They have accomplished extremely little, so that Franco evaluates their fighting quality as far inferior to that of his purely Spanish units.

Source: Documents on German Foreign Policy, vol. III, Series D, pp. 410, 411, 412

The progress of the war, 1936–37

The first six months of war saw a series of Nationalist victories in nearly every corner of the country. In the far north the frontier city of Irún fell to the rebels on 5 September, and, thanks to the relentless advance of the crack 'Navarre Brigades' in the northern region, much of the Basque country surrounding Bilbao, the Vizcayan capital, came under Nationalist control by the end of the month. In the same period, the strategically important Balearic islands of Majorca and Ibiza were secured by the Nationalists. Anti-Republican forces were also advancing on the Guadarrama front to the north of Madrid, the Castilian plains towards Toledo, and in the south and south-western regions. On 14 August, for example, Badajoz, a key city situated on the Spanish/Portuguese border, was captured by Colonel Yagüe's troops.

Although active on many fronts, the Nationalists were convinced that if they captured the capital city of Madrid the war would soon be over. Their string of military victories during the summer of 1936 strengthened both their confidence as a fighting force and their resolve to march on Madrid as soon as possible. By early September they were at the point of mounting such an offensive when Franco's attention was diverted by a drama that was being played out in the Republican-held city of Toledo. Shortly after the military rebellion had begun there, some 1,100 insurgents (mostly members of the civil guard and a few cadets) had, along with several hundred women and children and approximately a hundred Republican hostages, retreated to the Alcázar, a formidable structure towering over the Tagus River which also served as training facility for Spanish officers. Led by the indomitable Colonel José Moscardó, the Nationalists demonstrated remarkable perseverance in the face of repeated Republican attempts to blast through the thick walls of the ancient fortress (Document 2.14). By September news of the siege had spread far and wide and it was this publicity which had convinced Franco of the need to send relief forces to the region. This proved to be a calculated gamble on Franco's part. On the one hand, he must have known that his decision would inevitably dissipate the momentum of the Nationalists' advance on Madrid, thus prejudicing their chances of a quick and decisive victory. On the other hand, the political capital that could be gained from a dramatic rescue of the beleaguered insurgents in Toledo was too great to be ignored. At the time, the Junta de Defensa Nacional was at the point of selecting Franco as the supreme leader (Caudillo) of the Nationalist cause.

A successful rescue operation in Toledo would therefore go a long way towards enhancing Franco's public image in his new role. In the event, Franco's decision produced both results. By diverting troops from the Madrid front, Franco had allowed the mostly pro-Republican *madrileños* the time they needed to shore up their defences before the city was placed under siege. As we shall see, this meant that the Battle of Madrid would take a very different course than either side had anticipated. From a political standpoint, however, Franco's gamble had paid off. The troops he had dispatched to Toledo liberated the fortress on 26 September, and their dramatic rescue efforts provided an enormous boost for the morale and image of the Nationalists in general and of Franco in particular.

Document 2.14 The Siege of Alcázar

The personnel assembled in the Alcázar comprised:

MEN

Commanders and other officers	100
Civil Guards	800
Cadets (Academies)	150
Cadets (School of Gymnastics)	40
Falange Acción Popular and others	200

In all, there were some 1,300, of whom 1,200 were in charge of defence, while the non-combatants attending to the other services took no part in defence.

To this garrison must be added:

Women	550
Children	50

These consisted mainly of the families of the Civil Guards and of some professors of the Academy, and a number of Toledans who sought refuge at the Alcázar: the total population of the fortress amounting to some two thousand souls.

. . .

While the defenders were concentrated within the Alcázar, they were called upon daily to surrender. These messages were received by telephone. The first to call up was General Pozas who, as soon as he realized that neither the ammunition supplies nor the two hundred Civil Guards were leaving the fortress, threatened to destroy the Alcázar completely 'with not one stone left standing.' Then on July 21st General Riquelme telephoned and demanded an immediate surrender. He also demanded an explanation of our attitude. I replied that we took the position of all honorable men in view of the disasters which the Marxist government was bringing down on Spain, and that we were absolutely in accord with General Franco and wholly unwilling to see the ammunition belonging to the Academy and the Civil Guards delivered up to the rabble, to serve as weapons against us. General Riquelme insisted that our attitude was absurd, and promised to take active steps in the matter. I told the General that we preferred to die than to see the Alcázar transformed into a dung heap, as he proposed, by surrendering it to the enemies of our country. On the following day Barnés, the Minister of Education, tried to shake us from our patriotic duty by saying that resistance on our part would cause great damage to the city of Toledo, 'this precious jewel,' and we should bear this in mind, since it was certain that if we continued with our present attitude, violent measures would have to be adopted. He said he hoped things would not come to this, and he looked upon our attitude with sympathy, 'considering it rather childish than other-wise.' I replied that we could not conceivably change our attitude, and we would refuse to surrender to anybody or anything, in our determination to save the country by our efforts.

Source: Payne, R. (1962) *The Civil War in Spain, 1936–39*, New York, Putnam, p. 72

When Franco's troops reached the outskirts of the capital in early November, everyone, including the Republican government, believed that the city would soon fall to the Nationalists. On 6 November the prime minister and his cabinet transferred to the more distant Republican-held city of Valencia, leaving the administration of the defence of the city in its hour of crisis in the hands of a provisional ruling body known as the Defence Council (Junta de defensa). This consisted of representatives of the various Popular Front parties which were placed under the leadership of a General Miaja (Document 2.15). Though they faced overwhelming odds, the citizens of Madrid readied themselves for the inevitable attack. Overnight civilian groups were mobilized into work battalions used for digging trenches and fortifying the city's defences (Document 2.16). Their fighting spirit was also echoed in defiant messages that were broadcast on the radio and on banners emblazoned with such memorable slogans as 'Madrid will be the tomb of fascism' and 'They Shall not Pass'. The arrival on 8 November of the first shipments of Soviet arms, the newly formed units of the International Brigades, and Buenaventura Durruti's celebrated anarchist column further boosted the morale of the besieged Republicans (Document 2.17). The battle itself began a few days later. Some of the fiercest fighting took place in and around University City, where Franco's men were met by the determined resistance of the mixed units of the Republican army which were reinforced by the International Brigades. When it became clear in late January that the city was not going to be conquered, Franco decided to abandon his frontal offensive. The heroic defence of Madrid thus became one of the epic struggles of Spain's Civil War (Document 2.18).

Document 2.15 Facing the Enemy: Madrid under Fire

The siege of Madrid began in the night of the 7th of November 1936, and ended two years, four months, and three weeks later with the Spanish war itself.

When Luis Rubio Hidalgo told me that the Government was leaving and that Madrid would fall the next day, I found nothing to say.

Now I'm going to explain the situation to you. As I mentioned already, the Government will move to Valencia tonight, but no one knows it yet. Written instructions will be left with General Miaja, so that he can negotiate the surrender with the least possible loss of blood. But he doesn't yet know it himself, and he won't know until after the Government has gone. Now you will realize the task that falls upon you. It is absolutely necessary to keep the Government's move a secret, otherwise a frightful panic would break out.

Across the street a convoy of cars was lined up before the Gran Via Hotel. I went down to take leave of Rubio Hidalgo. The newspaper vendors were selling their morning papers. It was no longer a secret that the Government had gone to Valencia. Madrid came under military law and would be governed by a defence council, the *Junta de Defensa*.

Source: Barea, A. (1946) *The Forging of a Rebel*, London, pp. 571, 572 and 575.

Document 2.16 Madrid will be the Tomb of Fascism

And behind the lines, the civilian population poured into the streets to strengthen barricades. These grew in a week from the first amateur structures to solid fortifications, shoulder-high walls of cobblestones cemented into place by a military plan.

In all Madrid's streets towards the rebel front I saw them – these walls of rock and cement, with well-made holes for rifles and machine-guns. They reached from the buildings to the car-tracks, leaving a narrow traffic space. They repeated at intervals down the main thoroughfares; they guarded entrance[s] from every side-street and alley. Building these walls, and seeing how the people's forces held the enemy, the 'week of panic' steadily passed into the growing conviction that Madrid, defended by its citizens, need not be taken. And the slogan began to pass from mouth to mouth of the defenders: 'Madrid shall be the grave of fascism.'

Source: Strong, A. L. (1937) *Spain in Arms*, New York, p. 38.

Document 2.17 The Russians are Coming

Up the street from the direction of the Ministry of War came a long column of marching men. They wore a kind of khaki corduroy uniform, and loose brown Glengarry caps like those of the British tank corps.

They were marching in excellent formation. The tramp, tramp of their boots sounded in perfect unison. Over their shoulders were slung rifles of obviously modern design. Many had scarred tin helmets hanging from their belts. Some were young; others carried themselves like trained, experienced soldiers.

Each section had its officers, some carrying swords and revolvers. Behind rolled a small convoy of lorries, stacked high with machine guns and equipment. At the rear trotted a squadron of about fifty cavalry.

The few people who were about lined the roadway, shouting almost hysterically, 'Salud! Salud!', holding up their fists clenched in salute, or clapping vigorously. An old woman with tears streaming down her face, returning from a long wait in a queue, held up a baby girl, who, too, saluted with her tiny fist. One of the charwomen from the hotel stood with tears pouring down her face. The cars racing along the street stopped and blared their horns.

The troops in reply held up their fists and copied the call of 'Salud!' We did not know who they were. The crowd took them for Russians. The barman turned to me saying, 'The *Rusos* have come.'

But when I heard a clipped Prussian voice shout an order in German, followed by other shouts in French and Italian, I knew they were not Russians.

The International Column of Anti-Fascists had arrived in Madrid. We were watching the First Brigade of what was to develop into the most truly international army the world has seen since the Crusades.

Source: Cox, G. (1937) *Defence of Madrid*, London, pp. 66–7.

Document 2.18 An Epic Struggle

As far as the general feeling in Madrid is concerned, this has completely altered. The fashionable ladies stay at home. The safety measures against Mola's traitorous Fifth Column have given them something to think about. They carried out three attacks, but now the people are on the alert.

The bombardment with long-range guns is continued and takes its daily toll of victims. An extraordinary fight took place in the last few days above the roofs of Madrid. Sixteen republican aeroplanes attacked 17 fascist machines. As is known, five Heinckel and one Fiat plane crashed. The whole fight was followed by the populace, who came out on to the streets, despite the danger, and punctuated the progress of the fight with applause.

A counter-offensive on a big scale is being prepared. Fighting is going on with courage and confidence. But the military operations cannot be victorious in two or three days. At the moment the position of the republicans is favourable. I will express the wish that by the time these lines appear the position will be still more favourable and that Madrid will have cast off the terrible pressure of the siege. Then the anti-fascists throughout the world will remember the unknown heroes who, during these days, when the fate of civilisation is at stake, have given up their lives in the cause of freedom.

Source: Soria, G., in *International Press Correspondence*, vol. 17, no. 52, p. 1380.

In the meantime, at the southern end of the Republican zone, Nationalist forces were preparing an offensive against the Mediterranean port city of Málaga. Backed by some ten thousand Moors and eleven thousand Italian fascist volunteers who had only recently arrived as part of Mussolini's contribution to the anti-Republican cause, the Nationalists under the field command of Colonel Borbón (the Duke of Seville) struck the coastal capital at a time when it was most vulnerable to attack. For various reasons, including the fact that much of Republican attention had been focused on the struggle for Madrid, the some forty thousand Málaga militiamen were among the most poorly organized and ill-equipped of the forces fighting on the government side. Moreover, political and ideological feuding between the main defenders of the city itself, the anarchists of the CNT and the communists, effectively undermined any hope that the *malagueños* could mount the kind of organized and determined resistance that was being exhibited by their counterparts in Madrid (Document 2.19).

Document 2.19 The Fall of Málaga

Still, I can't help thinking that it was really to the credit of the Malagueñans that they did not on the whole show any disposition for war. They were people of peace and wanted to take as little part in this unnecessary struggle as possible. They never made any real attempt even to defend their city, which seems curious in Spain, the country of remarkable sieges. Malaga did not seem to us even at that time likely to be the scene of a second Numantia or Saragossa; and time was to prove that we were right.

I don't mean to suggest that Andalusians can't be extremely brave: they have proved their bravery in every war they have taken part in. But that extraordinary tenacity of whole populations, that screwing your courage to the sticking point and never wavering again, those forlorn hopes which last not for an hour but for months of taut agonizing endurance, that gaunt stoical holding-out against all rhyme and reason, that sublime or demoniac, stubborn, desperate insanity of courage seems only to exist in northern Spain out of all the countries of the world.

Source: Woolsey, G. (1998) *Málaga Burning*, Paris, p. 95.

The Nationalist offensive began in mid-January, and by February they were already advancing on the outskirts of Málaga. The city fell to the Nationalists on the 8th, causing the mass exodus not only of retreating militiamen but also of thousands of pro-Republican families. Yet, according to numerous eye-witness accounts, the huge number of non-combatants (approximately 150,000) evacuating Málaga were not allowed to escape the wrath of their enemies. For while fleeing along the narrow coastal roads leading northward out of the city, the winding stream of refugee men, women, and children were subjected to bombing and strafed by machine-gun fire of low-flying German and Italian planes. Their harrowing plight, as well as that of those civilians left behind to face a vengeful conquering army, was widely reported in the international press, thus highlighting one of the most disturbing aspects of modern warfare that would be underscored repeatedly throughout the Spanish conflict (Document 2.20). To the shock and horror of many native and foreign observers, it was now apparent that, with the line separating combatants from non-combatants becoming completely blurred, the age of total war had become a frightening reality.

Document 2.20 Counting the Civilian Victims

Mr. Ogilvie-Forbes to Viscount Halifax. – (Received February 14.)

Minister of State sent for me urgently this evening and introduced me to three members of Cabinet who have just visited Almeria to investigate circumstances attending the fall of Malaga. I was given at first hand an account of the terrible sufferings of refugees, estimated to number 150,000, who, fearing insurgent reprisals, abandoned Malaga before its capture, taking the road northward towards Almeria. These people, who for the first part of their flight were subjected to shell fire and bombing left without supplies of any kind, and are now in a deplorable state, having for a week lacked food, water, clothing and medical stores. They have completely overwhelmed the inhabitants and the authorities at Motril, and some 50,000 have already passed that place heading for Almeria.

Source: British Documents on Foreign Affairs, Series F, Europe, vol. 27, Document 70, pp. 86–7.

From a military standpoint, the fall of Málaga came as a major setback for the Republicans. Not only had they lost control of a key Andalusian city which allowed the Nationalists to complete their conquest of this strategically important region, but their inability to defend Málaga had revealed how far behind their forces outside of Madrid were in their efforts to transform the patchwork of civilian and military units into an effective army (Document 2.21).

Document 2.21 Explaining Defeat

I was on night-duty neither on February 6 nor on February 7. On February 8 a rebel army, consisting of motorised Italian units, entered Malaga. On none of these three days was ammunition sent to Malaga, for the simple reason that there was no ammunition to send.

Our forces at Malaga were still less organised than those on other fronts, and they asked not for thousands of shells, but simply for rifle ammunition. We had had three weeks' warning of the attack on Malaga. We knew that Italian troops had landed at Cadiz for the purpose, and we knew of the concentration of sixty German bombers. But we could do nothing to avoid the disaster. We hoped that a shipload of munitions might arrive to save us at the last moment.

Our forces in Malaga were behind schedule in the transformation from a militia into a regular army, and were worse off than other fronts both in quantity and quality of war material. Nevertheless I am convinced that if they had had ammunition, the 'glory' of the taking of Malaga of which Italy boasts would have been less glorious. Indeed, it is doubtful if they ever would have taken it at all.

Source: Blázquez, J. M. (1939) *I Helped to Build an Army*, London, p. 307.

By contrast, the Republican army of the centre was proving itself capable of stopping, if not defeating, the Nationalist army's relentless attempts to conquer Madrid. After his two frontal assaults on the capital in November and early January had ground to a halt, Franco decided to undertake a series of operations that would encircle the city. The first of these was the battle of Jarama, which coincided with the Nationalist assault on Málaga. The main aim of this offensive was to cut in two the Madrid–Valencia road, thus preventing much-needed food and war supplies from getting to the besieged city. Taking advantage of their superior artillery fire-power as well as the air support provided by German and Italian planes, the Nationalists subjected Republican forces to the most intense and concentrated shelling they had experienced up to this point in the war. The ferocity of the offensive tested the mettle of the Republic's new army and particularly that of the International Brigades, whose militarily inexperienced units were seriously demoralized by the disproportionate number of casualties (2,800) they suffered in combat (Document 2.22). Notwithstanding their staggering loses, however, the Republicans managed to blunt the offensive, which ended in a stalemate less than three weeks after it had begun.

Document 2.22 The Battle of Jarama

(a)

The bloody battle of the Jarama, which lasted most of February, was an unsuccessful attempt by the Nationalists to cut the Madrid Valencia road, the last remaining direct link between the capital and the Republican bases on the Mediterranean.

Spanish troops, *Requetés* particularly but also the crack Foreign Legion, seemed to think it undignified to dig trenches deep enough to give proper protection from shell fire.

When, therefore, the Republicans attacked us under cover of an artillery bombardment our casualties were much higher than they need have been, and we only just held on to the position after two days of hard fighting. It was partly the courage of the *Requetés* that saved us, partly the arrival at a critical moment of a squadron of our tanks, but chiefly the inept and suicidal tactics of the enemy. They put in a frontal assault in broad daylight across a plain dominated by our positions and almost devoid of cover. Their artillery preparation, though unpleasant enough for us, was quite inadequate for such a task, and their losses were appalling. They were Spanish troops and I greatly admired their bravery, but I wondered what kind of military cretin had ordered such an attack. I believe the main reason why the Republicans lost the war – apart from their initial failure to hold command of the sea – was their ignorance of tactics, planning, and logistics and – except in the International Brigades – the inferior quality of their officers.

Source: Toynbee, P. (ed.) (1976) *Distant Drum: Reflections on the Spanish Civil War*, London, p. 70.

(b)

It was terrifying to watch the uncanny ability of the Moorish infantry to exploit the slightest fold in the ground which could be used for cover, and to make themselves invisible. It is an art that only comes to a man after a lifetime spent with a rifle in his hand, whose very existence depends on his capacity to find safety where none apparently exists.

The effect of those brown, ferocious bundles suddenly appearing out of the ground at one's feet was utterly demoralizing. There appeared to be thousands of them popping up and disappearing all over the place, but seldom visible for long enough for anyone to get an effective shot at them. They were professionals, backed by a mass of artillery and heavy machine-gun fire supplied by the German Condor legion. It was a formidable opposition to be faced by a collection of city-bred young men with no experience of war, no idea of how to find cover on an open hillside, and no competence as marksmen. We were frightened by the sheer din of the battle and by the numbers of casualties. After the first few days I became indifferent to the noise, which was far louder and more furious than anything I had previously experienced. It was so intense as to seem to have an inescapably destructive force of its own. The horror of seeing close friends and comrades being killed and broken did not really penetrate my mind until later. It was all too fantastic for immediate realization, like something seen in a nightmare.

Source: Gurney, J. (1974) *Crusade in Spain*, London, p. 108.

Less than one month later, the Republicans achieved what would become their only major 'defensive victory' of the war at the Battle of Guadalajara. Buoyed by their recent success in Málaga, the some 35,000 Italian troops (organized as a Corpo di Truppe Volontarie, CTV) under the command of General Roatta were confident that they could outflank the Republican forces protecting the outer rings of Madrid by launching an attack in the Guadalajara sector on the Madrid–Saragossa road. On 8 March, four exclusively Italian divisions along with the Spanish Division Soria and Moorish and Spanish troops under General Moscardó, began the attack. Fortified by Italian motorized vehicles and assault tanks, the Nationalists immediately smashed through Republican lines at several points north of Guadalajara. Yet appalling weather conditions, which prevented effective air support, along with inadequate communications among the Nationalist units, kept the offensive from gaining sufficient forward momentum. There was little change on the front until 15 March, when the Republicans initiated their own offensive at Brihuega and along the Saragossa road. Soviet tanks, supported by some hundred republican fighter planes (Chatos and Ratas) and bombers (SB Katiuska), joined some of the best disciplined troops of the republican army. These included the communist Fifth Corps led by Enrique Líster, the anarchist 14 Division directed by Cipriano Mera, and the XII International Brigade (composed of Italian anti-fascists), which was attached to Mera's division. It was at this point in the campaign that a minor foreign civil war was played out on a Spanish battlefield. In the ruins of the Ibarra castle near Brihuega the Italian contingent (who adopted the name Garibaldi) of the International Brigade came face to face with their fellow countrymen fighting for the Nationalists. The irony of the moment was not lost on the Garibaldians, who used loud speakers and political leaflets dropped from planes in a remarkable propaganda feat aimed at convincing their fascist opponents to switch sides.

Whatever impact these efforts had on sowing seeds of defeatism among the Italian fascists, the next few days saw the Republicans effectively marshalling their air and ground forces (which included Russian-supplied T-26 tanks) in their offensive along the River Tajuña. On the 18th, the Republicans finally managed to push the Italian occupiers out of Brihuega, causing near-panic among thousands of Mussolini's much-vaunted Black Arrow and Littorio units. In their ignominious flight towards the Nationalist-held town of Sigüenza, many had abandoned their arms and munitions. The resulting Republican victory marked the first time they had defeated the Nationalists in large-scale military engagement. It also effectively derailed Franco's plan to encircle the capital. In the words of one contemporary observer, after Guadalajara, 'No one spoke of the fall of Madrid anymore'.[3] Equally important, at this juncture in the fighting, was the fact that the Popular Army demonstrated that the outcome of the war was not a foregone conclusion. The communists in particular proclaimed Guadalajara as a turning-point in the struggle against fascism, predicting that the tide would now shift in favour of the forces of democracy (Document 2.23).

Document 2.23 An Anti-Fascist Victory

(a)

The Battle of Guadalajara, in which the Italian expeditionary force was routed, also gave me an opportunity to contribute material to history, although not even my home office believed me at the time. When you put together all the elements – all the cynicism, immorality, timidity, and cruelty that formed the background of the Italian intervention – your heart must leap when you think of Guadalajara. I still believe I was right when I called it the 'Baylén of Fascism.' Baylén, in southern Spain, was Napoleon's first defeat, a turning point in his triumphant career, only realized in after years by historians. After Baylén he was to win many victories, but the spell had been broken. Guadalajara was Fascism's first defeat, and it, too, was followed by triumphs, but the world saw that Fascism could be fought and beaten. In vain Mussolini called it a victory, boasted how Italy won the war for Franco, displayed the strength and numbers of his military establishment. The mask was stripped off at Guadalajara.

Source: Matthews, H. L. (1946) *The Education of a Correspondent*, New York, pp. 94–5.

(b)

The First Defeat of Mussolini's Troops

is Above All a Victory for the Italian People

This is a victory for the policy of solidarity and the fraternisation of all workers which was laid down by the *Seventh World Congress of the Communist International*, and followed up most zealously by the heroic *Communist Party of Italy*. This is a victory for the soldiers and the people of Italy – who desire peace and freedom – over the fascist dictatorship of Mussolini.

The results of the battle of Guadalajara have proved that Mussolini, even if he is still in a position to hold the people inside Italy in chains, can no longer count on the 'loyalty' of the army, that in his policy of war provocation and the support of European reaction he has *not* at his disposal the army of Italy, that the soldiers and officers of Italy are true to the ideals of their people, the ideals of freedom and peace, and that they refuse to fight against other peoples, especially against their brother nations of France and Spain.

Source: Nicoletti, M., in *International Press Correspondence*, vol. 17, no. 15, p. 364.

3 | Volcanic eruptions: Popular experiences of revolution and violence

During its opening phases, it was apparent that the Civil War would entail more than just a clash between those who wanted to overthrow the Republic and those who sought to defend it. In fact, the military rebellion unleashed two major forces that irrevocably widened the dimensions of the Civil War. The first was a massive popular revolution which, in varying degrees, spread rapidly throughout much of the anti-rebel zone. The main features of this multilayered movement and the different ways in which it influenced the course of Republican affairs during the war are sketched out below. Parallel to the social, economic, and political changes being wrought by the popular revolution on the Republican side, the entire peninsula was engulfed in a wave of violence that saw the mass killings of civilians not directly involved in the fighting. In the Republican camp, the revolutionary left spear-headed a campaign of terror and extermination against individuals and groups who were perceived to be allied to the military rebellion. And though this largely improvised campaign of bloody purges began to subside within a few weeks, terror, repression, and the killing of suspected enemies or 'Fifth Columnists' became permanent features of Republican rule. In the opposing camp, the military and paramilitary 'repression brigades' of the Falange and Carlist organizations led the initial onslaught against individuals and organizations who were identified as being pro-Republican. As the war progressed these purges became more regularized, not least because terror and repression were regarded as necessary instruments of political rule in the Nationalist zone.

Revolutionary Spain: Transformation of the Republic?

Some of the most dramatic episodes in the Spanish Civil War occurred during the first months of the conflict. Collectively these incidents have been referred to as the July Revolution. It began when the military conspirators and their supporters rose up against the Republican government in mid-July, offering Spain's radical left-wing organizations (the anarchosyndicalists of the CNT-FAI, the left Socialists, and the POUM) the long-awaited opportunity to launch a sweeping revolutionary movement. Responding instinctively to the challenge presented by the rebelling forces, the revolutionaries did not (like many other Republican parties) hesitate to take to the streets with their own militias. In regions such as Catalonia, the weight of these civilian forces, combined with local and national military units loyal to the Republic, was enough to quash the rebellion. In the aftermath of the street-fighting, the revolutionaries emerged in Barcelona as the dominant force. According to one of the anarchosyndicalist participants, Juan García Oliver, the President of the Catalan government (Generalitat) offered to turn over the reins of government to the triumphant workers. But rather than take this historic step, the leaders of the libertarian movement decided to share power with the liberal-dominated Generalitat in a new ruling body called the Central Anti-fascist Militias Committe (CAMC) (Document 3.1). The anarchists' refusal to seize power was due partly to the short-comings of anarchist theory, which was silent on this vital issue, and partly to the fact that the anarchists themselves were loath to establish what would have amounted to a libertarian dictatorship. In all events, their decision to collaborate in a power-sharing scheme effectively set limits on the political revolution, above all because it granted the more politically astute and experienced anti-revolutionary parties a central role in governing the region (Document 3.2). The first unequivocal sign of this came early on: at the end of September 1936 the anarchists agreed to dissolve the CAMC and enter the fully reconstituted Generalitat. From that point on the struggle between the revolutionary forces on the one side and their pro-statist rivals on the other would take centre stage, culminating in the notorious May Events of 1937. (See below, Chapter 7.)

Document 3.1 The Central Anti-Fascist Militias Committee

The Central Committee of the Militia came into being immediately after the victory over the Revolt, and this was due to the initiative of President Companys, who united in his office the representatives of all Anti-Fascist Sectors. In the course of a memorable conference with men of the CNT and FAI he explained to them his views, recognising that we were absolutely masters of the situation in Catalonia. Companys, on giving expression to his definitely Liberal opinions, offers his unconditional assistance to the workers. If we considered that he would be an obstacle, then he was ready to retire. If, however, we were of the opinion that he can be useful, then he is prepared to make practical propositions calculated to bring about, within the shortest time possible, a normal state of affairs and to make it possible to give armed assistance to the other parts of Spain.

As a result of that conference with Companys and the contact with other Sectors (which actually represented very little at that time) the Central Militia Committee was formed. This was given executive powers and functioned in so excellent a manner as to become a most effective organ of the Government. Among various other less important sections, the Committee appointed a War Department which was charged with the organisation and preparation for the despatch of the militiamen to the Fronts. This Department had to deal with all questions in any way connected with the war. Another Department was that of Public Safety, which succeeded, in a very brief space of time, in establishing revolutionary order in the rear on a solid basis. The Propaganda

Department fulfilled an extremely useful task by encouraging the enthusiasm of the masses and by sending out communications abroad throwing light on the true character of our fight.

The Committee was composed of representatives from all Anti-Fascist Sectors, but the Libertarian Organisations were in the majority.

Source: Nettlau, M. (1990) 'Pages of Working Class History', in *Spain, 1936–1939*, London, pp. 28–9.

Document 3.2 Anarchists in Government

From the moment the leaders of the CNT-FAI entered into ministries and submitted to the conditions imposed upon them by Soviet Russia in return for some arms, I foresaw the inevitable price our comrades will have to pay. Actually all the foreign comrades present in Barcelona agreed that the concessions made by the CNT-FAI were the first wrong step taken in the rise of the Revolution. We foresaw, and we did not hesitate to call the attention of our Spanish comrades to it, that they were about to roll down a precipice.

If I nevertheless continued to defend the course taken by some of our comrades I did so because I felt that the gravity of the antifascist situation seemed to make the actions of the CNT-FAI inevitable. The other alternative that presented itself was Dictatorship, which the Spanish comrades justly considered the greatest menace. Nevertheless it is unfortunately true that the Anarchist participation in the Government and the concessions made to Russia have resulted in almost irreparable harm to the Revolution.

I can therefore understand perfectly the indignation of our French comrades and those in other countries against the CNT-FAI leaders. They have shown anything but clarity and judgement in dealing with their allies. My one objection to the manifesto issued by the comrades of the F.A.F. in France is the charge of treachery and political corruption against the leading comrades in the CNT-FAI. Anarchists are but human, all 'too human,' and therefore as likely to betray their cause as other men and women, nor do I think that their revolutionary past would always save Anarchists from being inconsistent. It has not done so in the case of the erstwhile Bolshevik revolutionists. There is a difference however. Lenin and his party aspired to the Dictatorship while the CNT-FAI have from the beginning of their inception repudiated Dictatorship and have held high the banner of Libertarian Communism.

Source: Goldman, E. (2 July 1937) 'Where I Stand', *Spain in the World*, London.

Not long after the anarchists decided to participate in the regional government of Catalonia, they reached another crossroads regarding the question of political collaboration. With the formation of a Popular Front government in September under the leadership of the socialist Francisco Largo Caballero, it became immediately apparent that the new administration was determined to reconstruct the apparatuses of the state at the expense of the popular revolution. In response some sections of the libertarian community began calling for the creation of a national council of defence, a national ruling body that would be dominated by left-wing working-class organizations. However, plans to establish a 'revolutionary government' were overruled by the more pragmatic leadership of the CNT-FAI. At a plenary conference held at the end of September 1936, Horacio Prieto and other reformist-minded anarchists argued that, given the relatively greater weight carried by the pro-Popular Front factions, the CNT-FAI had no choice but to solicit representation in Caballero's government (Document 3.3). Recognizing that his administration could function more smoothly with the anarchists inside rather than outside his cabinet, Largo Caballero offered the anarchists four ministries: justice, industry, commerce, and health. Though none of these could be regarded as a vital post (the portfolios of industry and commerce had previously been held by a single minister), the anarchists agreed on 3 November to accept Caballero's offer (Document 3.4). In so doing, the anarchists were not just violating the basic tenets of their anti-statist doctrine, they were committing themselves to a course of action that was fraught with uncertainties. As events would demonstrate, the anarchists never developed the knowledge and skills needed to survive in the political world they had entered. Even more problematic was the fact that the anarchists leaders' decision to join the government irrevocably split the libertarian community into pro- and anti-political factions. As a result, the policy of collaboration tended to weaken rather than strengthen the anarchists' position vis-à-vis their rivals in the Republican camp.

Document 3.3 Reasons for Anarchist Participation in the Popular Front Government

We are taking into consideration the scruples that the members of the government may have concerning the international situation, . . . and for this reason the CNT is ready to make the maximum concession compatible with its anti-authoritarian spirit: that of entering the government. This does not imply renouncing its intention of fully realizing its ideals in the future; it simply means that . . . in order to win the war and to save our people and the world, it is ready to collaborate with anyone in a directive organ, whether this organ be called a council or a government.

Source: Bolloten, B. and Esenwein, G. (1990) 'Anarchists in Government: A Paradox of the Spanish Civil War, 1936–1939', in Lannon, F. and Preston, P. (eds) *Elites and Power in 20th Century Spain*, London and Oxford, p. 161.

Document 3.4 A Government of a New Type

From Solidaridad Obrera, *anarchist newspaper*

The entry of the CNT into the central government is one of the most important events in the political history of our country. Both as a matter of principle and by conviction, the CNT has been antistatist and an enemy of every form of government.

But circumstances . . . have transformed the nature of the Spanish government and the Spanish State.

At the present time, the government, as the instrument that controls the organs of the State, has ceased to be a force of oppression against the working class, just as the State no longer represents a body that divides society into classes. And both will oppress the people even less now that members of the CNT have intervened.

Source: Bolloten, B. (1991) *The Spanish Civil War: Revolution and Counter-revolution*, Chapel Hill, p. 208.

Industrial collectives and agricultural collectives

Despite the fact that an estimated three million Spaniards (approximately one quarter of the Republican side) participated in the collectivist movement that unfolded inside Republican Spain during the war, this aspect of the civil war has generally been ill served by historians.[1] This is due in part to the fact that much of the documentation relating to collectives during the Spanish Civil War is both incomplete and difficult to assess, and in part to the inability of scholars and non-scholars alike to reach a consensus about the overall significance of the popular revolution. In the former case, the chief problem facing the historian is finding reliable evidence. Most extant first-hand accounts of collectives were written by anarchists or anarchist sympathizers, and as such they reflect the kind of political partisanship that was characteristic of nearly all the personal testimonies written during and after the Civil War. Equally challenging is the fact that few of these were written according to exacting standards. This is not to say that the factual information contained in these accounts is wholly unreliable. In fact, some of the pro-libertarian testimonies of the collectives written during and after the war faithfully recorded the details of collectivist activities – how many had been established, how production and distribution were handled, etc. – because they believed that the revolution would be weakened more by an uncritical admiration of the collectives than by a frank accounting of their shortcomings. And, finally, even if it is true that the vast majority of the eyewitness narratives attesting to the existence and performance of collectives must be read with caution, this (largely fragmented) body of evidence is the only window we have onto the remarkable revolutionary experiences that touched the lives of millions of Spaniards during the war.

Providing an interpretative framework that places the collectives in context has also proved exceedingly problematic. The debate over their historiographical significance has for many years revolved around three central questions: (1) whether collectives significantly transformed or revolutionized the economy on the Republican side; (2) whether those collectives which did operate throughout much of the war were an economic success or failure, and (3) whether the collectives (and the revolutionary order which they stood for) undermined or reinforced the war against the Nationalists. While it is beyond the scope of this study to answer these questions, the following section will highlight the reasons for their persistence over the past sixty years.

Geography of revolution

The revolutionary movement that was unleashed by the July uprising did not follow a single pattern of development. At least as far as the anarchists were concerned this was partly due to the fact that few, if any, libertarians were committed to a programmatic course of revolutionary action. Since it had been introduced to Spanish workers and peasants some sixty-seven years earlier, anarchist ideology had always represented an eclectic mix of left-wing anti-authoritarian and anti-capitalist ideas and practices. This does not mean that anarchists lacked a vision of how *comunismo libertario* would be realized (Document 3.5). Rather, it is to say that, unlike their counterparts in the Marxist parties, anarchists were not bound by a rigid theoretical understanding of revolution that followed a prescribed course of action. Thus, while the 'orthodox' Marxists of the PCE insisted that their 'reading' of the objective conditions at the time indicated that Spain was entering into the early stages of a 'modified' bourgeois rather than a proletarian revolution, the anarchists of the CNT-FAI believed that the power vacuum that had been created by the military rebellion and the sudden collapse of numerous local and national government institutions had created the ideal circumstances for launching a thoroughgoing workers' and peasants' revolutionary movement (Document 3.6). In industrial regions such as Barcelona, the economic aspects of this revolution took the form of a massive collectivization programme that embraced the entire spectrum of business enterprises. For the most part this movement was being led by members of the CNT-FAI, who took full advantage of the state of confusion and chaos that reigned throughout the city in the first weeks of fighting by bringing factories, hotels, restaurants, barber shops, public transportation facilities, and other sectors of the economy under workers' control. Where they already held a firm foothold or where the owners and their administrators had fled the scene, anarchist workers began immediately restructuring these businesses in accordance with libertarian principles (Document 3.7).

Document 3.5 A Blueprint for Communismo Libertario

Libertarian Communism is a society organised without the state and without private ownership. And there is no need to invent anything or conjure up some new organization for the purpose. The centres about which life in the future will be organised are already with us in the society of today: the free union and the free municipality.

The union: in it combine spontaneously the workers from factories and all places of collective exploitation.

And the *free municipality:* an assembly with roots stretching back into the past where, again in spontaneity, inhabitants of village and hamlet combine together, and which points the way to the solution of problems in social life in the countryside.

Both kinds of organisation, run on federal and democratic principles, will be sovereign in their decision making, without being beholden to any higher body, their only obligation being to federate one with another as dictated by the economic requirement for liaison and communications bodies organised in industrial federations.

The *union and the free municipality* will assume the collective or common ownership of everything which is under private ownership at present and will regulate production and consumption (in a word, the economy) in each locality.

The very bringing together of the two terms (communism and libertarian) is indicative in itself of the fusion of two ideals: one of them is collectivist, tending to bring about harmony in the whole through the contributions and cooperation of individuals, without undermining their independence in any way; while the other is individualist, seeking to reassure the individual that his independence will be respected.

Implementation

Libertarian communism is based on organisations that already exist, thanks to which economic life in the cities and villages can be carried on in the light of the particular needs of each locality. Those organisms are the union and free municipality. The union brings individuals together, grouping them according to the nature of their work or daily contact through the same. First, it groups the workers of a factory, workshop or firm together, this being the smallest cell enjoying autonomy with regard to whatever concerns it alone. Along with kindred cells, these make up a section within the industrial or departmental union. There is a general trades union to cope with those workers who have not sufficient numbers to constitute a union of their own. The local unions federate with one another, forming the local federation, composed of the committee elected by the unions, of the plenum of all the committees, and of the general assembly that, in the last analysis, holds supreme sovereignty.

Libertarian communism is an open channel through which society may organise freely and of its own accord, and through which the evolution of society may follow its course without artificial deviations.

It is the most rational of all solutions to the economic question in that it corresponds to an equitable sharing out of production and labour required to achieve a solution. No one must shirk this necessity to join in the comparative effort of production, for it is nature itself which imposes this harsh law of labour upon us in climates where our nourishment does not grow spontaneously.

Economic compulsion is the bond of society. But it is, and must be, the only compulsion which the whole should exercise over the individual. All other activities – cultural, artistic, and scientific – should remain beyond the control of the collective and stay in the hands of those groups keen upon pursuing and encouraging them.

Source: Puente, I. (1982) *Libertarian Communism*, Sydney, pp. 28–33.

Document 3.6 A Marxist Interpretation of the Spanish Revolution

The revolution in Spain, which is part and parcel of the anti-fascist struggle all over the world, is a revolution having the broadest social basis. It is a people's revolution. It is a national revolution. It is an anti-fascist revolution.

It would not be correct to draw a complete parallel between the present Spanish revolution and the Russian revolution of 1905, and still less with the Russian revolution of 1917. The Spanish revolution has its own peculiar features which arise out of the specific internal as well as international situation. Big events and movements in history do not repeat themselves with photographic exactness either in time or space.

The Spanish people are solving the tasks of the bourgeois-democratic revolution.

Source: Ercoli, M. (aka P. Togliatti) (1936) *The Spanish Revolution*, New York, pp. 6–7.

Document 3.7 Revolutionary Transformations in Barcelona

I looked over the road at the Ritz. Across its door was a huge new red lettered sign:

HOTEL GASTROMIC NO. 1
U.G.T. – F.O.S.I.G. – C.N.T.

The Hotel Ritz was nowhere to be seen. In May its waiters and cooks had refused to serve anyone at all; now they were serving thousands of poor men and women daily, for they had taken over the hotel and turned it into a Popular Kitchen. All along the beautiful wide Corts Catalans the windows of the ex-Ritz were flung wide open. Within, the huge chandeliers were a blaze of light. Outside was a queue hundreds long of men and women from the

Fifth District, the barri chino waiting their turn to sit at the table of Dives [archetype of the richman], who had gone abroad for his health.

Source: Langdon-Davies, J. (1936) *Behind the Spanish Barricades*, New York, pp. 118–20.

From the outset, however, the revolutionaries encountered a number of stumbling blocks that effectively circumscribed their efforts to restructure the economy radically. For example, while they found it relatively easy to commandeer factories and businesses where their unions were strong or which had been abandoned by their owners, it proved to be much more difficult for them to expropriate foreign businesses (Document 3.8). Another problem which the revolutionaries confronted from the outset – and which was to continue to haunt them throughout the Civil War – was that the fact that they did not control all the key levers of the economy. Because the regional and national authorities continued to regulate foreign exchange, commercial treaties, and the banks, the revolutionaries found it impossible to obtain financial assistance for their collectivist experiments. This gave the opponents of collectivization the leverage they needed to reduce greatly the revolutionaries' role in the economy (Document 3.9).

Document 3.8 The Economics of Revolution

The Outbreak of the Civil War – Seizure of Buildings

The effect of the outbreak of the rising was simply to hasten a process already in operation. In Madrid, for example, after the 19th July, the ministerial department began to requisition houses and other buildings for use as hospitals, barracks, &c., and the independent political authorities, and especially the trade unions, began to follow suit. Seizures by the militia or trade unions were carried out with a certain respect of legal form, in that an act of seizure was drawn up. As time went on, tenanted buildings and flats were also formally seized in the name of one or other of the political authorities, who hoped no doubt to collect the rents in due course.

Seizure of Businesses

On the outbreak of the civil war the Government attempted to obtain control for war purposes of vital industries and services, and a decree was made at the end of July providing for Government intervention in any industry or business where control was considered desirable, especially in those connected with public utility services. An 'Intervention Committee' was created for the purpose of recording the introduction of such control, and Government delegates were appointed in some industries as a result of this decree. In the main, however, control was exercised by the workers themselves or by their unions. Control by the workmen had, of course, a revolutionary object and was not intended as a war measure, but it was found possible to include the establishment of workers' committees under the terms of the Intervention Decree, with the result that the Government's measure served to give official sanction to actions which interfered with its original purpose, and to legalise innovations which were not defensible by any existing principles of law.

Where a committee did not appear spontaneously, pretexts for interference in the working of affairs were not lacking. The most obvious was the failure to pay wages in consequence of the moratorium imposed by decree upon drawing from, or paying into, bank accounts. (It may be mentioned that this moratorium has since been modified in certain respects, including the withdrawal of money for payment of wages.) In short, practically every industry of any importance in Government territory is now under the control of a Workers' Committee. The procedure adopted in each separate case of expropriation has varied little. In a firm where the manager was missing (he may have been removed by his own employees) a Workers' Committee was formed to continue the business. Where the manager was still present the committee formed was sometimes a 'Control Committee,' which nominally did not interfere with the running of the business; sometimes a 'Managing Committee.'

Source: British Documents on Foreign Affairs, Series F, Europe, vol. 27, Document no. 81, pp. 99–100.

Document 3.9 The Limits of Collectivization

When the war broke out, workingmen's committees, often Anarchist, took over the factories. Production fell. They paid themselves in wages everything they took in from sales. Now they have no money. They are coming to me for running expenses and for raw materials. We will take advantage of their plight to gain control of the factories. Catalan industry is in chaos and as a result we have to depend far too much on imports which, as you know, are expensive even when we can get them.

Source: Fischer, L. (1966) *Men and Politics: Europe Between the Two World Wars*, New York, p. 421.

No less impressive in its scope and depth was the economic revolution that swept through the rural hamlets and agricultural regions of Republican Spain.[2] Though a few collectives sprang up in the central (New Castile), eastern (Catalonia), and southern zones (Extremadura and Jaén), a significant number of them – over 1,300 – were established in Aragón and the Levant.[3] Most rural collectives sought to restructure local society from the bottom up according to libertarian principles. To this end, they began their construction of the new order by demolishing what were perceived as the pillars of the old regime: religion, capitalism, and the ruling structures of the old regime (Document 3.10). It should also be borne in mind that, in addition to its economic functions, the collective sought to attend to the social and cultural needs of its residents. In many collectives, for example, great emphasis was placed on expanding welfare and public services to the needy and on ending child labour and other exploitative practices. Equally important in the eyes of the revolutionaries was the need to develop and expand educational opportunities among a population that was largely illiterate. The building of libraries, *ateneos* (centres used for a variety of cultural activities), schools, and other types of cultural institutions was therefore given top priority (Document 3.11).

Document 3.10 Agrarian Anarchism in Practice

(a)

Structure of the Collectives in Aragon

The smallest unit of the collective in Aragon was the work group, usually numbering five to ten members, sometimes more. The group might consist of friends, or the neighbours on a certain street, or a group of small farmers, tenant farmers, or day labourers. When one group finished its work, it would help another group. Everyone was obliged to work. Each group member was given a worker's card. A group would go out to work together led by their delegate, who much of the time worked with his comrades as well as recording the members' work. Land was assigned to the groups by the collective. The tools, machinery, and animals needed for work were the property of the collective. The cultivation of the land assigned to them was the responsibility of the group.

The collective was the free community of labour of the villagers. It was created with the influence of anarchist ideas. The CNT and the FAI (National Confederation of Labour and Iberian Anarchist Federation) held general assemblies in all the villages. Peasants, small farmers and tenant farmers attended. That was how the collectives were born. They took possession of the land and the tools and machinery of the expropriated landholders. The small farmers and tenant farmers who joined the collective brought their tools and equipment. An inventory of all property and equipment was made. Whoever did not wish to join the collective could keep the land that he could cultivate without hired labour. Each collective proceeded along the following lines of development:

The distribution of land, labour, tools and fruit of their toil was taken care of first. The collective had to be concerned in the first place with the material survival of its members. The product of the fields was brought to a common warehouse; the most important foods were distributed equally among all. Surplus crops were used for trade with other communes or with collectives in the cities. Produce was distributed to the members free of charge. Depending on the wealth of the commune there would be bread and wine. Sometimes bread, meat and other foods were issued without limit and free of charge.

Whatever had to be acquired outside of the commune, through barter or purchase from other communes or the cities, or commodities that were in low supply in the commune, were rationed. Everyone, whether able to work or not, received the necessities of life as far as the collective could provide them. The underlying idea was no longer 'a good day's pay for a good day's work' but 'from each according to his ability, to each according to his needs.'

Source: Souchy, A. (1982) *With the Peasants of Aragon: Libertarian Communism in the Liberated Areas*, Minneapolis, pp. 20–1.

(b)

The village of Alcora has established 'libertarian communism'. One must not think that this system corresponds to scientific theories. Libertarian communism in Alcora is the work of the peasants who completely ignore all economic laws. The form which they have given to their community corresponds more in reality to the ideas of the early Christians than those of our industrial epoch. The peasants want to have 'everything in common' and they think that the best way to achieve equality for all is to abolish money. In fact money does not circulate amongst them any longer. Everybody receives what he needs. From whom? From the Committee, of course.

It is however impossible to provide for five thousand people through a single centre of distribution. Shops still exist in Alcora where it is possible to get what is necessary as before. But those shops are only distribution centres. They are the property of the whole village and the ex-owners do not make profits instead. The barber himself shaves only in exchange for a coupon. The coupons are distributed by the Committee. The principle according to which the needs of all the inhabitants will be satisfied is not perfectly put in practice as the coupons are distributed according to the idea that every body has the same needs. There is no individual discrimination; the family alone is recognised as a unit. Only unmarried people are considered as individuals.

Each family and person living alone has received a card. It is punched each day at the place of work, which nobody can therefore leave. The coupons are distributed according to the card. And here lies the great weakness of the system: for the lack hitherto of any other standard they have to resort to money to measure the work done. Everybody, workers, shopkeepers, doctors, receive for each day's work coupons to the value of five pesetas. On one side of the coupon the word bread is written; each coupon is worth one kilogram. But the other side of the coupon represents explicitly a counter-value in money. Nevertheless these coupons cannot be considered as bank-notes. They can only be exchanged against goods for consumption and in only a limited quantity. Even if the amount of coupons was greater it would be impossible to buy means of production and so become a capitalist, even on a small scale, for only consumer goods are on sale. The means of production are owned by the community. The community is represented by the Committee, here called the Regional Committee. It has in its hands all the money of Alcora, about a hundred thousand pesetas. The Committee exchanges the village products against products which it does not possess, and when it cannot obtain them by exchange it buys them. But money is considered as an unavoidable evil, only to be used as long as the rest of the world will not follow the example of Alcora.

Source: Kaminski, H.E. (1937) 'A Peasant Experiment', from *Ceux de Barcelone*, translated in *Anarchy*, no. 5, London, 1961, pp. 156–7.

Document 3.11 The Cultural Concerns of Anarchism

As everywhere else, Graus also gave high priority to education. The most striking achievement, due largely to a man inspired by his task and by his convictions, was an Art School which was used during the day by primary school pupils and in the evenings by young workers. Drawing, painting, sculpture (or its study), choral societies (which must have already existed as they were to be found throughout Spain); the mind was being cultivated and the soul of man and of the child was raised through Art.

Source: Leval, G. (1975) *Collectives in the Spanish Revolution*, London, p. 103.

The pattern of these revolutionary conquests was much the same. Where the revolutionary left was predominant (particularly anarchist and socialist militants belonging to the CNT and UGT), the community would move quickly towards establishing a collective. The organizational framework for collectivization was constructed by an administrative council (*consejo de administración*), whose members had been elected at a public assembly. Besides overseeing the steps needed to place the local economy on a collectivist footing, the council was responsible for enforcing the implementation of all policies decided by the members of the collective.[4]

Given that the authority of these ruling bodies was rarely, if ever, challenged and in view of the fact that many of the elections that established them were conducted under the pressure of wartime circumstances, the question arose both during and after the war as to whether collectivization was more of a coercive than a voluntary process. The communists of the PCE and other Republican parties that were strongly opposed to the anarchist-inspired popular revolution believed the former, arguing that collectivization was being forced upon an unwilling peasantry. As evidence of this, they pointed to the Council of Aragon, a ruling body that had been set up in the presence of Buenaventura Durruti's famous column of revolutionary militiamen and which these groups claimed was little more than a thinly veiled anarchist dictatorship (Document 3.12). On the other hand, defenders of the collectivist movement insisted that the vast majority of collectives were not enforced upon a hostile population (Document 3.13). Rather, they argued that collectivization was rapidly throwing down roots in rural communities throughout the Republican zone because it offered Spain's most downtrodden people the most desirable and practicable alternative to the outdated and exploitative modes of social and economic organizations that dominated their lives before the outbreak of civil war.

Document 3.12 A Communist Promotes Individualism

We declare that the peasant, like the worker, must be guaranteed the absolute freedom to dispose of the fruits of his labour as he pleases. No one dares to go to the worker and dictate to him how he shall spend his wages, and yet there are people who feel that a different policy should be pursued towards the peasants. Certain people are using violence in order to force the peasants to dispose of the fruits of their labour in a certain way.

That is not the state of affairs for which we are shedding our blood. That is loathsome and hateful dictatorship, no matter where it occurs. We are not in favour of individual licence without let or hindrance, and we do not agree with those who declare that the individual transcends everything. We declare that above the interests of the individual stand the collective interests of all individuals. However, unless the collective interests of all individuals demand intervention, the freedom of each individual is inviolable for all.

Source: International Press Correspondence, vol. 17, no. 8 (20 February) 1937, p. 212.

Document 3.13 An Anarchist Defends the Council of Aragón

During this period, Aragon was at the mercy of opposing factions, who regarded it as a colony ready to be robbed of its wheat, its oil, its artistic treasure, and, on top of that, to treat its citizens as mere minors.

It was then, when Aragon was faced with its own problems, complicated by outside forces, that the CNT issued its warning – only the CNT – that these developments that were taking place in the name of anti-fascism must stop.

It created the Aragon Council with the immediate mission of stopping this exploitation of this province and winning the respect that we deserved. Then, assured of their regional integrity, it proceeded to the laborious task of regulating the economy; to provide norms of living together and mutual relations in Aragon; to give the Aragonese a legal base that would reside in their Municipal Councils as well as in the Regional Council. All this was being done in spite of those who wanted to plunder Aragon and were continually intriguing in order to undermine the prestige of the Aragon Council.

Source: Spain and the World: Social Revolution and Counter-Revolution / Selections from the Anarchist Fortnightly, Spain and the World, 1936–1939 (1937), London: Freedom Press, p. 169.

In the end, the question of whether the libertarians' collectivist experiments were an expression of the popular will of the peasantry cannot be answered with a simple yes or no. The truth is that collectivization was at times forced upon the peasantry and local residents – especially where there were large pockets of resistance to it – and at times it arose spontaneously. What is beyond question is the fact that the collectivist revolution affected the lives of tens of thousands of Spaniards during the war.

Collectives: Success or failure?

When one draws up a balance sheet of the collectivization movement, it is nearly impossible to conclude whether this form of economic and social experimentation was a success or failure. From a strictly economic standpoint there is a mixed record. Because there are no reliable statistics of production figures, the general picture of economic life of the collectives throughout the Republican zone remains rather cloudy. Pro-revolutionary sources tend to emphasis the many achievements of collectives. For example, these usually cite government figures issued during the war which indicate that there was an increased output of wheat and other crops in those regions dominated by collectives (Aragón and Castile). The many successes of the worker-controlled industries in the towns and cities – such as the revolutionary restructuring of workshops and factories in Catalonia that allowed for the emergence of a viable war industry – can also be taken as evidence attesting to the benefits of collectivization. Yet this picture has to be balanced by the many defects of the movement (Document 3.14). Collectives encountered a number of difficulties owing to their own inherent shortcomings. Given that the overall collectivist movement itself did not conform to a unified and coherent plan of development, there was considerable variation in the organization and administration of individual rural collectives. In practice this meant that it was exceedingly difficult to mesh the activities of collectives that adopted extreme revolutionary measures – such as the root-and-branch eradication of capitalism – with those that opted to operate under a mixed-economic model. And while some progress was made during the war to bring about a greater co-ordination and standardization of the collectivist movement on a regional level, a fully functional overarching framework of this sort never materialized.

Document 3.14 Identifying the Obstacles to Anarchist Collectivism

The chief obstacles to the collectives were:

a) The existence of conservative strata, and parties and organisations representing them. Republicans of all factions, socialists of left and right (Largo Caballero and Prieto), Stalinist Communists, and often the POUMists. (Before their expulsion from the Catalan government – the *Generalidad* – the POUMists were not a truly revolutionary party. They became so when driven into opposition. Even in June, 1937, a manifesto distributed by the Aragon section of the POUM attacked the collectives). The UGT was the principal instrument of the various politicians.

b) The opposition of certain small landowners (peasants from Catalonia and the Pyrénées).

c) The fear, even among some members of collectives, that the government would destroy the organisations once the war was over. Many who were not really reactionary, and many small landowners who would otherwise have joined the collectives, held back on this account.

d) The open attack on the collectives: by which is not meant the obviously destructive acts of the Franco troops wherever they advanced. In Castile the attack on the collectivists was conducted, arms in hand, by Communist troops. In the Valencia region, there were battles in which even armoured cars took part. In the Huesca province the Karl Marx brigade persecuted the collectives. The Macia-Companys brigade did the same in Teruel province. (But both always fled from combat with the fascists. The Karl Marx brigade always remained inactive, while our troops fought for Huesca and other important points; the Marxist troops reserved themselves for the rearguard. The second gave up Vivel del Rio and other coal regions of Utrillos without a fight. These soldiers, who ran in panic before a small attack that other forces easily contained, were intrepid warriors against the unarmed peasants of the collectives.)

Source: Leval, G. (1974) 'The Characteristics of the Libertarian Collective', in Sam Dolgoff (ed.) *The Anarchist Collectives: Workers' Self-management in the Spanish Revolution 1936–1939*, Montreal: Black Rose Books, p. 169.

The parochialism of the collectives also militated against their success. In both the urban and rural collectives, it was not uncommon to see a strong sense of loyalty to a particular enterprise, union, or locality be expressed through the behaviour of the members of an individual collective. There is evidence, for instance, that workers with a strong attachment to a particular industry that had been collectivized placed the material interests of their own *sindicato* above the broader needs of industries engaged in the war effort. Collectives in the countryside, particularly those operating independently in remote regions, also exhibited this kind of group-centred behaviour. Though recognized by the leaders of the CNT-FAI as serious obstacles to the progressive development of collectivization, these manifestations of local 'patriotism' were nearly impossible to suppress (Document 3.15).

Document 3.15 Resistance to Revolutionary Ideology on the Factory Floor

Gaston Leval noted:

'Many times in Barcelona and in Valencia – the workers of each enterprise took possession of the factory, of the workshop, of the machines, of the raw materials, and taking advantage of the fact that there still existed the monetary system and the mercantile economy characteristic of the capitalist system, supported by the government, organized production for their own advantage, selling for their own benefit the production of their labour . . . This practice didn't create a true socialisation, but a species of workers' neo-capitalism . . .

'The collectivism we are living in Spain is not anarchist collectivism, it is the creation of a new capitalism, more inorganic than the old capitalist system we have destroyed . . . Rich collectives refuse to recognise any responsibilities, duties or solidarity towards poor collectives . . . No one understands the complexities of the economy, the dependence of one industry on another.'

Source: Alexander, R. (1999) *The Anarchists in the Spanish Civil War*, London, p. 475.

On a political level, the collectivization movement was perceived by its opponents as a major liability to the Republican cause (Document 3.16). This was true not just because these factions were in principle opposed to the idea of revolution but because they were convinced that the policies and practices associated with it were wholly impracticable. Over the course of the war, the struggle between the forces in favour of collectivism on the one side and those who strongly opposed it on the other became one of the main axes of conflict on the Republican side.

Document 3.16 Opposing the POUM's Revolutionary Economic Programme

'The P.O.U.M. advocates immediate collectivisation: is this possible?'

It is not possible without incurring a grave economic and political danger. Collectivisation can be applied when we have necessary and sufficient objective conditions; that is, intensive cultivation, the use of much agricultural machinery and technicians and experts for production on a large scale; and subjective conditions; that is, the conviction of the peasants that collec-tivisation will bring them advantages. Premature collectivisation would destroy the chances of winning the war, in so much as agricultural production would diminish without the good-will of the peasants, the march of the revolution would be retarded, and the very existence of the democratic republic endan-gered. At the moment, then, we are for the defence of small property, for the defence of the families who support themselves by their work on the land, for the creation of co-operative syndicates, whose duty it is to ensure the exchange of produce between city and country. For this reason we believe in the liberty of the small tradesmen, until he disappears in a natural way.

Of course we believe in collectivisation, but we must admit that the first efforts at collectivisation have failed miserably. Also, we must be on guard against trying to collectivise the great estates that were formerly worked by a single bailiff on behalf of an absentee landlord.

Source: The Spanish News Bulletin, issued by the PSUC / United Socialist
Party of Catalonia, Barcelona, 1937.

From a social perspective, there is a good deal of evidence that suggests that
collectivist revolution had a largely positive impact on the daily lives of those who
participated in these social experiments. The collectives appealed especially to the
many downtrodden and disenfranchised Spaniards. Under the collectivist system, the
economic and social barriers that had consigned this group to the bottom rungs of
society were broken down, and, for the first time ever, the dispossessed had access
not only to public resources that could improve their material conditions but also
to educational and cultural opportunities that could enrich their lives on a spiritual
level.

Red and White Terrors

The rebellion and revolution that began in July set in motion a wave of violence and
repression against the civilian population that swept through both the Republican
and Nationalist zones. Much of this terror was a product of the pent-up passions of
a country that was divided into mutually hostile ideological camps.

The most tragic aspect of any civil war is the violence done to the civilian
population on both sides. The violence that accompanied civil war in its opening
phases did not arise from any single emotion or political motivation. The breakdown
of traditional forms of authority – the courts, police services, etc. – opened the door
wide to popular vigilantism which was expressed during the first days and weeks
of the conflict (Document 3.17). According to many eyewitnesses, many of the
atrocities committed behind the lines during the opening phases of the war seemed
to be connected to deep-seated class and religious hatreds that had long divided
Spanish society. On the Republican side, for example, victims were usually identified
as members of the political, economic, and religious ruling classes, groups that
included members of right-wing political parties and organizations, business owners,
merchants, and clergy men and women (Document 3.18).

Document 3.17 Settling Political Scores

One of the most terrible features of the civil war has been the assassination or
execution of political opponents, of which both sides have been guilty. The
exasperation which the rebellion roused among the extremist parties found
vent in the immediate arrest in each locality of the leading members of the
parties of the Right. In some cases these persons were executed immediately,
often in circumstances of unbelievable ferocity. In other cases their death was
deferred until just before the entry of the national forces into the town or
village concerned. Sometimes the sudden advent of these troops prevented
the massacres from taking place, though there are few communities, it is
feared, where sooner or later they have not suffered molestation of some kind.

That this should be so is easily understandable, equally understandable is the vengeance taken by the friends and relations of those who died, and within a week of the outbreak of the movement orders were given that where elements of the Right had thus suffered, all the local leaders of the political parties concerned were to be summarily executed, and that failing their capture, an equal number of their political associates should be shot in their stead.

Source: British Documents on Foreign Affairs, Series F, Europe, vol. 27, Document no. 48, p. 55.

Document 3.18 Violence as an Instrument of Social Control

Summary of situation, August 28, 1936

The shooting of persons suspected of political affiliation with the Right continues. At Tarragona on one day seventy-two persons were taken from the prison ship and disappeared. In some cases, apparently, these people are thrown overboard with weights attached to their feet; in other cases they are taken into the country and shot, their bodies being left for their relatives to discover if possible.

Even local opinion was shocked a few days ago by the murder of Sr. Planas, a promising young journalist of the extreme Left, whose only crime seems to have been that he deprecated the use of too much violence in an article he wrote some weeks ago. The Anarcho-Syndicalists allowed no notice to appear of this murder in the press until after Sr. Planas was buried.

It is reported also that the Anarcho-Syndicalists are killing the members of the Somaten, a force of respectable householders, who had permission to carry firearms to repress local disorders.

Source: British Documents on Foreign Affairs, Series F, Europe, vol. 27, Document no. 25, p. 24.

During the war, there were at least three identifiable phases of violence. The first stage involved the armed struggle between the rebelling army and their supporters on the one side and the loyal Republican forces and civilian organizations on the other. After the military rebellion had been suppressed and the dividing line between Republican and anti-Republican Spain had been drawn, another, more harrowing stage of violence was unleashed. This was the so-called 'house cleaning' (*limpieza*) campaign aimed at eliminating suspected enemies. A third stage developed during the course of the war itself. On both sides, determined and often ruthless measures were taken to pacify opposition in the rearguard. In practice this usually meant either gaoling or executing refractory elements who challenged the policies of the reigning authorities.

Revolutionary violence

On the republican side, the breakdown of formal authority led directly to a kind of working-class vigilantism. In many cities and towns triumphant labour groups immediately began to round up suspected rebels or rebel sympathizers. Those who were known to belong to right-wing organizations were primary targets, though many innocent bystanders also fell prey to the 'street justice' that was meted out in the heat of the moment. In an effort to ferret out anti-republican elements behind the lines, a variety of investigation committees – known variously as 'revolutionary tribunals', 'committees of public health', and 'Investigation committees' – spontaneously sprang up at the local and regional levels. In Barcelona, for instance, these bodies immediately set about identifying citizens who were known to be on the right or who were engaged in what was perceived as 'fascist activity'. Countless so-named 'enemies' were brought before the impromptu tribunals, where convictions were handed down in a summary fashion. Little time passed between a conviction and execution. Those selected to die were usually 'taken for a ride' (*paseo*) – a euphemism adopted from American gangster movies which meant being carted off in the dead of night to a cemetery or other designated 'killing field' at the edge of town. After they had been executed, their bodies were left for public viewing, which served as a powerful visual reminder of the fate that awaited enemies of the new order. Other victims of 'revolutionary justice' suffered imprisonment and/or had their property confiscated or destroyed.

The high tide of activities for these unofficial tribunals was the summer of 1936. The early autumn saw the apparatuses of the central and local governments reasserting their authority. The intensity and scope of the 'Red Terror' described here began to abate in most regions following the reestablishment of central and local government authorities. As early as 23 August 1936 the Madrid government established Popular Tribunals, which attempted to regularize the trials of those suspected of being pro-Nationalist. Around the same time, the CNT-FAI and other trade-union groups began calling for a halt to arbitrary killings, particularly those which were motivated purely by personal vendettas and which were being carried out by criminals or street gangs. As a result, the myriad of revolutionary courts scattered throughout the Republican zone eventually disappeared (Document no. 3.19).

Document 3.19 Defining Revolutionary Terrorism and Popular Justice

(a)

Another circumstance on which they laid great stress was the execution of fascists. Some figures and notes may clear up that question. In Madrid, Valencia and Barcelona there were executions apart from the courts of justice, in the first days. But in these three cities armed fighting took place before these executions, bloody attacks on the town, monstrous provocation of the unarmed civil population who had to go with empty hands, strewing the road with their dead, to capture machine-guns and cannon from the enemy. Under such circumstances it cannot surprise anyone that in Barcelona seven thousand four hundred were killed. A city of a million and a half inhabitants driven into war could not help reacting in that way. The same can be said of Madrid, although the figures were not so high there, and where the absence of the passion for vengeance has allowed unmolested and free life not only to pacific people whose views and habits are strongly reactionary, but to Deputies of the Ceda and of its ally, the radical party, and thus to active political enemies. All those who abstained from actually taking up arms against the people not only have not been molested, but have enjoyed all the measures of protection given to the civil population by the Government, and afterwards by the Junta of Defence. We all know of many reactionaries in the background. We know who they are and where they live.

Source: Sender, R. (1937) *The War in Spain*, London, p. 94.

(b)

No. 128, December 2, 1936
Subject: Article by Mr. Lawrence A. Fernsworth, Concerning the Secret Reign of Terror in Barcelona and Catalonia

There is evidence that much of the terrorism was conducted by plain gang-sters, criminals who crawled out of their holes or flocked here from various parts of the world for motives of robbery and plunder under the cover of revolutionary terror. Such gangs frequently invaded the homes of wealthy persons under cover of night, robbing them of all that was valuable; in other cases [they] resorted to blackmail and they dealt death as suited their purpose. The dregs of Marseilles, of Paris and of Berlin seemed to have poured into Barcelona to prey on the terror-stricken wealthy.

Source: Perkins, Mahlon F., quoted in Cortada, J. W. (ed.) (1985) *A City in War: American Views on Barcelona and the Spanish Civil War, 1936–1939*, Wilmington: Scholarly Resources, pp. 50–1.

(c)

Barcelona, November 18, 1936

Sir,

I have the honour to refer to my despatches Nos. 217 and 220 of the 16th and 19th October respectively, on the subject of popular justice in Catalonia . . .

2. The popular tribunals must be distinguished from the popular juries which were set up soon after the uprising of last July, for the purpose of trying

military prisoners who took part therein. These juries have sat to conduct trials on board the steamship *Uruguay* which has, on this as on other occasions, served as a floating prison, but the prisoners have recently been transferred to the Montjuich fortress.

3. As reported in my despatch No. 220, sentences pronounced by the popular juries are extremely severe. The popular tribunals, or tribunals of popular justice, which formed the subject of my despatch No.217, are a more recent creation and only began to function about a month ago. They deal with offences of civilians described as: –

(1) Acts of 'fascism' which helped directly or indirectly the military rising and Fascist movement of the 19th July last.
(2) Anti-revolutionary acts such as espionage, sabotage, propaganda and defeatist activities.

Source: British Documents on Foreign Affairs, Series F, Europe, vol. 27, Document 46, p. 49.

(d)

The Government and the leaders of the Anarcho-Syndicalists appear to be attempting to check the atrocities which are still being carried out. A leading article in the local Labour press organ claims that arms should not be seen in the streets of Barcelona, their proper place being the Zaragoza front. It also points out that no executions are authorised except those approved by the Tribunal of Fifteen. The Councillor for the Interior has also published an order forbidding any house searching or detention, except when expressly ordered by the Government Executive or judicial authority or by the Central Committee of the Anti-Fascist Militia.

Source: British Documents on Foreign Affairs, Series F, Europe, vol. 27, Document 22, p. 22.

Where the Red Terror particularly distinguished itself from the White was in its massive onslaught against the Catholic Church. Since the late nineteenth century the anticlerical feelings of the Spanish left had grown ever more hostile, but it was not until civil war broke out that their long-simmering conflict with the Church violently boiled over. Apart from sacking and burning churches and convents, and attacking religious monuments, a certain number of revolutionaries set about killing clergy men and women in what turned out to be one of the greatest clerical bloodlettings in modern times. Close to seven thousand bishops (12), nuns (283), priests, and other religious officials (6,500) fell victim to this virulent and, for many, incomprehensible form of revolutionary rampage (Document 3.20).

Document 3.20 Catholic Victims of the 'Godless' Revolution

(a)

The total number of the assassinations which the Popular Front committed throughout the red zone, in the persons of Ministers of the catholic religion and members of the religious Orders, amounts to *seven thousand nine hundred and thirty-seven*, comprising Bishops (of whom 13 were murdered), priests (5,255), and monks and nuns (2,669); Madrid participating in the total number with *one thousand one hundred and fifty-eight* (111 of whom were nuns, murdered in the Capital); Barcelona with a total of *one thousand two hundred and fifteen* victims, the only motive being their religious character or profession; in Valencia, *seven hundred and five*; in Lérida *three hundred and sixty-six*; in Tarragona, *two hundred and fifty-nine*; and in the rest of the provinces suffering the Marxist terror, the assassinations reached high figures.

Source: The Red Domination in Spain: The General Cause, 4th edition (1961), Madrid, p. 195.

(b)

There is reason to hope, moreover, that the number of priests murdered, though no doubt lamentably great, was not nearly as large as originally stated. Some had had word beforehand of the rising and fled before it broke out. Others managed to hide until the outrages had ceased. The Catalan Government saved the lives of hundreds, also seven bishops and some at least of the monks of Montserrat, by sending them out of the country.

Some months later they were said to be keeping a large number of priests either in charitable institutions or under arrest – some of them, for their own safety.

It is probably owing to measures of this kind that, whereas the Spanish bishops originally estimated the number of priests killed at 15,000, in their recent letter, published July, 1937, they do not commit themselves to more than the statement that 'about 6,000 secular priests' had been murdered.

Source: Atholl, Katherine (1938) *Searchlight on Spain*, Harmondsworth, p. 97.

White Terror

On the Nationalist side, the cleaning-up (*limpieza*) of Republican sympathizers was conducted thoroughly and ruthlessly by the military, which was assisted in many regions by civilian groups such as the Falange (Document 3.21). In the large towns and cities the main targets of this grisly process were left-wing organizations (which possessed membership lists that could be used to identify potential enemies) and known critics of the right. The political composition of smaller towns and villages was so well-known to all that it was relatively easy to root out opponents of the rebellion. Because accurate records of these executions were not kept, it is impossible to know for certain just how many Spaniards were executed during these so-called 'house-cleanings'. Estimates derived from both pro-Nationalist and pro-Republican sources put the total at anywhere between sixty thousand and seventy thousand.

Document 3.21 House-Cleaning in the Nationalist Zone

Those who opposed this national movement were, therefore, declared rebels and traitors to the sacred cause of Spain, and were treated as such in whatever capacity they might exhibit such opposition. From the opening moves of the campaign, therefore, ruthless war, a war indeed of extermination, was declared on the leaders and prominent followers of the extremist parties, such as the Syndicalists, Anarchists and Communists.

Where the work of 'cleaning up' the villages had to be entrusted, as then happened, to the barely disciplined Falangist and Requeté militia, not infrequently composed of or led by members of the communities concerned, it is hardly to be wondered that this order was often given a ruthlessly elastic interpretation, which in its turn accentuated the ferocity of this vicious circle of extermination.

Source: Coultas, F.G. (1936) 'Paseos', *British Documents on Foreign Affairs*, Series F, Europe, vol. 27, 19 November.

More so than on the Republican side, the lines separating the cleaning-up efforts referred to above and military tactics were blurred. In August 1936, for example, invading Nationalist troops reputedly slaughtered nearly two thousand people trapped in the bullring at Badajoz. So great was the bloodbath, according to several reports filed shortly after the massacre, that blood was said to have flowed 'palm deep' in the streets of the city. Nationalist repression in cities such as Seville and Granada was also especially brutal. Not only ordinary people but also famous personalities were executed in these bloody purges. Among the many victims of the White Terror in Granada, for example, was the renowned homosexual playwright and poet Federico García Lorca. Rumours of Lorca's death shocked the outside world, most likely because his murder testified to the Nationalists' callous indifference to the fact that he was widely regarded as a citizen of the international literary community.

Repression behind the lines

A third stage of violence against non-combatants occurred during the war itself. Repressive measures taken by both the Republican and Nationalist governments often resulted in the deaths of civilians who had already been imprisoned or were identified as 'Fifth Columnists' (a term coined by General Mola during the Battle of Madrid in reference to the supposedly anonymous column of pro-Nationalists among the civilian population in Madrid who would rise up in support of the four 'columns' of rebel troops attacking the city). Attacks on civilians at this stage of the conflict would usually be triggered by news of a massacre or series of atrocities committed by the Nationalists. During the initial stages of the siege of Madrid, for example, a number of rightists who had been imprisoned in the city's main gaols were taken out (*sacas*) and summarily executed. What made this act of violence particularly horrific was the fact that the mass execution of some three thousand prisoners was carried out under the auspices of republican officials.[5]

After the initial wave of violence had swept through both zones, terrorism gave way to a form of repression that relied less on physical and more on psychological forms of intimidation. The Nationalists in particular were particularly adept at conducting this sort of psychological warfare through the media. The radio broadcasts of the 'Radio General' Queipo de Llano are a case in point. From the opening moments of the conflict, Queipo used the radio as an instrument of social control and terrorism. When his troops were in the process of securing Seville, the general reinforced their efforts by threatening the civilian population with reprisals. Thus, before concluding his first broadcast, the general warned the city's residents that Moroccan troops and Legionnaires of the African Army would soon be arriving to hunt down any trouble makers 'like wild animals'.[6] Quiepo continued to make broadcasts of this type throughout the first part of the war, no doubt because of the chilling effect they had on their intended audiences.

As the war dragged on, the morale of the Republicans became a major problem. Fearful of the corrosive effects of this development, the government grew increasingly suspicious of those who exhibited an attitude of 'defeatism' or disaffection from the Republican cause. This paranoia served as an impetus for yet another form of terrorism and repression in the rearguard, which reigned during the last year and a half of the war. This marked a particularly murky period of the Republic, one in which the political battles being waged among leftist organizations were merged with the general struggle against Franco's forces. On one level, the rivalry between the pro-revolutionary forces and the defenders of the moderate Popular Front policy of the government had opened deep rifts in the anti-fascist alliance that could not be bridged. This is illustrated by the negative fallout from the controversial May Events of 1937 (discussed below, Chapter 7). Following this highly disruptive episode, the communists became the dominant force in the coalition of forces which ruled Republican Spain from then onwards. With the tacit backing of the moderate elements of the socialist and Republican parties, the communists launched a sweeping campaign of repression aimed at eliminating all serious opposition to the Popular Front government. The political persecution and physical harassment of 'outcast' republicans culminated with the POUM trials in October 1938 but continued until the end of the war (see below, Chapter 9).

At the same time, the Republican government could not ignore the growing threat of a Fifth Column movement. Mounting republican defeats and rapidly deteriorating living conditions combined to undermine popular support for the anti-fascist cause, a development that played into the hands of Nationalist sympathizers who were already doing all they could to sabotage the Republican war effort. To all intents and purposes, then, the government's repressive measures did not discriminate between the activities of refractory left-wing groups and those of pro-Nationalist elements.

It was against this background, that Republican authorities established a vast network of spies and secret police, such as the infamous SIM (*Servicio de Información Militar*). Officially created in order to combat espionage and prevent acts of sabotage against the Republic, the SIM, under communist leadership, developed into a formidable organ of repression which was used both to eliminate 'Fifth Columnists' and also to repress left-wing anti-communist groups such as the POUM and dissidents of the CNT-FAI. Because it operated with very little interference from the government, courts, or other agencies which could have checked its activities, it is impossible to know precisely how many people fell victim to its extensive police network. What evidence we do have of its activities has been largely culled from sources hostile to the communists. According to these, the SIM developed into an instrument of Stalinist-like terror and repression and was responsible for torturing and killing a considerable number of Spaniards. And while it is reasonable to assume that these tendentious accounts somewhat exaggerate the extent of its excesses, there can be little doubt that the SIM was the government agency most responsible for sustaining an atmosphere of recrimination and terror in the Republican camp during the last stages of the war (Document 3.22).

Document 3.22 Political Repression Behind Enemy Lines

(a)

On August 15, 1937, a decree was issued creating the Military Investigation Service (SIM). The scope of the decree was not noticed by most Spaniards, possibly not even by the Minister of National Defence himself, who signed it. For it seemed natural in a time of war to set up an agency for counter-espionage: people were far from suspecting that an agency designed to counter enemy espionage activities could be turned into a powerful instrument of one party against opposition parties. This is what happened with SIM: it was converted from a secret service of the General Staff into a branch of the Soviet GPU.

On the homefront, SIM agents inspired fear even in the police. Every known SIM agent had another, secret one watching him. At first the Minister of National Defence was the only one who could name or remove agents, but a ruling in September, 1938, delegated this authority to the head of SIM.

The torture cells of SIM were often hidden in palatial mansions surrounded by trees and gardens. The Spanish people called all secret prisons '*chekas*'. At first the SIM jails were dark and spooky, located in old houses and convents. The regime of torture that they used in them included the normal kinds of brutality: beatings with rubber whips followed by very cold baths; simulated executions and other painful and bloody tortures. The 'Russian advisors' modernized these ancient techniques. The new cells were smaller, painted with bright colours and paved with sharp-edged tiles. The prisoners had to stand continually under a powerful red or green light. Other cells were narrow tombs with a sloping floor, where remaining on foot meant a complete tensing of nerves and muscles. In others there was an absolute darkness, and metallic noises could be heard that made the prisoners' heads ring.

Source: Peirats, J. (1974) *Anarchists in the Spanish Revolution*, Toronto, pp. 232–3.

(b)

The S.I.M. (Military Investigation Service) did not limit its activities to the sphere of military investigation as its title implies, but soon became the most sinister and dreadful branch of the political Police, imposing terror both at the battle front and in the rearguard, and committing numerous assassinations.

The S.I.M. of the Central Army (Madrid) remained in the hands of Angel Pedrero Garcia, a socialist school-teacher, a known thief, and friend of both Indalecio Prieto and Angel Galarza, being the latter's fellow-townsman. When he was named Demarcation-Chief of the S.I.M., with the rank of Lieutenant-Colonel, he distributed the more important posts under his command among his former companions at the afore-named 'checa' of Atadell, where he had held the position of Assistant Chief, completing his new staff by a number of socialist police agents, all of them former 'checa' members.

The S.I.M. of Madrid applied terrible tortures at its prison of San Lorenzo (formerly belonging to the D.E.D.I.D.E.), and committed numerous assassinations in the Capital.

Source: The Red Domination in Spain, (1961), Madrid p. 261.

Representations of violence and terror

In reading the many and varied accounts of atrocities committed during the war one is immediately struck by the numerous inconsistencies and contradictions that can be found in the various narratives describing these events. These were due to several factors. One was simply the difficulty in getting reliable information attesting to atrocities. Inside of Spain news of violent excesses against the civilian population could not be taken at face value, above all because the press on both the Republican and Nationalist sides was not only heavily censored but also being used more as an instrument of propaganda than as a vehicle for accurate investigative reporting. A further problem in this connection had to do with the sources for the stories themselves. For various reasons, including the fact that it was exceedingly difficult for surviving victims to develop a sense of detachment in their storytelling, eyewitnesses could not be relied on to report accurately what they had experienced.

The most exaggerated and lurid episodes were products of fear and of propaganda.[7] Reports of this sort were significant not for what they revealed about the atrocities themselves but for what they said about the moral and political narratives of the Civil War that were being constructed both by the participants themselves and by the outside world. The extent to which 'atrocities' were being used as instruments of propaganda is reflected in the numerous publications produced by several 'fact-finding' committees which were set up to investigate the nature and extent of atrocities. Each, such as the 'Committee of Investigation Appointed by the National Government at Burgos', claimed to offer an authentic account of alleged atrocities, though few, if any, of these bodies were composed of neutral observers and the conclusions of each were obviously aimed at exposing the 'falsehoods' of the opposing side and thereby convincing the intended reading audience of the moral and ideological superiority of the cause being promoted.

On the right, the recounting of brutal scenes from the revolution and terrorism behind Republican lines was done primarily to give legitimacy to their view that the military uprising was both a necessary and justified response to the breakdown of authority under left-wing rule (Document 3.23). Pro-Republican accounts of Nationalist excesses also served a variety of pointed ideological purposes. The horrific details of Nationalist executions were recounted in order to attest to the brutality of the 'fascist' enemy. In addition they were used to arouse anger and indignation against the enemy.

3.23 The Red Terror as Seen Through Nationalist Eyes

(a)

Communist technique was almost identical in every town and village. The plan carried out in the villages was usually as follows:

1. The churches were sacked and burnt.
2. Nuns and priests were tortured and murdered
3. Private houses were sacked and burnt.
4. Individuals were robbed or murdered (or both), for the following reasons:
    (a) because they belonged to the upper class.
    (b) because they were church-goers.
    (c) because they were anti-Communist or not sufficiently pro-Communist.

These appalling conditions continued everywhere until Franco's troops took the locality.

Source: Tennant, E. (1936) *Spanish Journey: Personal Experiences of the Civil War*, London, p. 70.

(b)

Lora Del Rio (Province of Seville)

This is one of the villages where the crimes of the revolutionaries were particularly atrocious. A large number of entirely unprovoked murders were committed in circumstances of the utmost barbarity.

It is impossible in this short preliminary report to describe in full detail all the atrocities committed in Lora. Many families had all their menfolk rounded up, and in most cases they were killed after revolting tortures. Cartloads of these wretched victims were taken at dawn to the cemetery, where they were made to dig a huge grave. Then the murderers fired on them, but they were careful to shoot them in the legs, so that they were not killed outright but fell writhing into the grave. Some were then buried alive and others left to linger in agony on the ground, where their cries and groans made the days and nights hideous, as they slowly died.

Puente Genil (Province of Cordova)

One hundred and fifty-four citizens were murdered here between July 24th and August 18th by the Communists, who also burnt seven churches, twenty-eight private houses, an almshouse for old men, and the barracks of the Civil Guard.

Seventeen of the murdered men were forced to remain with their arms raised above their heads for several hours – a boy of sixteen among them fainted from the pain – and they were then shot dead on the railway line near the station.

Source: A Preliminary Official Report on the Atrocities Committed in Southern Spain in July and August, 1936, by the Communist Forces of the Madrid Government (1936), London, pp. 48 and 58.

Another major difficulty in reporting accurately the atrocities being committed on both sides had to do with the shortcomings of the printed media. In some of the most sensationalist episodes of the war – most notably, the Badajoz massacres (August 1936) and the bombing of Guernica (April 1937) – no professional journalist was on scene and in a position to record details of the event as they were occurring. Published articles gathered after these two widely publicized episodes provoked endless controversies, not least because the descriptions contained in them were woven from a patchwork of both reliable and questionable sources that could be used to support diametrically opposed versions of what had happened (Document 3.24).

Document 3.24 Reporting the Terror: The Impact of 'Eyewitness' Testimonies

(a)

Blood Flows in Badajoz

Jay Allen, who wrote the following dispatch after a visit to Badajoz, was foreign correspondent in Spain for the Chicago Tribune Press Service.

Suddenly we saw two Phalanxists halt a strapping fellow in a workman's blouse and hold him while a third pulled back his shirt, baring his right shoulder. The black and blue marks of a rifle butt could be seen. Even after a week they showed. The report was unfavourable. To the bull ring with him.

We drove out along the walls to the ring in question. Its sandstone walls looked over the fertile valley of Guadiana. It is a fine ring of white plaster and red brick. I saw Juan Belmonte (bullfight idol) here once on the eve of the fight, on a night like this, when he came down to watch the bulls brought in. This night the fodder for tomorrow's show was being brought in, too. Files of men, arms in the air.

They were young, mostly peasants in blue blouses, mechanics in jumpers. 'The Reds.' They are still being rounded up. At four o'clock in the morning they are turned out into the ring through the gate by which the initial parade of the bullfight enters. There machine guns await them.

After the first night the blood was supposed to be palm deep on the far side of the lane. I don't doubt it. Eighteen hundred men – there were women, too – were mowed down there in some twelve hours. There is more blood than you would think in eighteen hundred bodies.

In a bullfight when the beast or some unlucky horse bleeds copiously, 'wise monkeys' come along and scatter fresh sand. Yet on hot afternoons you smell blood. It is all very invigorating. It was a hot night. There was a smell. I can't describe it and won't describe it. The 'wise monkeys' will have a lot of work to do to make this ring presentable for a ceremonial slaughter bullfight. As for me, no more bullfights – ever.

Source: Acier, M. (ed.) (1937) *From Spanish Trenches*, New York, pp. 6–7.

(b)

Webb [Miller, foreign correspondent for United Press] I have been summoned to Salamanca in connection with a paragraph appearing in a letter signed by Andrew Rothstein published in the Manchester Guardian of January the nineteenth quoting me as describing an eyewitness account of mass killings in Badajoz. The letter states that the article was published by the Paris edition of the New York Herald August sixteen and the message datelined Badajoz was dated August fifteen under my signature. Captain Bolin representing the nationalist military press authorities demands that you inform the Manchester Guardian that I never wrote such article also that I have never been in Badajoz if this is true. If you recall I pointed out to you months ago that there were a number of mysterious messages appearing under my name which I never wrote and datelined places that I have never been to. I give you my word of honour that I know nothing about this Badajoz message which obviously is one of them.

Reynolds Packard

Source: McNeill-Moss, Major G. (1936) *The Epic of the Alcazar: A History of the Siege of the Toledo*, London p. 310.

Reports filed by official representatives of foreign governments were somewhat more reliable, in part because they were based on a variety of secondary and primary sources and in part because they were meant to provide intelligence rather than to make political converts out of their prospective readers. Though these accounts reflect the ideological partisanship and personal prejudices – particularly as they related to the so-called 'national characteristics' of the Spaniards – of the observers, they had the advantage of offering an informed look at events that had not been filtered through the prism of indigenous political and emotional concerns (Document 3.25).

Document 3.25 Observing the Repression in 'White and 'Red' Spain

When I first went to Valencia there were still 'private' police and 'private' prisons (our Spanish butler spent a fortnight in one of the latter) and rare was the night that passed without shots. Sometimes the remains of the previous night's 'bumping-off' party would still be lying in the dust by the river during one's morning stroll. In the middle of the night there would occasionally be, as the result of a wrong number, a mysterious telephone call: 'Open the doors'! and in one's mind's eye would appear the not unfamiliar spectacle of five or six men slinking along the darkened streets to some unhappy doorway. During the late spring and early summer the position is improved as the Government – formed of men of very Left-Wing liberal tendencies, but neither assassins nor extremists – fought the Anarchists and shot them down in hundreds, chiefly in Barcelona. Recently, Valencia's deteriorating fortunes and the increasing miseries of the population have led to a revival of repression and a renewal of the offensive against the so-called 'Fifth Column' of supposed Nationalist sympathisers in Government territory, and the ever-present abuse of the anonymous denunciation has again come into its own.

3. After my transfer to Hendaye in June, my first short trips into Nationalist territory revealed, superficially, a very different state of affairs. Here was plenty of food and here were many comforts: public services functioning normally, no shortage of petrol, smartly-uniformed and well-gowned society sipping its

cocktails in cafés and being waited upon by obsequious waiters; bull-fights, the Guardia Civil, daily (and, judging from the onlookers' faces, boring) religious processions and, in short, virtually all the concomitants of Spanish life, plus the presence of Italian and German officers and soldiery. But it did not take me many visits, nor the perusal of many reports, nor many conversations with foreigners who were out of Spain for a week or so of respite, to find that there was another side to the picture – the spy, the *agent provocateur*, the secret police, the denunciation as a suspected 'Red' (and how easy it is to qualify as the latter!), the crowded prisons, the court-martial, the firing-party. Politically, just as the Valencia authorities have ceaselessly to struggle against the Anarchists, so does Franco have to combat the 'Falange Española,' the Spanish Fascist organisation whose membership corresponds in type and class to that of the Federación Anarquista on the other side. These men, the 'moppers up' of captured town, so far tolerate Franco as a general, but declare he is not their ideal as head of the State. There has already been street brawling with the Falange in Salamanca and elsewhere. If Franco wins he will have to shoot hundreds of them, just as Valencia have already liquidated large numbers of Anarchists.

4. Except for more outward order, more colour and more ease (for some) in Nationalist Spain, there is little basic difference in the atmosphere there and in Government territory. There is the same repression, the same terror, the same (if slightly more legal) executions. But, if such a thing be possible, there is less tolerance than on the Valencia side, and what is even more disagreeable, a great absorption of Italian Fascist ideas and methods. Thus, none will interfere with you in Valencia if you do not salute with clenched fist when the band plays the 'Internationale,' but Heaven help you if you fail, foreigner or no, to give the Fascist salute when the Colours come by in Franco Spain.

Source: Thompson, G.H., 'Memorandum Respecting Spain', *British Documents on Foreign Affairs*, Series F, Europe, vol. 27, Document 108, pp. 155–6.

Impact of violence and terror

While it was true that, at the very beginning of the conflict, executions were often treated as a public spectacles that were regarded by some as diversions or perverse forms of entertainment, the continued use or threat of violence gave way to more somber responses by civilians as they became increasingly inured to death and repression. On a cultural level, these twin forces had the effect of desensitizing and demoralizing the citizenry. Perhaps even more insidiously, the readiness of politicians and military authorities to use force against non-combatants whenever it was expedient to do so helped to give violence the status of normality. Over time the brutal policies associated with terror and repression fatally undermined the idea of tolerance on both sides. Among other things this facilitated the development of more autocratic forms of political rule over the civilian population. This would have far-reaching consequences for the conduct of both regimes, but particularly for the Nationalists, who, more so than the Republicans during the war, sought both to regularize and legitimate this form of social control by establishing a one-party state.

The mosaic of politics: Conflict and consensus in the Republican and Nationalist zones   **4**

The outbreak of civil war in July 1936 did more than just divide the country into two mutually opposing camps: it dramatically and permanently reshaped the whole of Spain's political landscape. On the Republican side, the rebellion produced a crisis of authority that led directly to the near-collapse of national and local government institutions. Above all, these events produced a significant realignment of political power on the left. The first and most significant casualties of this crisis were the middle-class Republican factions. The inability of either Martínez Barrio or José Giral to form a viable administration in the immediate aftermath of the uprising demonstrated beyond a doubt that the liberal politicians of the prewar Republic were in no position to play a leadership role. The fracturing of the Republic's political framework instead produced a new constellation of forces. One source of power radiated from the far-left organizations which had responded to the breakdown of traditional authority by launching a sweeping revolutionary movement. As we have seen, their control over a variety of economic and social institutions as well as over their own militias enabled them to rise to a commanding position in the Republican camp. The separatist Republican parties in Catalonia and portions of the Basque country also sought to fill the vacuum created by the dissolution of central government institutions by pressing hard to achieve their longstanding claims for greater regional autonomy. At least for a brief period, the creation of semi-autonomous regional governments within the boundaries of the wartime Republic represented yet another hub of power in the anti-Nationalist zone. The moderate socialists of the PSOE and Communists of the PCE constituted a third Republican force that vied for power during the war. Though they were divided over a number of fundamental ideological issues, these two factions were united over their opposition to the revolution as well as to the decentralizing efforts of the regionalists. Both groups also shared a common belief that the war against the Nationalists would not be won unless political and military unity prevailed on the Republican side. From 1937 on, an alliance between these two groups became the core of the 'Popular Front' coalition that ruled the Republic until the end of the war.

Like the Republican organizations, the Nationalist factions were linked not so much by a common ideology as by their shared fear and loathing of a common enemy. Yet, in contrast to the other side, the absence of formal government rule did not give rise to a corresponding devolution of power. In this chapter we shall see that this was partly because, from the outset, the military assumed a dominant role in Nationalist affairs and partly because the various factions on the right were more willing than their left-wing counterparts to defer to a unified and hierarchical chain of command.

The mosaic of Republican Spain: Madrid, Catalonia, Basque country

Shortly after the military rising divided Spain into two opposing camps, it became apparent that the pro-Republican zone was itself split into various geo-political blocs. In the beginning, Madrid became the focal point of the Republicans' struggle to keep the Nationalists from achieving an early victory. By early November the threat to Madrid was so great that the Republican government decided to transfer its headquarters to Valencia. After its hasty departure, the city was left in the hands of a military-dominated body, the Junta de Defensa de Madrid. To the astonishment of General Mola, who bragged that he would be taking tea in the Puerta del Sol before the end of the month, and Franco's troops, the people of Madrid did not capitulate. Bolstered by the recent arrival of the soon-to-be-famous International Brigades as well as fresh shipments of Soviet aeroplanes and war supplies, the *madrileños* and assortment of Republican militias threw their energies into erecting barricades, digging trenches, and defending the perimeters of the city (Document 4.1). The famous communist orator Dolores Ibárruri roused the people of Madrid into action by uttering memorable slogans like 'They Shall Not Pass! / ¡No pasarán!' and 'Madrid will be the tomb of fascism! / ¡Madrid será la tumba del fascismo!' (Document 4.2). The fierce fighting that took place in University City, Casa de Campo and other outlying districts drove home to the Nationalists how determined the Republicans were to stop their advance into the capital. Even the Nationalists' incessant shelling and bombing of the city itself failed to break the spirit of resistance. From then until the last month of the conflict Madrid was placed under a siege, and, as a result, ceased to be the centrepoint of the Civil War.

Document 4.1 Defending the Capital

Our party leaders met to discuss the grave matter of the defence of Madrid. Come what might, at any cost, Madrid must be defended. Madrid was not to fall into the hands of the insurgents. It was clear to all of us that the key to victory for the Republic was in the defence of Madrid. And we put all our efforts in explaining this to the people and the government.

The people understood and supported our efforts. In the face of the delays and vacillations of those who believed it was impossible to defend an open city like Madrid, we called on the people to build barricades. Setting the example, we were the first to wield the picks and shovels and surround Madrid with a belt of barricades. Every day thousands of men and women, young and old, even children, joined us in digging trenches and antitank ditches, building a defensive belt around our beloved Madrid.

Source: Ibárruri, D. (1966) *They Shall Not Pass: The Autobiography of La Pasionaria*, New York, pp. 245–6.

Document 4.2 Mobilizing the Masses

I turned on the radio for the Government news reports. And then I first heard the voice of Dolores Ibarruri, 'La Pasionaria.' This woman of the people, this living symbol of Spanish courage, spoke to the people of Spain at the grave moment when Madrid faced the enemy at its very gates.

'*They shall not pass! No pasarán!*' Her beautiful voice, vibrant, strong, filled the room. We straightened up. After the long day of panic and fear, after the weeks of tense waiting which had weighed on even the children, this stirring voice called us all back to our faith in Spain, to our faith in ourselves.

'*The fascists will not pass! They will not pass because we are not alone!*'

The strong voice, powerful and sure, went on, growing more vibrant, more electric. '*The lives and future of our children are at stake! This is not the time for hesitation; this is not the time for timidity. We women must demand that our men be courageous. We must inspire them with the thought that a man must know how to die worthily. Preferimos ser viudas de héroes antes que esposas de cobardes!*'

'We prefer to be the widows of heroes rather than wives of cowards!'

Source: De la Mora, C. (1939) *In Place of Splendor: The Autobiography of a Spanish Woman*, New York, pp. 272–3.

In Catalonia, the industrial base for the Republican war effort, the political and economic situation was markedly different. Both the military rebellion and popular revolution had an enormous impact on local politics in Catalonia. Perhaps the most striking consequence of these events was the empowerment of revolutionary groups such as the CNT-FAI and POUM which claimed to represent the vast majority of the working population but which nevertheless had been consigned by the ruling parties during the prewar Republican period to the fringes of the 'official' political and economic system.[1] On the economic front, the libertarians spearheaded a collectivization movement that embraced both land and industry. For their part, the much smaller POUM called for the immediate re-ordering of the region's social and political life along Marxist-Leninist revolutionary lines. Yet, from the beginning, the revolutionaries' attempts to establish their hegemony were challenged by a coalition of disparate parties. Foremost among them was the Esquerra (ERC), the left-liberal Catalan party which had formerly served as the ruling party in Catalonia, now forced to share political power with groups as diverse as the CNT-FAI, the communist-dominated PSUC, and an assortment of liberal and conservative Catalan parties. In political terms this meant that the separatist Nationalist forces – the Estat Català, for example – which had previously sought to establish an independent Catalan state either disappeared or were pushed into the background. This did not mean that the Generalitat would cease to define itself as an autonomous region. In fact, the period from October 1936 until October 1937 saw the ascendancy of the 'Nationalist' but non-separatist ERC. Under the leadership of two of the party's most able politicians, Lluis Companys and Josep Taradellas, the Catalan parliament achieved a high degree of autonomy, issuing its own currency, maintaining its own army, and conducting diplomatic relations with foreign countries (Document 4.3).

Document 4.3 Defining Catalan Independence

(a)

Since July 19th, Catalonia has been compelled to organize the struggle against Fascism as well as its own internal life with absolutely nothing but its own resources. The very fact that Catalonia has been able to pull through such a profound crisis without any outside help, shows clearly that such assistance is not indispensable. On the other hand the armed forces of the Catalan Generalitat are today fighting outside the limits of Catalan territory and are collaborating efficiently in the defence of the loyal regions. This war will bring about an increase of Catalan influence in the life of the peninsula; the characteristics and personality of Catalonia will emerge from the struggle greatly fortified.

Such a 'de facto' state of complete independence as that now existing, allows the Catalans to fully comprehend their own real desires to collaborate freely in an Iberian Commonwealth of nations, without the old centralist or state coercions, and in the spirit of the League of Nations Covenant. The most representative men of Catalonia have repeatedly presented this as the political ideal of the Catalan people.

Source: Martin, J. G. (1936) *Political and Social Changes in Catalonia during the Revolution (July 19th – December 31st 1936)*, edited by the Generalitat de Catalunya, Barcelona, p. 6.

(b)

John Langdon-Davies interviews Lluis Companys, President of the Generalitat

Is Catalunya now in fact and in law independent of Madrid?

No. The common front of anti-fascism has drawn us closer to the rest of Spain than ever before. In face of the common danger of Fascism the Madrid Government has given us independence of action, but we are making no attempt to make capital out of it. When it is all over we shall, however, expect to retain the greater freedom that the moment has put in our hand.

Source: Langdon-Davies, J. (1936) *Behind the Spanish Barricades*, New York, p. 152.

The regionalism expressed in Catalonia was equally pronounced in the Basque country (Document 4.4). Unfortunately for the Basque nationalists their hopes for establishing an autonomous (or separate) regional government hinged on the survival of Vizcaya and Guipúzcoa, the only Basque provinces that did not fall to the Nationalists in the early weeks of the war. Physically separated from the rest of Republican Spain, the Basques nevertheless seized the opportunity to press for their much-desired self-government. The first step in this direction came about when the conservative and solidly middle-class Basque National Party (PNV) emerged as the most powerful political force in the region. Working through the provisional juntas that had been established in the wake of the military rebellion, the PNV quickly outflanked the much smaller pro-revolutionary forces pressing for radical changes by expanding local government control over the economy and social relations. As a result, the Basque region escaped the socio-economic convulsions that shook regions under left-wing control. At the same time, the PNV worked in tandem with other nationalists who were eager to begin laying the groundwork for an independent Basque state. By the end of the summer, the anti-revolutionary forces had matters well in hand and the political climate of the Basque region was one of calm and order (Document 4.5).

Document 4.4 Regionalist Sentiments in the Basque Country

(a)

Basque Nationalists aim at having the Basque people recognised as a minority of the League of Nations, and they wish to enlist the aid of His Majesty's Government for this purpose.

All the Basques are not Basque Nationalists, *i.e.*, Separatists. An important section of them, the Navarrese, refuse to admit their Basque blood as a political fact and are Traditionalists almost to a man. Of the other three Basque provinces, Guipozcoa and Alava, now in General Franco's hands, are mainly rural in character, and their normal population has a large Basque Nationalist majority. The Province of Vizcaya, however (which is all that President Aguirre now rules), is mixed in character. Of its normal population of half a million, three-fifths live in agricultural areas, and of these between 80 per cent and 90 per cent are Basque Nationalists. Bilbao and its industrial suburbs, on the other hand, have a normal population which is by no means all Basque by blood nor Basque Nationalist in politics. According to a fair estimate, 40 per cent of these 200,000 people are supporters of the 'Frente Popular.' 30 per cent of them are supporters of General Franco, and the remaining 30 per cent are Basque Nationalists.

Source: British Documents on Foreign Affairs, Series F, Europe, vol. 27, Document no. 88, p. 116.

(b)

Consul Stevenson to Sir H. Chilton

Bilbao, October 21, 1936

The relationship of the Basque State to the Government of the republic is that of ward to tutor. The latter through the instrument of the statute, has reserved to itself the right of control, in manifold ways, of the Judicature, the Legislature, and the Administration, and there is a clear warning as to the observance of the treaty obligations. It will require considerable ingenuity and skill of argument to circumvent or pass through the hedge of articles of the Constitution of the republic in order to exercise that form of self-government to which these people aspire. The highest Basque court of law is only the 'Tribunal Superior,' and there is appeal from it to the Supreme Court of the Spanish Republic, and, in certain cases, to the Tribunal of Constitutional Guarantees at Madrid. It would not be an exaggeration to say that the majority of Basques, who have troubled to study their new Constitution, are under no delusion as to the difference between a Constitution granted by the grace of Madrid and one born in their own travail.

Source: British Documents on Foreign Affairs, Series F, Europe, vol. 27, Document no. 40, p. 43.

Document 4.5 Basques Establish a Non-Revolutionary Government

(a)

The Government has given its approval to projects which permit the just and orderly intervention of labour in the administration and management of business enterprises, trusting that within a short time this will bring a greater harmony among all the elements which create the country's wealth; all of which must be fulfilled observing the strictest order and legality, inexorably exacted and imposed by the Government, which has more than the necessary means to carry out its purpose, and above all it has the approval of the people, who will help, ever increasingly, to establish in our Country the social reforms – which have elsewhere been preceded by disturbances – amidst the general understanding of a people which has known how to harmonize the collectivity's paramount interest with the smallest possible harm to private interests, especially when these interests have been, as is often the case in our country, the result of long years of personal labour.

Source: Aguirre, J. de, An Address by His Excellency the President of the Government of Euzkadi, H.E.A. José de Aguirre. Broadcast from Radio Euzkadi, 22 December 1936.

(b)

A Council of Commissars was constituted, with the department of War, Public Order, Commerce and Provisions, Transport, Industry and Exchequer. The Civil Governor (top representative of the Madrid Government) was absent from this newly-created power structure. It was done against his advice and against the advice of many leaders of the working class parties. The workers proceeded without hesitation to confiscate all means of transport, all arms, the food necessary for the column marching to Vitoria and for the volunteers who stayed behind.

Even while things were running under the new order, its destruction was being planned behind the scene: The Civil Governor, who was also Governor of the provinces of Asturias, Guipuzcoa and Santander, had watched passively the decisions taken by the representatives of the working class parties. He was, however, pushed into action by the party of 'order' the Basque Nationalist Party. The Nationalists, who had not participated in the fighting during the first few days, now intervened by putting pressure on the authorities, (as they did in October 1934). They contributed nothing to the fight; they simply sat behind the Civil Governor wielding their influence. They did not proclaim open support for the movement, but they did proclaim their condemnation of working class violence. The Nationalist influence soon produced results . . .

In a short time, the political climate of the Basque country changed radically. The Nationalists participated in the Junta de Defensa with some reserve, but in the villages the delegates of the Junta took all power from the committees. The Nationalists could now legally monopolise the commanding posts. Meanwhile the young were being prepared for active participation in the war. In Madrid governments changed constantly. Aguirre, who is now president of the Basque Council, was proposed by Prieto for a ministerial job, but the nationalist party decided not to accept this offer. One of the ministries remained vacant while negotiations were going on between the nationalists and the Government on future policy for the Basque Country, which led to the granting of the Estatuto (autonomous status). In order to win nationalist support, which meant the support of financial capital, the Government granted autonomy to the Basque country, and the nationalist party, represented by Irujo, then joined the Government.

Source: Arenillas, J. M. (1974) *The Basque Country, Euzkadi*: The Nationalist Question and the Socialist Revolution, Leeds, pp. 12–16.

Document 4.6 Celebrating Basque Autonomy

An address by His Excellency the President of the Government of Euzkadi, H.E. José de Aguirre broadcast from 'Radio Euzkadi', 22 December 1936.

To all of you listening in, here in Euzkadi, the rest of the Republic and abroad, the greetings full of hope for the future, from the President of a young Government representing the ancient Basque People. Two and a half months ago, the autonomy of Euzkadi was proclaimed, after having been solemnly voted by the Cortes of the Republic in their meeting of October the first. A persistent and tenacious campaign of the Basque people to regain their liberty destroyed by the Spanish monarchy a hundred years ago, had as a result, amid tragic days, the recognition of the Basque personality by the establishment of an Autonomous State, and by virtue of the law recognizing this Autonomous State, the first autonomous Government of Euzkadi was issued.

Under the guidance of the PNV, a Basque statute recognizing autonomy was approved by the Valencian-based Republican government in early October 1936 (Document 4.6). The Basque nationalists – or at least those living in Vizcaya, the only surviving pro-Republican province at this time – had finally attained their goal. The existence of the tiny Euzkadi presented an interesting paradox of the Civil War: It was a pro-Catholic and non-revolutionary state that was allied to the left-wing forces which dominated the rest of Republican Spain. Euzkadi was therefore destined to play an independent role during the war. Basque forces fought bravely to defend their homeland against the Nationalists but their militias contributed little to the Republican war effort elsewhere.[2] Equally telling of the fact that the Basque government was at first intent on pursuing its own agenda were the strained relations it maintained with the Republic.

By the spring of 1937, however, the Basque struggle for survival transcended its regional boundaries when the advancing Nationalist forces, supported by both Italian artillery units and the German Condor Legion, shocked the world with their 'total war' tactics. The bombing and consequent near-destruction of the historic Basque town Guernica (Gernika), on 26 April 1937 produced a scandal of immense proportions (see below, Chapter 8). When news of the incident hit the headlines of major newspapers around the globe, the fate of the Republic (and not just Euzkadi) became the focus of international attention. Pablo Picasso, the renowned Spanish painter who was living in Paris at the time, was inspired to paint his most famous masterpiece, *Guernica*, which immortalized the agony of all Spaniards who were being consumed by the fires of civil war.

Following this highly publicized episode, the fighting in the Basque country became increasingly identified with the greater Republican war cause. When the regional capital of Bilbao fell to the Nationalists in June, Basque resistance to the Nationalists ended. The official government, headed by the thirty-three-year-old José Antonio de Aguirre, transferred its seat first to France and finally to the Republican capital in Barcelona, where it threw its support behind Republican efforts to defeat Franco's troops.

The Nationalists

Though not everyone on the Nationalist side shared the same vision of Spain's future – the authoritarian Alfonsine monarchists and reactionary Carlists wanted the immediate restoration of the monarchy, while the Falangists advocated the formation of a corporatist-fascist state – they all accepted the military's leadership role throughout the civil war. During the early months of the conflict, this allowed the leaders of the rebellion to give priority to winning a war that they thought would be over before long.

A junta set up shortly after the uprising, the National Defence Committee (Junta de Defensa Nacional), served as a co-ordinating body for military operations throughout the rebel zone. But, by the end of summer, visions of a quick victory were beginning to fade and it was becoming apparent that a greater political-military structure was needed to run the increasingly complex affairs of the Nationalist movement. A meeting of the Defence Committee in late September sought to overcome this problem by appointing a supreme commander of the army. From a pool of candidates that included Generals Mola and Quiepo de Llano, General Franciso Franco was chosen as the new Commander-in-Chief or Generalissimo of the Nationalists (Document 4.7).

Document 4.7 The Generalissimo of Nationalist Spain

'Every reason,' read the decree of the National Defence Council of September 29, 1936, 'points to the convenience of concentrating in one person all those powers which will lead to a final victory, and to the establishment, consolidation, and development of the new State, with the loyal assistance of the Nation. An organic and efficient regime has been established, in effect, which may answer adequately to the realities of present-day Spain, and may plan its future with absolute authority.'

And so His Excellency, Divisional General Francisco Franco Baamonde was named as the head of the Nationalist government, 'who shall assume all of the powers of the new State.' Article II of this decree also named him 'Generalissimo of the national forces of land, sea, and air.'

The Generalissimo and head of the government of Nationalist Spain was now installed in the Episcopal Palace at Salamanca. From that vantage point he could envisage with clear detail the whole national scene, and there he felt the full weight of growing responsibilities.

By the decree of September 29, 1936, General Franco was vested with absolute civil and military authority. However, the basic structure of the government remained unchanged. It was a war measure. To quote Franco: 'The implanting of the most severe principles of authority, which this movement implies, is not exclusively military in character, rather it is the establishment of a hierarchical regime, through the harmonious functioning of which all the powers and energies of the Nation will develop . . . When the new Spanish

State becomes stronger and its development becomes more normal, it will advance farther towards the decentralization of those functions which are not essential, and every region, municipality, association, and individual will enjoy more ample liberties, within the supreme interest of the State.'

Source: Arrarás, J. (1938) *Francisco Franco*, London, pp. 214–15.

There are several reasons why Franco had been selected. First and foremost was the fact that he had from the outset played a critical role in the uprising. When it became apparent towards the end of July that his troops could not be transported across the Straits of Gibraltar to the mainland, he appealed to both Italy and Germany for assistance. In so doing, he not only placed himself at the forefront of the rebellion but he also irrevocably widened the dimensions of Spain's domestic conflict. Fate also intervened on Franco's behalf. General Sanjurjo, whom the chief conspirators had designated as the primary leader of the revolt, was killed in an aeroplane crash on 20 July. His death, along with the early demise or disappearance of other Nationalist leaders – the charismatic leader of the Falangist movement, José Antonio Primo de Rivera, for example – paved the way for Franco's rise to the top of the rebel movement. What secured his position were the early military successes for which he was credited. A string of swift and resounding triumphs, that culminated with Franco's widely publicized liberation of the Alcázar (Toledo) fortress in late September, catapulted him beyond the reach of his nearest contenders for the coveted post of Generalissimo.

In what would turn out to be an even more fateful development, Franco was also invested with complete political authority over the Nationalist government. Significantly, this title, as well as his designation as the Commander-in-Chief of the military, was officially conferred on him only for the duration of the war. Yet when his appointment was announced in the Official Bulletin of the National Defence Committee on 30 September, this qualifying phrase had been expunged.[3] Because this bold behind-the-scenes move to crown Franco as the permanent ruler of Nationalist Spain went unchallenged, he became more than just the person in charge of all military operations during the civil war: he was from now on to serve as the political head of the 'Spanish state' (*el Caudillo*).

The challenge Franco now faced was how to achieve his twin goals of winning the war and laying the foundations for a new government. Given the dominant position that his armies continued to hold on all military fronts, Franco was especially preoccupied with the problem of establishing control over the disparate and sometimes conflicting right-wing forces on which he relied (Document 4.8). To this end, Franco and his advisers began devising in the late autumn of 1936 a political blueprint that called for the forging of a single party out of the existing factions. Such an 'organic' unity was not easily realized, not least because of the profound differences between the two largest and most important Nationalist parties, the fascist Falange and the monarchist Traditionalist Party (Comunión Tradicionalista, CT) (Document 4.9). From an ideological perspective the two groups were poles apart. Whereas the Falange tended to be forward-looking and revolutionary, the CT was a reactionary monarchist party. On the other hand, Franco and his closest political advisers recognized that, as different as they were from one another, the two parties had much in common. Both were rabidly anti-liberal and anti-Marxist, and both were totally opposed to the separatism and factionalism that had characterized the political life of the Second Republic. Franco therefore concluded that it was possible to create a single party that took into account these commonalities.[4]

Document 4.8 Keeping a Tight Rein on Nationalist Supporters

The Carlists are now the blue-eyed boys and the 'Falangists' are out of favour, apparently for good. Mutual attacks in the two parties' press are frequent. The Carlists pride themselves on their catholicism and imply that the Fascists are a godless riff-raff. The Fascists protest that they, too, are good Catholics and believe that although Largo Caballero's son was held hostage expressly as a guarantee against the execution of José Antonio Primo de Rivera, General Franco deliberately made no move towards an exchange, preferring to let the Fascist idol perish. The inference is that Franco does not intend to let the Fascists make the running in 'his' new Spain as at one time seemed likely. He deals severely with Fascists who 'go too far' in captured towns and villages, and a number have been shot. Gil Robles is 'nowhere.'

Source: British Documents on Foreign Affairs, Series F, Europe, vol. 27, Document no. 54, p. 64.

Document 4.9 Conflicting Goals of Carlists and Falangists

The 'Roquetes,' as the Carlist Volunteers are called, are the flower of the youth of Spain. They are far superior, physically and mentally, to the Fascists, who for the most part come from a distinctly lower social level. The Carlists cut a dashing figure in their khaki uniforms and brilliant red berets, and are easily the favorites of the señoritas who promenade the *ramblas* of the Spanish towns in the early evening hours. The Carlists are convinced Royalists who want to see the old regime restored.

It is quite different with the Spanish Fascists, who call themselves the 'Falanges Españols.' These youths in their dark blue shirts and blue forage caps adorned with red stripes, who are obviously modelled on their Italian namesakes and Hitler's Nazis, are merely rebels by propaganda. One feels that under different circumstances they might easily be ardent Communists. While the war cry of the Roquetes is '*Viva España!*' the Fascists shout '*Arriba España!*' – '*Up Spain!*' They have a rollicking song with that name, just as the Nazis have their 'Horst Wessel Lied' and the Italian Fascists their 'Giovinezza.' The Spanish Fascists are not at all anxious to have the monarchy back. Their leader is the eldest son of the late Primo de Rivera, the Spanish dictator, who certainly gave Spain the most efficient government she has had in recent years, only to be left in the lurch by the King when he became unpopular.

While the Fascists are willing to accept a republic, like the Nazis prior to 1933, they do not want the existing republic. They desire a republican regime free from Marxist influences and based on an authoritarian order. The Fascists were regarded by the Spanish Republicans as their most deadly enemies. This feeling of animosity was partly due to the fact that the Blue Shirts were competitors for the favor of the masses. Their members mostly belong to the lower middle classes, but many come from the proletarian quarters of the big cities. While in the mountainous districts of the Pyrenees the red-capped Carlists furnish the nucleus of the village guards, the Fascist youth are more numerous in the sun-baked plains of Spain's central plateau.

Source: Elliott, J. (November 1936) 'With the Rebels', *The Atlantic Monthly*, vol. 158, issue 5, 538 and 539.

(b)

Now that the war has reached an advanced stage and the hour of victory nears, it is urgent to undertake the great task of peace and to crystallize in the New State the thought and style of our National Revolution . . .

The unification which I am demanding in the name of Spain and in the sacred name of those who have sacrificed their lives for it – both heroes and martyrs – and to whom we shall always look with fidelity, does not mean a conglomeration of forces or a mere governmental concentration, or a temporary union . . . We must avoid the creation of an artificial party, but rather bring together all our recruits in such a way as to integrate and synthesize them into a single national political entity that will link State and Society and guarantee the political continuity and loyalty of the people to the State . . .

In Spain, as in other countries where there are totalitarian regimes, traditional forces are now beginning to integrate themselves with new forces. The Falange Española has attracted masses of young people by its program, its new-style propaganda, and has provided a new political and heroic framework for the present and a promise of Spanish fulfilment in the future. The Requetés, in addition to possessing martial qualities, have served through the centuries as the sacred repository of the Spanish tradition and of Catholic spirituality, which have been the principal formative elements in our nationality – and whose eternal principles of morality and justice shall continue to inspire us . . .

Source: Delzell, C. F. (ed.) (1970) *Mediterranean Fascism, 1919–1945*, London, p. 294.

In order to prepare the ground for such a fusion, Franco still needed the co-operation of the two movements. Of the two the Traditionalists were the most difficult to win over, above all because they were single mindedly determined to use the Civil War to enthrone the Carlist pretender, Don Francisco Javier de Borbón. In addition, Carlist leaders such as Manuel Fal Conde displayed a degree of independence that challenged Franco's newly asserted authority. When, in December 1936, he attempted to set up a parallel military structure in the Nationalist camp under Carlist control, Franco forced him into exile. By removing Fal Conde Franco effectively eliminated the Carlist threat to his own political agenda.

Domesticating the Falange was less problematic, thanks primarily to the badly fractured leadership of the movement. Following the death of its national chief, José Antonio, in November 1936, an intense rivalry developed among provincial party chieftains, including the veterans (*Camisas Viejas*) Agustín Aznar, Sancho Dávila and the acting head of the Falange, Manuel Hedilla. Taking full advantage of this power struggle, Franco moved forward with his thinly veiled plans to create a single Nationalist party.

Just as the Falangist search for a party leader was reaching a climax in the spring of 1937, Franco made a daring pre-emptive move. On 19 April he issued the 'Decree of Unification', which not only merged the Falange and Traditionalist parties but also abolished all other rightist factions. Henceforth Nationalists of all stripes would be represented by only one party under Franco's control, the Falange Española Tradicionalista de las Jons (FET) (Document 4.10). Significantly, the new party represented a careful blending of the principal ideas and beliefs of the right-wing parties that complemented one another (Document 4.11). The fascist economic principles of the new party appealed to the Falangists, whereas the political structure they implied resonated with both the Traditionalists, who favoured an authoritarian government that promised national unity, and the Alfonsine monarchists, who believed that the new regime intimated in the decree was not irreconcilable with the idea of a monarchist restoration. In this way, Franco's move to consolidate his power did not appear as a direct threat to any one group on the Nationalist side.

Document 4.10 Franco Decrees a One-party State

(a)

Franco's Call for Unification of the Fighting Forces (18 April 1937)

We are confronted by a war that every day is taking on more of the character of a crusade, of a transcendental struggle of historic grandeur on the part of whole peoples and civilizations – a war in which Spain once again has been selected by history to serve as the field of tragedy and honor in order to bring peace to today's enraged world.

What started out on July 17 [1936] as our own civil war has today turned into a conflagration that is going to illuminate the future for centuries.

At this time, with a clear conscience and a firm sense of my mission in behalf of Spain and in accordance with the will of the Spanish fighters, I demand of everyone but one thing: Unity.

Unity, in order to bring the war speedily to an end; unity, in order to undertake the great new task of peace, crystallizing in the New Spain the thought and style of our National Revolution.

This unity which I call for in the name of Spain and in the sacred name of those who have given their lives for her does not mean a mere *conglomeration* of forces, or a governmental *concentration* of political factions, or a *sacred union* of more or less patriotic type. There is nothing inorganic, fleeting, or temporary in what I am calling for.

I demand unity in our march toward a common goal – unity both internally and externally, both in faith and in doctrine, both as regards the forms to be manifested to the outside world and in those to be manifested to ourselves.

. . . The Movement that we are leading today is precisely that – a movement, not a program. And as such, it is in process of elaboration and subject to constant revision and improvement to the extent that is realistically possible.

Source: Delzell, C. F. (ed.) (1970) *Mediterranean Fascism 1919–1945*, London, pp. 289 and 290

(b)

Franco's call for the Unification of the Militias (19 April 1937)

Now that the war has reached an advanced stage and the hour of victory nears, it is urgent to undertake the great task of peace and to crystallize in the New State the thought and style of our National Revolution . . .

In Spain, as in other countries where there are totalitarian regimes, traditional forces are now beginning to integrate themselves with new forces. The Falange Española has attracted masses of young people by its program, its new-style propaganda, and has provided a new political and heroic framework for the present and a promise of Spanish fulfilment in the future. The Requetés, in addition to possessing martial qualities, have served through the centuries as the sacred repository of the Spanish tradition and of Catholic spirituality, which have been the principal formative elements in our nationality – and whose eternal principles of morality and justice shall continue to inspire us . . .

Source: Delzell, Charles F. (ed.) (1970) *Mediterranean Fascism 1919–1945*, London, p. 294.

Document 4.11 Political Factions under One Banner

Within the 'Party of Unity' built by Franco, the 'Falange Tradicionalista y de las JONS,' there are several sharply defined tendencies:

1. The old fighters and adherents of the original Falange (*Camisas viejas*), founded by José Antonio Primo de Rivera, who are urging thorough social reforms;

2. The very pro-Vatican and reactionary Requetés, which developed out of former Carlist units;

3. The adherents of the Acción Española, a small party consisting of highly placed intellectuals of a conservative and monarchistic trend;

4. The Acción Popular, representatives of political Catholicism (Center!);

5. The 'Tradicionalistas,' a small group of pure monarchists.

The 'Party of Unity' exists therefore only on paper. After the victory these divergences may, under certain circumstances, be intensified.

Franco cleverly keeps himself above these parties. Around him there are at present strong forces at work to give Catholicism its dominant position in Spain again. The Vatican has lately put itself entirely on the Nationalist side. The prospects for the establishment of a Spanish National Church independent of Rome are not very great. There are, moreover, increased efforts, supported by Italy (and England), to re-establish the monarchy. The Spanish people are sharply divided on this latter point. Restoration must nevertheless be reckoned with.

On the other hand, there is a prospect that certain social reforms will be carried out to eliminate the previous domination of the nobility, capital, and landownership, and improve the situation of the working classes.

Source: Documents on German Foreign Policy, 1919–1939, Series D, vol. 3, Washington, DC, pp. 481–2.

On the other hand, tensions on the right did not disappear overnight, and some persisted throughout the Civil War. In the wake of Franco's *fait accompli* this was underscored by the fact that Manuel Hedilla and other leaders of the Falange were not content with playing a subordinate role to the Generalissimo. Fearful that the fascist ideals to which they aspired would not be realized in a 'hybridized' regime, they resolved to conspire against it. Before an opposition movement even materialized, Hedilla and his fellow plotters were arrested and tried for treason. Hedilla himself was condemned to death, though, presumably in the interests of safeguarding Falangist support for the Nationalist cause, Franco spared his life by commuting his death sentence (Document 4.12).

Document 4.12 Spanish Fascists Challenge Franco's Authority

(a)

The Ambassador in Spain to the Foreign Ministry

The last few days have led to a temporary, severe tension in the internal situation.

Through the *Gobernadores Civiles* (corresponding to our Regierungs-spräsident or Oberregierungspräsident), thereby circumventing Hedilla, Franco had sent the *Jefes Provinciales* (corresponding to our Gauleiters) the command that in future they were to follow only orders given by him, Franco. In this manner Hedilla was eliminated from his own party. He answered this measure of Franco with a telegram to the Gauleiters to obey the instructions of the Chief of State only if they came through him, Hedilla. As Franco at the same time became convinced that Hedilla had told him untruths in various previous conversations, and since he received other news which made the situation more serious, the Chief of State had Hedilla and 20 other leading Falangists arrested. The decisive factor seems to have been as Franco told me, that a young Falangist from one of the provincial capitals reported to headquarters, naming witnesses, that the local Gauleiter had ordered his subordinate leaders immediately to initiate strong propaganda against Franco.

Franco told me a few days ago that he was determined, since he was fighting a war, to nip in the bud any action directed against him and his Government by shooting the guilty parties.

Both sides are to blame for this momentary deterioration in the situation. Franco overlooked the fact that one can, to be sure, make one brigade out of two regiments by an order, but that the merging and fusing of two parties takes some time even if, as in this case, their social programs are very similar. Franco therefore had to give Hedilla the time and the opportunity partly to integrate the numerically much weaker Requetés and partly, insofar as that was not possible, to eliminate them. On the other hand, Hedilla, under pressure from his subordinates, who accused him of treason toward the party, sent the above-mentioned telegram to the *Jefes Provinciales*, which meant open rebellion against Franco.

Source: Documents on German Foreign Policy, 1919–1939, Series D, vol. 3, Washington, DC, Document no. 248, p. 277.

(b)

Anatoly Krasikov interviews Dionisio Ridruejo.

The next year, 1937, I was appointed 'leader' of Valladolid province. I was very young, but I owed this rapid promotion to a speech made at a meeting in Segovia. It was an impromptu speech but it drew loud applause. I said that the hour had come for all of us to unite in order to cross out the past and start a new life. I believed in what I said and for that reason my speech sounded convincing. Franco liked it. Later it transpired that he had already decided to merge the Falange and other political organisations of the insurgents into a single party. I had no inkling of this at all, but I scored a direct hit. This gave a great boost to my career.

There were, however, incidents. Early in February 1937 we distributed the text of one of José Antonio's old speeches containing sharp criticism of those whom we called rightists and calling for a 'revolutionary dismantling of capitalism'. In the eyes of the military leaders of the insurgence this was impermissible 'leftist extremism'. Those guilty of such a serious 'political error' were arrested and tried. I voluntarily joined the defendants and stood trial together with them.

We were all acquitted, of course, and the whole thing was treated as a misunderstanding which was not to disrupt the unity of the 'national forces' at a critical moment of the fight against the 'reds'.

Source: Krasikov, A. (1984) *From Dictatorship to Democracy: Spanish Reportage*, New York, p. 52.

Opposition to the new regime was not always directed at Franco himself. Occasionally clashes between Falangists and members of the clergy and monarchist forces would break out behind the lines. It was not until Franco's first government was formed in early 1938 that these and similar signs of opposition were finally brought under control.

Though it was not formally defined as 'fascist' the main structures of this evolving system incorporated many fascist ideas and organizational principles. For example, the Trade Union Unity Act (TUUA) passed in 1938 was closely patterned after the Labour Charter earlier adopted in Mussolini's Italy (Document 4.13). As a result, all unions in the Nationalist camp were merged into a state-controlled vertical structure, the Spanish Syndical Organization (Organización Sindical Española, OSE).

Document 4.13 Labor Policy in the *Nuevo Estado*

Reviving the Catholic tradition of social justice and the lofty sense of humanity that inspired the laws of the Empire, the State – which is national by reason of being an instrument wholly at the service of the entire Nation and syndical in so far as it represents a reaction against nineteenth century capitalism and communistic materialism – embarks upon the task of carrying out, with a disciplined constructive and soberly religious demeanor, the revolution that Spain is achieving to ensure that Spaniards may once more possess, for good and all, their Country, Bread and Justice.

Basing itself on the postulate that Spain is one and indivisible as regards her destiny, it hereby declares its aim to make Spanish industry – in the fellowship of all its components – one and indivisible, so that it may minister to the needs of the country and uphold the instruments of its power.

1. Work is the participation of man in production through the voluntary exercise of his intellectual and manual faculties according to his personal vocation and with due regard to the decorum and breadth of his life and the better development of the national economy . . .

3. The right to work is the result of the duty imposed by God for the fulfilment of man's individual ends and the prosperity and greatness of the Fatherland . . .

4. The State values and exalts work, the fruitful expression of the creative spirit of man, and, in this sense, will protect it with the force of the law, will grant it the greatest consideration and make it compatible with the fulfilment of all other individual, family and social aims. . . .

6. Work constitutes one of the most noble attributes of hierarchy and honor and has sufficient title to demand the assistance and tutelage of the State.

XIII

The Syndicalist Organization of the State will be inspired by the principles of Unity, Totality and Hierarchy.

2. All the economic elements will be joined together in vertical syndicates formed according to branches of production or service. The liberal and technical professions will be organized along similar lines, as determined by law.

3. The vertical syndicate is a Corporation of public Right which is constituted by the integration, in a centralized organization, of all the elements which dedicate their activities to the fulfilment of the economic process within a determined branch or service of the production, which corporation is hieratically governed under the direction of the State.

Source: The Labor Charter for New Spain, 9 March 1938, Peninsular News Service Inc., New York.

But not all aspects of the Francoist state conformed to the fascist model. Both because it fostered social cohesion and supplied his rule with a moral basis of authority, the Catholic Church became a major pillar of Franco's regime both during and following the war. More than any other Spanish institution, the Catholic Church embodied the beliefs and values of the Nationalists, most of whom followed Bishop Plá y Deniel and other church officials in picturing the Civil War as a crusade against the godless enemies of the 'spiritual' Spain they were defending. Of particular importance in this connection was the 'Collective Letter of the Spanish Bishops' issued on 1 July 1937 (See below, Chapter 6). By arguing that the Civil War was both necessary and justified, the Bishops hoped to convince the outside world that the Church was compelled to take sides. On a practical level, the Bishops also knew that by endorsing the idea of a Nationalist crusade the Church stood to gain a great deal. Above all, it was assured of playing a major role in defining the social and intellectual life of the Francoist state. Under its influence, all vestiges of the liberal Republic were erased. In schools, religious instruction returned to the classrooms and in public places men, and especially women, were expected to observe a strict moral code of behaviour.

Franco's efforts to unify the Nationalist movement greatly benefited from the relative economic stability which his side enjoyed throughout the war. Though they could not rely on Spain's traditional financial institutions to fund their cause, the Nationalists managed to secure support through private funding and foreign loans.

Much of Franco's war was underwritten by economic arrangements with Italy, Germany and capitalist concerns. In the latter case, multinationalist firms such as Texas Oil and Firestone who were sympathetic to the Nationalists willingly provided supplies on credit. No less important was the economic assistance provided by the Axis powers. In exchange for generous mining concessions, Germany set up an export–import company (HISMA-ROWAK) which was used to supply the Nationalists with war materials. The Italians were even more generous with their aid. Mussolini extended credit to Franco so that he could pay for weapons, military equipment and supplies which Italy shipped to the Nationalists throughout the Civil War.

Territorial gains also strengthened the Nationalists' economy. Besides possessing the greater part of Spain's food-producing regions, they controlled much of the country's mineral resources. All of this had a stabilizing effect on Nationalist social and political affairs, allowing Franco to devote his full attention to the conduct of war on the battlefields (Document 4.14).

Document 4.14 Business as Usual in Nationalist Territory

(a)

The standard of living in Nationalist Spain

The continuity and the normalcy of economic existence is especially evident in the cost of living and the average wage. The riches of Nationalist Spain in foodstuffs and the lack of inflation, have made it possible to maintain or even to diminish the cost of living . . .

Life in Nationalist Spain is therefore absolutely normal. 'As normal,' wrote the London *Times* in its edition of April 1st, 'as life in England in 1915, or in any other country under such conditions. Business is organized, new industries spring up, the railroad service functions normally and on seas communications are on a regular basis.' This opinion is confirmed by numerous foreign enterprises set up in Spain, thus for instance, the French Societe des Mines of Pena Roya, in its report sent out in the course of the year 1936, states that in the territory belonging to General Franco's government the exploitation of the mines continues as heretofore, and that 'the coal mines and the foundries in territory occupied by the government troops (Reds) are practically at a standstill.'

Source: One Year of War, 1936–1937 (1937), New York, pp. 14 and 15.

(b)

June–July, 1937. F.G. Coultas

In spite of the fact that Spain has for nearly a year been waging a civil war of the most bitter description, life in those parts of this consular district dominated by Franco's forces still runs a relatively normal course. The principal activities of the district are agriculture and mining, and for the products of both the demand is great at the moment. Although, therefore, the movement remains largely what it was to start with, namely, the uprising of a relatively small band of enthusiasts, based on a few groups of patriots of high but perhaps rather hazy ideals, the law and order maintained throughout the area controlled bring them the support of the bulk of the population above the working-class line, and probably some of the latter too. It is obvious, however, that the divergencies that led to the civil war are being reproduced among Franco's supporters in the same way as in but in much less violent form than among his opponents. The political sense and patriotism of the Conservative classes, however, check a natural desire for a more violent expression of their opinions, and permit lip-service to the more radical ideas of their bed-fellows which cloaks, in the interest of an immediate common objective, the essential differences that divide them, and which even the conclusion of a successful peace is unlikely to heal unless Franco proves to be at least as skilful a statesman as he is a soldier.

Source: British Documents on Foreign Affairs, Series F, Europe, vol. 27, Document no. 92, p. 126.

While Franco's one-party rule in the Nationalist camp proved to be an effective means of overcoming the ideological divisions among the various rightist parties, the great distances separating the political parties on the left were not so easily bridged. In fact, except for brief periods, profound differences between the left-wing factions persisted throughout the war and ultimately proved to be a major source of weakness to the Republic.

The dynamics of political discord

Tensions on the left were not simply the result of inter-party rivalries. Within each movement, there were currents that were opposed to one another. This was especially true of the socialists and anarchists. As mentioned in an earlier chapter, the former was divided into three distinct tendencies during the last years of the Second Republic. One was a reformist or centrist wing led by Indalecio Prieto. Prieto was a moderate socialist who believed that a democratic and pluralistic Republic was the best vehicle for advancing the interests of Spain's labouring classes. Along with republicans such as Manuel Azaña he worked hard to cobble together an alliance between the socialists and the middle-class parties on the left. Largo Caballero, the veteran trade-union activist and leader of the massive UGT, represented the revolutionary wing of the movement. Though he had long been identified as a reformist and political opportunist (he held a government post in Miguel Primo de Rivera's right-wing dictatorship), Largo underwent a political conversion after the break up of the socialist-republican coalition in 1933. By the spring of 1936 he was widely viewed as the 'Spanish Lenin', an uncompromising critic of the bourgeois

Republic who would lead the working-class revolution that many on the left (and right) believed was imminent (Document 4.15). Occupying the right-wing position of the socialist movement was an orthodox Marxist faction headed by Julián Besteiro. His refusal to commit to either the reformist or radical wings of the movement caused him to retire to the background. It was not until the final moments of conflict, when he joined a multi-party coalition that sought to overthrow the Negrín's communist-dominated government, that Besteiro returned to the limelight of the political stage.

Document 4.15 The 'Spanish Lenin'

(a)

There is no course but to destroy its roots . . . Imperceptibly, the dictator-ship of the proletariat or workers' democracy will be converted into a full democracy, without classes, from which the coercive state will gradually disappear. The instrument of the dictatorship will be the Socialist party, which will exercise this dictatorship during the period of transition from one society to another and as long as the surrounding capitalist states make a strong proletarian state necessary.

Source: Bolloten, B. (1991) *The Spanish Civil War*, Chapel Hill, p. 24.

(b)

'Some persons,' in an unmistakable reference to the Communists, 'are saying: "Let us crush fascism first, let us finish the war victoriously, and then there will be time to speak of revolution and to make it if necessary." Those who express themselves in this way have obviously not reflected maturely upon the formidable dialectical process that is carrying us all along. The war and the Revolution are one and the same thing. Not only do they not exclude or hinder each other but they complement and support each other. The war needs the Revolution for its triumph in the same way that the Revolution needed the war to bring it into being.'

Source: Bolloten, B. (1991) *The Spanish Civil War*, Chapel Hill, p. 116.

The divisions referred to here were affected by the Civil War in several impor-tant ways. On one level, the differences among the factions intensified. Thus, the reformists were placed increasingly at odds with the revolutionary elements. But at the same time the circumstances of war were reinforcing old divisions they were creating new ones. This was true because of the ever-shifting political positions of the leaders of the different tendencies. For example, when he became prime minister in September, Largo Caballero abruptly jettisoned his revolutionary rhetoric and projected himself to the outside world as the moderate leader of a democratic government that embraced all left-wing views. Despite this apparent volte-face, Largo's policies as premier rekindled opposition from his old political enemies and made new ones. While his administration made great strides towards unifying the left – the government he formed in early November 1936 was comprised of representatives from every major party – few saw Largo as an effective premier. A string of Republican military debacles in late 1936 and early 1937 further eroded his credibility as a leader. By then Largo had also incurred the wrath of the communists, who increasingly viewed him as an obstacle to their plans to dominate Republican affairs. For very different reasons, Prieto and the reformist elements of the socialist and Republican parties joined the communists' efforts to unseat him as premier. As we shall see, their opportunity finally presented itself in late spring of 1937 when Barcelona became the scene of a political battleground.

Like the socialists, the anarchosyndicalists possessed left, right, and centre factions. This was largely a result of a multi-dimensional movement which was divided along various fault-lines. By the time war broke out in 1936, the massive CNT, which included both radical and moderate syndicalist elements, was largely under the control of the FAI, a vanguard organization that sought at all costs to prevent the anarchosyndicalist movement from losing its revolutionary character. The revolutionary movement unleashed in the wake of the rebellion initially reinforced the radicalism of the CNT-FAI. But as the uprising developed into a more protracted conflict, the anarchosyndicalists faced a number of insoluble dilemmas. The foremost of these was whether they should pursue their own revolutionary agenda or whether they should compromise their hallowed anti-statist beliefs by co-operating with political parties (see below, Chapter 7). The decision of anarchist leaders to collaborate in governments at both local and national levels opened deep wounds in the movement from which they would never recover. The infamous Iron Column (see Chapter 8), the Libertarian Youth organization FIJL, foreign anarchists such as Camillo Berneri, and the Friends of Durruti group were among those anarchist groups which stridently opposed the non-revolutionary drift of the movement (Document 4.16). Over time, these splits fatally undermined the anarchosyndicalists' ability to defend themselves against their leftist rivals. Among other things, this paved the way for the communists and their allies to establish their hegemony over the war time Republic.

Document 4.16 Dissenting Voices in the Libertarian Community

(a)

Our programme

Revolutions cannot succeed if they have no guiding lights, no immediate objectives. That is what we find lacking in the July revolution. Although it had the strength, the CNT did not know how to mould and shape the activity that arose spontaneously in the street. The very leadership was startled by events which were, as far as they were concerned, totally unexpected.

They had no idea which course of action to pursue. There was no theory. Year after year we had spent speculating around abstractions. What is to be done? The leaders were asking themselves then. And they allowed the revolution to be lost.

Such exalted moments leave no time for hesitancy. Rather, one must know where one is headed. This is precisely the vacuum we seek to fill, since we feel that what happened in July and May must never happen again.

Source: Hacia una nueva revolucion (Towards a Fresh Revolution) (1938), New Anarchist Library, 2, Orkney, 1978.

(b)

Open Letter to Comrade Federica Montseny

Dear Comrade,

It was my intention to address myself to all your comrade ministers, but once the pen was in my hand, I addressed myself spontaneously to you alone and I did not wish to go against this instinctive impulse.

The fact that I am not always in agreement with you neither astonishes you nor irritates you, and you have shown yourself cordially oblivious to criticisms which it would almost always have been fair, because it is human, to consider as unjust and excessive . . .

In your speech of 3rd January, you said,

'The anarchists have come into the Government in order to prevent the Revolution from deviating from its course and in order to pursue it beyond the war, and also in order to oppose all possibility of dictatorial endeavours, wherever they should come from.'

Well then, comrade, in April, after three months of collaborationist experience, we find ourselves face to face with a situation in the course of which serious actions are taking place. While other, worse ones are taking shape . . .

The time has come to find out whether the anarchists are in the Government to be the vestal virgins tending a fire that is on the point of going out, or even if they are there from now on to serve as a 'Phrygian cap' for politicians flirting with the enemy or with the forces for the restoration of the 'Republic of all classes'. The problem is set by the clear evidence of a crisis which is outstripping the men who are the personages who embody it.

The dilemma: war or revolution no longer has any meaning. The only dilemma is this one: either victory over Franco thanks to the revolutionary war, or defeat.

The problem for you and the other comrades is to choose between the Versailles of Thiers and the Paris of the Commune, before Thiers and Bismarck form the *holy alliance*. It is up to you to reply, for you are the 'light under the bushel'.

C. Berneri

Source: Mintz, F. 'The Writings of Camillo Berneri', *Anarchist Review*, vol. 1, no. 4, 58–9.

Politics of the popular front

The factionalism which characterized the socialist and anarchist groupings was not a serious problem for the official communist party of Spain, the *Partido Comunista de España* (PCE). This was true primarily because the PCE was a relatively small organization which enforced a strict code of discipline over its membership. Dissenters were either excommunicated or forced to toe the party line. The fact that, ever since it was founded in 1921, the affairs of the PCE were inextricably tied and subordinated to the policies and personalities of the international communist movement headquartered in Moscow also explains the homogeneity and cohesiveness of the Spanish communist movement.

In the years leading up to the Civil War, the communists never managed to attract a mass following, partly because the socialist and anarchosyndicalists retained their hold over the majority of organized workers and partly because the communists' ideology was marked by a heavy Moscow accent that was hard to translate into a Spanish idiom. This all changed after the July uprising. Within a few weeks, there was a new and rapidly growing communist party in Catalonia, the PSUC, and, thanks in part to the intervention of the Soviet Union, the Madrid-based PCE had become one of the most dynamic forces on the Republican side.

The prodigious and unprecedented expansion of Communist ranks during the civil war owed a great deal as well to their carefully crafted military and political strategies. Both were based on the Popular Front formula which had been adopted by the Communist International in 1935. According to this, communists were instructed to abandon their 'class against class' tactics (which had proved disastrous in countries such as Germany and Austria) and form alliances with a broad band of left-wing middle-class and labour parties. This type of class collaboration was seen as the most effective way of combating fascism and promoting the foreign policy aims of the Soviet Union. As we saw in Chapter 1, this policy had been appropriated and modified by the socialist and Republican parties who were seeking to re-establish a left-coalition government after two years of right-wing rule. The triumph of the Popular Front electoral coalition in February 1936 underscored its potential value as a political tool.

By the time civil war broke out in July, however, what remained of the socialist-Republican-led Popular Front coalition – already in a state of advanced decomposition – completely disintegrated. When both the moderate socialists and middle-class Republican parties either refused or were unable to play a leadership role in the chaotic days following the July uprising, the door was opened for the communists to reclaim the leadership of the Popular Front strategy. Like the Popular Front coalition that had been cobbled together in February 1936, the communist-led Popular Front programme aimed to unite the disparate left-wing groups in Republican Spain under the banner of anti-fascism. Yet, once the military revolt had been suppressed in Madrid, Barcelona, and other key cities, and once the popular revolution had been unleashed in zones that had fallen under the rule of left-wing unions, politics in Republican Spain entered a new phase.

As far as the communists were concerned, this meant that the Popular Front strategy would no longer be used as a vehicle for effecting democratic rule. Instead, it was to be used as instrument for conducting both the political and military policies in the Republican war effort. In addition, the communists were determined to put the Popular Front policy to the use for which it was originally intended, namely, to promote the collective security interests of the Soviet Union (Document 4.17). From a diplomatic perspective this meant that Republican Spain would have to accept Soviet interference in Republican foreign policy affairs. Thus, for example, the Popular Front cabinet formed by Largo Caballero in the autumn of 1936 included the pro-communist Álvarez del Vayo as Foreign Minister, not because he was the prime minister's choice but because he had been hand-picked by the Soviets. Adjusting Spain's Popular Front government to conform to the policies of Moscow sometimes meant importing some of Stalin's own obsessive concerns into the Spanish arena. The communists' ferocious and relentless persecution of the anti-Stalinist POUM is a case in point. More than any other political contest, this intense and very public rivalry poisoned the political atmosphere of Republican Spain.

Document 4.17 The Popular Front in Defence of the Soviet Union

(a)

In other words, comrades, we believe that in the present international situation it is advantageous and necessary for us to carry out a policy that would preserve our opportunity to organize, educate, unify the masses and to strengthen our own positions in a number of countries – in Spain, France, Belgium and so on – where there are governments dependent on the Popular Front and where the Communist party has extensive opportunities. When our positions have been strengthened, then we can go further.

We have been interested for some time in having a democratic regime like this, so that through the general pressure of the masses and the Popular Front in a number of European countries (among which are the fascist countries – Germany, Italy, and so on), we [could] influence the mass of workers. The example of Spain shows how the masses operate, how the proletariat, the petty-bourgeois, radical intelligentsia, and peasants can form a common democratic platform against reaction and fascism. We have a number of examples in European circumstances where the masses, through the policy of the

Popular Front, under pressure from fascism and reaction, are strengthening their position and are shaping conditions for the final victory of the proletariat.

We should be able to influence the masses of these countries a great deal and therefore the struggle in Spain has immense significance. It seems to me that we must push this point, and we hope that we will in fact be victorious over the enemies of the Popular Front, who desire the destruction and discrediting of the Popular Front.

Source: Radosh, R., Habek, M. R. and Sevostianov, G. (eds) (2001) *Spain Betrayed: The Soviet Union in the Spanish Civil War*, New Haven, pp. 11–12.

(b)

The ECCI [Executive Committee of Communist International] presidium regards as wholly correct the Spanish party's policy designed to strengthen the popular front in every way, to fuse still more closely all anti-fascist forces, to consolidate still further the fighting community and fraternal relations between republicans, socialists, communists, and anarcho-syndicalists, for complete unity in the ranks of the people's front is the decisive requisite for defeating fascism.

Source: Degras, J. (ed.) (1965) *The Communist International 1919–1943 Documents*, vol. III, 1929–1943, Oxford, London and New York, p. 398.

In pursuit of these aforementioned goals, the communists forged alliances with parties on the left that shared their belief that the PF policy – whether dominated by the communists or not – was the only realistic means of achieving victory over the Nationalists. The communists were able to maintain their dominance of this coalition throughout the latter half of the war partly because of the splintered nature of their rivals (see above and below) but not least because of continued Republican reliance on Soviet aid.

Communist dissidents: POUM

When the military rebellion broke out in July the POUM was the only Marxist party that stood unequivocally for socialist revolution. This is true despite its adherence to the prewar Popular Front coalition, which the POUM had always understood not as a policy of class collaboration but as an electoral pact that could be used to further the working-class struggle against the bourgeoisie. The onset of war and the spontaneous grass-roots collectivization movement it unleashed was thus interpreted by them as an opportunity to establish the dictatorship of the working classes. Indeed, it was their unwavering commitment to a policy of waging war and revolution simultaneously as well as their persistently strident opposition to Stalinist policies which later proved to be an enormous liability for the party.

Possessing a mere handful of cadres scattered throughout the peninsula, the POUM was one of the smallest parties on the left end of Spain's political spectrum. Yet, its relative weight as a political force cannot be measured by numbers alone. Thanks to the prestige enjoyed by *poumista* intellectuals such as Joaquín Maurín, Julián Gorkin, Jordi Arquer, and Andreu Nin, the POUM exerted an influence throughout Spain that was disproportionate to its size.[5] Furthermore, the Catalanist sympathies expressed by many *poumistas* helped to enhance their political leverage at the regional level. Even so, the POUM never managed to build on these strengths, and throughout the war the POUM lacked both the popular support and material resources they needed to pursue their ambitious revolutionary agenda. Perhaps more than any other single factor, however, it was the POUM's ideological position which consigned them to a state of political limbo during the war. Though accused of being 'Trotskyite' – a term synonymous with fascist in communist circles – by its political enemies, the POUM was actually a Marxist-Leninist party that sought to steer a course between the Scylla of Stalinism and the Charybdis of Trotskyism. Joaquín Maurín, the party's principal leader and co-founder, was firmly opposed to Trotskyism, as were most members of the BOC, the majority current in the POUM. Nevertheless it is true that several key party members, notably Juan Andrade, Julián Gorkin and Andreu Nin, were deeply influenced by Trotskyist ideas. All three had figured prominently in the Trotskyist-oriented Izquierda Comunista Española, and Nin himself had maintained a close personal relationship with Trotsky until 1934.[6] Yet however sympathetic some poumistas were to Trotsky, the fact is that the party never adhered to what can be regarded as a Trotskyist programme. Trotsky himself made this clear both before and during the war when he frequently inveighed against Nin and the party leaders for failing to give the POUM a true revolutionary orientation (Document 4.18).

Document 4.18 POUM's relation to Trotsky and the Fourth International

(a)

The P.O.U.M. is not Trotskyist. Its membership and leadership come predominantly from the Communist Party, the Catalonian section of which was expelled in bloc during the ultra-left wave of 1929, for rejecting union-splitting, for advocating the tactics of the united front, for opposing the stupid theory that the rest of the working class was 'social fascist', for objecting to the mechanical transference of tactics to Spain which had no connection with Spanish realities. Its outstanding leader was Joaquin Maurin, repeatedly and bitterly attacked by Trotsky as 'centrist', 'opportunist', 'petty-bourgeois', 'main misleaders of the Spanish proletariat', 'Menshevik traitor' and similar choice epithets.

Two of the leaders of the P.O.U.M., Andres Nin and Juan Andrade, were former followers of Trotsky. They broke with him almost five years ago when they rejected his instructions to enter the Second International. They fused with the Maurinists to form the P.O.U.M. as a united organization in September 1935. Since then, Trotsky has variously honoured them as 'a mere tail on the "left" bourgeoisie', 'the traitors Nin and Andrade' (this after the outbreak of the Spanish civil war!) and has declared that 'in Spain, genuine revolutionists will no doubt be found who will mercilessly expose the betrayal of Maurin, Nin, Andrade and Co., and lay the foundation for the Spanish Section of the Fourth International' (January 22, 1936).

Source: Wolfe, B. D. (1937) *Civil War in Spain*, New York, pp. 68–9.

(b)

The POUM is merely slavishly conducting the same policy that the Seventh Congress of the Comintern foisted on all its sections, absolutely independently of their 'national peculiarities.' The real difference in the Spanish policy this time lies only in the fact that a section of the London International has also adhered officially to the bloc with the bourgeoisie. So much the worse for it. As far as we are concerned, we prefer clarity. In Spain, genuine revolutionists will no doubt be found who will mercilessly expose the betrayal of Maurin, Nin, Andrade, and their associates, and lay the foundation for the Spanish section of the Fourth International!

Source: Trotsky, L. (1973) *The Spanish Revolution, 1931–1939*, New York, pp. 210–11.

No less hostile to the POUM's politics were the anarchosyndicalists of the CNT-FAI. Before the war, friction between the two organizations was caused primarily by the POUM's persistent efforts to wrest control of the CNT from the purists of the FAI. Once the war had begun, however, the POUM abandoned its confrontational tactics towards its former trade-union rivals. This was true above all because, though both were in the forefront of the revolutionary movement that was sweeping through Catalonia, the POUM was clearly too weak to influence the course of events. To the leading militants of the POUM the rapidly changing circumstances dictated a new course of action. Rather than challenge the anarchosyndicalists' supremacy among the workers head-on, they believed that the POUM ought to take on the role of a revolutionary vanguard party. In so doing they hoped to convince the majority of libertarians that the Marxist-Leninist model they were promoting was superior to their own (Document 4.19). However their reasoning proved to be faulty on several counts. Not only did they overestimate the POUM's ability to play a leadership role, but they also underestimated the anarchosyndicalists' determination to conduct the revolution on their own terms.

Document 4.19 The POUM appeals to the CNT for a Revolutionary Alliance

The P.O.U.M., the C.N.T. and the F.A.I. are the real revolutionary vanguard of the Spanish workers. Between us and the C.N.T. there is not a perfect agreement concerning the significance of events and the interpretation of their development, but at least we both know that the workers are not fighting the civil war to install capitalist democracy in power again. Last Sunday's edition of the 'Solidaridad Obrera', the organ of the C.N.T., stated this clearly in the following terms: 'The chief thing at the present time is to conquer fascism and put the direction of public affairs and economy into the hands of the working class. We must begin building the new Worker's Spain'.

If there is a slight difference between our language and that used by the anarcho-syndicalist newspaper, it is not the basic interest. We both want to see Spain completely in the hands of the workers and neither of us believe that winning the war and making the revolution can be considered apart. We may differ over some aspects of workers' power, but while we of the P.O.U.M. are demanding the dictatorship of the proletariat, we wish with our anarchist Comrades for the broadest possible democracy within the regime of this class dictatorship.

Source: The Spanish Revolution: Weekly Bulletin of the Workers' Party of Marxist Unification of Spain, vol. 1, no. 7 (2 December 1936), p. 6.

Far more significant for the future of the POUM during the Civil War was its relationship with the Catalan orthodox Marxist party, Partit de Unificat de Catalunya (PSUC). The rivalry between these two parties grew increasingly virulent over time and would led ultimately to open warfare between them during the spring of 1937.

Orthodox communists in Catalonia: PSUC

Although negotiations for creating another Marxist party in Catalonia were being conducted before the war, the unresolved question as to whether such a party would be affiliated with the Comintern had prevented any merger from coming about. Then, following the outbreak of civil war and social revolution, the pressures to consolidate intensified. Fearful that the moderate forces might be completely swallowed up in areas where the revolutionaries were in the ascendant, four Catalan parties decided to merge, forming the Partit Socialist de Unificat de Catalunya (PSUC). Despite its socialist label – two of the four constituent parties were the Unió Socialista de Catalunya (USC) and the Federació Catalana del PSOE – the PSUC was in fact dominated by the communists. This was true both because the PSUC's ruling faction, the Partit Comunista de Catalunya (PCC), controlled all of the party's vital functions (including its press and trade union activities) and because of its structural links to the PCE and Comintern.[7] In practice this meant that the policies of the PSUC and the communists were indistinguishable from one another throughout the war (Document 4.20).

Document 4.20 The Creation of a Communist Party of Catalonia

A few days after the revolt of the reactionary forces, and immediately following upon the defeat of the people of the military-fascist insurrectionary movement in Barcelona and other localities of Catalonia, the *United Socialist Party of Catalonia* (P.S.U.C.) was formed on July 24 by the amalgamation of the four working-class parties formerly existing in Catalonia.

The relations between the four amalgamating parties, i.e., the Communist Party of Catalonia, the Socialist Union of Catalonia, the Catalan Federation of the Spanish Socialist Workers' Party, and the Catalan Proletarian Party, were most cordial long before the fascist rising.

In spite of the fact that they belonged to different international organisations, the four parties were already united prior to the military-fascist rising by their absolute acceptance of the decisions of the 7th Congress of the Communist International, and particularly by their complete acceptance of the masterly report of our great comrade, *Dimitrov*. They were united by the conviction that proletarian unity and a solid People's Front were absolute necessities in face of the everyday more aggressive and provocative attitude of the fascists, whose sinister machinations were making themselves felt more and more in Spain as the days went by. They were further united by the firm determination to defend unreservedly the U.S.S.R., fatherland of all the workers of the world. They were united by the conviction that only by following the road traced by the glorious Communist International, only by creating a mass proletarian party, which is a revolutionary Marxist-Leninist party, could the road be barred to fascism, and the working class and the people of Catalonia and of all Spain be liberated later on.

Source: Comorera, J. (17 May 1938) *International Press Correspondence*, Special Spain Number, vol. 18, no. 24, p. 566.

Possessing fewer than six thousand members, the newly formed party hardly appeared as a threat to its principal rivals, the CNT-FAI and the POUM. Yet thanks largely to its strong opposition to the maximalist revolutionary programme of the left – the party insisted that the war had to be won before any revolution could take place – and the power and prestige they acquired when Soviet supplies began arriving in October, the PSUC rose rapidly to become one of the principal parties in Catalonia. By 1937 party membership had surpassed the fifty thousand mark, while the PSUC-dominated Catalan section of the UGT counted nearly half a million members. Apart from the rank and file support it derived from its trade-union partner, the party appealed mostly to the small peasants (*rabaissaires*), small manufacturers, tradesmen, and middle- and lower-middle-class Catalans – whose interests they sought to protect by creating organizations such as the GEPCI (Federación Catalana de Gremios y Entidades de Pequeños Comerciantes e Industriales) (Document 4.21).

Document 4.21 The Social Composition of the PSUC

The P.S.U.C. does not hold interests that differ or are contrary to the people and the proletariat. Already it is a proletarian party; flesh and blood of the working class, and of an anti-Fascist people. In our party more than 60 per cent of the militants are industrial workers, and some 20 per cent are land workers. And if to these percentages we add the office employees, school masters, and in short all the wage earners, we can affirm that our Party is made up of 97 per cent of salaried workers, and the remaining 3 per cent of members of free professions, and a small part of the petite bourgeoisie. We are the authentic proletarian party of Catalonia, a Marxist-Leninist party that follows the teachings of Marx, Engels, Lenin and Stalin, adhering to the Communist International, and being the brother party of the great and heroic Communist Party of Spain, the self-denying champion of the Spanish United Proletarian Party.

Source: Comorera, J. (9 September 1937) 'Catalonia and Communism', *The Labour Monthly*, vol. 19, pp. 557–8.

5 | Spain in the international arena

Because the origins and causes of Spain's Civil War stemmed from deeply rooted domestic problems, few observers at the time could have predicted that the course and outcome of this internal conflict would be partially determined by foreign powers. But this is exactly what happened. Throughout the war both sides received and increasingly relied on foreign aid to sustain their struggle. To understand this internationalization process, it is necessary to bear in mind how the outbreak of civil war on the Iberian peninsula forced the rest of Europe to reassess Spain's importance in the international community. Ever since its humiliating defeat in the Spanish–American War of 1898, Spain was widely viewed as a second-rate power the affairs of which were largely irrelevant to its European neighbours. However, this view changed after July 1936. In Foreign Offices everywhere questions were raised about the meaning of Spain's troubles, not least being what bearing they would have on the precarious balance of power in Europe. At the time, diplomatic tensions were already running high. Italy's invasion and occupation of Abyssinia in 1935–36 provoked a negative reaction from Britain and the smaller states of the international community. And the failure of the League of Nations to take decisive action against the aggressor nation did little to allay the growing fear that Europe's peace could easily be shattered. Then, just three months before the July uprising in Spain, Hitler blatantly repudiated the Versailles Treaty and Locarno Pacts by ordering German troops to re-occupy the Rhineland. Thus, after years of relative isolation, Spain burst upon the world stage when the frailty of the European diplomatic order was becoming more and more apparent.

Because it was generally believed at the time that the rebellion would be a short-lived affair, it is hardly surprising that, apart from Germany and Italy, most governments adopted a 'wait and see' attitude. By August, however, the war was gaining rather than losing momentum and both Italy and Germany showed no sign of limiting their commitment to the Nationalist forces. Now better able to appreciate the strategic and diplomatic significance of what was unfolding in Spain, the Great Power countries of Britain and France decided to formulate a more concrete policy towards the Spanish crisis.

Non-intervention and the Western powers

Of the two, France was at first willing to aid the Republicans. But before any substantial arms shipments could make their way to Spain the socialist prime minister, Leon Blum, was forced to reconsider his commitment. Partly because he feared the grave domestic consequences of committing his government to a left-wing cause, partly because his own administration was split over the issue, and partly because France's principal ally, Britain, adamantly opposed intervention, Blum's government was impelled to pursue a new course of action. By the beginning of August, France renounced its plans to furnish arms to the ailing Spanish Republic and instead joined Britain in promoting the idea of sealing Spain's war off from the rest of Europe (Document 5.1).

Document 5.1 French Denials of Arms Shipments to Republican Spain

(a)

The Ambassador in France to the Foreign Ministry

Telegram
CONFIDENTIAL   PARIS, July 30, 1936 – 1:00 p.m.
No. 400

Regarding the question of arms deliveries to the Spanish Government, the following statement was made to the Embassy by the Press Department at the Quai d'Orsay: No arms deliveries had ever been made, and they had furthermore been denied officially and formally. In this connection reference was made to the denial circulated by the Agence Fournier, which was reported by DNB. The phraseology used there, that France would not intervene, was entirely clear and could refer only to arms deliveries. When the question had arisen for the French Government, the Foreign Ministry had been consulted. The latter had taken the stand that, while arms deliveries were quite permissible from the viewpoint of international law, they would be contradictory to the tradition of French diplomacy not to support civil war [*ne pas alimenter guerre civile*].

Source: Documents on German Foreign Policy, Series D, vol. 3, Washington, DC, 1949, pp. 16–17

(b)

Welczeck [former German Ambassador to Spain]

The Ambassador in France to the Foreign Ministry

Telegram
URGENT   PARIS, August 10, 1936.
No. 454 of August 10   Received August 10 – 9:35 p.m.
                                          Pol. III 987.

Delbos asked me to call on him today in order to tell me in the name of his Government how much the German Government's understanding reception of the French neutrality proposal had been appreciated and how much importance was attached to German–French collaboration in isolating the Spanish conflagration. France would see in this collaboration a favorable omen for future negotiations on the questions of concern to our nations, the settlement of which was, no doubt, very much desired by both Governments.

Source: Documents on German Foreign Policy, Series D, vol. 3, Washington, DC, 1949, p. 35.

Britain's refusal to involve itself directly in the Spanish conflict was consistent with its foreign policy since 1919. Above all, Britain was concerned with maintaining the status quo in Europe and in practice this meant avoiding taking on any commitment that might disrupt the fragile order of Europe. By the early 1930s Europe's economic and political stability was being precariously held together by both France and Britain, both of whom were being increasingly pressured to accept the revisions to the postwar settlements that both Italy and Germany were bent on making. Further complicating the picture for the British was the Soviet Union. Largely because of its suspect political and social doctrines, Russia had not yet been granted a major role in European affairs. Britain was content to keep the USSR isolated as much as possible and therefore did not want to see Stalin benefit from the Spanish imbroglio.

The British response to the Spanish Civil War was also predicated on its own strategic and economic interests. In the former case, the British wanted to make certain that Gibraltar and other key areas of the Mediterranean did not fall into the hands of a hostile power. Additionally, Britain wanted to protect its considerable business interests in Spain, particularly its investments in mineral resources. Not taking sides in the conflict was thus seen as the best way of achieving these goals (Document 5.2).

Document 5.2 Origins of the Non-intervention Policy

The revolution broke out on the 19th July.

For the first few days the attention of foreign Governments was concentrated on the evacuation of their nationals from Spain.

It soon became clear, however, that supplies of arms and ammunition were being received by the two parties in increasing quantities from foreign sources, and that the Powers were beginning to group themselves round the combatants in accordance with their own political doctrines. The danger in the supply of war material and military assistance to the two factions by these groups became immediately clear.

On the 25th July the French Government, appreciating this danger, announced their intention, as a unilateral gesture, of prohibiting the export of arms and war material from France to Spain.

On the 2nd August, learning that the insurgents were receiving large quantities of war material from abroad, and instigated particularly by the fact that a number of Italian military aircraft had flown over French Morocco to the insurgents' headquarters without permission, the French Government informed His Majesty's Government and the Italian Government, through their Ambassadors in London and Rome, that they would find it difficult to continue refusing arms to the legally constituted Government of Spain, and would be obliged to recover liberty of action, unless His Majesty's Government and the Italian Government would agree to accept the principle of non-intervention as a common rule.

His Majesty's Government replied on the 4th August that they would welcome an early non-intervention agreement between all Powers who might be in a position to supply arms and ammunition to Spain, but suggested that it ought in the first instance at any rate, to be accepted by the Governments of the United Kingdom, France, Germany, Italy and Portugal, 'who are primarily affected by the course of events in Spain, owing to their paramount material interests in, or close geographical connection with, that country.'

The Italian Government, though accepting in principle the 'thesis' of non-intervention, raised difficult points regarding the interpretation of the French note, particularly on the phrase 'moral solidarity,' and on the universality of the agreement and measures of control.

The German Government also accepted the principle of non-intervention, provided that Russia would be a party to the agreement, and the Soviet Government, who had also been consulted by the French Government, were understood to be willing to join.

Source: British Documents on Foreign Affairs, Series F, Europe, vol. 27, Document 37, pp. 39–40.

The joint Anglo-French effort to get other countries to adopt a hands-off policy towards Spain came to fruition in August 1936, when a series of unilateral pacts – collectively known as the Non-Intervention Agreement (NIA) – were signed by some twenty-seven nations. In September the Non-Intervention Committee (NIC) was set up in London to monitor outside interference in the Civil War. However, from the beginning the effectiveness of this body was in doubt. Not only did it lack the means to enforce its policies, but its leading members included Italy, Germany, and the Soviet Union – the three countries that openly intervened in the conflict between 1936 and 1939. A further strike against the NIC was the ambiguity of its mandate. This caused critics such as Manuel Azaña, the president of the Republic, to denounce the NIC as having been conceived, 'as it was, to tie the hands of the League'.[1] Later in the war Álvarez del Vayo, the Republic's representative to the League, tried to counter the NIC's policy by appealing directly to the world community[2] (Document 5.3).

Document 5.3 Alvarez del Vayo decries Italian Aid to the Nationalists

From the statements made by the Italian officers and men taken prisoner on the Guadalajara front the following facts emerge: On February 6th and the following days, numbers of Italian regular troops, equipped, armed and supplied, landed at Cadiz from the Italian steamer *Sicilia* and other ships. They were concentrated in the port of Santa Maria and subsequently conveyed to the Guadalajara front to take part in the present offensive.

The participation in the struggle of military contingents forming part of the Italian regular army not only constitutes the most scandalous violation perpetrated on the European continent since the Great War of the very principles on which any juridically organised international community is founded and which form the essence and basis of the League of Nations, but openly raises a political issue on the importance of which it is hardly necessary to insist. This is a clear case of the very danger to which the Spanish delegate drew the attention of the Assembly of the League of Nations, of war being openly waged without a previous declaration.

It is impossible for anyone to confuse a more or less open infringement of the obligation not to authorise the departure of 'volunteers' for Spain with the organisation and despatch by the Italian Government itself of a veritable military expedition to fight on the side of the rebels. The former can be checked by a more or less perfect technical system of control. The latter raises a political question of the utmost gravity and importance which can certainly not be settled by the application of control, no matter how perfect, but requires the direct collaboration of those countries on which fall the honour and responsibility of applying the fundamental principles governing international relations today.

In the opinion of the Spanish Government, this question has already been raised and the responsibilities resulting from it are quite clear; moreover, its opinion is based on definite and categorical evidence. The Spanish Government asks that this should be examined and a final decision reached to the effect that its opinion coincides with the facts.

This is the purpose of the present Note.

The Government of the Republic declares its readiness to co-operate fully in the measures which the Non-Intervention Committee may consider it necessary to adopt for this purpose.

(*Signed*) Julio ALVAREZ DEL VAYO

Source: League of Nations Official Journal, Special Supplement no. 165, Appeal by the Spanish Government, WHITE BOOK, Published by the Spanish Government and presented to the Council on 28 May 1937, pp. 4–5.

Monitoring intervention

In order to fulfil its mandate as a 'watch-dog' agency, the Non-Intervention Committee was obliged to adopted various schemes aimed at preventing the export to Spain of aircraft, arms, and other war materials from the some twenty-seven countries that were signatories of the non-intervention agreement. To ensure that violations of this agreement were not occurring, the NIC subcommittees set up a naval patrol scheme in the spring of 1937. But, as the historian Michael Alpert has pointed out, the major flaw with this plan was that ships registered in Spain or in non-participating countries were not covered.[3] Thus, the Germans easily evaded monitoring by flying the flag of exempt Panama, and both Italy and the Soviet Union could similarly avoid detection by shipping arms via Spanish ships.

The difficulties members of the Control Commission of the Naval Patrol faced in their efforts to stop arms from coming to Spain were further compounded by the presence of numerous foreign warships and naval vessels in the harbours and off the coasts of the Iberian peninsula. Though most of these countries maintained a naval presence in order to evacuate refugees and to protect their commercial and strategic interests, both Germany and Italy – whose warships were assigned to the Naval Patrol – demonstrated a willingness to engage in hostilities. For example, when the Republican airforce bombed the Italian cruiser *Barletta* and the German pocket battleship *Deutschland* at the end of May 1937, the Germans were quick to retaliate (Document 5.4). Hitler was so enraged by the attack that he ordered two other warships in the vicinity, the *Leipzig* and *Admiral Scheer*, into action. A couple of days later the small port city of Almería was heavily bombarded, resulting in some 74 casualties (Document 5.5).

Document 5.4 Diplomatic Responses to the *Deutschland* Incident

(a)

[No. 216]   BERLIN, May 30, 1937.

The Foreign Minister to the Embassy in Great Britain

After Red airplanes bombed British, German, and Italian ships lying in the harbour of Majorca a few days ago and killed six officers on an Italian ship, German ships were forbidden to remain in the harbor any longer. On Saturday, May 29, 1937, the pocket battleship *Deutschland* was lying in the roadstead of Iviza. The ship belongs to the forces assigned to the international sea patrol. In spite of this, the pocket battleship was suddenly bombed between 6 and 7 p.m. by two planes of the Red Valencia Government in a gliding attack.

Since the Red Valencia Government was twice warned by the Non-Intervention Committee and the German Government against further attacks on the ships engaged in the international patrol, this new criminal attack on the German ship compels the German Government to take measures of which it will immediately inform the Non-Intervention Committee.

NEURATH

Source: Documents on German Foreign Policy, Series D, vol. 3, Washington, DC, 1949, Document 267, pp. 296–7.

(b)

Note from Maisky to the Non-Intervention Committee on the Deutschland *incident and the naval patrol*

8 *June* 1937

Mirovoe Khoziaistvo, 1937, 7, p. 151

As regards questions of a more general nature which arise out of the bombing of the Deutschland, I am compelled to draw your attention to the fact that the aggressive actions of the insurgents, directed against British ships, French aircraft, and French territory, have, so far, never been the subject of discussion by the non-intervention committee.

While not objecting in principle to the adoption by the non-intervention committee of measures guaranteeing the ships participating in naval control from various incidents which may arise in connection with the military operations, I must declare that, in my opinion, all negotiations on such measures ought to be undertaken only after the entire question has been discussed by the non-intervention committee, and, in any case, on condition that all the countries represented on the committee should be fully informed about them.

Source: Degras, J. (1951) *Soviet Documents on Foreign Policy*, New York, pp. 240–1.

Document 5.5 The Bombardment of Almería

Description of the destruction caused by the Nazis, according to a despatch from the correspondent of the Daily Telegraph, *in Almería (5 June 1937)*

The destruction caused last Monday in Almería in one hour by the German 'pocket battleship' *Admiral Scheer* is greater than that wrought by any single bombardment during the Spanish war, with the possible exception of the bombing of Guernica, on the Basque front.

I have spent two days touring the ruins and examining the havoc done. The figures already given, of 24 dead and 100 injured, are no real indication of what happened when for sixty minutes the *Admiral Scheer* and her escort of four destroyers shelled this old white-washed town.

Source: How the German Fleet Shelled Almeria (n.d.), London, p. 17 and 19.

The reprisal almost sparked off an international incident. The Republican Defence Minister, Indalecio Prieto, wanted the Republic to respond by declaring war on Germany. Yet, given that such a move threatened to provoke a wider European crisis, his suggestion was immediately overruled by Juan Negrín and the rest of his cabinet. The Valencian government's efforts to use diplomatic channels to draw attention to Germany's egregious behaviour were also to no avail. For when Álvarez del Vayo asked the Secretary of the League of Nations to convene a special session in order to condemn Germany's assault on an undefended city, the Council refused to do so. The NIC's response to the crisis was predictable. Rather than censure the Germans, the Committee invited them, along with the Italians, to resume their activities in the coastal patrol.

However, the NIC's strategy to appease both Italy and Germany in order to keep them as partners in its multinational effort to contain the Spanish conflict suffered a serious setback just two months after the Almería affair. During the latter part of August, navigation in the Mediterranean around Spain was interrupted by a series of maritime attacks on Russian and British vessels. Though it was widely known that Italian submarines were responsible for the torpedoing incidents, the British in particular wanted to find a way of stopping them without provoking Italy. To this end the British, at the urging of the French, hosted a diplomatic gathering in Nyon (near Geneva, Switzerland) in September. Significantly, Italy and Germany did not attend. None the less, it was decided at the meeting that it was necessary for various nations to police the Mediterranean. Because Italy was invited to join these patrols, the effectiveness of the so-called Nyon agreements was rendered null and void.

In view of its cynical political underpinnings and its overall ineffectiveness in preventing foreign intervention, the policy of non-intervention must be judged a failure. For even though its adoption most likely helped to prevent the Spanish Civil War from boiling up into a general European war, its overall activities fatally undermined the belief that crises of this sort could be satisfactorily resolved through international diplomacy.

The fascist powers

Because there were strong fascist currents on the Nationalist side, and because the insurgents received support from Europe's principal fascist powers, it was rumoured at the time that the military coup was part of an international fascist plot. Yet there was no irrefutable evidence supporting this claim. In fact, Germany had not paid much attention to Spain before 1936, and, despite having supported anti-Republican groups that had been conspiring against the Republic before 1936, Italy was not directly involved in the July rebellion.

Prior to the July rebellion, Germany had generally ignored Spanish affairs. After all, in modern times Spain had never been regarded as a member of the Great Power system and the fact that it was a Mediterranean country meant that it held no special geographic importance to a Nazi government which was mainly concerned with establishing German hegemony in central and eastern Europe. But, shortly after the July military uprising, Germany's interest in Spain suddenly changed.

Only five days after civil war had erupted, General Franco dispatched a delegation consisting of a Spanish representative, Captain Francisco Arranz Monasterio, and two Germans resident in Spanish Morocco, the businessman Johannes Bernhardt and the Nazi official Adolf Langenheim, to Germany in order to request troop-transport planes from the Führer. In Franco's eyes their mission was of the utmost importance, not least because he feared that, without planes to ferry his troops across the Gibraltar straits, the rebel forces would face certain defeat.

Through his connections to high-ranking Nazi officials, Bernhardt managed to bypass bureaucratic diplomatic channels, and on 25 July he gained access to Hitler himself. Upon reading Franco's desperate pleas for support in his crusade against Bolshevism, Hitler decided to commit German resources to the Nationalist cause by launching Operation 'Magic Fire' (*Feuerzauber*). Within days twenty Junkers-52 were making their way to Morocco.[4]

But Hitler's decision to aid Franco was based on more than just ideological considerations (Document 5.6). From a diplomatic standpoint, he was determined to undermine France's role as a major power and he reasoned that the defeat of a left-wing government in Spain would most likely further this goal. A war in Spain also provided Hitler with a much welcomed opportunity to divert international attention from his efforts to further Germany's hegemonic aims in central and eastern Europe.

Document 5.6 Goebbels Outlines the Significance of the Spanish Conflict

For more than a year the Spanish question has held the public of the whole world in suspense. Now, if we are to form a decisive judgement on the possible consequences and far-reaching effects of what is happening in Spain we must in this case, as in all cases where we have to deal with acute and complex problems, clearly differentiate between the opposing sides.

The Spanish problem concerns the whole world. There is no further cause to divide Europe into two sections. Bolshevism and the Comintern have already seen to that. This is the meaning of the Red Revolution which has spread its fearful convulsions all over Spain. The question whether and how the affair will be further pursued can no longer depend on our wills alone. For what is happening now is partly the outer effect on internal dynamic laws that have been set in motion. Of course there are elements that have remained neutral in this struggle; but what is of decisive importance is that the struggle has begun and that it cannot be broken off at will. Here also Europe's stand on the international Jewish question must be decided. For the Jews want this war. They are preparing it with all the means at their disposal. For them it is necessary as a prelude to the Bolshevic world hegemony.

Source: Goebbels, J. (1937) *'The Truth About Spain', Speech Delivered at the National Socialist Party Congress, Nürnberg,* Berlin

Hitler was also eager to exploit any material advantage he could from the Spanish situation. German economic relations with the rebels was early on secured by the creation of the import–export companies HISMA (Hispano-Marroquí de Transportes, Sociedad Limitada) and ROWAK (Rohstoffe- und Waren-Einkaufsgesellschaft). During the war, these companies served as a conduit not only for funnelling supplies to the Nationalists but also for extracting mining concessions from Franco[5] (Document 5.7).

Document 5.7 German Economic Relations with Franco's Government

(a)

The Director of the Economic Policy Department to the Embassy in Spain Telegram

Berlin, May 13, 1937

As the first reason we would recall that the Hisma–Rowak machinery was set up earlier primarily to insure that the possibilities for procuring German goods of any kind might be utilized by one person only, namely, General Franco. We therefore regarded Hisma–Rowak not as a merely German organization but also as a confidential and control agency of General Franco.

The second reason is the following: There had thus far been complete and friendly agreement that if Germany, on the one hand, rendered assistance to Nationalist Spain in every way possible, she should, on the other hand, also receive something in return within the scope of Spain's potentialities, and specifically through the procurement of essential raw materials and foods.

Source: Documents on German Foreign Policy, Series D, vol. 3, Washington, DC, 1949, p. 288.

(b)

The Ambassador in Spain to the Foreign Ministry

SALAMANCA, January 21, 1938.

Subject: Ore shipments from Nationalist Spain and Spanish Morocco to Germany.

Director Johannes Bernhardt of Hisma Ltd., Seville, has transmitted to the Embassy a report, a copy of which is enclosed and which gives a picture of the quantities of ore shipped to Germany during the past year, from Spanish Morocco and Nationalist Spain.

[ANNEX]

For your information we wish to report to you that ore exports were as follows during the month of December:

Iron ores:	Bilbao shipments, approximately	90,000 tons
	Morocco shipments, approximately	100,000 tons
	Other shipments, approximately	15,000 tons
	Total	205,000 tons

Shipments of pyrites, approximately	55,000 tons
Shipments of ores such as tungsten, copper, and bronze, approximately	152 tons

Thus during the month of December we achieved a record of approximately 260,000 tons.

The figures for the year 1937 are also now available. We shipped a total of 2,584,000 tons of ores, including:

Iron ores	1,620,000 tons
Pyrites	956,000 tons
Miscellaneous ores, approximately	7,000 tons

The figures speak for themselves.

Source: Documents on German Foreign Policy, Series D, vol. 3, Washington, DC, 1949, pp. 565–6.

While this economic arrangement did not prove profitable for the Germans, there were other palpable ways in which they benefited from their investment in the Nationalist cause. Chief among these was the fact that the Germans gained valuable battlefield experiences which were used for testing their military tactics and weapons. In fact, the Condor Legion, the military force sent to Spain in October 1936, was able to develop under combat conditions many techniques – dive-bombing, for example – which were later put to use during the opening stages of the Second World War.[6]

Besides the transport planes and fighters they had delivered to Franco at the beginning of the war, the Germans also sent fighter pilots and specialists needed to operate and maintain the equipment they were supplying the Nationalists (Document 5.8). In September 1936, Lieutenant Colonel Walther Warlimont of the German General Staff arrived as the German commander and military adviser to General Francisco Franco. By late October, Berlin decided to formalize its air combat role in Spain by creating the Condor Legion, a force which comprised not only aircraft of various types – Heinkel-51 fighters and Heinkel-99 and Heinkel-70 reconnaissance bombers, for example – but also several thousand German pilots recruited from the Luftwaffe. General Hugo Sperrle was appointed commander of the Condor Legion in November 1936. His chief of staff was Wolfram von Richthofen, the cousin of the First World War flying ace Manfred von Richthofen. Wilhelm von Thoma was placed in charge of all German ground troops in the war. The Condor Legion was initially equipped with around a hundred aircraft and 5,136 men but by the end of the war over nineteen thousand Germans had fought alongside the Nationalist Army.

Document 5.8 Italian and German Military Aid to the Nationalist Cause

(a)

The Chargé d'Affaires in Spain to the Foreign Ministry

SALAMANCA, January 7, 1937.

The arrival of the first German instructors, who immediately started their work of training the Falange units, likewise resulted in improving morale. Since we have anticipated the Italians in this field, and Spain's future depends on the ideas held by the Falangists, I consider that cooperation with the Falangists holds certain possibilities for the future.

Altogether approximately 50 German instructors can be expected to arrive in the course of the next 6 weeks, most of whom were active in Spain until a few months ago as merchants, etc., and who will now have the opportunity of reestablishing themselves here in their former occupations as soon as the situation permits.

FAUPEL

Source: Documents on German Foreign Policy, Series D, vol. 3, Washington, DC, 1949, pp. 206–7.

(b)

Up to 29 September, the arrivals of German and Italian aircraft had been as follows:

German: 20 Junkers-52 transports/bombers arrived between 28 July and 10 August
24 Heinkel-52 fighters arrived on 6 and 17 August, and in early September
29 Heinkel-46 reconnaissance machines arrived in mid and late September

TOTAL   73

Italian: 9 Savoia S.81 bombers arrived on 30 July: 36 Fiat CR32 fighters arrived on 14 and 28 August and 3 and 29 September.
1 Cant Z.501 naval reconnaissance seaplane arrived 20 September.
10 IMAM Ro37 reconnaissance biplanes arrived 29 September 1936.

TOTAL   56

Source: Coverdale, J. in Alpert, M. (1994) *A New International History of the Spanish Civil War*, Basingstoke, p. 78.

(c)

Reuter's correspondent considers that German help has been probably larger in quantity and certainly better in quality than the Italian. The Fiat tanks, he says, though beautifully made, are too light and continually break down, just as they did in Abyssinia. The Italians, moreover, lose many of their tanks and aircraft through carelessness. (Two Italian tanks were being repaired by their crews one night in a village south of Madrid when four Russian tanks appeared, put the Italians to flight and towed away their tanks.) The Russian 'Vickers' tanks are very good. They mount 45-mm, quick-firing guns, which do great execution. Captain Strunck (German, part pilot, part correspondent for the *Völkischer Beobachter* and in close touch with Hitler) told Reuter's correspondent, who had known him in Abyssinia, that these Russian 'Vickers' tanks were the only foreign type of which the German War Office had no model. The first one to be captured was accordingly rushed off to Berlin for inspection.

In mid-October General Franco had at his disposal a contingent of seventy-seven German 'instructors' with eighteen whippet tanks (? two squadrons) complete with trailors for carrying them and motor trucks for hauling the trailers. There was also at least one German A.A. battery of four 88-mm, guns, firing in couples by the 'scissors' method. There are plenty of Germans about, all officially 'instructors' for German mechanical equipment. Heinkel 'Blitz' fighters have now arrived, though the Russian fighters are still the faster.

Source: Malcol, A.F.C., in *British Documents on Foreign Affairs*, Series F, Europe vol. 27, Document no. 53 (enclosure in Document no. 52), p. 63.

News of the uprising did not solicit a definitive response from Italy, which was not overly concerned with what appeared to be just another military *pronunciamiento*. Though representatives of the insurgent forces approached the Italian government for military aid in the critical early days of the rebellion, Mussolini was at first reluctant to intervene. Yet for several reasons Mussolini, his newly appointed Foreign Minister, Count Ciano, and his other close advisers did not take much prodding to change their minds. First and foremost was the fact that the timing of Spain's war coincided with a dynamic period in Italian foreign affairs.[7] After all, Ethiopia had only recently been conquered (spring of 1936), and the Duce was anxious to realize his plans to turn the Mediterranean into an 'Italian lake'. There were as well longstanding ideological and political ties between Italy and the Nationalists. Primo de Rivera's quasi-fascistic military rule during the 1920s paralleled developments in Italy, and Italian assistance to anti-democratic right-wing causes – notably the Alfonsine monarchists and the Carlists – during the Second Republic (1931–36) provided further links that Nationalist representatives who hurried to Italy in the early moments of the rebellion hoped to expand upon in their quest for military supplies.

All of this is not to say that Mussolini had a direct hand in fomenting the *alzamiento* or military rising of July. Nor is it to suggest the Italian dictator had specific designs on Spanish territory. Rather, the point here is that Mussolini decided to assist the Nationalists for a variety of political and pragmatic reasons. The Italian fascists viewed the Spanish situation with great interest above all because they wanted to see the demise of the Popular Front government. The success of a right-wing coup would assure this and thus make it possible for Italy to achieve a major foreign policy goal, namely to eclipse both French and British influence in the Mediterranean, the two major stumbling blocks to Italy's hegemonic aims in southern Europe.

There was a further reason why Mussolini committed himself to aiding the Nationalist cause. *Il Duce* was convinced that the future of Italian interests was bound up with its image as an aggressive power. Demonstrating Italy's growing military prowess in the Spanish arena could only enhance the 'forceful' image that Mussolini was seeking to cultivate in the face of what he perceived as the 'decadent' and increasingly enfeebled Western powers. In addition, Mussolini hoped that Italy's military accomplishments in Spain would impress others, particularly Germany, of its value as a potential ally. In fact, it was largely thanks to the common ground they established while assisting the Nationalists that both Germany and Italy began to draw closer together, forming a bond that first took shape with the Rome–Berlin Axis alliance announced in Milan in November 1936 and which developed into a full partnership during the Second World War (Document 5.9).

Document 5.9 Forging an Anti-Bolshevik Alliance

(a)

The Ambassador in Italy to the Foreign Ministry

Rome, December 18, 1936.
Received December 19.

The interests of Germany and Italy in the Spanish troubles coincide to the extent that both countries are seeking to prevent a victory of Bolshevism in Spain or Catalonia. However, while Germany is not pursuing any immediate diplomatic interests in Spain beyond this, the efforts of Rome undoubtedly extend toward having Spain fall in line with its Mediterranean policy, or at least toward preventing political cooperation between Spain on the one hand and France and/or England on the other.

In connection with the general policy indicated above, Germany has in my opinion every reason for being gratified if Italy continues to interest herself deeply in the Spanish affair.

The struggle for dominant political influence in Spain lays bare the natural opposition between Italy and France; at the same time the position of Italy as a power in the western Mediterranean comes into competition with that of Britain. All the more clearly will Italy recognize the advisability of confronting the Western powers shoulder to shoulder with Germany – particularly when considering the desirability of a future general understanding between Western and Central Europe on the basis of complete equality.

HASSELL

Source: Documents on German Foreign Policy, Series D, vol. 3, Washington, DC, 1949, pp. 171–3.

(b)

In Spain the two fronts have formed – on the one side the Germans and Italians, on the other the French, Belgians and Russians. The Duce agrees with Hitler that the formation of the two fronts is now an accomplished fact.

Italy has helped the Spaniards, and at the present moment numerous acts of help are being performed without conditions, though much Italian blood has been shed and the Balearics were saved only by Italian men and Italian material. For the present it is necessary to win. After the victory we will ask nothing of Spain which might modify the geographical situation in the Mediterranean, but will only ask her to follow a policy which is not contrary to the interest of Italy.

Our actions in Spain are an effective proof of our participation in the anti-Bolshevik struggle.

Source: Muggeridge, M. (ed.) (1948) *Ciano's Diplomatic Papers*, London, pp. 45–6.

Towards the end of December, the Italians landed their first groups of volunteers known as CTV (Corpo di Truppe Volontarie) in Cádiz, and further reinforcements, including members of Mussolini's elite Black Shirts, arrived shortly afterwards. There they joined the Nationalist forces under the command of General Quiepo de Llano, who were swiftly advancing along the Mediterranean coast towards Málaga. In early February, the Italian commanding the CTV, General Mario Roatta, led his troops to their first resounding victory on Spanish soil in the battle of Málaga. Thereafter the Italians sought to play an even greater role in the fighting, though their unexpected and humiliating defeat at the battle of Guadalajara in March, 1937 considerably cooled their hopes in this regard and proved to be acutely embarrassing for Mussolini who had hoped to use Spain as a showcase for Italy's growing military might.

Though its assistance to the Nationalists was of less importance, Portuguese intervention during the Spanish Civil War also deserves mention.[8] In power since 1928, the corporatist-fascist government of Antonio Oliveira Salazar had been inverterately hostile to the liberal democratic Second Republic. Not surprisingly, then, the Portuguese government was exceedingly sympathetic to the July coup. Though publicly maintaining its neutrality – under British pressure Salazar had signed on to the NIA – Portugal would, in various ways, support the rebels throughout the war. Besides providing both a safe haven for the plotters of the rebellion (Sanjurjo's plane took off from Lisbon on 20 July 1936) and a secure route for German supplies being channelled into Spain, the Portuguese government sent medical supplies, war *matériel*, and several thousand 'volunteers' to fight alongside the Nationalists.

Impact of Italian and German aid

There can be no doubt that the contribution of the Axis powers gave the Nationalists a clear-cut advantage in military terms. This was particularly evident in the case of German assistance. Over time the Condor Legion became ever more vital to the Nationalist war effort. In addition to providing tactical support for ground troops, the Legion helped the Nationalists gain air superiority, a factor that turned the tide in numerous campaigns fought in the last year and a half of the war. If they did not necessarily tip the balance in favour of Franco's side – internecine bickering among the parties in the republican camp was equally important – they none the less assured Franco of a complete and total defeat of the Republicans.

For all the aid they provided, both Italy and Germany never managed to bring Spain completely into the Axis orbit. Hitler found this out in the early months of the Second World War. At their famous summit meeting held near the French– Spanish border in October 1940, Franco delivered a marathon speech to the German leader in which he outlined the precise conditions under which Spain would join the war on the Axis's side. Given his superior bargaining position, it is scarcely surprising that Hitler rejected these demands. In the end, he was forced to accept Spain not as an ally but as a friendly neutral power in the Mediterranean.

United States and Latin America

Primarily because of its location, the Spanish Civil War posed no immediate concern to non-European countries. This was true despite Spain's longstanding and deeply rooted cultural ties to Latin America. Most of Spain's former colonies, however, were so preoccupied with their own domestic problems that few were willing to take a committed stand on the war. In the end, only Lázaro Cárdenas's Mexico was prepared to send aid to the Republic. Mexico sent some 3.5 million pesos' worth of (mostly outdated) arms and served as a broker for Republican arms sales during the war. Further attempts to aid the Republic were sharply curtailed by the pressures the United States brought to bear on its southern neighbour.

When war broke out in 1936 the United States was still in the grip of an isolationist mood that had descended upon the country following the First World War and which had been reinforced by the onset of the Great Depression. Seeking to avoid foreign entanglements, the US had since 1919 consistently pursued an independent course of diplomacy. During the Abyssinian crisis, for example, it refused to co-operate with the League's sanctions and in 1935 (reinforced in 1937) the US imposed an arms embargo (Neutrality Act) on foreign wars. This did not mean that the left-leaning administration of Franklin Roosevelt was entirely indifferent to the Spanish conflict. In fact, his government were generally sympathetic to the Republic, though fearful of taking sides because of pressing domestic concerns. With much of the energy of his administration directed at the economy, there was little Roosevelt could do for a foreign country that had little relevance to the average American (Document 5.10). Besides, the Civil War had erupted in an election year, and Roosevelt could not afford to alienate the large community of Catholic voters, the majority of whom tended to be pro-Nationalist.

Document 5.10 President Roosevelt Makes the Case for American Neutrality

The Department of State, with my entire approval, soon after the beginning of the Civil War in Spain, took a definite stand on the subject of the export of arms to that country – a stand which was in entire conformity with our well-established policy of non-intervention and with the spirit of the recent neutrality act.

. . . it [is] clear that the civil conflict in Spain involves so many non-Spanish elements and has such wide international implications that a policy of attempting to discriminate between the parties would be dangerous in the extreme. Not only would we, by permitting unchecked the flow of arms to one party in the conflict, be involving ourselves directly in that European strife from which our people desire so deeply to remain aloof, but we would be deliberately encouraging those nations which would be glad of this pretext to continue their assistance to one side or the other in Spain and aggravating those disagreements among the European nations which are a constant menace to the peace of the world.

Source: Taylor, F. J. (1956) *The United States and the Spanish Civil War*, New York, p. 83.

A further step to keep America out of Spain's war came in August 1936, when the government announced its 'moral embargo' on arms supplies. In practice this meant that individual contributions from Americans would not be permitted and that Americans travelling abroad could not go to Spain. Despite these measures, however, there were several notable breaches of the aforementioned embargoes. During the war some 3,200 American men and women managed to make their way to Spain as members of the International Brigades. Forced to assume false identities and smuggled into Spain by communist organizers of the IBs, these idealistic volunteers defied their government in order to support a cause in which they deeply believed. Many would lose their lives on the battlefields of Spain, and those who returned after the war were greeted not as heroes but as communist sympathizers who were later branded by some as 'pre-mature' antifascists.

Several US companies violated the spirit if not the letter of the US government's injunction against participation in the Spanish conflict. Texas Oil and Firestone, for example, were so confident of a Nationalist victory that they extended credit to Franco so that he could purchase badly needed oil, tyres, and other raw materials for his army. It was in these and other informal ways that the United States 'intervened' in the Spanish Civil War.

Soviet Union

When civil war broke out in July, the Soviet Union was experiencing a series of domestic crises. Soviet society was still in the disrupting throes of Stalin's massive collectivist programme. Then, as the period of the first Five Year Plan (1929–34) drew to a close, Stalin sought to consolidate his rule by launching a series of purges that struck at the heart of his system. Political and military leaders were the main targets of the show trials that began in 1936, events which would have ominous echoes in Spain during the Civil War.

On the diplomatic front, the Soviet Union was by 1934–35 emerging from the state of limbo to which it had been consigned following the Russian Revolution. By this time, the Soviets were embarked on a new diplomatic course, one that was aimed at drawing Russia into a closer relationship with the liberal-democratic Western powers. A pact of mutual assistance signed with France in May 1935 was a clear indication of this *démarche*. The Spanish Civil War thus occurred at a time and place in Europe when Soviet diplomatic relations were at a critical crossroads. Since a victory for the rebels would mean that France would be surrounded by fascist or pro-fascist countries, the Spanish conflict directly threatened the Soviets' newly forged 'collective security' link to the West. The Soviets were also compelled to respond to the glaring shortcomings of the policy of non-intervention articulated by Britain and France. From the beginning, it was clear that, by preventing the legitimate Spanish government from gaining access to arms from the rest of

Europe and beyond, non-intervention favoured the Nationalists. It was also apparent that two of the signatories of the NIA, Germany and Italy, were flouting the agreement.

Ever cautious and slow to take action, Stalin himself was at first reluctant to get involved in a situation fraught with such thorny diplomatic complications. But growing pressures from the Soviet public, his foreign advisers as well as from the international communist movement, were impossible to ignore. Then, following the fall of San Sebastián on 13 September, the precariousness of the Spanish Republic was underscored. It was at this point that Stalin decided to cross the threshold of commitment. A shipload of arms and supplies arrived in Alicante in late September, and from then until the last year of the war, Soviet involvement in the republican cause deepened (Document 5.11).

Document 5.11 Reasons for Soviet Intervention

(a)

Chairman of the Council of Ministers
Madrid, 25 July 1936
To the Ambassadors of the USSR in France

Dear Sir:

The government of the Republic of Spain needs to supply its army with modern armaments in significant quantities to conduct the struggle against those who began and are continuing the civil war against the legal authority and constitutional government and who are being supplied with weapons and ammunition from abroad in abundant quantities. The government I head, knowing what sorts of means and availability of military matériel are at the disposal of the USSR, decided to appeal to you to notify your government about the desire and necessity, which our government is experiencing, for supplies of armaments and ammunition of all categories, and in very great quantities, from your country.

Taking the opportunity, etc.

Signature: José Giral

Source: Radosh, R. Habeck, M.R. and Seviostianor, G. (eds) (2001) *Spain Betrayed: The Soviet Union in the Spanish Civil War*, New Haven, Document no. 10, p. 21.

(b)

It was late in August, and the Franco forces were firmly organized and marching successfully on Madrid, when three high officials of the Spanish Republic were finally received in Russia. They came to buy war supplies, and they offered in exchange huge sums of Spanish gold. Even now, however, they were not conveyed to Moscow but kept incognito in a hotel in Odessa. And to conceal the operation, Stalin issued, on Friday, August 28, 1936, through the Commissar of Foreign Trade, a decree forbidding 'the export, re-export, or transit to Spain of all kinds of arms, munitions, war materials, aeroplanes and warships.' The decree was published and broadcast to the world on the following Monday.

Stalin was in reality sneaking to the support of the Spanish Republic. While its high officials waited in Odessa, Stalin called an extraordinary session of the Politbureau, and presented his plan for cautious intervention in the Spanish civil war – all this under cover of his proclamation of neutrality.

Stalin argued that the old Spain was gone and that the new Spain could not stand alone. It must join either the camp of Italy and Germany, or the camp of their opponents. Stalin said that neither France nor Great Britain would willingly allow Spain, which commands the entrance to the Mediterranean, to be controlled by Rome and Berlin. A friendly Spain was vital to Paris and London.

Source: Krivitsky, W.G. (1939) *I Was Stalin's Agent*, London, p. 98.

(c)

FOREIGN OFFICE, *November 3, 1936*

His Excellency went on to give what he described as an exposition of the motives which had actuated the Soviet Government in the Spanish conflict. He was emphatic that the Soviet Government's admitted sympathy with the Government in Spain was not due to their desire to set up a Communist régime in that country. I remarked that the Ambassador could hardly be surprised if other people thought differently in view of the declared objective of the upholders of Communism to make their method of Government universal. The Ambassador replied that it was quite true that this was their ultimate objective but it was a very distant one – nobody [in] Russia today thought that it could be achieved for instance in our lifetime – and the Soviet Government's purpose in attempting to assist the Spanish Government was far more immediate than that.

The Ambassador confessed that he really could not understand our attitude in this matter – surely we could not wish to see another Fascist Government in the Mediterranean. Perhaps we thought that we could influence General Franco – and to some extent no doubt this belief was justified – but we could scarcely expect our influence to be as great as that of the German or Italian Governments who had given him active help. The Soviet Government were convinced that if General Franco were to win, the encouragement given to Germany and Italy would be such as to bring nearer the day when another active aggression would be committed – this time perhaps in Central or Eastern Europe. That was a state of affairs that Russia wished at all costs to avoid and that was her main reason for wishing the Spanish Government to win in this civil strife.

Source: Documents on British Foreign Policy, London 1949 (1936–37), vol. XVII, Document no. 348, pp. 495–6.

The impact of Soviet intervention

It is well known that Soviet involvement was a complicated affair that had both positive and negative consequences for the Republic. On the one hand, Soviet military aid – later underwritten by the transfer of the bulk of Spain's enormous gold reserves – undoubtedly saved the Republicans from certain defeat in the early months of the war. This is illustrated by the famous Battle of Madrid, during which Soviet planes, arms, and military advisers played a major role in thwarting the Nationalists' bid to take the capital. Soviet advisers, including both military and NKVD agents, used the commissariat, police, and other means to penetrate every layer of the Republic's military apparatuses. Without doubt their presence shored up the infrastructure of the Popular Army, enabling it to continue fighting against the generally superior Nationalist forces until late in the war.

Yet there is also little doubt that Soviet assistance came at a high price. Above all, Soviet intervention had an enormous impact on the general course of Republican affairs. Before the war, the Spanish Communist Party (PCE) was a relatively minor force on the left. But using the leverage they obtained from Soviet support, the communists quickly saw their political fortunes reversed. For example, in their campaign to build a Popular Front army, the communists could count on the help of experienced Soviet and communist *apparatchiks* in securing for themselves a commanding role in the Republican army. The formation of the communist-controlled International Brigades in October 1936 also greatly contributed to the rise of the PCE's influence over military operations. Numbering between forty thousand and sixty thousand men and women, the International Brigades were made up of volunteers from some fifty-nine countries who went to Spain, not just to support the aims of international communism but to do what they could to stop the spread of fascism. As we shall see, from the time they arrived in October 1936 until the last unit left Spain in November 1938, the International Brigades played an important role in nearly every major military campaign of the war.

The Spanish Communists benefited from the support of the International Brigades in several ways, but above all because the volunteers helped the Communists expand their power and influence in military matters. The Spanish communists took full advantage of Soviet presence in their rivalry with other parties. The most notorious of these contests pitted the communists against the POUM, the anti-Stalinist Marxist-Leninist party that George Orwell made famous in *Homage to Catalonia*. Backed by the extensive network of NKVD agents and the highly effective propaganda machine of the Communist International, the communists successfully silenced not only the POUM but also the voices of all Republican groups that dared to challenge their agenda. The result was that the communists became the most potent political force on the Republican side.

To say that the Soviet Union was largely responsible for the meteoric rise of communist power and influence during the Civil War is not to deny the role of other important factors. Certainly the relative strengths and weaknesses of their principal rivals contributed to their ascendancy. For example, the socialists were unable to provide effective leadership during the war because their movement was hopelessly divided into warring factions. Largo Caballero, the veteran trade-union leader and socialist premier from September 1936 to May 1937, not only resisted the communists' efforts to establish their hegemony but also opposed the moderate socialists who supported them. The anarchosyndicalist movement was also fractured along several ideological fault-lines. Those who decided to compromise libertarian principles in order to co-operate with the Popular Front parties drove a wedge between themselves and the purist elements. The latter were loath to abandon classical anarchist beliefs and values, arguing that fighting the Nationalists was meaningless if the revolution did not go forward. These splits inevitably weakened their position vis-à-vis the communists and other political rivals.

It should also be pointed out in this connection that the divisions referred to here predated the war and were in fact symptomatic of the Spanish left even before the creation of the PCE in 1921. On the other hand, it would be misleading to explain the failure of the various non-communist movements to check the prodigious growth of communism during the war solely in terms of these structural flaws. Were it not for the backing they received from the Soviet Union and its international organizations (support which was vital to the success of their predatory behaviour towards their key rivals), it is highly unlikely that the communists would have been catapulted into a position of political dominance during the last year and a half of the war (Document 5.12).

Document 5.12 Snapshot of Soviet Military Aid to the Republic

Estimates of Soviet war material supplied to the Spanish Republicans as found in numerous publications between 1950 and 1996:

Aircraft	1,000–1,400
Tanks	c.900
Armoured cars	c.300
Artillery pieces	1,500–c.2,000
Machine-guns	c.30,000
Rifles	c.500,000

Plus huge quantities of munitions and military equipment of all kinds.

Soviet war material supplied to the Spanish Republicans, as shown by the documents in the Russian State Military Archives (RGVA). Material sent in 1939 excluded:

Aircraft	623 plus 4 UTI trainers
Tanks	331
Armoured cars	60
Artillery:	
Field-guns	302 (− 30)
Howitzers	191 (− 8)
Mine-throwers	4
Anti-aircraft guns	64
Infantry-support and anti-tank guns,	
37 mm and 45 mm	427
Grenade-throwers	240 or 340
Small arms:	
Machine-guns	15,008 (− 2,430)
Rifles	379,645 (− 85,000)

N.B. Figures in parenthesis show material that did not come from the USSR. Total medium and light artillery = 493 pieces.

Source: Howson, G. (1998) *Arms for Spain*, London, pp. 141–2.

Non-government responses

In sharp contrast to the pragmatic and calculating attitudes of their governments, individuals and civilian groups from around the globe responded to the Spanish Civil War with a strong sense of idealism and moral commitment. Everyone, from the average citizen to Hollywood stars, seemed to have an opinion on the war. Rallies, street demonstrations, newspapers, pamphlets, and the radio became the principal vehicles for expressing concerns about the issues thrown up by Spain's struggles. The debates and discussion aroused by the war revealed that public opinion was not only polarized but also clouded by emotions and passions. Most saw the conflict as a Manichean struggle in which the meaning of the war was reduced to one-dimensional terms like Christianity versus Communism or fascism versus democracy. Some people, like those who joined the now legendary International Brigades, felt compelled to act on their convictions by going to Spain to fight. Others, like many journalists, writers, intellectuals, and artists, became participants of sorts by lending their celebrity to whichever cause they supported. Stage and film actors were, like the Hollywood stars of today, particularly successful at drawing attention to the plight of the Spaniards since they could exploit their easy access to the public media. The vast majority of those who took a stand on the Spanish Civil War sympathized with the Republican cause. Writers George Orwell, W.H. Auden, Ernest Hemingway, John Dos Passos, Dorothy Parker, and Langston Hughes; artists Henry Moore and Ben Shahn; and actors Errol Flynn, Paul Robeson, Joan Crawford, and Shirley Temple were among the many famous people of their era who rallied behind the Republicans.

To liberals and leftists the Spanish Civil War became the test case for the future of democracy. The triumph of the 'fascism' in Spain was thus seen by them as the beginning of the end of liberal-democratic regimes in Europe and beyond. Conservatives and the majority of Catholics naturally rejected this reading of the Civil War. For them, Spain's struggle was not about the fate of democracy but about the preservation of Western spiritual and social values against the onslaught of communist paganism and collectivism. In their eyes, the anti-clerical fury that left thousands of clergy men and women dead and the revolutionary workers' expropriation of countless business enterprises testified to the validity of their interpretation of events.

Public interest in the war was kept alive by the many dramatic episodes of the war. The atrocities committed at Badajoz and Guernica and major sieges such as those that took place at Toledo's Alcázar and Madrid were widely reported in the international press. Civilian groups from around Europe and the Americas also became directly involved in the welfare of the innocent victims of war, particularly children orphaned by the fighting. During the siege of Bilbao, foreign relief agencies such as the Basque Children's Relief Committee in Britain helped to evacuate several thousand Basque children, many of whom were taken in by families for the duration of the war.

Popular interest in the Civil War also stemmed from humanitarian impulses. A variety of non-government international organizations were involved in relief work in Spain. Some, like the British-based Society of Friends and Save the Children Fund, were interested in providing assistance to the victims of war regardless of which side they were on. More commonly, however, humanitarian relief was channelled by parties and agencies in a partisan political direction. A number of the humanitarian relief organizations in Britain and the United States – the Spanish Medical Aid Committee and the North American Committee to Aid Spanish Democracy, among many others – were affiliated with the Communist International. Similar organizations were set up by conservative and Catholic groups, though, like their left-wing counterparts, their 'humanitarian' interests lay primarily with the side they supported.

The coming of the Second World War

As the war dragged on, the political spotlight shifted away from Spain and towards other, more menacing events. In March 1938 Hitler ordered his troops into Austria and, without firing a shot, managed to annex Austria as the first step in his long-range goal to expand the Nazi empire. A few months later Hitler once again captured the headlines when he threatened to go to war over an area of Czechoslovakia. Hitler's tactics forced not only Britain, France, and Italy but also the rest of the world to take heed of his reckless attempts to redefine the boundaries of Europe.

Against this ominous background, general interest in the Spanish Civil War faded rapidly. In April 1939 the Nationalists defeated the Republicans, and General Franco became dictator of Spain. Then, with the outbreak of the Second World War in

September 1939, Spain fell even further from the limelight. While much of the world was enmeshed in this century's most devastating conflict, Spain's citizens were too emotionally exhausted and physically depleted of resources to become involved in another war.

Race, religion and gender | **6**

In most general narratives of the Spanish Civil War one rarely finds an analysis of the social and cultural factors relating to the categories of race, religion and gender. This is true despite the growing interest being shown in developing an interdisciplinary approach to the study of these themes in other periods of Spanish history. In this chapter a special effort has been made to highlight the different and often contradictory messages relating to race, gender and religion that were to be found on both the Nationalist and Republican sides. By doing so, it is hoped that some light will be shed on the differing ways in which social values and practices relating to these complex issues were refracted through the lenses of the political cultures that were constructed during the Civil War.

Race and war

It was a peculiarity of the Spanish Civil War that, even though it was primarily a domestic conflict which pitted Spaniards against Spaniards, it developed into a struggle with racial dimensions. On one level, this was due to Moroccan intervention in the Nationalist war effort. The Moors had long been viewed as a menacing outsider in Spain, and it was this belief that largely shaped the racialist responses to their involvement in the war. The participation of African Americans and African volunteers in the Republican army, which was partly motivated by their identification of fascism with racism, also reflected the extent to which race was embedded in the ideological disputes that helped to define the two opposing sides.

From the outset of the rebellion, Moorish *tabores* (companies) of *regulares* and *mehallas* (militia) attached to the Army of Africa fought alongside the insurgents who seized control of Spain's Moroccan Protectorate. Moorish troops were then airlifted to the mainland, where their forces were rapidly reorganized and expanded In the course of the war, some sixty thousand to seventy thousand Moroccans served in the Nationalist army, the vast majority of whom were used as shock troops in nearly every major engagement of the conflict.

That Islamic tribesmen under Spanish colonial control were prepared to sacrifice their lives for a movement that projected itself as a Christian crusade was one of the true paradoxes of the Civil War. Yet the reasons for Moroccan involvement are understandable, if not entirely logical from an ideological perspective. Formal Moroccan ties to the Spanish army can be traced to 1911, when General Berenguer organized the first company of Moorish volunteers. This development inevitably gave rise to a contradictory situation in which Moroccan members of the Army of Africa were from then on used to repress the anti-colonial aspirations of indigenous forces.

The colonial wars proved to be a particularly brutal contest in which Moroccan troops on both sides earned a reputation as being both fearless and ruthless fighters. This image fitted the demonized stereotype which Moors had long been saddled with in Christian Spain. Not surprisingly, then, the vast majority of Spaniards came to regard even the Moroccan soldiers who fought in their army as a fearsome breed of bloodthirsty warriors. Spanish authorities later exploited this widely held view, such as during the infamous Asturian repression of 1934 when *regulares* were sent up from Africa in order to terrorize local populations into submission.

The outbreak of civil war afforded the insurgents based in Africa the opportunity to employ Moroccans as a special fighting force. The advantage of using them was twofold. Not only were they among the best trained soldiers in the Spanish army, but their macabre reputation could be used as a psychological weapon to generate fear and panic among the troops and civilian inhabitants of the opposing side.

Throughout the war, the Nationalists could count on a constant supply of Moroccan volunteers. Recruitment was made possible by several factors. First, Franco himself seems to have commanded the loyal following of a number of Moroccan tribesmen, especially among those who saw him as the divinely inspired leader of a Christian jihad against the godless forces of the Republic (Document 6.1). Others participated in the war because they were coerced into doing so. This was especially true late in the war, when an increasing number of Moroccans faced being arrested, imprisoned, or summarily executed if they deserted or refused to join the crusade.[1] Most of those who volunteered for service, however, did so for economic reasons. The war broke out in the wake of a series of poor harvests which had ushered in a period of hard times throughout the zone of Spanish occupation. The promise of high wages and steady pay was thus the biggest incentive for enlisting in Franco's army.

Document 6.1 Nationalists defend Moorish involvement

(a)

The Madrid government then attempted to stir up the Moroccan tribes. They were stirred up over the radio with rabid speeches in Arabic, undesirables were bribed, and agents were sent out to foment insurrection. It was all in vain. Morocco remained loyal to the army. The Moors reverenced Franco, whose military prowess overawed them. They called him 'The Victorious,' 'Chief of Chiefs,' 'The Sacred One,' and 'Bold as the Lion.'

Source: Arrarás, J. (1938) *Francisco Franco*, London, p. 202.

(b)

The use of Moorish troops

General Franco and his colleagues have been criticised for employing Moorish troops against the white troops of the Communists. The misunderstanding in regard to this has been carefully fostered.

The Spanish Foreign Legion and the 'Regulares' are an integral part of the Spanish Regular Army. The Foreign Legion is entirely recruited from Spaniards, except as to about 8 to 9 per cent of foreigners, no foreigners being enlisted after expiration of their service. The 'Regulares' are Moors who enlist voluntarily under Spanish officers; their discipline is excellent.

When it is remembered that, during the war of 1914–18, Great Britain, France, and America all used coloured troops, Indian, Algerian, and Negro, it is rather difficult to understand the moral indignation professed in certain quarters against the employment of the Moorish troops.

Source: O'Duffy, E. (1938) *Crusade in Spain*, Clonskeagh, p. 27.

To justify their recruitment of Moroccans in their holy crusade against fellow Spaniards, the Nationalists and their supporters were obliged to project a positive view of their Islamic ally. Pro-Nationalist propaganda, for example, attempted to deconstruct the Moroccan soldier as a menacing outsider or 'other' by attributing to him the racial and cultural traits of the Western European (Document 6.2). It was an ideological project that was clearly at odds with the army's attempts to trade on the vicious stereotype of the Moor in their campaign of terror and repression against the Republicans.

Document 6.2 Racial profile of Moors

In my younger days I laboured under a very false impression that the Moors were savages, without culture or civilisation, and not until I went to Spain was the idea altogether dispelled.

The Moors are not Negroes; the shape of the head, nose, and mouth, their hair and eyes, are more characteristic of the European. Many Moors are fairer in colour than either the Italian or the Spaniard. They are splendid soldiers, brave, loyal, reliable and well-disciplined.

Source: O'Duffy, E. (1938) *Crusade in Spain*, Clonskeagh, pp. 200–1.

Given their commitment to liberal and leftist principles it is perhaps more surprising that the Republicans constructed a racialist image of Moroccan participants. Drawing upon the popular European stereotype of Africans, Republican propaganda tended to portray the Moors as a racially inferior and culturally backward people. In poster art and political cartoons, for example, Moroccans were depicted as caricatures of the discriminatory image of the archetypical black African, someone who was thick-lipped, dark-skinned, and wide-eyed. In their effort to solicit foreign sympathy for their cause, Republican and pro-Republican publications also promoted the image of the Moroccan as a barbarian invader (Document 6.3).

Document 6.3 Republican images of Moorish invaders

(a)

I appeal to the universal conscience against the monstrous fact that traitor generals in rebellion should utilize black mercenary forces to combat, harass and murder their own compatriots. Imagine the indignation of the British people, if British generals paid by the people, who had sworn loyalty to the Empire, should transport to their country black colonial forces, to be launched against their compatriots, who had democratically elected a Government, and their bombs and shells should reach Piccadilly Circus? Is not the case of the Republic, that of our Basque Country a problem of universal value? How long will the silence of the voices with authority, those which represent the universal conscience, continue?

Source: An Address by His Excellency the President of the Government of Euzkadi H.E. José A. de Aguirre. Broadcast from Radio Euzkadi, 22 December 1936.

(b)

The sexual question has also a certain military importance. In the small towns hitherto occupied by the Rebels, the commanders of the Moorish detachments have had in some cases to share out the captured women supporters of the Government among the Moors in the ration of only one woman to twenty men. It is naturally expected that in Madrid there will be many more women available. Moorish prisoners state that this expectation is of very considerable value in keeping up the spirit of the African section of the invading troops.

Source: 'Spain: American Friends of Spanish Democracy' (n.d.), *The Week* (New York), 6.

(c)

Cast your eyes for one moment on that tragic pyramid of grotesques: generals, bishops, Moors, Carlists in red berets they are like some fantastic mumming-show of Death.

You have placed in the barbarous hands of Legionaries and Moors the sacred vessels, the riches and treasure which you never offered to your people, the poor, the disinherited, the hungry. And you either give these things as sacrilegious booty, or to convert them into weapons dealing death to your people and your flock.

Source: Bergamin, J. (1936) Radio broadcast, 20 September 1936, from *Catholics and the Civil War in Spain*, London, pp. 11–12.

Notwithstanding their blinkered attitude towards Moroccans, Republicans saw themselves and were generally perceived by others as the defenders of liberal, progressive values when it came to issues involving race. Outside of Spain, this view owed a great deal to the propagandizing efforts of the international communist movement. Much of the communist literature of the day focusing on the 'Negro' question offered a class analysis of racial discrimination and exploitation under capitalism that equated fascism with racism. Blacks inside the movement, such as Walter Garland, an African-American soldier in the International Brigades, uncritically accepted this interpretation. According to him, the social, political, and economic oppression of blacks in America was 'nothing more than a very concrete form, the clearest expression, of fascism'.[2] Italy's recent invasion of Ethiopia was cited by others as a motive for taking up arms against fascism in Spain, an attitude famously summed up by a writer who reputedly quipped: 'This aint Ethiopia, but it'll do' (Document 6.4). Thus, black volunteers from Africa, Europe, and the Americas who had been recruited through the Comintern and its affiliate organizations came to Spain precisely because they believed that taking a stand against the Nationalists was equivalent to fighting Jim Crow politics in America and fascist imperialism in Africa.

Document 6.4 From Ethiopia to Spain

Most Blacks saw the war in Ethiopia as merely another malicious attempt by whites to destroy Blacks.

Ethiopia had been defeated by Mussolini's troops and modern air force. The League of Nations looked the other way while Haile Selassie fled into exile and another piece of Africa was colonized. The date was May 2, 1936, scarcely ten weeks before the Spanish fascist's rebellion.

Source: Yates, J. (1986) *Mississippi to Madrid*, New York, pp. 94–5.

At least for this small group of politically conscious men and women (perhaps numbering around a hundred) their experiences in Spain were largely positive ones. Black volunteers and visitors rarely suffered the kind of racial discrimination that was common in the United States and elsewhere at the time. And, apart from those occasions when they were mistaken as Moors, blacks were warmly received by the Spanish people. Moreover, thanks to the multi-ethnic tolerance shown in the Republican army, blacks not only served in fully integrated military and medical units (a feat not achieved until after the Second World War in the United States) but also managed, in the cases of Oliver Law and Walter Garland, to rise to a position of authority over white Europeans (Document 6.5).

Document 6.5 Anti-Semitism in the International Brigades

The nationality question is the weakest spot in the international units and is the main hindrance impeding the growth of our potential. Very little is said about relations between the nationalities within the international units, or, more truthfully, it is completely hushed up, but it is just this [problem] that gives rise to almost all our weaknesses.

The francophobia was most transparently obvious, for instance (although it is difficult to see why, when in all the brigades it was precisely the French who filled in all of the most unpleasant 'holes' during battle), anti-Semitism flourished (and indeed it still has not been completely extinguished), but in general this was, if one can talk like this, a family quarrel, very diligently hidden from strangers', that is, Spanish, eyes. However, the conditions of that period allowed neither the time nor the opportunity to investigate thoroughly this veiled issue.

Source: Radosh, R., Habeck, M. R. and Sevostianov, G. (eds) (2001) *Spain Betrayed: The Soviet Union in the Spanish Civil War*, New Haven, pp. 448–9.

Despite the limited success they enjoyed in overcoming racial barriers of their era, blacks who volunteered to go to Spain had little impact on the overall development of race relations in the countries from which they hailed. This was true in part because they constituted only a tiny fraction of the overall number of foreigners who went to Spain during war and partly because of their association with the international communist movement. In the latter case, the achievements of blacks were generally ignored by a mostly anti-communist public who tended to believe that black involvement in Spain was little more than a communist propaganda exercise that aimed to win over minorities in countries such as the United States. In the end, even the singer/actor Paul Robeson, an internationally renowned African American who was not afraid to use his celebrity to highlight the social issues at stake in the Spanish Civil War, found that his message was obscured by his affiliation with the communist cause (Document 6.6).

Document 6.6 An Anti-fascist Speaks Out against Racism

'What reasons led you to come to Spain.'

'My devotion to democracy,' he answers rapidly. 'As an artist, I know that it is dishonourable to put yourself on a plane above the masses, without marching at their side, participating in their anxieties and sorrows, since we artists owe everything to the masses, from our formation to our well-being; and it is not only as an artist that I love the cause of democracy in Spain, but also as a Black. I belong to an oppressed race, discriminated against, one that could not live if fascism triumphed in the world. My father was a slave, and I do not want my children to become slaves . . . During these last months I have worked a great deal in London, singing to raise funds to send to the Spanish people, and I will continue doing it, not only there, but everywhere that I am able to do it.'

Source: Foner, P. S. (ed.) (1978) *Paul Robeson Speaks: Writings, Speeches, Interviews, 1918–1974*, New York, pp. 124–5.

The same internationalist spirit that drew black volunteers to Spain was shared by Jews who rallied to the Republican cause.[3] While many of those who enlisted in the International Brigades did not identify themselves as religious Jews, they were none the less the targets of racism. In the case of the Jewish volunteers, however, perse-cution was not based so much on skin colour but on the fact that, for cultural, social, and political reasons, they were regarded as outsiders in Germany and elsewhere in Europe where national identity was constructed around race or ethnicity. The some seven thousand to ten thousand Jewish volunteers from Europe and the United States thus saw the Spanish conflict as part of the larger struggle that involved Jews as well as all minority groups that were being menaced by the racist agenda being promoted by fascist movements (Document 6.7).

Document 6.7 Jewish Motives for Fighting against Franco

(a)

Madrid, 1937

I came to Spain because I felt I had to. Look at the world situation. We didn't worry when Mussolini came to power in Italy. We felt bad when Hitler became Chancellor of Germany, but what could we do? We felt – though we tried to help and sympathize – that it was their problem and wouldn't affect us. Then the fascist governments sent out agents and began to gain power in other countries.

Seeing all these things – how fascism is grasping power in many countries (including the U.S., where there are many Nazi organizations and Nazi agents and spies) – can't you see that fascism is our own problem – that it may come to us as it came to other countries? And don't you realize that we Jews will be the first to suffer if fascism comes?

But if we didn't see clearly the hand of Mussolini and Hitler in all these countries, in Spain we can't help seeing it.

Together with their agent, Franco, they are trying to set up the same anti-progressive, anti-Semitic regime in Spain, as they have in Italy and Germany.

If we sit by and let them grow stronger by taking Spain, they will move on to France and will not stop there; and it won't be long before they get to America.

Realizing this, can I sit by and wait until the beasts get to my very door – until it is too late, and there is no one I can call on for help? And would I even deserve help from others when the trouble comes upon me, if I were to refuse help to those who need it today? If I permitted such a time to come – and as a Jew and a progressive, I would be among the first to fall under the axe of the fascists – all I could do then would be to curse myself and say, 'Why didn't I wake up when the alarm-clock rang?'

Source: From a letter by Hyman Katz, 25 November 1937. Reprinted in Nelson, C. and Hendricks, J. (eds) *Madrid 1937: Letters of the Abraham Lincoln Brigade from the Spanish Civil War*, London and New York: Routledge, 1996.

(b)

Fascism, breeder of the most vicious anti-Semitism, is being fought in Spain. Anti-fascists the world over have come to Spain to fight their enemies. Jews the world over have also come, conscious of the fact that a defeat of Italy, Germany and Fascism in Spain is an integral part of the world struggle against anti-Semitism.

Source: Singerman, R. (1977) 'American–Jewish Reactions to the Spanish Civil War', *Journal of Church and State*, vol. 19, no. 2, 268.

The idealism of the Jewish volunteers was, at least for some, leavened by their personal encounters with anti-Semitic volunteers from various European countries. Such discriminatory behaviour obviously violated the internationalist principles of the brigades and was therefore frowned upon by communist commanders (Document 6.8). In any case, manifestations of racism were treated as an 'internal' matter within the units and thus publicly did not mar the International Brigades' reputation as being a classless and prejudice-free organization. None the less, the varying degrees of prejudice exhibited towards the Jews and other ethnic groups within the IBs illustrates the complex nature of the race issue during the war. Above all, it also demonstrates that, in many instances involving the day-to-day operations of the war, it was difficult even for the ideologically committed to live up to the principles of their own doctrine.

Document 6.8 Racial Tensions Inside International Brigade Units

An even more serious offence in the International Brigades was racism, but there was little evidence of this. The British Battalion contained many members of the Irish Republican Army and there were also a number of Jews, mainly from Manchester, Leeds and London. In the Washington-Lincoln Battalion there were Jews and Negroes. In the Canadian Mackenzie-Papineau Battalion there were French Canadians and Finns. In the International Brigades all were equal, and I seldom came across any serious friction between men of different race or nationality.

Source: Jump, J.R., in Toynbee, P. (ed.) (1976) *The Distant Drum: Reflections on the Spanish Civil War*, London, p. 117.

The Church in war and revolution

Following the introduction of liberal and left-wing doctrines into the Spanish arena, the Catholic Church became progressively estranged from certain sectors of the population. This was partly due to the policies and practices of the Church itself, which, from the late nineteenth century on, tended to adopt an embattled attitude towards all those secularizing groups in Spanish society who sought to diminish its power and influence. The Church's persistent fear of losing the contest which pitted the forces of Catholic spirituality against those of materialism drove it to seek the protection and support of the monarchy and Spain's traditional economic and political ruling classes. It was thus widely perceived among the rural and industrial workers who had fallen under the influence of left-wing ideologies as an extension of the oppressive state system which they were striving to overthrow.

Over time conflicts between the Church and its secular opponents grew both in their frequency and in their intensity. One particularly violent episode in this ever escalating cycle of hostilities occurred during the so-called Tragic Week of 1909. Though this five-day period of rioting in Barcelona was triggered by a crisis over Spain's colonial role in Morocco, workers expressed the depth of their hatred towards the Church by destroying dozens of churches, convents, and other Catholic buildings. Such bloody confrontations served only to deepen the distrust between the Church on the one side and their liberal and left-wing opponents on the other. This was especially apparent during the Second Republic (1931–36), when the battle lines between the pro- and anti-Catholic segments of society finally hardened.

The degree to which the Spanish working classes and peasantry were alienated from the Church was strikingly revealed during the opening phases of the Civil War and July Revolution. Given its strong political and institutional ties to the military and civilian organizations which launched the armed rising against the Republic, it is not surprising that the Catholic Church became a chief target of the revolutionary elements of the pro-Republican forces. Led by the anarchosyndicalists of the CNT-FAI, these groups mounted a murderous onslaught on representatives of the Catholic Church. Some 4,100 priests and over 2,600 male and female ecclesiastical personnel were slaughtered during July and August of 1936, making this anti-clerical fury the worst of its kind in modern European history.

The two Catholic Spains

The Civil War had a profound impact on Spain's Catholic community. Above all it deepened political divisions among Catholics, particularly within the Church hierarchy, that had been developing in the years leading up to the Civil War. On the one side, were traditional Catholics who had condemned the secularizing policies of the Republic, which they believed had undermined not only the spiritual life of society but also the core identity of all Spaniards. Understandably, this group of Catholics immediately sided with the rebels when they rose up against the secular Republic in July 1936. At the end of September, an official justification for the Church's support of the Nationalist cause came from the Bishop of Salamanca, Enrique Plá y Deniel. In his pastoral letter entitled 'The Two Cities', Plá pictured the war as a genuine crusade (*la cruzada*) against communism, an analogy that was later adopted by other Catholic spiritual leaders and even by Francisco Franco himself. In the latter case, this was because Franco wanted to be seen not as a renegade military leader but as the head of a national movement that was defending both Catholic Spain and the Christian values of Western civilization.[4]

In their interpretation of the war as a modern-day crusade, the Church's leaders could count on the support of the various Nationalist political factions, all of whom saw the defence of religion as being bound up with their efforts not only to preserve the country's Catholic identity but also to defend private property, the family, and Spain's traditional institutions. In this sense, religion became the ideological glue that held together the various right-wing groups on the Nationalist side.

Not surprisingly, pro-Republican Catholics interpreted the war differently, and thus challenged this blatant attempt to dress up the military coup in 'spiritual' clothing (Document 6.9). While most Catholics abhorred the violent outbursts directed against the clergy and Church during the first months of the Civil War, these tragic episodes did not turn all of them against the Republican cause. For some liberal-minded Catholics in particular the assault against the Church was regrettable but entirely understandable given that they believed that the powerful elites – including the Church hierarchy – in Spanish society had, over the course of many years, imposed excessive burdens on the oppressed classes. The Church had incurred the wrath of the poor, it was argued, precisely because it had consistently supported these ruling powers instead of assisting the victims of an unjust socio-economic system. They were supportive of the Republican cause because it promoted the very values and beliefs that aimed to bridge the 'infinite gulfs' that existed between Spain's haves and have-nots (Document 6.10).

Document 6.9 A Catholic Clergyman Rejects the Notion of a Holy War

A Holy War? Them, it is not possible to abstain from it? It is not possible to condemn this fearful war? Must the Christian teaching of peace and brotherhood and charity be refused and denied for an action of violence and blood? A Holy War? . . .

A Holy War? Then the great mass which struggles against the 'Nationalists', the half of Spain, almost the entire population of the workers – are these to be, for us Christians, souls damned beyond hope or redemption, fanatical desperados, fit only for fire and death?

Do not these paradoxical conclusions prove clearly enough that the question has been badly stated, that we have no right to speak of a Holy War?

Above the political question, we are faced with a much graver question of conscience, which we must decide with serenity, by reason, and without prejudice.

Source: Rocafull, J. M. G., Canon of Cordova Cathedral (1936) in *Catholics and the Civil War in Spain*, London.

Document 6.10 Republican workers and Catholicism

(a)

Father Leocadio Lobo Defends the Spanish Workers

The Spanish people has been and always will be a GOOD people.

'They do not believe, you say? They have become pagan? They are Marxist?

'They are against an absurd and brutal economic system? Then I am with them, for the Church has long been with them in this.

'They demand social justice, the lessening or the total disappearance of the infinite gulfs between those who have all and those who have nothing? Then they are right, and because they are right they must demand, and claim, and insist, and prevent the continuance of this wrong state.

Source: Lobo, L. (1936) in *Catholics and the Civil War in Spain*, London, p. 9.

(b)

We, the Catholics, are not only tolerated and accepted by the people sympathetic with the government in Spain, but we are welcomed by them enthusiastically.

The first time after the rebellion that I spoke at a meeting I was a little nervous as to what my reception, as a Catholic, would be. Immense overflowing enthusiasm stilled all my doubts. The same things always happen. The people see the official church as the ally and the friend of its oppressors. Religion means money, power, domination, inhumanity, capitalism, fascism. The anti-clericals were, at least until recently, very moderate, rather in the style of Lerroux. They were neither Socialists nor Communists. The youth of Spain . . . had passed beyond the anti-clerical state of mind. And if this hatred of the clericals returned it was self-provoked before the elections. A certain Bishop in Catalonia distinguished himself by his violence against the Popular Front and against democracy, and insisted that Christ was with the Rightists.

Source: Bergamin, J. (1937) in *Catholics Speak for Spain*, New York, pp. 16–17.

Popular Front supporters constituted yet another group of Republicans who did not see the war as a struggle against religion in general and Catholicism in particular. After the tide of revolution had receded and the moderate forces were in the ascendant, Republican authorities went to great lengths to play down its anti-clerical past and project a pro-Catholic image to the outside world. This was particularly true after the Popular Front government under Juan Negrín was formed in May 1937. One of the main aims of his anti-revolutionary administration was to present the Republic as a democratic regime that respected the fundamental freedoms of a liberal society, including that of religion. To this end, the government enlisted the support of prominent Catholic propagandists such as the polemical José Bergamín, the editor of the influential Catholic review *Cruz y Raza*.

The divisions within the Spanish Church were further complicated by the regionalist issue. Both Catalan and Basque Catholics who supported regional autonomy and/or separatism tended to be pro-Republican. This was primarily because both groups believed that it was only in the context of the kind of cultural and democratic pluralism promised by a federal form of republicanism that they could give full expression to their respective regional identities. During the war, the alliance formed between Catholic regionalists and the secular defenders of the Republic presented an especially thorny dilemma for the Nationalists, who were adamantly opposed to the 'separatist' movements that threatened Spain's unity. An exchange between José Antonio de Aguirre, the president of the autonomous Basque state (Euzkadi), and the Cardinal Primate of Spain, Cardinal Gomá y Tomás, highlighted the ideological differences separating the two camps (Document 6.11). For his part, Aguirre defended the Republic on the grounds that the Civil War was not a religious struggle but rather a conflict between two diametrically opposed political systems, democracy and fascism. He also criticized the Church hierarchy for remaining silent while the side they supported used bullets and bombs against innocent civilians (Document 6.12). In January 1937, Gomá y Tomás, appointed by the Pope as the 'official agent' of the Holy See, defended the pro-Nationalist clergy in an Open Letter to Aguirre. According to this, the war was not about class or politics but a confrontation between two irreconcilable civilizations: Catholic Spain and the godless, materialist anti-Spain of the liberals and Marxist 'Reds'.[5]

Document 6.11 The Sources of Anti-clericalism

It is, basically, a war of love or hatred for religion. The love for the God of our fathers has placed weapons in the hands of half Spain, irrespective of less spiritual motives in the war; hatred whipped up against God has placed weapons in the hands of the other half. And thus the camps turned into churches, the religious fervour, the feeling of providence on one side; on the other, thousands of priests murdered and churches destroyed, the satanic fury, the drive against all signs of religion. And now a hundred and two atheists have come from Russia to give doctrinal form to this great religio-social ruin.

Source: Aguirre Prado, L. (1965) *The Church and the Spanish War*, Madrid, pp. 23 and 25

Document 6.12 Religion and the War against Social Injustice

The struggle now taking place in the Spanish Republic, let the entire world know it, is not a religious war, as they would have you believe: it is a war of an economic type, of an archaic economic type, it is a war of social content. It is not a religious war, nor can Christian doctrine be invoked, because the Christian doctrine is one of love, peace and renouncement in favour of one's fellow beings; the Christian doctrine is one and inflexible and it cannot be utilized as a means when convenient and trampled down when [in]convenient.

Source: An Address by the President of the Government of Euzkadi, H.E. José A. de Aguirre. Broadcast from Radio Euzkadi, 22 December 1936.

The Nationalist invasion of the Basque region in early 1937 brought the political conflict of these two Catholic communities into sharper focus. For his part, Franco was determined to use force to resolve the Basque question. His intransigence on this point not only reinforced the divide within the Spanish Church but also caused the international Catholic community and particularly the Vatican to withhold their unconditional support of the Nationalist cause. When Franco's military campaign resulted in the arrest and assassination of Basque priests and the bombing of civilians in Durango, Guernica, and other Basque towns, the controversy over the Basque issue heated up. In the wake of these highly publicized events, a significant number of foreign Catholics in France, Britain and the United States turned against the Nationalists, condemning them for their brutal massacre of a 'Christian people'.

It was against this background that Cardinal Gomá was asked by Franco to prepare an address which formally expressed this interpretation of the war to the outside world. The collective pastoral letter he issued to the bishops of the entire Catholic Church on 1 July 1937 sought to justify the Church hierarchy's pro-Nationalist position as well as to defend their active role in supporting Franco and his troops (Document 6.13). Citing the Nationalists' unsubstantiated claim that the July rebellion was a response to the Communist International's plans to spearhead a revolution in Spain, the pastoral letter pointed out that, since both the representatives and institutions of Christendom were under attack, it was necessary to conduct an armed crusade against the barbarities of communism. Only by defeating these anti-Spanish and Christian forces, it was further argued, would peace and justice be restored to a divided nation.

Document 6.13 Justifying the Holy War against the Republic

Our country is undergoing a profound upheaval; it is not only one of the bloodiest of civil wars which fills us with tribulation, it is a tremendous commotion which is shaking the very foundations of social life, and has put in danger our very existence as a nation. You have understood it, Venerable Brethren, and 'Your words and your heart have opened unto us'.

The nature of this Letter

This document will not be the demonstration of a thesis but a mere explanation, made rapidly, of the events which characterise our war and give it its historical complexion. The Spanish war is the result of the struggle between irreconcilable ideologies; in its very origins are involved the gravest questions of moral, juridical, religious, and historical order. It would not be difficult to develop the essential points of doctrine applied to our present situation . . .

The Church has neither wished for this war nor provoked it, and we do not think it necessary to vindicate her from the charge of belligerency with which the Spanish Church has been censured in foreign newspapers. It is true that thousands of her sons, obeying the promptings of their conscience and of their patriotism and under their own responsibility, revolted in arms in order to safeguard the principles of religion and Christian justice which had for ages informed the nation's life; but whoever accuses her of having provoked this war or of having conspired for it and even of not having done all that in her lay to avoid it, does not know or falsifies the reality.

Source: Aguirre Prado, L. (1965) *The Church and the Spanish War,* Madrid, pp. 28 and 30.

In the end, the opposing positions held by Spain's pro- and anti-Republican Catholic groups could not be reconciled. Because they insisted on interpreting the war as a contest between democracy and fascism, those who defended the Republic refused to accept the argument that the Nationalist cause was fighting a 'just war' that demanded the backing of the Catholic Church. On the other side, the Catholic community was convinced that the spiritual and physical regeneration of Spain could not come about until the enemies of the Church had been vanquished.

Women at war: Republican and Nationalist women

When the Civil War broke out in July 1936, Spanish society was still largely divided along traditional gender lines. This was true despite the liberal reforms initiated during the Second Republic (1931–36) which were aimed at expanding women's political and civil rights. For example, it was during this period that women were allowed for the first time to vote and obtain a legal divorce under certain conditions. But while the steps taken towards 'modernizing' females by granting them the legal status of men may have opened the door to greater gender equality, it did not bring about a fundamental shift in the pattern of male–female relations in Spanish society. In part this was due to the mixed reception such liberalizing efforts had on Spain's ideologically diverse and politically fragmented feminine community. For example, left-wing women who either belonged to or identified with the working classes saw their liberation in revolutionary rather than in liberal terms. Because they gave primacy to the class struggle, they tended to dismiss demands for women's suffrage and equal rights as bourgeois concerns that were aimed at furthering the interests of the dominant capitalist classes.

The political agenda defined by liberal feminist notions also did not resound with women activists who promoted nationalist or regionalist causes. As the historian Mary Nash has pointed out, the 'feminism' that developed among certain Catalan women was influenced more by their struggle for political nationalism and civil rights than by their commitment to the political emancipation of women per se.[6]

Conservative Catholic Spanish women rejected the liberal feminist model because it threatened to undermine their ties to the Catholic Church and other traditional institutions that had long defined a female's place in society. According to these, men were expected to dominate the public world of work and politics, whereas female activities were largely confined to the private or domestic realm. Thus the liberal effort to transform Spanish women into citizens of a secularized Republic threatened one of the core beliefs of many Catholic females, namely that a woman's primary duty as a 'Christian, wife and mother' was to play a central role in maintaining the sanctity of the family.

But irrespective of what views they held on women's issues and no matter how attached they were to the conventional views on male and female identities, women during the Second Republic found themselves playing a more public role in society. This was above all due to their changed political status. Now that they could influence the outcome of elections, women were increasingly mobilized into party organizations across the political spectrum. Even parties on the right, the conservative Catholic CEDA, for example, overcame their ideological aversion to women participating in politics by actively recruiting female members.

Ironically, women's increased visibility in the public arena was also due to their growing involvement in religious and social movements that were opposed to the progress of liberal feminism. As noted above, a number of Spanish women were hostile to progressive-minded policies which blurred the distinction between male and female roles. To prevent the further erosion of these boundaries, women activists on the right joined organizations such as the Falangist Sección Femenina and the Carlist Margaritas (Document 6.14). Falangist feminists in particular promoted a virulently anti-feminist ideology which argued for the submission of Spanish women to a bellicose male order.

Document 6.14 A Woman's Role in the Crusade against the Left

The good National-Syndicalist state rests on the family. It will be strong if the woman at home is healthy, fecund, hard-working and happy, with the windows of her home and soul open to the sweet imperial dawn that the sun of the Falange is bringing us.

Azul (Editorial on the 2nd national council of the women's section of the Falange, February 1938)

The Margaritas of Tafalla

Solemnly promise on the Sacred Heart of Jesus

1. To observe modesty in dress: long sleeves, high necks, skirts to the ankle, blouses full at the chest.

2. To read no novels, newspapers or magazines, to go to no cinema or theatre, without ecclesiastical licence.

3. Neither publicly nor in private to dance dances of this century but to study and learn the old dances of Navarre and Spain.

4. Not to wear makeup as long as the war lasts.

Long live Christ the King! Long live Spain!

Source: Fraser, R. (1979) *Blood of Spain: An Oral History of the Spanish Civil War*, New York, p. 309.

Following the outbreak of civil war on 18 July 1936, the public activities of all Spanish women were greatly expanded. This was especially true of women such as the anarchist Federica Montseny and the communist Dolores Ibárruri (better known as 'La Pasionaria') who were already playing prominent roles in political and social causes. Because the war was highly disruptive of domestic home-life, the majority of women were cast into unfamiliar roles. Some were drawn into 'men's work' in munitions factories and social services, and some briefly participated as combatants. But despite the increased visibility and involvement of women in public life, the fact remained that women themselves never exercised a significant influence over the conduct of war. This was above all due to the fact that men – whether on the left or the right – were often confused and conflicted about the place of women in it. Most were uncomfortable with the idea of women bearing arms and most assumed that women were by nature best suited to perform a supportive role in the war effort.

Nationalist women

From the outset of the rebellion, the Nationalists made it clear that their regime had a conservatively defined social agenda. Shortly after it was established, the Junta de Defensa Nacional took special aim at the liberal customs associated with the Second Republic by decreeing an end to divorce, civil marriages, and coeducation. The 'pagan' morality of the liberal Republic was also rejected in favour of one based exclusively on the teachings of the Catholic Church. This 'new' direction in social relations had obvious implications regarding the behaviour and treatment of women. Under Franco's rule, for example, women were required not only to respect the traditional hierarchy of gender in which women deferred to the masculine-dominated institutions of Church and state but also to play a private as opposed to a public role in society. Mothers and wives were expected to aspire to an ideal type of the Nationalist woman. According to this, she was supposed to accept her primary social duties, which were to reproduce and preserve the stability of the family. The Catholic Church instructed married women to aspire to the role of the *perfecta casada*, the loving and self-sacrificing wife who is devoted to the needs of her children and husband.

Given this rigid interpretation of a woman's position in society, it is scarcely surprising that Nationalist women were not allowed to express their sexual feelings publicly. A strict dress-code was therefore enforced for women of all ages. Wearing lipstick or provocative clothing were signs of loose morals and those caught dressing this way were branded accordingly. Unmarried women, particularly adolescents, were the main targets of the Church's propaganda campaign to provide moral guidance during a period when formal means of social controls were difficult to regulate. A stern reminder of how young women should conduct themselves at a time of national crisis can be found in a manifesto issued by the Catholic women of the Diocesan Union of Seville (Document 6.15).

Document 6.15 Public Behaviour of Nationalist Women

While our soldiers and volunteers working for God and our country are sacrificing their lives in the fields of battle, you, the woman of Spain who is dedicating yourself to personal pleasures, to flirting and falling into bad habits, you are: A traitor to your country, a traitor to your faith, contemptible to all and deserving of our repulsion.

Spanish woman, in these grave moments of our beloved country, your daily life should not be one of frivolity, but of austerity; your place is not at the movies, the public walkways and the cafes, but in church and at home. Your fineries and your dresses should not be in the obscene style of the French jewess and traitor, but in the modest and retiring style of the moral Christian, rather than exhibit salacious behaviour to stir up feelings of carnal desire, you should devote yourself to assuaging those suffering in the hospitals and homes. Your duty now is not to procure for yourself an easy life, but to educate your children, to sacrifice your pleasures in order to help Spain.

Source: Nationalist women, 'Spanish Woman', issued by the Catholic Union of Women of Seville, in Abella, R., *La vida cotidiana durante la guerra civil*, Barcelona, Planeta, 1973.

One irony associated with the Nationalist attitude towards women was the fact that prostitution flourished in the rearguard during the war. More so than representing a breakdown of morals or an incomplete imposition of the Nationalist code of behaviour, this practice was due to economic circumstances. Women who lost their husbands, brothers, and fathers could easily slip into poverty. (After all, women were being discouraged by the government from taking on the role as chief 'breadwinner' of the family.) The result was that a number of women were forced into selling their bodies in order to make ends meet – a reality that was generally ignored by the conservative men who paid for their services.

The Franco government attitude towards women was informed also by the fascist model. Like Mussolini, for example, Franco took steps to take women out of the workplace and factory and put them back in the home.[7] Both the March Labour Charter and the Fundamental Law of July 1938 made it clear that at least married women would be (1) freed from the public workplace and (2) no longer required to work in order for their families to receive a subsidy from the state (Document 6.16).

This did not mean that women were to be denied a role in the war effort. From the beginning, women were mobilized by ideological organizations such as the Carlist Margaritas or the Sección Femenina, the Falangist women's organization that was founded in 1934 and directed by Pilar Primo de Rivera, the sister of José Antonio. In October, 1937 a decree was passed that required all able-bodied women to support the Nationalist cause by enlisting in some type of social service. Unmarried women in particular were expected to assist in the running of youth centres, health services, and the physical education of children (Document 6.17). As the historian Aurora Morcillo has pointed out, this order was 'the first step towards the nationalization of Spanish women'.[8] Yet, as Morcillo also notes, the document itself contains conflicting ideological messages. At the same time that women were being told to join the war effort by participating in the public sphere, they were also being told to remember that their primary duties were to be mothers and supportive wives.

Document 6.16 Women and the Labour Force in the Nuevo Estado

The State promises to exercise a constant and effective action in defense of the worker, his life and his work. It will conveniently limit the length of the working day, so that hours of labor will not be excessive. It will provide work for all classes and offer guarantees of humane treatment. The State will prohibit night work for women and children, it will regulate piece work performed at home, and it will free the married women from workshops and factories.

Source: The Labor Charter for New Spain, issued 9 March 1938, Peninsular News Service, Inc.

Document 6.17 Welfare Role of Sección Femenina

The Woman's Section of the Spanish Traditionalist Phalanx, with Pilar Primo de Rivera at its head, is undoubtedly the leader of the organisations for women in National Spain. Its branch institution, the Sisterhood of City and Country (Hermandad de la Ciudad y del Campo) does a splendid work; the young girls place themselves at the service of those families, either in city or in country, who are in need of extra assistance, owing to the fact that the men whose hands had previously performed the tasks are now occupied fighting in the National trenches. Much good and important work has been accomplished during the past year; at the reaping of the large crops of grain in Castille, at the vintage of the grape and at the harvesting of the olive in the southern provinces, these 'sisters' are ever to be seen, full of life and enthusiasm, carrying out their duties to the letter and glad of the opportunity of lending a helping hand to their country.

And the Social Aid or Welfare Institution (Auxilio Social)! I should like to have several hours at my disposal to describe all its endless activities. It had its birth in Valladolid, under the direction of Mercedes Sanz Bachiller, and began by opening one dining-room in the city and ten in the villages of the province; now there are hundreds distributed throughout National Spain.

Source: Farmborough, F. (1938) *Life and People in National Spain,* London, p. 37.

The double-sided gender significance of this and other policies associated with activist Nationalist women has been underscored by recent research. According to the testimonies of surviving members of Sección Femenina, which was dissolved by the Spanish government in 1977, at least some of the women who belonged to the movement saw themselves as crusaders for 'social justice'. They were particularly interested in improving the welfare services and educational standards of the rural poor and other dispossessed elements in Spanish society (Document 6.18). Viewed in this way, it is apparent that the self-perception of some, if not all, members of SF was at odds with the image of women that was being projected by the male-dominated authorities of the Nationalist movement.

Document 6.18 Fascist Women in the Public Sphere

Social justice means that each child on being born has the same possibilities that other children have, without his birth having been privileged, or whatever, playing a part. It was José Antonio's, and it was ours: social justice before all . . . To educate so that a child who is born can have the same rights; but if he doesn't have sufficient formation, or sufficient education, he will always be on a lower level. Thus, for us, social justice begins with education . . .

In 1937 . . . the *Sección Femenina* realized that the role of women in Spain had to be revitalized. Women were relegated to be no more than . . . what they traditionally had been: in their homes, at their work. And the poor thing that remained single . . . ! Then the *Sección Femenina* realized that women did not participate . . . that culturally, they were very backward in relation to men; that there was much more illiteracy among women than among men; that women did not participate in sports, for example – except some select minorities, four *señoras* that played tennis, or rode horseback; that in health there were some huge problems due to the ignorance of the women of the common people, the working class women, who did not know how to care for their children; that there was a very high infant mortality rate in Spain.

Source: Enders, V. L. and Radcliff, P. B. (eds) (1999) *Constructing Spanish Womanhood: Female Identity in Modern Spain,* Albany, pp. 383 and 385.

Republican women

The gender question on the Republican side was complicated by the fact that the women's movement there was far from being homogenous. Republican women were grouped into various types of organizations, each reflecting a specific viewpoint regarding women's issues. Middle-class women's organizations tended to define feminism in terms that were at variance with working-class organizations. Thus, while the former accepted the liberal view that the emancipation of women necessarily involved a struggle for political or legal rights, working-class groups such as the anarchosyndicalist Mujeres Libres rejected both the practice and the ideas associated with the liberal feminist cause. Nationalism provided a further dividing line among female groups. Women who supported the movement for a separate Catalan identity, for example, were able to see their struggle for female rights through the lens of political nationalism (Document 6.19).

Document 6.19 Catalan Feminism

Our censor was a tiny, curly-headed English teacher, and an ardent Catalan nationalist. She brought our papers back to the Inn and offered to show us around the town.

For her, the Revolution meant Catalan independence from the Madrid government and the right to speak their beloved mother tongue. 'Imagine, the central government won't even let us speak our own language in the schools, or in public business. We had to speak Castilian.'

'Now the revolution has made Catalonia independent of Madrid, Spain will have a federal government, like your United States. Each of our provinces will have its autonomy.'

She told us about the Committee for the New Unified Schools (CENU, *Comite por la Escuela Nueva Unificada*). Its aim was to get every child enrolled, to eliminate illiteracy. It would of course teach in Catalan, with Spanish as a second language. They had plenty of confiscated buildings, but not enough teachers, as the religious had all fled abroad. All the men with education and ability, she told us, were at the front or working to build up the Catalan war industries so the antifascists could be self-supporting in munitions.

Source: Cusick, L. (1978) *The Anarchist Millenium: Memories of the Spanish Revolution, 1936–37*, unpublished manuscript, Gainesville, p. 11.

Public behaviour

It was ironic that, though Republican women could express their sexuality in relations with men in ways that were forbidden on the Nationalist side, not every women's group condoned or encouraged the sexualized behaviour of women in public. In the first months of the war this was due to the imposition of a proletarian aesthetic in cities where the revolution had triumphed. In Barcelona many women donned blue overalls (*mono azul*), adorned only with the colourful kerchiefs and insignia representing the left-wing organization to which they belonged. In an atmosphere charged with class tensions, it was not surprising that middle-class women felt obliged to defer to this anti-feminine, 'proletarian' style (Document 6.20). The receding tide of revolution saw the return of a 'bourgeois' couture, and by the end of 1936 high heels, French dresses, and well-coiffured women could be seen in the prosperous areas of the city, though no one dared to wear the traditional mantilla, which was identified with the religious symbolism of Catholic Spain.

Document 6.20 Proletarian Couture

(a)

Also among those who donned *monos* [workmen's overalls, literally 'blue monkeys'] were a considerable number of upper-class girls – members of the hated aristocracy. Most of these volunteered their services during the first days of the war when the Loyalist rearguard was engaged in the extermination of all those of the wealthiest classes it could find. By joining the militia these young women not only succeeded in saving their own lives but in many cases those of members of their families. Volunteers were given placards by the various enlistment bureaux urging militia raiding units to respect the homes of those actively helping the Loyalist cause. Few of these young society women served at the front. Most of them became office assistants for Leftist officials and were much publicized in the Loyalist press as examples of women who had 'repudiated' their hateful places in the upper brackets. Later some of these girls were executed on charges of furnishing information to enemies of the cause.

Source: Knoblaugh, E. (1937) *Correspondent in Spain*, New York, p. 3.

(b)

One remarkable aspect of the streets becomes more conspicuous with time: the changed position of women. Young working-class girls in hundreds and perhaps thousands are walking up and down the streets, and are especially to be seen in the elegant cafés of the Alcalá and the Gran Via. They collect for the 'International Red Help', an organization 'in favour of the victims of class war', here mostly working for the wounded and for the relatives of the victims of the civil war; it was sponsored originally all over the world by the Comintern, but is run in Spain by socialists and communists jointly. There is no collecting either in Barcelona or in Valencia, whereas the couples of girls (they never go alone; walking through the streets completely unchaperoned would still be unthinkable for any decent Spanish girl), well dressed in working-class fashion, who ask everybody for a contribution, are almost a nuisance in Madrid, or at least would be were they not so pleasant to look at. They enjoy it enormously; for most of them it is obviously their first appearance in public, and now they are even allowed to talk to foreigners and sit down at their ease in the cafés for a chat with the militia-men.

Source: Borkenau, F. (1974) *The Spanish Cockpit: An Eye Witness Account of the Political and Social Conflicts of the Spanish Civil War*, Ann Arbor, pp. 126–7.

Breaking gender barriers

A certain number of women transgressed well-established gender lines by enlisting in popular militias. While many Spaniards saw this as shockingly inappropriate behaviour, revolutionary women in particular did not hesitate to answer the call to fight. For the most part, these were spontaneous responses to the outbreak of civil war, which occurred during the period when the traditional lines of political and military authority in Republican Spain had broken down. The motives for becoming women warriors were mixed. As the historian Mary Nash has pointed out, some of these daring women were already active in left-wing circles and organizations and they simply joined militias to which their friends, lovers, and husbands belonged.[9] In fact, whether consciously or not, they were following in the footsteps of the brave women who had participated alongside men in the infamous Asturias Rising of 1934 and other revolutionary struggles during the Second Republic. Others were driven by their ardent desire to defend the political and social rights they had won under the Second Republic and which they knew would be taken away under a right-wing regime.

Almost overnight, it seemed as though the Republic had embraced the idea of women serving in the military (Document 6.21). Posters, pamphlets, and popular slogans featured women in their new role. This new image of woman was early on reinforced by the heroic exploits of *milicianas* such as Lina Odena, a leader of the communist youth movement, JSU, who died on the Granada front, and Rosario La Dinamitera (the Dynamiter), whose fearless behaviour inspired the well-known left-wing poet Miguel Hernández to dedicate a poem to her.[10]

Document 6.21 Women in Arms

(a)

Since its formation only a few weeks ago, the Women's Secretariat has enjoyed a rapid and soaring success.

Up till the present, individual women had gone to the front in various columns of the militias, serving bravely with the men and doing their share as well as they could, but no effort had been made to provide them with adequate military training. The P.O.U.M. was the first to put forward the idea that so much eager willingness should be properly trained and organised, and in this way our plan for military instruction began. We believe that every working woman should be familiar with the use of firearms and military terms, not necessarily because we think women should go to the front, but because the time may come when our women comrades will be compelled by force of circumstances to take up arms in the defence of our cities and fight side by side with the men.

Source: The Spanish Revolution, no. 7, p. 4, The First Women's Batallion, reprinted New York, 1978.

(b)

The regiment was composed in large part of these runaways. We used to meet at seven o'clock in front of the local, with the winter morning mist still rolling up the Ramblas and round the trunks of the trees, strapped into our new blue woollen uniforms with divided skirts and stand there blowing on our hands and most of us hoping that our families wouldn't catch us.

I have seldom seen such spirits. They were so glad and gay and seemed like children. While we waited for the members of the Directive Committee to come and lead us to the barracks they skipped on the hard pavement and played little girls' games, singing and holding hands and dancing in their pointed shoes. (It was a long time before we could make them all understand that they must go to drill in flat heels and leave their earrings at home.) In the excitement of being free, they were able to get up carelessly time after time in the rough morning air. They would wait endlessly on the drill-field in the wind. Even the weight of centuries of indolence did not deter them.

Source: Low, M. and Breá, J. (1979) *The Red Spanish Notebook: The First Six Months of the Revolution and the Civil War*, San Francisco, pp. 186–7.

(c)

The heights of Guadarrama, Madrid and many other cities have witnessed the heroism of women who are battling a strong and brutal enemy. They march to death merrily singing. They cheer those who have lost heart, infuse courage into them and inspire them with the fighting spirit. So it was at Alto de Leon, in Somosierra and elsewhere. These places, drenched in the blood of many a nameless hero, will shine with an inextinguishable flame in the history of our country's struggle against reaction.

With them will be bound up the revolutionary traditions of our people, with them, the women who are fighting at the front, who are donating their blood to save the wounded, who, forgetting their own fatigue, watch at the bedside of wounded heroes, who died exclaiming: 'Long live liberty!'

We dip our colours in honour of you, dear women comrades, who march into battle together with the men.

All honour to you, women anti-fascists!

Defense, September 4, 1936

Source: Ibárruri, D. (1938) *Speeches and Articles 1936–1938*, London, p. 23.

By the end of the summer of 1936, however, the initial enthusiasm expressed for women taking up arms had all but evaporated. Not only males but also prominent Republican women – La Pasionaria, for example – began calling for women to return from the front lines and support the anti-fascist struggle by performing war-related tasks at home and in the workplace. Several developments during this period contributed to this changed attitude towards female militia members. Catapulting women into male roles so quickly rankled with their male comrades who had, despite their left-wing sentiments, internalized the beliefs of a society deeply imbued with machismo values. Even those on the far left (and therefore presumably more inclined to accept such dramatic revisions of traditional roles than were their conservative counterparts) were uneasy about having women bearing arms and sacrificing their lives on the battlefield. Resistance to the notion of females assuming a traditionally defined masculine role was also common. Some complained that women at the front were not contributing to fighting as much as they were contributing to the spread of venereal diseases. The latter was indeed a serious problem during the war, though it was simplistic (and characteristically chauvinistic) to attribute this solely to the presence of *milicianas* at the front (Document 6.22).

Document 6.22 Women at the Front

Spaniards are very critical. They called the milicianas prostitutes and the milicianos thieves. And when the brigades arrived, they called them every name in the book. I don't understand it. Precisely the reason I came here today was to explain this to you. I never saw anything. First of all, one would have to be very stupid to go to the front lines to be a prostitute, where you can get your head blown off . . . We women wore overalls like the men. They criticized us a lot for that: 'How shameful for women to wear overalls!' When overalls cover you up more than anything! Women went to jail after the war for having worn overalls and for having carried a gun! You didn't have to have used it, just carried it, and worn overalls! If you go to war, naturally you have to be armed!

Source: Mangini, S. (1995) *Memories of Resistance: Women's Voices from the Spanish Civil War*, New Haven and London, p. 84.

Above all, however, the movement to restrict women's participation in the army was due to the restoration of male-dominated military structures. The pressing need to militarize the militias inevitably meant eliminating activities that ran counter to the customary practices of a traditional army. Furthermore, having women fight alongside men reflected a radical conception of the war, and the Republican forces pushing for the creation of a military force run along conventional lines wanted to divest the militias of their revolutionary character. In the event, as soon as a formal military organization, the People's Army, began taking shape in the autumn of 1936, women were no longer welcome at the front.

The home front and social relations

Republican women's activities in the rearguard ranged over a wide spectrum. In addition to working in factories and war-related industries, they were placed in charge of running many of the social services vital for sustaining the war effort. But while these activities inevitably open doors to women in the public sphere, it should be noted that their mass mobilization was justified by the government and anti-fascist organizations on the grounds of wartime needs. The question as to whether it was a woman's natural or social right to work or play a public role remained unanswered. Rather, women were expected to take over war-related jobs and activities abandoned by men who were urged to go to the front to fight while women remained behind in their 'proper place', the home front.

Responding to the urgent need for more labourers, thousands of women began entering the workforce. For most, however, it was not an easy transition. Women frequently incurred the wrath of male trade unionists and others who saw the introduction of women in the workplace as a major setback to their organizational efforts. Furthermore, these males felt their masculine culture threatened by the 'feminization' of the factory: women set up crèches and promoted services designed for the needs of wives and mothers who had to carry on their family obligations while away from home.

In the countryside, there was a less radical shift in gender relations, not least because women already comprised a significant percentage of the agricultural labour force. What's more, in this sector women seemed to have made limited progress towards achieving equality with men. This was evident even in many of the agricultural collectives set up by the anarchosyndicalists and revolutionary Marxists. Despite the revolutionary nature of these social and economic experiments, the policies of many collectives none the less reflected gender-based prejudices, such as the belief in the concept of the patriarchal family. According to one eyewitness, peasant attempts to establish libertarian communism in remote rural regions inevitably reflected the backward economic and cultural conditions that existed up till then. It was scarcely surprising, therefore, that their efforts to define a 'free' society fell far short of libertarian ideals. In at least half, wage differentials between males and females persisted, and, though a woman's right to livelihood was recognized, she was still expected to perform household chores.[11]

Progress for Republican women?

Were women in Republican Spain, on the whole, more emancipated than before as a result of the war and revolution? The answer to this question is both yes and no.

Steps were taken, especially by the revolutionary parties, to redefine gender relations in Republican Spain. This was particularly true during the early months of the war and revolution. One of the remarkable developments in this regard was the adoption of a marriage code in Catalonia which, at least in principle, placed women on an equal footing with men. The initial acceptance of women fighting alongside men was another 'conceptual' breakthrough for Spanish women.

The many-sided character of the Republicans' women's movement makes it exceedingly difficult to gauge the progress women in general were making during this period of intense social and economic change. With so many different groups and theoretical perspectives, clashes over gender-related policies inevitably occurred. For example, the anarchist Mujeres Libres split with the female branch of the libertarian youth (FIJL) over the question of whether an independent female organization was necessary. Even more problematic were the ideological differences among the various women's groups. Politically, the communist Agrupación de Mujeres Antifascistas and Unió de Dones de Catalunya were at odds with the revolutionary policies being promoted by both the women's section of the POUM and the Mujeres Libres. The latter, for example, rejected the idea of fusing all women's organization on the ground that the social advances of women relied on the diversity of opinion. In the end, it proved impossible for women's organizations to escape the effects of the overarching political struggle that dominated Republican affairs. As a result, women's issues tended to be pushed to the background for most of the war.

In practice, the greatest obstacle to the forward progress of women seems to have been entrenched male attitudes and behaviour. Attempts to emancipate females on many fronts revealed just how much men continued to draw upon pre-existing definitions of male/female relations. This was mainly because attitudes towards women were largely shaped and conditioned by deeply rooted social conventions. Catholic values permeated Spanish society and even libertarian men seemed unaware how their 'Catholic' home life and conservative relations with their wives could affect their views on gender questions. Male attitudes towards prostitution were particularly illustrative of the double standards that persisted even during the high tide of revolutionary changes (Document 6.23).

Document 6.23 Free Women against Prostitution

(a)

The Anarchist women were more ambitious as far as posters were concerned. They attacked all kinds of problems with their slogans.

I was riding in the tram down the Ramblas the first time I saw their poster against prostitution. It was the first time I had seen the matter raised. I felt very pleased at this new sight.

The poster was huge and covered a whole hoarding. Everyone was looking at it.

A group of Anarchists from the militias, the young beards fresh on their faces, were standing round me on the rattling front of the tram. When they saw it they were disturbed.

'Finish with prostitution,' read one of them. 'What do you think of that?'

They stood around uneasily, obviously annoyed, and awkward at finding themselves annoyed.

'Our women, too. They don't mind getting their hand in, do they?'

'Nothing to do with them. They're free, aren't they?'

'Well, what's a man going to do if they start really suppressing it? It's not as though they were so oncoming themselves that we could do without it.'

At night the narrow streets in the prostitute quarter swarmed with militias back from the front.

'Well, what can you do?' people answered me with a shrug. 'You can stop it growing, or beginning again, but what can you do with those women who are there already? How can you change them?'

In the end, the prostitutes began to look after their own interests. A little time had elapsed before they began thinking of vindicating themselves. One day they realised that they also could be in the revolution.

Source: Low, M. and Breá, J. (1979) *The Red Spanish Notebook: The First Six Months of the Revolution and the Civil War,* San Francisco, pp. 196–7.

(b)

Free Women, unlike the bourgeois feminists, linked the social and political struggle with feminism and fought against machismo even among anarchists. It was all very well for them to say that men and women were all the same, were equals; machismo still existed. Men were quite happy to have a woman who understood them, as activists; but they were not happy for her to be an activist. They still thought that most women were incapable. They thought a lot of Federica Montseny because she was cultured; but what of the rest? The men thought women knew nothing about economic and social problems.

As for those who had activist wives, well, they were there to take in new arrivals, to get the food and act as hostesses. Activists were often in prison. The lot of men in the CNT was three years in prison, two years' freedom, four years in prison, three years' freedom; so they needed to have someone there for when hard times struck. If their women too were activists then they too would be liable to arrest. Activists could not start a family – the risks of imprisonment were too great. The men in the CNT saw no further than giving women a social conscience. The anarcho-syndicalists did not go beyond that.

Source: Gadant, M. (ed.) (1986) *Women of the Mediterranean,* London and New Jersey, p. 52.

On the other hand, the war and revolution thrust women into roles that impelled men to treat them, if not as equals, as participants in the public sphere of society.

Federica Montseny, Dolores Ibárruri (La Pasionaria), Isabel Palencia, Constancia de la Mora are notable examples of the tiny handful of women who not only played a major role in defining policies relating to gender issues but also in exercising power and influence in institutions formerly the exclusive preserve of males. Yet, even for this select group of women, it was clear that females would be granted only limited access to the main corridors of power. The anarchist Federica Montseny, the first female in Europe to be named to a cabinet post in a national government, was placed in charge of Public Health and Assistance. In this capacity, she was responsible for overseeing domestic issues that, though essential, were identified more with activities in the rearguard than on the front lines. Even the primary responsibilities of the indomitable La Pasionaria, a high-ranking member of the Communist Party (PCE), were defined along gender lines. So while she was, because of her exceptional oratory skills, frequently called upon to make public speeches and radio broadcasts on behalf of the Republican cause, she was also delegated tasks traditionally assigned to women, like heading organizations that mobilized women in the war effort and that looked after the welfare of the wounded and orphaned children.

It was the public personae of prominent women that spoke to the advances that were being made on the Republican side towards redefining the role of females in society. In their many and varied tasks performed during the war both Montseny and Ibárruri, for example, projected an image of women which contrasted sharply with that of the protected, submissive female of traditional Spain. The iconography that grew up around La Pasionaria during the war is a case in point. Usually portrayed in the media as an indefatigable and formidable spokesperson for the anti-fascist cause, La Pasionaria's image replaced that of the seductive and feminine 'Marianne' as the personification of Republican Spain (Document 6.24).

Document 6.24 La Pasionaria

There is our great Comrade La Pasionaria, the most popular person in all Spain, an almost legendary figure: 'When she goes into the countryside, into a village or house, the people touch her to see if she is really made of flesh, or if she is imaginary,' says Diaz. The flaming words of Pasionaria have become historic – her cry which brought 50,000 Paris workers to their feet with enthusiasm in September, 1936: 'The Spanish people would rather die on their feet than live on their knees,' or that phrase to the soldiers defending Madrid: 'The Spanish women prefer to be widows of heroes than companions of slaves.'

Source: Marty, A. (1937) *Heroic Spain*, New York, p. 30.

For the average woman, too, the war and revolution had had a significant impact. By occupying public spaces that had long been controlled by men, women were able to begin the process of developing a greater sense of self and agency. This 'new woman' was hardly the emancipated female we are today familiar with in Western society. Yet she was not the woman of 'old' Spain, and could look forward, at least as long as the war against the Nationalists was not lost, to gaining ground in the struggle to acquire greater personal and social freedoms.

Non-political and 'forgotten' women

To these groups of Nationalist and Republican women can be added one more category, namely, women who did not see themselves as belonging to any political or social group that espoused allegiance to either the Nationalist or Republican sides. These were not party leaders or public figures, but anonymous women who were more concerned with securing their own (or their family's) survival than supporting a particular cause. For them, the meaning of the war and revolution could be expressed not in terms of an ideological perspective but rather as a bleak daily reality of struggling to keep their households running in harsh circumstances. These women went about their routines unnoticed, except perhaps by foreign observers who had come to Spain to record in pictures and in writings war scenes for newspapers and magazines. Typically they were, along with children and the elderly, portrayed as the nameless 'victims' of war (Document 6.25).

Document 6.25 Anonymous Heroines

(*a*)

Nowhere in any other country had I seen so much participation in the daily work with the men as I saw in this short drive among these Spanish women.

During the first months of the Spanish civil war the papers were filled with the part the loyalist women were playing in the conflict. The early heroes of the war were heroines. John Langdon Davies has told of the matter-of-fact way the girls fell into line to march off to the front. He says that there was absolutely no sex-glorification . . . Even the Fascist countries took a right-about-face and began to organize their women and look to their development. It was not long before the Loyalists began to recognize that women could serve at other places better than they could in the front-line trenches. But the work of the women went on.

Source: 'Gibraltar to Malaga. The "real" Spanish women and the women of the people' *The Fight*, August 1937.

(*b*)

They put up a sign on the shop door, and word flies through the neighborhood that you can get food today. Then the lines form. Sometimes they are five blocks long. Sometimes you wait all that time but just before your turn comes the shop closes. There is no more food. The women wait in line and talk or knit, the children invent games that they can play standing in one place.

The pinched women file into the shop and hand their food cards over the high bare counter. The girls behind the counter look healthy because they are wearing rouge. Then the food is doled out in little gray paper sacks. The girl behind the counter pulls out a slab of the gray-white flat fish and cuts off a little piece with a pair of scissors. She cuts it with scissors, not a knife, because scissors are more accurate.

The woman with gray hair and a gray frozen face and exhausted eyes reaches out to get her piece of fish. She holds it a minute in her hand, looking at it. They all look at it, and say nothing. Then she turns and pushes her way through the crowd and out the door.

Source: Gellhorn, M. (1988) *The Face of War*, New York, p. 39.

Among this same group of anonymous women were those whose experiences were not 'visible' to the public eye. For example, in the Nationalist zone, it was not uncommon for women to be harassed or even imprisoned simply because they were known to be related to or associated with pro-Republican men. Once gaoled, they soon became forgotten casualties of the war (Document 6.26).

Document 6.26 The Price of being Republican in Nationalist Spain

They placed my bag inside, the officers took their places, the driver – an armed air force private – took the wheel and off we went towards the higher section of town. In a hoarse tone I asked:

'Where are we going?'

'To the prison, madam!'

'To prison? Why?'

'We have been ordered to take you there.'

And then Librada broke into tears: 'Do I go to prison too?'

'You too.'

'But we have done nothing.'

'Then you have nothing to worry about. If you have done nothing, you have nothing to fear.'

. . . And here we were, the prison rising before us, hardly distinguishable in the darkness. The car stopped in front of this heap of dark stones, thick dungeon stones, for this was more dungeon than prison. The iron doors swung open and we passed through the wrought iron gate. We were now inside the prison.

Source: O'Neill, C. (1978) *Trapped in Spain*, Toronto, p. 28.

Not all women passively endured the hardships imposed on them. As in all wars, there were a number of reported instances of women (and men) who exhibited anti-social or selfish behaviour. According to the US historian Michael Seidman, some women during the war asserted their own interests against the demands of various causes and collectivities.[12] Seidman further contends that this type of woman was involved in a number of different anti-social and sometimes subversive activities. On the Republican side, for example, these so-called 'individualist' woman demanded to work overtime when laws were passed that prohibited night work and they readily defended their sources of income when these were threatened.

Conclusion

On the Republican side, the question of whether the experiences of war either promoted or undermined equality between the sexes cannot be answered with any certainty. For even though some women broke new ground by participating on an equal footing with men both behind and on the front lines, the general tendency during the war was to confine women to activities that did not violate traditional gender boundaries. On the Nationalist side, where gender lines were rarely transgressed, women were expected throughout the war and beyond to conform to norms established by the male-dominated military government and the Catholic Church. This is not to deny the increased public presence of women under Francoism. In fact, the Sección Femenina continued to promote educational and social welfare programmes that sought to revitalize the role of women in Spanish society.[13]

7 | Political life behind the lines

Shortly after the military rising divided Spain into two opposing camps, it became apparent that the pro-Republican zone was itself split into various geo-political blocs. In the beginning, Madrid became the centre of the Republicans' struggle to keep the Nationalists from achieving an early victory. Then, following the Republican government's removal to Valencia in early November, Madrid was placed under a siege that would last for over two years. No longer the capital, the city was governed by a multi-party executive body called the Madrid Defence Junta (*Junta de Defensa de Madrid*). From then until the last month of the conflict, Madrid ceased to be the geographical centre-point of the Civil War.

Political struggles in Republican Spain: The case of Catalonia

In Catalonia, the industrial base for the Republican war effort, the political and economic situation was markedly different. Because it was initially far removed from the front lines of the conflict, Catalonia managed to conserve its status as a self-governing region of four provinces. However, its government, the Generalitat, was at first forced to share political power with a revolutionary body known as the Central Anti-fascist Militias Committee (Comitè Central de Milícies Antifeixistes), which remained in existence until the end of September 1936.

Even after it had recovered its independent status, however, the Generalitat was unable to rule without the assistance of the constellation of left-wing parties that had risen to prominence following the July Rebellion. The anarchosyndicalists of the CNT-FAI in particular dominated significant segments of the economy and exercised power through their control of numerous anti-fascist committees.

Both the military rebellion and popular revolution had an enormous impact on local politics in Catalonia. As we have already seen, the July Revolution had led to the ascendancy of the revolutionary forces in this region as represented by the anarchosyndicalists of the CNT-FAI and the Marxist-Leninist POUM. On the economic front, the libertarians spearheaded a collectivization movement that embraced both land and industry. For their part, the much smaller POUM called for the immediate re-ordering of the region's social and political life along Marxist-Leninist revolutionary lines. Yet, from the beginning, the revolutionaries' attempts to establish their hegemony were challenged by a coalition of parties. Foremost among them was the Esquerra (ERC), the left-liberal Catalan party which had formerly served as the ruling party in Catalonia, which was forced to share political power with parties as diverse as the CNT-FAI, the communists' regional party, PSUC, and an assortment of liberal and conservative Catalan parties.

Perhaps the most striking consequence of this shift of the traditional lines of authority was the empowerment of groups (such as the CNT-FAI) which claimed to represent the vast majority of the working population but which nevertheless had been consigned by the ruling parties during the prewar Republican period to the fringes of the 'official' political and economic system. The resulting new constellation of forces clashed more than they complemented each other. As a result, a power struggle ensued which led first to the re-establishment of the Catalan regional government, the Generalitat, and, in the wake of the May disturbances, to the sub-ordination of this body to the centralizing forces of the government based in Valencia.

The coalition of reformist liberal forces was strengthened by the fact that they had not been fatally weakened by the revolutionaries' bid for power. Not only did they retain control of important bases of economic interests – the banks, for example – but they also continued to exercise their oversight of the machinery of local or regional government. The latter was possible largely because their revolutionary rivals were ill equipped from both an ideological and an organizational standpoint to seize complete control of the region. Given their long-standing hostility to the state and all forms of state control, it is scarcely surprising that the anarchosyndicalists lacked a blueprint for political action. In fact, as one prominent anarchist put it, remaining true to this theoretical heritage meant that the idea of establishing a libertarian dictatorship was anathema to most anarchosyndicalists. Another important legacy of the past was the anarchosyndicalists' aversion to highly centralized labour organizations. Anarchist unions were organized along confederative as opposed to vertical lines, and, while this served the movement well during the chaotic days immediately following the July military uprising, it tended to militate against their efforts to exercise control over the economic revolution to which they were committed throughout the Civil War. The development of the anarchosyndicalist-inspired structures that emerged during the first months of the civil war were conditioned by several factors. First and foremost was the fact that key sectors of the economy remained outside of their control.

Following Nin's ejection from the Cabinet in December and the reorganization of Josep Tarradellas's administration, PSUC councillors stepped up their efforts to strip the anarchosyndicalists of the economic and political authority they exercised through their revolutionary committees and armed forces.[1] (Document 7.1).

Document 7.1 Background to the May Day Crisis

(a)

I have just spent a further three weeks in Spain, visiting Aragon, Catalonia, Valencia, Alicante and Murcia. The impressions which follow are open to contradiction and will probably be contradicted; but so far as possible they are unbiased and the result of checking up on many conversations with many different kinds of people. Spain is a country where it is impossible to get accurate figures about anything important and where rumours gather force in proportion as the censorship grows more severe. There have been considerable changes in the political, economic, and military situations since I was there in December and I should describe them as all for the worse, though not irremediably for the worse. The outstanding political fact is the greatly increased power of the moderate elements in the Government backed up officially by the Communists, whose policy is to support a bourgeois democratic Spain against what they consider the premature revolutionary activities of the Anarchists and the P.O.U.M. Their reasons for this are: (1) that it fits in with Stalin's foreign policy elsewhere, which is to do nothing to weaken the anti-Fascist democracies, who might be less able to defend themselves in war if extremists have provoked internal dissensions; (2) that only by presenting England and France with authentic evidence of a legitimate and moderate government in power in Spain will they win over those fearful and hesitant countries, and possibly deflect Mussolini from his threat not to tolerate a Red Catalonia; (3) that it also enables the numerically weak Communist Party to get power through supporting the Liberals and the Marxian Socialists, using the vast bulk of the U.G.T. as a hermit crab takes possession of a winkle; and (4) that it enables them to attack, on patriotic grounds, their ideological enemies, the anarchists of the C.N.T. and the Trotskyites of the P.O.U.M.

The position of the P.O.U.M. is the most precarious, for they are severely condemned by the Communist and Socialist press on charges of being Trotskyites, and hence Fascists, of running away in battle and undermining the Government (from which they have been driven out), of consisting of criminals and the rejected members of other parties, and of preparing a counter-revolutionary coup. They are defended by the Anarchists with very much less zeal than they are attacked.

Source: The New Statesman and Nation, 20 February 1937, p. 278.

(b)

Acting Consul-General Vaughan to Mr. Eden – Received January 6 [1937]

In the recently reconstructed Catalan Government the Anarchist Minister of Supplies, Sr. Domenech, and the Socialist Minister of Public Services, Sr. Comorera, have changed places. The latter played a leading part in the crisis and was most outspoken against the extremists and, in particular, the C.N.T. by blaming them for the inadequacy of the steps taken by them while they were in control of the Department of Supplies.

Sr. Comorera has already taken a number of steps to give the Supplies Department full powers. He has dissolved all the Supplies Councils in the provincial capitals and replaced them by delegations in each of the forty districts or 'comarcas.' The presidents of these delegations are appointed by him and they are subject to the orders of the Generality. He has withdrawn from the municipalities all control over the purchase of supplies, and their functions are limited to rationing and hygiene. He has also taken into his own hands stocks of wheat and flour, and their distribution. Furthermore, he has dismissed many of the officials in his department and replaced them by his own men.

It is to be feared that these brave words on behalf of a strong Government will not lead to much improvement, but there are signs that some attempt is being made to suppress what are referred to in the press as the incontrollable and irresponsible elements.

A new chief of police, a Socialist, has been appointed, and he is working to restore the authority of the police force. He has already made several arrests for acts of terrorism. Police and National Republican Guards have been brought back from the front, and there is some idea of amalgamating all the forces in charge of public order, the police, the National Republican Guards, and the control patrols of the militias, into one body. At the same time many death sentences passed by the popular tribunals have been commuted by the Government to life sentences, and the Minister of Justice has announced his intention of reforming the popular tribunals by changing their personnel, and by introducing more persons with legal experience. A scheme is also being considered for the establishment of concentration camps.

Source: British Documents on Foreign Affairs, Series F, Europe, vol. 27 (January, 1937) Document nos 56 and 57, pp. 67 and 69.

The Popular Front at War: May Events of 1937

The early months of 1937 saw the tensions between the pro- and anti-Popular Front forces in Catalonia sharpen. The highly charged political atmosphere finally exploded in May, when the opposing sides were locked in a series of bloody street battles. The 'May Events', the 'war within a war' so vividly captured in George Orwell's *Homage to Catalonia*, would have far-reaching consequences.[2] Above all it marked a turning point in Republican politics, signalling the end of the revolutionary drive that had begun ten months earlier and the beginning of communist hegemony in the Republican camp.

Despite the fact that the Generalitat had, since the end of September, become the principal ruling body of Catalonia, the revolutionary organizations refused to relinquish their control over certain sectors of society. The anarchosyndicalists, for example, ignored a government decree which called for the establishment of a centralized police constabulary, above all because they saw their Patrols of Control (*patrullas de control*) as one of their fulcrums of revolutionary power in the region. And though they continued to participate as members of the government, the anarchosyndicalists increasingly found their revolutionary base being whittled away by the pro-statist parties.

By mid-April the escalating infighting between the pro- and anti-revolutionary elements inside the Generalitat had brought the government to a standstill. At the end of the month two highly publicized assassinations – the one of PSUC official Roldán Cortada and the other of Antonio Martín, the anarchist head of the revolutionary council in Puigcerdá – generated so much palpable tension in the region that the approaching May Day celebrations had to be cancelled. Two days later the political storm that had been building for months finally broke, and for the next few days the streets of Barcelona and the surrounding areas became the battleground for a mini-civil-war inside Republican Spain.

The storm breaks

The political drama that has since been immortalized in George Orwell's *Homage to Catalonia* began at three in the afternoon when several truckloads of police arrived in front of La Telefónica, Barcelona's principal telephone exchange located in the city's centre on the Plaza de Catalunya. Their orders, taken directly from Artemio Ayguadé, the Catalan republican Councillor of Public Order and Internal Security, and Rodríguez Salas, the communist (PSUC) police commissioner, were to eject the anarchists from the building. The guards quickly occupied the first floor, but their efforts to take complete control of the building were met with bursts of gunfire. As soon as they secured their positions, anarchist workers blocked all access to the upper floors and gave the alarm to the rest of the libertarian community. The much anticipated showdown between the revolutionaries and their political adversaries had begun.

Though the official justification for launching the raid was to stop the CNT-FAI from interfering with government communiqués – anarchists frequently eavesdropped and even interrupted communications of the Generalitat as well as those between the Valencian government and its representatives abroad – the real motives behind this bold manoeuvre were obvious to all the major protagonists involved. Above all it was intended to end the duality of power-sharing in the region. As far as the pro-statist forces were concerned, the CNT-FAI's continued *de facto* control over essential government operations had to end in order for the Generalitat to become the sole authority in the region. For their part, the anarchosyndicalists were determined to hold on to any lever of power that they believed was necessary to defend the revolutionary conquests they had gained since July 1936 (Document 7.2).

Document 7.2 The Fighting Begins

Although there is no official explanation as to the exact cause of the outbreak, it would appear that it undoubtedly originated with an attempt on the part of the Government to install their delegate in the telephone central building last Monday. It is obvious that the control of the telephone is of vital importance to the Government in times of crisis, and the Anarchists had had the effrontery to interrupt a conversation on the telephone between Sr. Companys and Sr.

Largo Caballero. The F.A.I. received the Commissioner of Public Order, when he reached the telephone building, with shots, and it is possible that the Anarchists thought that a serious attempt was about to be made by the Government to assert their hitherto flouted authority. The occasion was therefore taken by the F.A.I. and C.N.T. to call out their adherents and test their mobilisation arrangements. The more moderate parties, who support the Government, did likewise, and only a few shots were necessary to precipitate the general engagement. The result was bound to be indecisive, as neither side was strong enough to oust the others from their fortified positions. Spaniards have indulged in periodical house-to-house fighting ever since they have had firearms, and they are adepts at it. They have little talent for taking places by assault, and tanks and artillery would have been necessary for any force desirous of dominating the situation in Barcelona.

Source: Norman King (May 1937) *British Documents on Foreign Affairs*, Series F, Europe, vol. 27, document no. 87, p. 113.

As soon as news of the assault on La Telefónica began spreading throughout the city, hundreds of CNT-FAI militants began occupying the streets. Barricades were hastily erected in working-class districts, and public buildings and commercial enterprises under anarchist control became redoubts of revolutionary resistance (Document 7.3). On one side of the barricades stood militants of the regional and local committees of the CNT-FAI, who were joined in the following days by the POUM, the maverick anarchist group known as the 'Friends of Durruti' ('Amigos de Durruti'), and a handful of foreign leftists who described themselves as 'Bolshevik-Leninists' (read Trotskyist), (Document 7.4). Because the POUM was later unjustly accused by the communists and others of having provoked the May crisis, It should be underscored here that they were in no way responsible for instigating the uprising. Nor were they, as they were later portrayed in pointedly slanderous communist propaganda, acting in collusion with the so-called 'uncontrollable' elements of the anarchosyndicalist movement. The fact is that the coalition of parties referred to above was loosely knitted together after the street fighting had erupted on 3 May. Moreover, the leaders of the CNT-FAI showed little interest in joining forces with either the Marxist POUM or the independent libertarian faction Friends of Durruti, whose policies during the conflict were roundly criticized by the anarchosyndicalist leadership.[3] The only attempt to form a united front among the diverse groups involved in the fighting occurred on 5 May when the Amigos issued a leaflet calling for the establishment of a revolutionary junta composed of the CNT-FAI and POUM. But while it is true that the Friends were willing to play a vanguard role in building such an alliance, their initiative was denounced by the official representatives of the CNT-FAI and ultimately rejected by the leaders of the POUM (Document 7.5).

Document 7.3 Revolutionaries Strike Back

(a)

The events of 3rd May [1937]

About three o'clock in the afternoon of May 3rd, three motor lorries of police drove up to the telephone building under his [Eusabio Rodríguez Salas] personal command. They entered the building, wanting to occupy it. The manner of their approach was, of necessity, regarded as an insulting provocation by the workers. They were asked to put up their hands and turn over their weapons.

The workers defended themselves. A machine gun covered the police from an upper storey. They could not go beyond the first floor. While all this was taking place inside the building, word of the assault spread in the square and, soon after, throughout the city. It was as though a match had been set to gunpowder.

Workers and police ran about excitedly in every section of the city. The union headquarters were full of people. Everybody wanted arms. Everybody wanted to be ready to defend buildings from similar assaults.

A few hours later, the entire city of Barcelona was in arms.

Source: Souchy, A. (1937) *The Tragic Week in May*, Barcelona, pp. 9–10.

(b)

There was a sound of firing in the distance and the streets were completely empty of people. Everyone said that it was impossible to go up the Ramblas. The Civil Guards had seized buildings in commanding positions and were letting fly at everyone who passed. I would have risked it and gone back to the hotel, but there was a vague idea floating round that the Comite Local was likely to be attacked at any moment and we had better stand by. All over the building, on the stairs and on the pavement outside, small knots of people were standing and talking excitedly. No one seemed to have a very clear idea of what was happening. All I could gather was that the Civil Guards had attacked the Telephone Exchange and seized various strategic spots that commanded other buildings belonging to the workers. There was a general impression that the Civil Guards were 'after' the C.N.T. and the working class generally.

Source: Orwell, G. (1964) *Homage to Catalonia*, Boston, p. 123.

Document 7.4 Steps Towards a Revolutionary Junta

(a)

A newly founded group, called 'Friends of Durruti', functioning on the fringes of the CNT-FAI, published a proclamation declaring that 'A Revolutionary Junta has been constituted in Barcelona. All those responsible for the putsch, maneuvering under the protection of the government, shall be executed. The POUM shall be a member of the Revolutionary Junta because they stood by the workers.'

The Regional Committee decided not to concur with this proclamation. The Libertarian Youth likewise rejected it. On the next day, Thursday, May 6th, their official statement was printed in the entire press of Barcelona.

Source: Souchy, A. (1937) *The Tragic Week in May*, Barcelona, p. 17.

(b)

The confederal policy of pacification led to a deep disgust among the union fighters, and an extremist group emerged called 'Friends of Durruti'. This group's paper, *El Amigo del Pueblo* (The Friend of the People) used revolutionary Jacobin language: 'In Barcelona a Revolutionary Junta has been formed. Those responsible for the attempted subversion, people acting under government protection, will be shot. The POUM will be admitted to the Revolutionary Junta because it sides with the workers.' The higher committees of the CNT immediately disavowed this group, which never had the importance ascribed to it by some foreign historians. The relative unimportance of its members, POUM participation, and the Marxist flavour of some of its communiqués all served to dilute the real influence of the 'Friends of Durruti'.

Source: Peirats, J. (1974) *Anarchists in the Spanish Revolution*, Toronto, p. 215.

Document 7.5 Relations between Anarchist Militants and the POUM

(a)

The Friends of Durruti, the Left Anarchists, issued their first leaflet to the working people, to the fighters on the barricades. It was joyously greeted. The possessors of membership cards in the Friends of Durruti were honoured highly by all barricade defenders. The leaflet was a clarion: 'Disarm all the Bourgeois Forces. Socialization of Economy. Dissolution of the political parties opposed to the working class. We will not surrender the streets. The Revolution before everything. We greet our comrades of the POUM who have fraternized with us in the streets. For the Social Revolution. Down with the Counter-Revolution.'

On Wednesday a second effort was made, with the backing of the Friends of Durruti, to establish a revolutionary junta. It failed. The City Committee of the FAI coordinated its defense committees, but did not measure up to the vital needs of the time; they would not act for an organized offensive against the Generality. In the afternoon the Durruti group sent a delegation to the POUM, inviting participation in the forming of the revolutionary junta. Nothing materialized from the ensuing discussion; each blamed the other for the failure.

Source: Oehler, H. (1937) *Barricades in Barcelona: The First Revolt of the Proletariat against the Capitalist People's Front, Eyewitness Account – Barcelona May 15, 1937*, New York, p. 10.

(b)

The Communist Party could not refrain from using this occasion to launch an attack against its special enemy, the so-called Trotskyist party, i.e., the POUM, a small Marxist anti-Stalinist party which has developed in certain working class circles in Catalonia. The POUM, however, denies being under Trotskyist influence. We do not intend to discuss this point, not being qualified to define the subtle differences existing between the various opposition groups of the Communists. By their form, which is organisationally trade union, and by their anarchist ideology, the CNT and the FAI are widely separated from this group as from all other antifascist organisations.

The POUM identified itself with the protest movement of the Anarcho-Syndicalist workers. But to present it as the determining factor, dragging in its wake, the workers of the CNT is only another version of the nazi tactics that makes a political scape goat of the Jews by holding them responsible for everything; for the war, the peace treaty, the revolution and the reaction . . .

We have no connection with the POUM, but the CNT has insisted that it shall be recognized as an antifascist organisation. On May 9th, the organ of the CNT, 'Solidaridad Obrero', demanded that the police should give up the POUM printing office which had been seized. This was done.

To credit the POUM with having taken the initiative and the responsibility for the protest movement in Barcelona is merely another lie spread by the news hawks of the International Press.

Source: International Workingmen's Association/Anarchosyndicalists (1937), *IWMA Bulletin of Information*, Barcelona, p. 9.

Opposing the revolutionary forces were government troops (Assault Guards, Civil Guards, and Catalan City Guards), who were supported by a coalition of anti-revolutionary parties, which included the PSUC, the Catalan branch of its trade union affiliate, UGT, and an assortment of Catalan middle-class (Esquerra) and separatist parties (Estat Català). Despite their common opposition to the far-left working-class organizations, this disparate collection of political factions was divided over the question of how to regain control of public order. The primary aim of the Catalanistas belonging to the Esquerra, Estat Català, and other regional parties was to break the revolutionary power of the workers without compromising the local autonomy they cherished so dearly. However, the PSUC and the pro-Popular Front factions in Barcelona and Valencia saw the May crisis as an opportunity for the central government to extend its control over all of Republican Spain. This is precisely what happened once it became apparent that the Catalan authorities found themselves unable to put down the rebellion without outside reinforcements. On the 5th, the Valencian government dispatched over five thousand Assault Guards to quell the rebellion, and, at the same time, steps were taken to assert greater central government rule over the forces of public order in the region. And while this transfer of authority was made in accordance with provisions that had established Catalan self-government, it henceforth ended the Generalitat's ability to exercise independent power in the region.

In the meantime, local political leaders from both sides were desperately appealing for a ceasefire. National representatives of both the UGT and CNT-FAI arrived in Barcelona on the 5th, though they, too, were unable to use their influence to bring about an end to hostilities (Document 7.6). Even the announcement later that day that a new Catalan government had been formed – a move which satisfied the CNT-FAI demand that both Aiguadé and Rodríguez Salas should be ousted from their posts – failed to defuse the situation.

Document 7.6 An Anarchist Pleads for a Ceasefire

Garcia Oliver:

Think of the pain, think of the anguish . . . of those antifascist workers in that part of Spain dominated by the whip of Hitler and Mussolini when they learn . . . That in [Catalonia] we are killing one another . . . All of you should remain in your respective positions . . . but should cease firing, even though provoked by persons not interested in finding a solution to this conflict.

Source: Bolloten, B. (1991) *The Spanish Civil War*, Chapel Hill, p. 439.

The fiercest fighting took place during the first two days of the conflict, during which time dozens of casualties were reported on both sides.[4] A more sinister form of violence occurred behind the scenes. On the 5th, for example, the noted Italian anti-fascist and libertarian philosopher Camillo Berneri and his comrade Barbieri were murdered by unknown assailants. Though it was believed at the time that he had been abducted by communist militiamen, it is possible that he had been assassinated by police agents OVRA operating underground in Barcelona (Document 7.7). That suspicion was immediately cast in the direction of the communists was not surprising. It soon became apparent, particularly to the small group of foreign revolutionaries who were identified as enemies of the Popular Front government, that the communists were using the cover of the May disturbances to round up their political adversaries (Document 7.8). Whether the communists were guilty of carrying out the Berneri/Barbieri executions or not, there can be no doubt that they were responsible for settling countless political scores once the revolutionary movement had been subdued.

Document 7.7 Silencing Dissent: The Death of Camillo Berneri

On the morning of Tuesday, May 4th, the Catalan and Communist guards came to the house and told the Italian Anarchists to be careful because there was a lot of shooting in the neighborhood. There was another visit in the afternoon for the purpose of registering the house and confiscating the arms, which belonged to Italian militiamen in leave in Barcelona. The next day, Wednesday, May 5th, at about 5 o'clock in the afternoon, Berneri and Barbieri were taken away by 12 guards, half of them city police and the other half members of the PSUC as evidenced by their red arm bands.

Both men were shot during the following night, by machine guns, as the autopsy proved. It was cold blooded murder, since both men were unarmed. The murder was committed near the Palace of the Generality. Soon after the bodies of the two Anarchists were delivered at the morgue of the Hospital Clinico. The lists show that the Red Cross had found both bodies near the Generality.

The evidence is irrefutable. Berneri and Barbieri were shot, because they were Anarchists, by police and members of the PSUC, i.e., faithful Moscow Communists.

Source: Souchy, A. (1937) *The Tragic Week in May*, Barcelona, p. 19.

Document 7.8 Rounding up Foreign Revolutionaries

(a)

I had gotten up from my sick-bed in hopes the May Days would change things, reverse the tide, but it had only sped up the communist drive for control. I was fired from my Generality job by the PSUCists. Eileen Blair and Lt. Col. George Kopp tried to raise my spirits by feeding me.

George had tried to persuade me to leave Barcelona even before the May Days. He said we were children, playing with fire, and should get out. I didn't take him seriously, but he knew whereof he spoke. The next day, June 15, 1937 the Russian-led police arrested Nin and the POUM Executive Committee. They didn't get to us until two days later. June 17, 1937, they raided the Hotel Falcon at 2 am and arrested all the foreigners there. At 8 am they came to our apartment at Republica de Argentina 2 bis to arrest us and two other foreign comrades who lived with us.

That night, they separated out the POUM foreigners and marched us through the blacked-out streets of the Old City to Puerta del Angel, 24.

Puerta del Angel, 24 was a Russian checka, an old house, elegant upstairs. They put us eight women in a windowless basement room about 15' square. Outside the door was an air vent that ran up for five stories. The walls of our cell were dirty grey plaster, covered with graffitti by the prisoners before us, in all the languages of the International Brigade. One prisoner had lovingly traced out a map of the Soviet Union. The fifteen men (with whom we could exchange remarks when we went to the toilet) had a big picture of Stalin on the wall of their cell.

Source: Cusick, L. (1978) *The Anarchist Millenium: Memories of the Spanish Revolution, 1936–37*, unpublished manuscript, Gainesville, pp. 303–5.

(b)

For four of us the position was very different: George Orwell, Eileen, Stafford Cottman and myself, I had been informed that we were all on the lists of suspects and warrants were out for our arrests. We had a council of war and decided to stay together and leave Spain at the same time. George and Eileen would not separate, and Orwell summed it up when he said: 'Let's all stick together and fight it through – damn them all.'

In the meantime I had seen the other foreign friends. I saw Max Petel but as he was a member of the French Socialist Party and there were a lot of French people in Barcelona his position was not dangerous. Then I met my old friend, Willy Brandt. Willy was making his own arrangements to leave by steamer. I fixed up a final appointment for the three of us next morning.

Source: McNair, J. (1973) *Spanish Diary*, Manchester, p. 24.

It was not until the morning of the 6th that there was a noticeable break in the gunfire. By this time the vast majority of the rank-and-file of the CNT and FAI had lost their will to fight. With their leaders insisting that the workers should not offer any further resistance, it made little sense for them to continue to man the barricades. When the bulk of the troops from Valencia arrived in Barcelona the next day, they entered the working-class districts unopposed. The state of siege that had abruptly descended on Barcelona on the 3rd had finally lifted[5] (Document 7.9).

Document 7.9 Taking Down the Barricades

Friday 7 May [1937]

A few hours later, Barcelona had undergone an almost complete change. True to their agreement, the workers had left the barricades. In many places the barricades had already been torn down. They had withdrawn from the buildings. But they were keeping their arms.

In the center of the city, however, the air was still tense. The barricades of the assault guards, of the Catalan Nationalists, and of the PSUC remained intact. And guarded. Taking advantage of the good will of the workers, groups of assault guards were walking about disarming workers wherever they could get hold of them. New friction arose between the assault guards and the Libertarian Youth in the Plaza del Pino and the Puertafer. And once more it was thanks to the initiative of the Anarchist Youth, who went unarmed to the headquarters of the assault guards to negotiate, that finally, after hours of discussion, the assault guards decided to show a more peaceful attitude and the barricades could come down.

Source: Souchy, A. (1937) *The Tragic Week in May*, Barcelona, p. 28.

Significance of the May Events

Most of the contemporary accounts of the May disturbances underscore the political importance it held for the future of the Republic. While each camp saw it as a tragedy for the Republican side, each interpreted the tragedy differently. For the Popular Front forces the fighting was symptomatic of the unruliness of those who were critical of their pro-statist policies. In their eyes, this indiscipline amounted to an act of insubordination, above all because it undermined the Republic's ability to fight and thus played into the hands of the Nationalists. On the other hand, the far-left parties saw the May events as the culmination of their ongoing struggle against the bourgeois parties who wanted to recover the power they had lost to the revolutionary workers' movement after 19 July 1936. As far as they were concerned the May conflict underscored the fundamentally different ways in which the two sides viewed the war itself. The Popular Front supporters saw it as a national war against foreign invaders which had to be won before the question of social, political and economic reform in the Republic could be addressed. For the CNT-FAI and POUM the war was about social revolution and therefore they insisted that the war and revolution had to be conducted simultaneously.[6]

In emphasizing the political character of the crisis, these contemporary accounts do not necessary imply that the meaning of the May disturbances was reducible to a one-dimensional conflict between pro- and anti-revolutionary forces which had arisen as a result of the war. On the contrary, references are made in these publications to the longstanding complex web of dialectical conflicts in the region that were embedded in class (workers versus middle classes), economic (unions versus entrepreneurs), and political (bourgeois republicanism and Catalan separatism versus socialist internationalism) issues.

Yet, while it was true that the May fighting had its roots in conflicts that predated the Civil War, it was also true that the disturbances themselves were intimately bound up with the unique set of political circumstances in Catalonia that had developed since July 1936. First and foremost was the fact that the power and influence of the dominant political parties in the region – notably, the Esquerra and the Estat Català – had been significantly compromised by the emergence of new political forces. The formation of the communist-dominated PSUC in late July 1936 was perhaps the most significant development in this regard. Although it had been in existence only a short while, the PSUC and its trade union affiliate, UGT, had rapidly grown into the most dynamic and effective political organizations in Catalonia. This was not least due to these organizations' ability to draw upon two very different constituencies. For example, while the UGT siphoned off non-revolutionary workers from the militant CNT-FAI and POUM, middle-class shopkeepers and peasant property owners, who had belonged to the Esquerra and other regional parties before the war, were now flocking to the PSUC because it appeared to offer the best protection against the expropriating policies of the revolutionaries.

The prewar power equation in the region was also significantly affected by the debut of the revolutionary organizations (CNT-FAI and POUM) onto the formal political stage. Among other things, their unprecedented participation in government rule had not only exacerbated old tensions but also created new ones. The fact that middle-class parties were forced to rule in co-operation with organizations that promoted a political and economic agenda that was diametrically opposed to their own meant that a stable underlying political consensus would be nearly impossible to achieve. As events would show, the marriage of convenience that had been hastily cobbled together between the revolutionary and anti-revolutionary parties at the beginning of the war was never meant to last. For, as soon as the balance tipped in favour of the pro-government parties, the idea of power-sharing was immediately abandoned.

It must also be emphasized that the regional political conflicts referred to here did not take place in a vacuum. Most were inextricably intertwined with the rapidly evolving national political context of the Republic. This is illustrated by the PSUC's reciprocal relationship with the native and foreign communists, who collectively represented the most potent political force on the left from 1937 until late in the war. Because the PSUC was used as a conduit for promoting Stalinist policies in the region, events in Catalonia were unavoidably linked to the ever-expanding Popular Front state-building projects that were increasingly being dominated by the communists throughout Republican Spain.

War of words

And, finally, the May Events exercised a profound impact on the propaganda struggle that was being waged among left-wing parties inside Republican Spain. As we have seen, the main parties on the left were divided into pro- and anti-Popular Front camps. Led by the communists, the former group were pursuing policies that were consistent with the view that Spain's Civil War was intimately bound up with the international conflict between fascism and democracy. The revolutionaries also saw the war as an expression of a global process. But instead of defining it in terms of middle-class democracy versus fascism, they insisted on picturing the war as a life-and-death struggle between the working classes and bourgeois capitalism and its fascist defenders. Not surprisingly, the May disturbances were interpreted very differently by the two opposing groups. The defenders of the Popular Front line argued that they should be understood as a failed 'criminal putsch' provoked by disloyal elements in the Republican camp who were acting in collusion with the Nationalists (Document 7.10). On the other hand, the far-left organizations maintained that, far from being an act of subversion, the May Events were about defending the people's revolution that had been set in motion in July 1936 against the bourgeois elements who were trying to reassert their hegemony (Document 7.11). For various reasons, including the fact that the pro-government forces emerged victorious in the wake of the May riots, the Popular Front view summarized here became the dominant version of events both inside and outside of Spain. As far as the revolutionary movement was concerned, this propaganda victory had far-reaching consequences. Above all it provided the Valencian government the formal pretext needed to substantially reduce worker-power in Catalonia and elsewhere in Republican Spain. In the months following the May crisis, for example, the government stepped up its efforts to nationalize industries that had formerly been under union control. The government also succeeded in rolling back the revolutionary movement in the countryside. In Republican-held Aragon – where the CNT-FAI had established their own libertarian fiefdom – anarchosyndicalist militias were disarmed and their agricultural collectives were forcibly dismantled.

Document 7.10 Identifying 'Enemies of the People'

(a)

The fascist rebellion of July, 1936, came. At that time the slogan of the day was defense of the democratic republic, the only slogan capable of rallying all the anti-fascist forces, the only one capable of creating the conditions necessary for a struggle for the real liberation of the proletariat and all the people of Spain. The reply of the Trotskyists to this was to demand the immediate estab-lishment of the dictatorship of the proletariat, a slogan calculated to smash the People's Front by separating the middle classes from the proletariat and depriving the latter of their allies, thereby facilitating German and Italian fascist intervention.

It was a criminal act of provocation designed to arouse the hatred of honest Anarchist workers against the international brigades engaged in rendering such great aid to the Spanish people. Only an agent of Franco could express himself in these terms.

Source: Marty, A. (1937) *Heroic Spain*, New York, pp. 21–2.

(b)

The Anarcho-Trotskyite putsch of May, which was inevitably to lead to a crisis in the Largo Caballero government, had been in the making for months. The time for the outbreak was not chosen in Catalonia, but in the General Staff offices of Franco, as proved by the document already quoted from German Ambassador Faupel, which gives testimony of the ties of the POUM and FAI with the enemy.

And if they bloodied the streets of Barcelona with a criminal revolt, it was because neither the Catalán nor Madrid governments wanted, for different reasons, to end the shameful, violent provocation.

Source: Ibárruri, D. (1966) *They Shall Not Pass*, New York, p. 285.

(c)

José Díaz declared at a public meeting on May 9 [1937]:

Our principal enemies are the fascists. However, the fascists have their agents who work for them. Of course, if these agents were to say, 'We are fascists and we want to work among you in order to create difficulties,' they would immediately be eliminated by us. For this reason they have to give themselves other names . . . Some call themselves Trotskyists, which is the name used by many disguised fascists who talk of revolution in order to spread disorder. I therefore ask: If everyone knows this, if the government knows it, why does it not treat them like fascists and exterminate them pitilessly?

Source: Bolloten, B. (1991) *The Spanish Civil War*, Chapel Hill, pp. 462–3.

Document 7.11 POUM Calls for Renewal of Revolutionary Struggle

May 13 in 'La Batalla.'

1. The unceasing provocations of the counter-revolution, embodied in the reformist parties of the PSUC and the petty bourgeoisie – provocations aimed at liquidating in the spheres of economy, war and the public order, the revolutionary gains won by the workers, weapon in hand, on July 19, provocations which reached their climax on May 3 with the attempt to storm the telephone exchange building – these provocations produced the armed protest of the proletariat . . .

The experience of the May struggles has clearly shown that the only solution lies in the seizure of power by the working class and that it is therefore absolutely necessary for the revolutionary activity of the working masses to be coordinated thru the formation of a revolutionary workers front uniting all organizations ready to fight for the complete annihilation of fascism. This can be accomplished only thru military victory at the front and the victory of the revolution at home.

Source: Lambda (1937) *The Truth about the Barcelona Events*, New York, pp. 13–14.

The fall of Largo Caballero

Because he had refused to act decisively and effectively to put down the May rebellion, Caballero was vulnerable to barbed criticisms of the communists and his opponents within the PSOE. In the immediate aftermath of the uprising his authority was once again assailed by the communists who had just launched their campaign of persecution against the POUM. Denouncing *poumistas* as fascist agents and provocateurs who had inspired the 'criminal putsch' in Barcelona, the PCE insisted that the rearguard could not be secured until the POUM had been 'swept away' by the government. His stubborn refusal to do so prompted Uribe and Hernández, the two communist ministers, to storm out of his cabinet. Though he was confident that he could continue to rule without them, Caballero underestimated the extent to which the political tide of opinion had turned against him. In the weeks leading up to the May crisis the anti-Caballerista forces had been gaining momentum. Much of this opposition was centred around the Republicans' inability to defeat the Nationalists. A string of setbacks in the spring only reinforced the view that Caballero lacked the strategic acumen needed to reverse Republican military fortunes. Thus the May crisis had merely solidified the anti-Caballero alliances in the government, particularly the one formed between the *prietista* wing of the socialist movement and the communists. It was the pressure of this coalition of forces that forced Caballero on 17 May to step down from his posts as war minister and premier. He was replaced by the moderate socialist Juan Negrín, who would rule the Popular Front government until the end of the war.

The decline of the left socialists

Largo's dismissal threw into sharper relief the longstanding strains and fractures within the socialist movement, especially those which revolved around the Largo/Prieto rivalry. Up till now doctrinal and tactical differences between the reformist and revolutionary wings had been kept under control, above all because of their collective desire to uphold the banner of Popular Front unity in the face of Nationalist aggression. But the more it became apparent that this commitment meant different things to the competing socialist factions, the more this unity began to break down. As far as the left socialists were concerned, for example, Popular Frontism and the class collaboration it implied was acceptable as long as it did not mean sacrificing the social and economic gains that had been achieved during the revolutionary phase of the war. But this was not true for the reformist socialists, who made it clear in the aftermath of the May crisis that they were determined to liquidate the revolution for the sake of political expediency.

The new direction of Republican politics inevitably raised the question as to whether the radical tendencies within the socialist movement would continue to support the Popular Front coalition or whether they would retaliate by directly challenging the anti-revolutionary drift of the government. For several reasons the latter alternative had little chance of succeeding. Foremost was the fact that, since

July 1936, the relative strengths of the rival tendencies had been irrevocably altered. Although they maintained their numerical superiority within the socialist movement, the left socialists increasingly found themselves unable to prevent the moderates and their friends from imposing their will on the trade unions.[7] Yet the ascendancy of the moderate socialists was not simply the result of the failure of political leadership on the left. What tipped the balance in their favour was the informal partnership that had been cobbled together between the *prietistas* and the communists.[8]

The co-operation between the reformist wing of the socialist movement and the PCE represented a major departure from the pre-Civil War pattern of political alignments. Before July 1936 the two had clashed with one another over a number of fundamental issues. This was true even during the brief Popular Front period, during which time Prieto's efforts to rebuild the alliance between the Republicans and the Socialists were being supported by the communists. But this did not stop Prieto from spurning the communists' friendly overtures. He was particularly hostile to the latter's bid to bring about the fusion of the two parties. Needless to say, Prieto's steadfast refusal to countenance what he termed the 'fraud of unification' earned him the opprobrium of the communists (Document 7.12).

Document 7.12 Prieto Versus the Communists

Then Prieto, who was excited, spoke, delivering a speech on the theme of co-operation with the Communists, in which, by the way, he declared, 'We will speak openly. It's no use playing. The Communists are capable people. They have a certain way of working. I would not even object if the minister of internal affairs were a Communist. But I would not want to have Communists as my own subordinates. For the Communist is not a human being – he's a party, he's a line . . .

If in questions of internal politics Prieto wants to push aside the Communists, then this [attitude] was also noticeable in the army.

On 26 June, Prieto published his famous order on forbidding 'prose-lytizing' (I enclose a translation of the text of the order). At that time it seemed to many that this was done by accident, that Rojo or someone else had slipped that law to Prieto and that it was then, as is well known, quickly taken up by the Caballeristas, anarchists, and used against the Communists. But later, during the time of the Madrid operation, it was revealed that Prieto had really actively tried to reduce the influence of the party in the army. This effort took a special form – an overemphasis on the supposed military illiteracy of the Communist commanders, a disparagement of their contribution, and so on.

Source: Radosh, R., Habeck, M.R. and Sevostianov, G. (eds) (2001) *Spain Betrayed*, New Haven, pp. 215–17.

After the outbreak of civil war in July 1936, however, relations between the two former antagonists underwent significant changes. Apart from appreciating the fact that the PCE were, like themselves, adamantly opposed to the revolutionary trajectory of Republican politics, the *prietistas* recognized that they needed another powerful ally if they ever were to dislodge the *caballeristas* from the commanding positions they held in the government and the trade unions. For their part, the communists were willing to collaborate with the moderates because this would bring them closer to realizing their own long-range hegemonic designs, which, as we have seen, included their desire to dominate the Spanish left by effecting a fusion of the communist and socialist movements.

Of the two partners, it was the communists who were largely responsible for systematically eroding the organizational strength and discipline of the left socialists. In the period immediately following the May Events they were particularly successful at whittling away at the power of the *caballeristas* in the unions. To understand how the communists eroded socialist influence within their own organizations it is necessary to appreciate the different ways in which the socialists co-operated with the communists. During the war a certain number of socialists – notably the Foreign Minister, Álvarez del Vayo – transferred their political allegiance to the communists in order to facilitate the amalgamation of the two movements (Document 7.13). But, for various reasons, including the fact that they were following the instructions of the communists who did not want to force such a unification, they did not leave the PSOE and UGT. Just how many socialists became 'fellow travellers' during the war is difficult to determine, though, judging from the postwar memoirs of leading socialist and ex-communist figures it is reasonable to assume that defectors of this kind were present throughout the party and union structures, from the upper echelons right down to the rank and file. While the degree to which they contributed to the communists' penetration of the socialist movement cannot be accurately measured, there can be no doubt that the duplicitous behaviour of fellow travellers who occupied key government and trade union positions undermined socialist unity.[9] This was true because in public their true allegiances were veiled not only to those working closely with them but also to the rank-and-file. If we are to accept the testimony of anti-communist eyewitnesses, many socialists sincerely believed that fellow travellers such as Santiago Carrillo, Álvarez del Vayo, and Amaro del Rosal were acting on behalf of the socialists.[10]

Document 7.13 Álvarez del Vayo as a Fellow Traveller

The label 'fellow traveller' has been attached to me too. Here our opponents and accusers have a better case, judged by surface appearances. I have never made any secret of my sympathies for the Russian Revolution; I have visited Russia many times and written several books about it; in the Socialist party I have advocated unity of action with the Communists against fascist or reactionary attempts to seize power . . .

Anybody lacking in scruples and a respect for truth might find material with which to build up Del Vayo as a 'fellow traveller.'

Source: Alvarez del Vayo, J. (1950) *The Last Optimist*, New York, pp. 288 and 289.

For yet another group of socialists, and here we can include Indalecio Prieto, Juan Negrín, and Ramón Lamoneda, allying with communists did not entail joining their cause since their co-operation was motivated largely by political opportunism. Particularly in the period leading up to and immediately following the May Events of 1937, Prieto, Ramón Lamoneda and other reformist members of the PSOE executive believed that they had much to gain by co-operating with the communists.

It soon became apparent that the more the communists applied pressure against the ramparts of the left socialists, the more the *caballeristas* lost ground to their adversaries. Towards the end of May 1937, control of Caballero's principal mouthpiece *Claridad* (Madrid) fell into the hands of the communist 'fellow traveller' Amaro del Rosal. Shortly afterwards *Adelante*, the daily newspaper of the Caballero-dominated Federación Socialista Valenciana, was forcibly taken over (Document 7.14). The remaining public organ of the *caballeristas*, the evening paper *La Correspondencia de Valencia*, was shut down on 13 November on the grounds that it fomented a 'rebellious' (read anti-Popular Front) attitude among the workers. These setbacks were not offset by Caballero's own efforts to mount an anti-communist crusade from within the trade-union movement. For even though he resumed his secretaryship of the UGT, the reality was that Caballero was daily growing, in the words of one sympathetic eyewitness, increasingly 'weak and indecisive'.[11]

Document 7.14 Campaign against Largo Caballero and his Supporters

(a)

For three weeks the Caballeristas have been endeavoring to organize a dissenting congress of the Socialist party. Lamoneda, the general secretary of the Socialist party, who up to now has not inspired us with any great confidence in his efficiency on the matter of unity, has now become the most fervent defender of unity. Several days ago, in the name of the executive committee of the Socialist party, he dismissed the provincial committee of the Communist party, which had taken an anti-unity position, and replaced it with another committee that was pro-unity. He also expelled the anti-unity Caballeristas from the editorship of the newspaper *Adelante* and turned *Adelante* into a pro-unity organ of the Socialist party.

Source: Radosh, R., Habeck, M.R. and Sevastianov, G. (eds) (2001) *Spain Betrayed*, New Haven, pp. 229–30.

(b)

The Caballeristas have in their hands the leadership of the regional committee of the city's unions. Therefore they have the opportunity to publish the daily organ *Correspondencia de Valencia* – the organ of Valencia's unions. This newspaper is now Caballero's organ, leading the dirtiest campaign against the

Communist party. This question was before the secretariat up to the time that I came here; the comrades are convincing me every day that they are driving the Caballeristas out of the leadership of the union regional committee and from the editorial staff of the newspaper. The comrades want to enter into an agreement with the Socialists (centrists) who are in the leadership of the regional committee, which will give them the majority, and then to make a sort of semi-legal revolution, driving out the Caballerista editors and putting in their place a new editorial staff. They assure [me] that this is possible, that it is possible to accomplish it with the help of the authorities and they promise every day that everything will be done in twenty-four hours. Luis inspires them and energetically pushes down this path.

Source: Radosh, R., Habeck, M.R. and Sevastianov, G. (eds) (2001) *Spain Betrayed*, New Haven, pp. 417–18.

However, the political eclipse of Caballero did not put an end to the struggle for control of the PSOE and UGT. From 1937 on the left socialists, under the leadership of the head of the militant land-workers' federation (FNTT), Ricardo Zabalza, fought hard against the governments' aggressive anti-collectivist programmes in the countryside (Document 7.15). As we shall see, the final round of the socialists' internecine struggle occurred during the last weeks of the war, when the left socialists joined other anti-communists in their effort to unseat the Negrín government.

Document 7.15 Socialists Promote Collectivisation in the Countryside

As a result, the wage workers remain without land in many places or have to content themselves with the worst soil or with that farthest from the villages because the rest of the land, or nearly all of it, is in the hands of small owners and tenant farmers. This makes friction inevitable, for it is impossible to accept the galling injustice of a situation whereby the sycophants of the former political bosses still enjoy a privileged position at the expense of those persons who were unable to rent even the smallest parcel of land because they were revolutionaries.

Source: Bolloten, B. (1991) *The Spanish Civil War*, Chapel Hill, pp. 239–40.

Repression of the POUM

As we saw earlier, it was in the wake of the May Events that the new leaders of the new Popular Front government vigorously pursued a programme aimed at establishing centralized control over the political and economic life in the Republican zone. One of the first 'casualties' of this drive was the semi-autonomous Catalan government. It will be recalled that, having failed on its own to resolve the May crisis, the Generalitat had opened the door to outside interference. The arrival of thousands of Assault Guards and *carabineros* (the customs and excise guards who were increasingly being used by the government as an auxillary police force) during the last days of the conflict along with the appointment of General Sebastián Pozas as military commander of Catalonia on 5 May effectively divested the Generalitat of its control over public order. Further encroachments on Catalan autonomy occurred in the following months, climaxing when the central government decided to transfer to Barcelona in late October 1937.

Taking full advantage of the changed political climate, the communists and the PSUC spearheaded an all-out offensive against the much-vilified POUM. Because of its relatively small size and because it lacked any firm political allies, the POUM was particularly vulnerable to the campaign of repression against it that began in June, 1937 and continued until the end of the war. Acting on the orders of Alexander Orlov and other agents of the NKVD, the Soviet security police, communists in the government's security forces began gaoling POUM leaders. By mid-June, Nin, Andrade, Jordi Arquer, Gorkín and other members of the party executive had been arrested, and, in the following weeks, *poumistas* throughout the Republican camp were hounded into exile or driven underground. Nin himself was taken to a prison on the outskirts of Madrid, where, under torture, he was murdered by his communist captors. Because his unexplained disappearance proved to be an embarrassment to the recently formed Negrín government, the communists attempted to cover their crime by circulating a variety of rumours, the most preposterous being one that had Nin escaping from prison with the aid of the German Gestapo and Nationalist soldiers who had disguised themselves as International Brigaders. In the end, only those who wilfully ignored Nin's untarnished revolutionary pedigree could accept that he was secretly an agent of fascism.

Having been made the scapegoats of the May disturbances, *poumistas* were pilloried not just in the communist media but also in much of the national and international press. The communists' appeal to the unity of the Popular Front proved to be an effective way of silencing criticism of their anti-POUM persecutions. Few people either inside or outside of Spain dared to speak out on the POUM's behalf. The eyewitness revelations and documented testimonies of those who did, including the writings of well-known public figures such as Fenner Brockway and John McNair of the British Independent Labour Party (ILP) and George Orwell, did little to change public opinion, which had already weighed in against the POUM (Document 7.16). As we shall see in a later chapter, the anti-POUM campaign culminated in October 1938, when several prominent *poumistas* were finally tried by a special tribunal on espionage.

Document 7.16 In Defence of the POUM

Because the P.O.U.M. was the main instrument in resisting the counter-revolutionary tendencies of the Government it was fiercely attacked by the Communist International, which feared that Britain, France and the 'democratic' capitalist countries might be estranged from Russia by a Socialist revolution. The Communists went to astounding lengths of calumny against the P.O.U.M. They charged it with being engaged in conspiracies to assassinate Largo Caballero, the Premier, and other Spanish leaders. They asserted that the P.O.U.M. was General Franco's 'Fifth Column,' serving as Fascist spies and planning to sabotage the anti-Fascist Forces. They actually made the charge that the P.O.U.M. militia had deliberately refused to advance at the Front at critical moments in order to enable the Fascists to win victories!

The Communists have never produced one jot or tittle of evidence in support of these outrageous statements. When challenged they have been unable to substantiate a single charge.

Source: Brockway, F. (1937) *The Truth about Barcelona*, London, p. 6.

Anarchosyndicalists in disarray

It was a testament to the political character of the May crisis that the anarchosyndicalists of the CNT-FAI were not called to account for their role in the disturbances. This was partly because the relative strength and influence of the organizations were still considerable in Catalonia and parts of Aragón and partly because the anti-revolutionary parties did not feel compelled to prosecute a movement that was increasingly being rent asunder by internal discord. Though temporarily repressed in the weeks that followed the May Events, dissident anarchists belonging to the Anarchist Youth organizations (FIJL) and the Friends of Durruti movement continued to agitate for a complete reversal of official libertarian policy (Document 7.17). Yet for the majority of *cenetistas*, especially those who believed that unity in the anti-fascist coalition was necessary in order to defeat fascism, it was too late to chart an alternative course. Instead they opted for the collaboration line being advocated by Mariano Vásquez, Horatio Prieto and other prominent libertarian representatives. They did so not because they believed in the state-building goals of Popular Frontism but because they had resigned themselves to the fact that Negrín's policy of resistance was the only diplomatic weapon the Spanish left had in their arsenal against the Nationalists. In the end, their co-operation with the pro-statist parties cost them dearly. For in the last year of the war their attempts to win over the pro-Revolutionary elements were to no avail, and the chasm separating the two tendencies continued to widen.

Document 7.17 Exposing the 'Betrayals' of the Counter-revolutionaries

For our part, we must point out that we can no longer remain in silence nor tolerate all the counter-revolutionary activities which are taking place; so much Governmental injustice and so much political unfaithfulness – all in the name of the war and anti-fascist unity.

The Revolutionary Working Class Alliance, sought long before the fascist revolt and so eagerly desired by the workers in general, has not been accomplished because governmental socialism is more interested in an alliance with the republican bourgeoisie.

Source: 'Protest of Libertarian Youth', *Man!* (San Francisco), June 1937.

In addition to the problems caused by their internal feuding, the anarchosyndicalists were forced in the coming months to adjust to a political reality in which their bargaining position in the Popular Front coalition had been greatly diminished. Before the May Events, local and national governments found it necessary to solicit anarchist representation in their administrations. Yet, when Juan Negrín announced the formation of his first administration on 17 May, not a single anarchosyndicalist was named to the cabinet. Even in Catalonia, one of the traditional libertarian strongholds, the regional administration cobbled together by Luis Companys at the end of June did not include an anarchist minister.

Realizing that they could no longer participate in the political arena on their own terms, leading members of the CNT-FAI began searching for other ways to recover their strength and influence. Overtures to the left cadres of the UGT during the summer of 1937 led to preliminary discussions of a fusion of the two movements. Yet finding common ground between organizations that held differing programmes and overall goals was not easily negotiated. The rise of the communists and their Popular Front allies and the consequent rapid decline of Largo Caballero's wing of the socialist movement represented another stumbling block to the formation of an anarchist-socialist coalition. For their part, the communists recognized that the best way of domesticating the anarchists was to bring about a fusion of the CNT organizations and those sections of the UGT under communist influence (Document 7.18). This was not possible until the spring of 1938, above all because the *caballeristas* had by then lost their commanding position in the UGT. A pact between the age-old rivals was concluded on 18 March 1938. But because the terms of the contract effectively subordinated the Republic's two largest unions to the will of the central government, this historic fusion was hardly more than a symbolic gesture made in order to demonstrate working-class solidarity during a time when the Republic was at the point of military defeat. In this sense, the CNT–UGT concordance represented the denouement of one of the principal rivalries on the left that had characterized Republican politics since July 1936. From this point on the Republic would be effectively under the administrative control of the Popular Front government of Juan Negrín.

Document 7.18 Communist Strategy for Domesticating the Anarchosyndicalists

There is significant disorder within the anarchist movement. There are two tendencies. The adventuristic tendency, represented mainly by the leadership of the Iberian Anarchist Federation (FAI), the regional Catalan committee of the National Labor Confederation (CNT), and also by part of the leadership of the anarchist youth, has close ties with the Caballero group and with the Trotskyist POUM. This tendency suffered a defeat at the plenum of the entire anarchist movement, which took place at the end of October. The other, healthier tendency is represented by the leadership of the National Labor Confederation (CNT) and the majority of its organization. It is standing up for supporting the government, for the Popular Front, for the struggle for the country's independence . . .

To further strengthen unity, it is necessary to intensify the struggle against the enemies of unity – the POUM, the Caballeristas, adventurers from the Iberian Anarchist Federation (FAI), defeatists – coordinating this struggle with the struggle for a closer unity between the Communist party and the Soc. Party, for a union of the youth, for an activation of the Popular Front, and, most of all, for the creation of a unified union center as the vitally important question of the war itself. To achieve this last objective, it would be necessary to concretely raise and resolve the question not only about the further improvement of the party's work in the General Workers' Union (UGT) and in the enterprises, but also about the work in the National Labor Confederation (CNT). This would be done to get some prominent leaders of the CNT, from the most honest elements, to enter the Communist party and the Unified Socialist Party of Catalonia. [We could then] use cases like these to develop a large-scale political campaign.

Source: Gerö, E. 25 November 1938 in Radosh, R., Habeck, M.R. and Sevastianov, G. (eds) (2001) *Spain Betrayed*, New Haven, pp. 508–9.

After they had repeatedly failed to take Madrid by the spring of 1937, the Nationalists decided to shift the focus of their military operations. Franco himself had not given up on the idea of capturing the capital, but at this point in the fighting he believed that defeating the isolated northern zone of the Republic would greatly improve his chances of achieving this goal. At the end of March General Mola, chief of the Army of the North, launched a major offensive in the Basque country. This was to be the opening battle the Nationalist campaign to conquer republican territory not only in Vizcaya but also in the adjoining regions of Santander, Gijón, and Oviedo. It was shortly after the Basque offensive had begun that one of the most controversial and emotionally stirring episodes of the war occurred. On the afternoon of 26 April several squadrons of German and Italian aircraft carrying an estimated 60,000 pounds of high-explosive and incendiary bombs took off from airfields in Burgos and Vitoria en route to the small market town of Guernica. Their mission was to destroy a bridge (Rentería) and railway station that linked the Basque town nestled in a mountain valley with the outside world. The first planes arrived in the late afternoon. The incoming HE-111 bombers immediately swooped down over the station area, dropping high-explosive and incendiary bombs. Soon afterwards, the target area was hit again by a wave of Heinkels and Junkers-52 bombers.[1] Within half an hour the smoke and dust surrounding the town was so thick that further bombing sweeps carried out by both German and Italian aircraft were done blindly. As a result, a number of houses and public buildings which could not be regarded as legitimate military targets were also hit. By the time the last planes departed around 7.30 p.m., most of the town lay in ruins. In the mounds of rubble and debris left from the burning buildings were the charred and mutilated remains of several hundred men, women, and children. (Estimates of those actually killed range from fewer than a dozen to more than three thousand.) An untold number of other civilians had been wounded by the fighter planes who strafed men, women, and children scrambling to find shelter in the closest *refugio*. Those who survived the attack could not easily erase from their memories the scenes of devastation and carnage to which they were subjected that fateful afternoon (Document 8.1). News of their anguish and suffering inspired the renowned Spanish artist Pablo Picasso to immortalize Guernica's tragedy in what many critics now regard as his most famous painting. Across the massive canvas of this daring work – first exhibited on 4 June 1937 at the International Exhibition in Paris – are strewn grotesque figures painted in the sombre hues of white, black, and grey. Through his use of colour and startling imagery Picasso managed to tell to the world a profoundly moving story not only of the aerial bombardment of Guernica but also of the senseless death and destruction that inevitably results from the tactics of modern warfare.

Document 8.1 The Bombing of Guernica

(a)

Today we flew to Guernica. It has been totally destroyed, and not by the Reds, as all the local newspapers report, but by German and Italian bombers. It is the opinion of all of us that it was a rotten trick to destroy such a militarily unimportant city as Guernica. There are certainly thousands more dead beneath the rubble, unnecessary victims. Everywhere is smoking rubble, bomb craters, empty facades.

Source: Ries, K. and Ring, H. (1992) *The Legion Condor*, West Chester, PA, p. 62.

(b)

– The fighters dived down and machine-gunned people trying to flee across the plain. The bombers were flying so low you could see the crewmen, recalled Father Dionisio AJANGUIZ. It was a magnificent clear April evening after a showery morning . . .

– People started to panic, recalled Ignacia OZAMIZ. 'The house is on fire, we're going to be burnt alive,' they screamed. *Gudaris* guarding the shelter let no one leave. One man tried to force his way out with his young child. 'I don't care if they kill me, I can't stand it here.' He was pushed back. 'Keep calm,' the soldiers shouted . . .

Source: Fraser, Ronald (1979) *The Blood of Spain*, New York, pp. 399 and 400.

(c)

We were still a good ten miles away when I saw the reflection of Guernica's flames in the sky. As we drew nearer, on both sides of the road, men, women and children were sitting, dazed. I saw a priest in one group. I stopped the car and went up to him, 'What happened, Father?' I asked. His face was blackened, his clothes in tatters. He couldn't talk. He just pointed to the flames, still about four miles away, then whispered: 'Aviones . . . bombas . . . mucho, mucho.'

In the good 'I' tradition of the day, I was the first correspondent to reach Guernica, and was immediately pressed into service by some Basque soldiers collecting charred bodies that the flames had passed over. Some of the soldiers were sobbing like children. There were flames and smoke and grit, and the smell of burning human flesh was nauseating. Houses were collapsing into the inferno.

In the Plaza, surrounded almost by a wall of fire, were about a hundred figures. They were wailing and weeping and rocking to and fro. One middle-aged man spoke English. He told me: 'At four, before the market closed, many aeroplanes came. They dropped bombs. Some came low and shot bullets into the streets. Father Aronategui was wonderful. He prayed with the people in the Plaza while the bombs fell.' The man had no idea who I was, as far as I know. He was telling me what had happened at Guernica.

Source: Monks, N. (1955) *Eyewitness*, London, pp. 96–7.

In purely military terms the bombing of Guernica could not be judged a complete success. For though nearly every major building in the town's centre had been severely damaged or destroyed and thousands had been terrorized by the assault, one of the designated targets, the Rentería bridge, remained intact. On the other hand, the attack did pave the way for the Nationalist ground forces who were pressing towards Guernica. Less than three days after the bombing raid, Spanish, Moroccan, and Italian troops met little resistance as they marched into the smouldering city.

Compared to the aerial bombing raids conducted during the Second World War, the scale of death and destruction in Guernica is not remarkable. Yet, at the time, the idea of attacking a civilian population in order to achieve military objectives was shocking to most people. Thus, as soon as news of the events there became widely known, Guernica sparked a scandal of international proportions, becoming, in the words of the historian Herbert Southworth, 'one of the most discussed events of the war'. The publicity surrounding the Guernica tragedy was fuelled by the many questions that arose in its immediate aftermath, not least being who should be held accountable for attacking the city. Republicans and their supporters insisted that the brutal assault on a town of minor strategic importance was proof of the annihilation tactics that the Nationalists were adopting in their relentless drive to terminate the northern offensive as soon as possible. Yet the Nationalists were quick to deny any responsibility for what had happened. Instead, Franco's press agents accused the Reds of destroying Guernica as they had done early on in the war at Irún and elsewhere by dynamiting and setting fire to the city's buildings. Their decision to shift the blame in this way gave rise to bitter mutual recriminations which would persist until long after the war had ended (Document 8.2).

Document 8.2 The Origins of the Guernica Myth

(a)

St Jean de Luz, Wednesday

Franco's headquarters at Salamanca today formally denied all knowledge of the air raid which on Tuesday destroyed Guernica, ancient capital of the Basque country, North Spain.

No plane left the Vitoria aerodrome after Monday afternoon, it is stated. There was no flying on Tuesday.

The anti-Reds do not deny that the raid occurred, but they say they had not part in it.

The Basque (Red) authorities say the town had no military importance. A British Bilbao business man, however, stated today there is a large munitions factory at Guernica belonging to the Esperanza Unceta Co.

A new proclamation, denying suggestions that Guernica was destroyed by the Reds themselves, was today made by Señor Aguirre, Basque President, who stated: 'I affirm that for three and a half hours German planes bombarded the civil population of Guernica with unexampled savagery.' – Reuter.

The conclusions to be drawn from the facts summarized under these headings are clear and unmistakable. By far the greater part of the destruction worked in Guernica was the deliberate work of the retreating forces, and that part, if any, which was the result of the air raid of the 26th could have been localized and, in so far as the fires were concerned, substantially mitigated by prompt action on the early evening of the 26th.

Source: Reuters dispatch *Daily Mail*, London, 29 April, 1937

(b)

There is direct and unassailable evidence that, at the very most, only a quarter of the town was on fire at 8 p.m on April 26 after the last aeroplane had, by common consent, disappeared. There is also clear evidence that certain houses, some of them isolated, found burnt on the 29th, were not burnt at all on the 26th, but were set alight on the 27th or 28th and actually in one case on the 29th . . .

There is direct and unassailable evidence that explosions were heard through the night of the 26th – 27th. It is common ground that no aeroplanes were on the scene at that time.

Source: Guernica: Being the Official Report of a Commission Appointed by the Spanish National Government to Investigate the Causes of the Destruction of Guernica on April 26–28, 1937 (1938), London.

The fact that a relatively minor military operation could so rapidly escalate into a major episode illustrates the degree to which propaganda had become an integral feature of the war. So much so that the publicity surrounding events like the Guernica air attack would often overshadow or distort its actual military significance. Beginning with the uprising itself and continuing with widely publicized events such as the massacre at Badajoz, the siege of Alcázar, and the battle for Madrid, propaganda was used as an instrument of war on both sides. Winning the support and sympathy of the outside world, which could possibly be parlayed into some form of foreign assistance, was not the sole reason propaganda was seen as an indispensable weapon. Equally important was the need to sustain the loyalty of civilians and troops who were increasingly compelled to make great sacrifices for their respective causes. As far as the Guernica affair was concerned, the Republicans scored a major victory in the battle for world opinion, but, unfortunately for them, they were not able to reap substantial benefits from it. By this time, the Republicans appeared to be losing the war on every front, and the sympathy they gained from the international court of public opinion over the Guernica bombing did nothing to sway foreign governments from abandoning their hands-off policy towards Spain.

Following the destruction of Guernica, the Nationalists' northern offensive was briefly stalled by bad weather and the slow progress of troop movements through the rugged Basque terrain. One month later, however, improved weather conditions allowed further Nationalist advances into the Basque country. By mid-June only the key city of Bilbao had not yet fallen to the enemy. Yet, with the port to the city blockaded and supplies rapidly running out, the citizens of Bilbao faced overwhelming odds. Despite their determination to keep on fighting, they were forced to surrender on 19 June. Within a few weeks, the remaining pockets of Basque territory fell under Nationalist control (Document 8.3).

Document 8.3 The Collapse of the Basque Front

Apart from strategical damage of this nature and a comparatively small amount of destruction caused by aerial bombardment, the town of Bilbao and its industrial hinterland have suffered comparatively little. This is undoubtedly due in great measure to the rapidity of the military advance and to protective intervention by the Basque militias, who prevented their extremist allies from committing barbarities . . .

General Franco's forces are in complete control of Bilbao and have undertaken with commendable rapidity and success the reorganisation of the public institutions and services . . .

The chief impression derived at Bilbao today is the quiet determination evinced by the military and civil authorities, and by the civil population of the town itself, to cope with the numerous problems that beset them, in a spirit of cordial co-operation and friendship. There is no doubt in my mind that this spirit will result in the town being promptly restored to conditions of peace, happiness and industrial activity. There is considerable evidence that the principal factories will be working at reasonable pressure in a short space of time.

Source: British Documents on Foreign Affairs, series F, Europe, 1919–1939, vol. 27, Document no. 94, 19 June 1937, p. 129.

Not long after the Nationalists had mounted their northern campaign, the Popular Front command began gearing up for its own offensive. By this point in the war, the Popular Army had grown to around 360,000 men, and, thanks in part to increased Soviet military aid, now possessed a formidable array of artillery (750), tanks and armoured cars (250), and planes (200). Republican forces had also made great strides towards achieving a degree of organizational coherence and combat readiness that made it possible for them to undertake their own large-scale offensives (Document 8.4).

Document 8.4 Overview of the Military Situation in Republican and Nationalist Zones

General Franco's Government controls today three fifths of Spanish peninsular territory, including the Canaries and the Balearic Islands with the exception of Minorca. In addition, the Spanish Protectorate of Morocco and Ifni, Rio de Oro, and Spanish territory in the Gulf of Guinea and on the River Muni are likewise under General Franco's Administration. The Nationalist press states that in twelve months' operations General Franco's army has doubled the area in its occupation, increasing it from 147,000 square kilom. held in July 1936 to 310,000 kilom. in July 1937, the Government territory having decreased correspondingly in that period from 358,000 to 195,000 kilom. With this extension of their territory the Nationalists claim to have doubled the population under General Franco, which is now given as 14 to 15 million, leaving 9 to 10 million in Government territory. These figures, however, are founded on pre-war statistics and are probably inaccurate owing to the departure of a considerable proportion of the inhabitants of the larger towns before their occupation by General Franco's troops. Of fifty provincial capitals, thirty-three (including three in the islands) are under General Franco, of which six (Huelva, Badajoz, San Sebastian, Toledo, Malaga and Bilbao) have been captured in military operations.

The Two Armies

(a) Government Army

Don Indalecio Prieto, Minister for National Defence, stated in June 1937 that the Government army would soon reach 500,000 men. Time, the Government says, has been on its side, enabling it to convert all the heterogeneous elements at its disposal into an organised army. This army is well-equipped and, in general, well armed; but the scarcity of offices, the constant changes decreed in regard to organisation, administration and command; the lack of unity, discipline and training, have prevented the army as a whole from reaching any degree of efficiency; although in individual formations, particularly in the force defending Madrid, there are notable exceptions. There is no reliable information regarding the number of foreigners fighting in the ranks of the Government army; possibly no true record exists.

(b) General Franco's Army

With regard to General Franco's army no figures are ever disclosed enabling one to form an accurate idea of its strength. Nevertheless, in view of the length of the front, extending as it does 2,500 kilom. through the country, and the important forces engaged on two, at least, of the four main fronts (northern, central, southern and eastern), each with its several sectors, his army in the field cannot be less than 250,000 exclusive of reserves. The foreigners in his ranks have been estimated at different times at 75,000 to 100,000, but no accurate figure can be given. Like the Government army, General Franco does not depend on foreigners for number (such, at least, should not be the case considering the large man-power of the nation), but for experience and technical knowledge, for aviation above all, and for organisation in the distribution of supplies, movement of troops, &c. As to officers, at the outbreak of war General Franco was definitely at an advantage, for, in addition to the two-thirds or three-quarters of those on the active list who declared in his favour, the 12,000 to 14,000 officers who retired under the Azaña scheme in 1931 supported him to a man, though a proportion of them were caught in Government territory and were unavailable for service. Casualties among his officers, however, were very heavy in the first weeks of the war, several hundreds losing their lives in each of the defeated garrisons, including the smaller garrison towns of San Sebastian, Gijon, &c.

Source: British Documents on Foreign Affairs, series F, Europe, 1919–1939, vol. 27, Document no. 100, enclosure in document 99, pp. 138–9.

Throughout the spring of 1937, the Republicans had done little to stop the Nationalists' relentless advances in the north. Two ill-conceived and poorly executed attempts at drawing their attention away from the Basque front were made in May and June. The first took place north-west of Madrid and was focused on the towns of La Granja and Balsaín. The attack began on 30 May but was immediately met with fierce resistance from the enemy, whose state of preparedness suggests that they might have had advance knowledge of the operation. Lacking both the troops and supplies necessary to achieve their objectives, the Republicans suspended their offensive on 4 June.

In the same period another attack occurred near the town of Huesca in Aragón, where the Republicans were hoping to break through at a weak point on this otherwise idle front. Once again the enemy seemed to be fully aware of the Republicans' military plans and once again the attack failed. Both of these minor engagements did little to delay the Nationalists' drive to conquer the Basque territory. On 19 June, the day after the Huesca offensive was called off, Bilbao was occupied and the remainder of Vizcaya (Biscay) fell to the Nationalists shortly afterwards.

While these military failures were indicative of the shortcomings of the Republican army, they did not by themselves tell the whole story. In fact, the Republicans were making great strides towards creating a more cohesive and effective military force. One of the important developments in this regard was the fact that the army had lost its spontaneous and independent character. From the late autumn of 1936 until the spring of 1937, the government had succeeded in militarizing the militias, and, as a result, the revolutionary or political militias under trade-union control had all but disappeared. A new army was emerging in which Republican troops were now divided into brigades, battalions, army corps and armies, all of which were incorporated into a centralized command structure (*mando único*). In the central zone, where the bulk of the Republican forces were fighting, this process of reorganization was evidenced in the formation of the eighty-thousand-strong Army of Manoeuvre. Not surprisingly, then, it was on the Madrid front that the Republicans launched their first major offensive of the war.

In July 1937 the Republicans sought to relieve Nationalist pressure in the northern zone by mounting their own assault. The Battle of Brunete, as this operation came to be called, reflected both the strengths and weaknesses of the Popular Front army. Unlike their ill-fated attacks at La Granja and Huesca, the Republicans' assault on Brunete was a well-guarded secret that enabled them to achieve complete surprise. Altogether some 59,000 Republican troops organized into ten divisions and three army corps were thrown into the initial stage of fighting. Backed by effective artillery, tanks (Russian T-26) and aerial support, Republican forces were buoyed by the prospects of a great victory. The astute General Vicente Rojo, the top Republican military leader and master strategist of this and other major offensives, later remarked that the Battle of Brunete was one of the Republicans' most perfectly prepared operations of the war (Document 8.5).

Document 8.5 Battle of Brunete

Two operations had been made in our war whose preparation embodied a rigorous technical beauty, almost perfect. There were Brunete and the Ebro. The General Staff of the Central Army had seen to the most insignificant details, and had complied with the directives of the superior command with an absolute precision, especially concerning the secrecy of the attack. On the afternoon of the assault, the Minister of Defence, Indalecio Prieto, made an automobile reconnaissance of the zone of troop concentration in the oak and pine groves extending from Torrelodones to Valdemorillo. It was at these points that the entire strength of the 18th and 5th Army Corps had been gathered without discovery by the enemy. The artillery was in place and the infantry in positions for attack. Enthusiasm was vibrant in the very air and the men evinced pride in participating in an enterprise of such importance.

They exhibited discipline and perfect order. On the night of that day, at the appointed hour, the attack began impetuously. Each officer knew his mission and set out to comply with it without the least hesitation. The 46th Division broke the front on the right flank at dawn, driving to the town of Quijorna where enemy troops, recovering from their surprise, held the town with tenacity. The 11th Division of Lister had also broken the front with its surprise attack; then, infiltrating through the retreating ranks of the disorganized enemy, the advance units marched audaciously straight to Brunete. They stormed the town, overwhelming the heavy command garrison, then waited for the troops on their flanks to arrive. The 34th Division of the 18th Corps fell directly upon the town of Villanueva de la Cañada. The town did not fall immediately. The Division suffered the attraction of fire and was left strung out in combat against pillboxes and organized resistance of the line. Nevertheless, good use was made of our tanks and artillery; to such an extent that by evening, when all roads and communications from the town had been cut, elements of the garrison pulled back and the town was overwhelmed. The first day closed with an indubitable triumph. For the second day the plan would proceed without alterations.

Source: Landis, A. (1967) *The Abraham Lincoln Brigade*, New York, pp. 185–6.

On 6 July Republican troops smashed through the thinly held Nationalist lines around the village of Brunete, fifteen miles west of Madrid. In just two days, they had taken not only Brunete but also the nearby villages of Quijorna, Villanueva del Parillo, and Villanueva de la Cañada. The air superiority that the Republicans enjoyed during the opening phases of the assault helped to underscore their initial successes.

But it did not take long before the shortcomings of the Republican military organization were revealed. The biggest problem they faced was how to exploit their early gains. Rather than pressing forward and broadening the scope of the offensive, field officers allowed their troops to be tied down by the vastly outnumbered Nationalists who were doggedly defending nearby villages. Above all, this allowed the defenders enough time to send in much-needed reinforcements.

From the beginning, the discipline and organization of the Republican troops were also put to the test. Apart from being exposed to the withering effects of a scorching summer heat, ground troops were subject day and night to unrelenting machine gunning and shelling from artillery and air strikes. On top of all of this, Republican communications were so poor (field telephone lines either melted in the sun-baked plains or were severed by shellfire) that soldiers often found themselves unable to communicate with each other or with their superior officers. In these appalling conditions, it was hardly surprising that many soldiers began to crack on the battlefield and that discipline within the front-line units began breaking down (Document 8.6). As a result, less than a week after it began, the Republican offensive was already grinding to a halt.

Document 8.6 A Hard-Won Victory for International Brigades

All of the International Brigades, except for the 14th, took part in the immense Brunete operation (July), but their presence was not distinguished by anything special compared to the other Spanish brigades, among which were many young units experiencing battle for the first time. Thus, for example, the 11th had a very sluggish start at Brunete, but then after two days, on 8 July, they showed an exceptional brilliance, rushing to the attack on the 'Cemeterio' in Quijorna and, with the seizure of this cemetery on the morning of 9 July, deciding the fate of the village that the Campesino division had been unsuccessfully attacking for three days. But then again, after a few days, this same brigade, showing a rare lack of talent attributable to its commanders, attempted unsuccessfully to seize Hill 610, which was not very well fortified. In that same operation the number of International Brigades was reduced by one, the 12th (this number was later appropriated by the Polish Dombrowski Brigade), which was disbanded by the Spanish command for its poor fighting ability and for its refusal to carry out a military order.

On the disturbing day of 26 July, when there was a general panic and flight, the International Brigades, except for the 11th and units of the 15th, which held their positions, were not much slower [than other units] in their inexplicable but hasty movement backward.

Source: Radosh, R., Habek, M.R. and Sevostianov, G. (eds) (2001) *Spain Betrayed*, New Haven, p. 437.

Meanwhile, the Nationalists, who had moved rapidly and effectively to bring down reinforcements from the north, were able to launch a sustained counter-offensive on 18 July. Bolstered by the arrival of a fresh shipment of German aircraft (including the formidable Messerschmidt 109 fighters), the better equipped and organized Nationalist forces took only a week to recover much of the territory that had been captured by the enemy. By 25 July the Republicans were in full retreat, and the battle itself ended a few days later.

Given the huge losses on both sides – some 25,000 republican and 17,000 Nationalist casualties – neither side could claim victory. So far as the Republicans were concerned, the results of the campaign were not entirely negative. First and foremost, the Republicans had forced Franco to transfer some of his best troops and most of his air units (Italian, German and Spanish fighters, bombers and reconnaissance aircraft) from the northern sector, which inevitably interrupted the Nationalists' preparations for their assault on Santander. No less significant, as the communists were quick to point out in their publications, was the fact that the Brunete campaign demonstrated that the Republicans were capable of waging an active war. And, though Republican territorial gains had been rather small – they had succeeded only in expanding their territory by some twenty square miles – the hope was that the newly reorganized Popular Army would inspire Spaniards and foreigners alike to have faith in the fighting capacity of the Republic. (Document 8.7).

Document 8.7 Renewed Hope for the Republican Army?

The Recent Fighting on the Madrid Front

In one word, the fascist counter-offensive having collapsed, the Republicans could hold all their newly-won positions with the exception of *Brunete*, razed to the ground by a terrible bombardment and merely a smoking heap of ruins.

The lesson to be learnt from this series of operations will be a valuable asset in future. If one studies the characteristics of these battles, the really extra-ordinary discipline shown by the armies of the central front, their offensive power and the excellent coordination of their organisational machinery, one must say that the victory is due to the good operation and co-operation of the technical resources. Considering these technical resources used by the Government troops, i.e., aeroplanes, fleets of tanks and lorries, the slightest mistake might have thrown into confusion the best thought-out plan of operation. If, in addition, one keeps in mind that this perfect co-ordination of technical resources was put into operation for the first time in this offensive in a series of actions planned in advance, the friends of the Spanish people have every reason to look with confidence to the future.

Source: International Press Correspondence, vol. 17, no. 33, p. 747.

On the other hand, in purely military terms, the Battle of Brunete had underscored the structural weaknesses of the Republican army. Above all, the logistical problems they encountered and tactical mistakes made during the offensive undoubtedly contributed to its ultimate failure. Complaints from the field officers of ill-coordinated military manoeuvres (the poor co-operation between the tanks and infantry, for example) and the lack of proper communications between the commanders and the men on the front lines all pointed to the lessons that the Popular Army still needed to learn. Beyond the control of the military, however, were the shortages of planes, tanks, and other war supplies. It was clear in this regard that Republican offensives would be doomed to fail as long as they ran short of critical supplies. Yet this would be the fate of the Popular Army throughout the war. As the Nationalists gained greater control over the flow of arms to the Republic (after 1937 they were effectively blockading Soviet shipments to ports in the Mediterranean), it became increasingly apparent that the Republicans had little chance of reversing their fortunes on the battlefield.

The extent to which political preoccupations on the Republican side determined strategical and tactical decisions was also made clear at this time. The Brunete offensive was the first major military operation to reflect the power struggle between the pro- and anti-communist factions that was taking place behind the lines. The decision to launch an attack in the central region had come about after the fall of Largo Caballero's government in May 1937. Up till then, Largo's military planning staff had suggested a major offensive in Estremadura. If successful, such an attack would have divided Nationalist Spain in two, cutting off the main forces based in the north from troops and supplies to the south. In addition, a victory would have undoubtedly strengthened Largo's hand against his critics, who argued that the premier was not prosecuting the war vigorously and effectively. Though there were compelling reasons for launching such an operation, including the fact that the Nationalists were particularly vulnerable to an attack in this region, the plan was resisted by Largo's political adversaries in both the socialist and communist movements. After Largo was forced to step down from the premiership in May, plans for the Estremadura offensive were shelved. The new defence minister, Indalecio Prieto, backed the communists' proposal to stage an attack near Madrid. The main architect of this strategy, Vicente Rojo, was convinced that an offensive near the capital had the best chance of succeeding, above all because it was possible for the Republicans to amass troops in that area without raising the suspicions of the enemy. Though under the command of General Miaja, the commander of the Republican forces in Madrid, it was clear from the outset that the offensive would be used to showcase the results of the communists' efforts to reorganize the Popular Army.

In the wake of Brunete, the Republican general staff decided against another assault in the central region. Yet their forces could not stay idle given that the Nationalists were once again fully engaged in the northern sector. Another diversionary offensive was thus planned. The Aragón front was selected for various reasons but not least because of the Negrín's government's intention of establishing its authority in that part of the Republic which was still under 'cantonal' or provincial rule. Since the May Events of 1937, the central government had assumed control over Catalonian affairs. However, most of Republican-held Aragón remained under the sway of the anarchosyndicalists, whose political and military forces were concentrated in the north-eastern front of Republican Spain.

To end this state of affairs as well as to integrate the military forces there fully into the Popular Front army became the focus of government activities following the Brunete offensive (Document 8.8). The first stage of this campaign was to wrest political control from the anarchosyndicalists. Using the leverage they obtained through the communist-controlled army units recently transferred from the central front, the government issued a decree on 11 August which officially dissolved the anarchist-dominated Council of Aragón. In the following weeks, government troops struck at the roots of the anarchosyndicalist power-base among the local population by forcibly dismantling anarchist collectives in Aragón that had operated since the beginning of the war. According to government and communist propaganda, these collectives were unpopular because they had been established against the will of the majority of the people in the region. But while it was true that some independent peasants were both relieved and pleased to be liberated from the anarchist-dominated agricultural collectives that had sprung up throughout the region, many others strongly objected to the military authorities' heavy-handed methods (Document 8.9).

Document 8.8 Communist Plans to Strengthen the Popular Front Government

The following testimony is provided by the Comintern agent Palmiro Togliatti, aka 'Alfredo' and 'Ercoli'.

It is beyond doubt that the fall of the Largo Caballero government and the creation of the Negrin government set up a more favorable environment for solving the tasks before the entire Spanish people on how to win the war, and also for the work of the party. In several sectors, thanks to the new environment and the policies of the new government, there have already been successes. The party succeeded in strengthening its authority among the people and in the eyes of the other parties, especially after it defeated the offensive by Caballero and his group. A positive side in the current environment is also the fact that a number of measures against the POUM were successfully adopted. This makes strengthening the rear easier. The disbanding of the Council of Aragon also was a blow against 'irresponsible' and 'responsible' elements of anarchism and produced the same positive results. What is more, the fact that the anarchist organization was not able to oppose these measures of the government, which were directed precisely against them, helped to lessen their authority and sowed dissension among their ranks.

Source: Radosh, R., Habek, M.R. and Sevostianov, G. (eds) (2001) *Spain Betrayed*, New Haven, p. 382.

Document 8.9 Reasons For and Against the Disbanding of the Council of Aragón

(a)

The authority bestowed upon it by the Government was only used by the 'Council of Aragon' in order to support those who were fighting against the Government. Many members of the Council took part in the criminal putsch of May 5, in Barcelona. This putsch was instigated by a letter which was obviously sent by Ascaso's brother, and which was intercepted. But when this movement had been suppressed and the officials of the Republic were endeavouring to bring to justice those who were behind the putsch, these people found in Aragon a city of refuge. There they were able with impunity to laugh at the attempts of law and justice to bring them to book. Many of them who had taken part, weapon in hand, in the Barcelona putsch, started to march to Aragon, they did not, however, march to the front, but into the safe hinterland. And they would certainly have used their weapons in Aragon had the opportunity presented itself, in the same way as they used them in Barcelona.

In view of this situation it was necessary, if the hinterland were to be cleansed, to set to work resolutely to wipe out the so-called 'Council of

Aragon.' The Negrin Government has done this, and it has done it despite the threats which, more or less openly, were uttered against it. Approximately three weeks ago when the resolve of the Government to establish order in Aragon began to be recognised, the Anarchist Press opened a campaign on a large scale, in favour of the existing system of Aragon, and its 'unblemished' administration. In this way it hoped to create an atmosphere which would make it impossible for the Government to carry out this indispensable measure of dissolving the Council of Aragon. The Anarchist Press was supported in its endeavours by the Press which is in close touch with Caballero, and which, when it is a question of attacking the Communist Party or the Government, is a temporary ally of the Anarchists.

Source: International Press Correspondence, vol. 17, no. 35, 21 August 1937, p. 790.

(b)

A short time before the Aragon council was deposed, the Lister Division was sent there, not to fight at the fronts established by Durruti but rather to achieve victories in the rear akin to those which were accomplished in Mora de Toledo and Cobena. Before the arrival of the Lister Division in Aragon there had been a meeting of the representatives of the Aragon Popular Front, at which time unanimous approval of the work of the Regional Council was adopted. Nevertheless, the Stalin–Negrin–Prieto government decided to depose that Council.

The '*Chamber Press*' of the Communist Party and Senor Prieto prepared a series of misleading publicity items. Articles were brought out about Aragon, distorting conditions. The most scandalous statements were made by the same character assassins who had previously, time without number, dared abuse and insult the Aragon militiamen who suffered and fought under the most atrocious conditions imaginable, soldiers who never knew retreat . . .

So what was Lister sent to Aragon for? Was it to establish order where there was no disorder or to bring about a reign of terror? All Aragon was startled with the announcement of the government that the Council was to be dissolved and the knowledge that its President, Joachim Ascaso, was to be jailed, but it did nothing to prevent it. It was just this attitude of resignation that made Lister fail in his mission. He went there in high hopes and well equipped to handle any likely resistance. The real purpose was to create a situation which would warrant execution of the sinister plans of the Communist Party in Spain as laid down by Stalin as the price of England's and France's support of Soviet Russia, namely, to crush all semblance of revolutionary organization.

Source: Spanish Revolution, vol. II, no. 3, New York, 22 October 1937.

Notwithstanding the disruptive effects of these measures, the Republicans pressed ahead with their plans to mount a spoiling offensive. Their objective was to take the regional capital city of Saragossa, a key communications centre that had been a left-wing stronghold before the war broke out in July 1936 (Document 8.10). On 24 August, only two days before Santander fell to the Nationalists, some 75,000 Republican troops were sent into action on a 50–60-mile front. The heaviest fighting took place in and around the villages of Belchite and Quinto. In Belchite Republican forces were met by fierce resistance from a small contingent of Nationalist troops (1,500) (Document 8.11). The town fell on 3 September, but at the cost of many casualties on both sides. Attacks in the direction of Sarragossa were even less successful. By early September the campaign was already winding down, though sporadic fighting – including a concerted effort to take the town of Fuentes de Ebro – continued until 24 October. As at Brunete, the Republican forces demonstrated that they were incapable of sustaining an offensive. This was true despite the numerical superiority they enjoyed against the enemy and despite the fact that the Republican army was well-trained and under a single command.

Document 8.10 Republican Action on the Aragón Front

General Rojo:

We had elected to concentrate our forces for an attack in strength against Zaragoza, for, as at Brunete, it was an area and a citadel of sufficient importance to draw enemy strength from the north. And, too, the front was, at the moment of attack, weakly held – though with strongly fortified defences. This weakness led us to believe that if the attack went well there would be an excellent chance of achieving all of our immediate objectives. And if these successes could then be expanded the result would be a tactical victory which was sorely needed by the Republic: especially to impress those outside of Spain who had seen only Fascist victories to date.

Source: Landis, A. (1967) *The Abraham Lincoln Brigade*, New York, p. 259.

Document 8.11 The Battle of Belchite

The Great Victory on the Aragon Front and the Situation in Catalonia

With the capture of the strongly fortified city of Belchite the first phase of the Republican offensive on the Aragon front has come to its close. The results of the offensive achieved up to the present can be summarised as follows: Despite the violent resistance of the minions of Hitler and Mussolini, the Republican People's Army has won more than 900 square kilometres; the places captured were: Pueblo de Alberton, a fort the great strategic importance of which was recently emphasised by Franco in a wireless speech, that portion of Pinas which still remained in the hands of the fascists, the position of the Ermita de la Virgen de Bonaster, and finally the towns of Quinto and Belchite, which had been turned into fortresses by the fascists. The number of prisoners captured by the Republicans exceeds 3,000. The casualties of the enemy amount to some 5,000 dead. In the air as well the superiority of the Republican arms was displayed – alone in the last three days of the offensive 20 fascist machines were shot down.

Source: International Press Correspondence, vol. 17, no. 38, 11 September 1937, p. 855.

In the meantime, the Nationalists had completed their conquest of the north. For all the determined resistance of Republican troops defending their last strongholds in Oviedo and Gijón, Asturias fell on 22 October. As a result, the Nationalists now controlled not only the important arms factories in the Basque country but also the considerable mineral resources (coal and iron ore) of the northern region.

After nearly one and a half years of fighting, it had become apparent that the balance of war had shifted decisively in favour of the Nationalists. Despite their attempts to check Nationalist advances in the north and to take on an offensive military role, the Republicans had lost considerable ground to the enemy. Their failures were even more frustrating given that, since the spring of 1937, much progress had been made in the reorganization of Republican forces. A unified command had finally been imposed throughout Republican Spain. With better organized military units (now consisting of five army corps) and with improved training and discipline among the troops, the fighting capacity of the 'People's Army' was greater than ever before. Yet serious problems remained. The task of transforming the recently organized military units into a united army was a difficult and painfully slow process. Among the persistent stumbling blocks in this regard were the poor organization of supplies, the unreliability of communications, and the absence of a well-coordinated command structure.

On another level, the overall performance of the armed forces continued to be affected by political rivalries in the rearguard and at the front. This was especially apparent after 1938 when conflicts between the communists and those who opposed their control of the military (and Republican politics generally) gave rise to an enduring atmosphere of distrust and recriminations. Though the anarchosyndicalists and left socialists were no longer in a position to challenge forcefully the anti-revolutionary measures of the government, their resistance of the communists' ascendancy in the armed forces persisted. Ironically, the communists themselves tended to fan these flames of resentment through their blinkered efforts to create unity among the disparate Republican factions. Because they believed that the future of the war depended on the proper political orientation of those fighting it, the communists were determined to forge a unified People's Army by aggressively proselytizing among the soldiers and purging the military (and the rearguard) of those who resisted their ideas and policies. In the latter case the communists quickly gained notoriety for their reliance on heavy-handed methods to achieve their ends. After 1938, for example, the communists gained control of the special government espionage agency known as the SIM (Military Investigation Service), which they used as an instrument of repression against not only 'Fifth Columnists' but also anti-communist leftists. In resorting to such ruthless methods to obtain their political goals, the communists may have sincerely thought they were laying the groundwork for a unified fighting front on the Republican side. The reality was, however, that their excessive propagandizing measures and strong-arm tactics used to overcome opposition to their policies served only to widen the chasm separating the pro- and anti-communist factions (Documents 8.12).

Document 8.12 Opposition to Communist Methods in Military Operations

(a)

Our Communist comrades have a press which deserves our most serious attention. The outstanding feature in it is the agility with which they adopt slogans, and defend certain 'urgent necessities', adapting their arguments to tactics of the moment, which naturally have the party approval. But perhaps the most notable of all that is to be observed in the papers of the Communist Party, is that they always are and always have been right. They preach newly discovered doctrine in the confidence that other parties will lend ear to them. For this is a fact. If today our communist comrades have to defend the precise opposite of what they were preaching and defending yesterday, they quite conclusively prove to us, as they perform the manoeuvres, that they have never upheld the same thesis, that they always showed us the right way, and that they never failed to point out the direction that we should take to avoid the dangers that they were good enough to detail for us.

Source: Tierra y Liberdad (Barcelona), 4 March 1938, reprinted in *Spain and the World*, London, 1990.

(b)

In their press they ardently defended unity of command and the greatest possible measure of authority for the commander; stronger discipline was a slogan of theirs and they advised the union of all anti-Fascists to strengthen our resistance. But though they propounded these theories every day in their papers, they were contradicted by the sad reality that the Communist Party in practice did exactly the opposite. Its members did everything they could to coerce commanders into bowing to their wishes. They abused military discipline because it interfered with their political activities in the trenches, where they organised frequent meetings for senior officers, officers, N.C.O.s and privates, often presided over by a soldier, at which critical opinions were given about the conduct of the commanding officers, and it was not rare that an order from superior officers was critically considered to decide whether it would be a good thing to obey it or not. And lastly, they advocated the greatest cordiality between the anti-Fascist forces, but they kept the flames of jealousy constantly alight, and never for a moment ceased to sow discord amongst the syndicalist organisations and the political parties.

Source: Casado, Colonel S. (1939) *The Last Days of Madrid: The End of the Second Spanish Republic*, London, pp. 84–5.

Although the shortcomings of Republican military policy referred to here help to explain why the army failed to capitalize on their initial victories against the Nationalists, this is not to say that their defeats during the summer and winter of 1937 can be solely attributed to political causes. Owing to external factors largely beyond their control, the Republicans could not overcome the many obstacles they faced in obtaining arms and supplies. The Brunete, Aragon, and Teruel offensives had shown that the Republicans were not always outfought on the battlefield but rather were ultimately defeated by the superior firepower of the enemy. The effectiveness of the Nationalists' blockade of republican ports meant that getting *matériel* from the outside was becoming increasingly difficult. From 1938 on, shipments via Republican ports slowed to a trickle, and what deliveries of materials did come in were smuggled across the French–Spanish border. Moreover, the quality of weaponry that the Republicans were receiving from their main supplier, the Soviet Union, was clearly inferior to that being provided by the Nationalists' allies.

A turning point? Battle of Teruel

Following the Nationalists' conquest of the north, Franco turned his attention once again to Madrid. Since past experience showed that a frontal assault on the well-defended capital was likely to fail, the Nationalists laid plans for an offensive on the Guadalajara front. In anticipation of a fresh Nationalist offensive, Vicente Rojo decided to launch a pre-emptive strike where the enemy least expected one: some 200 miles east of Madrid at the southern end of the Aragón front. The principal target was the small provincial capital of Teruel. The surprise attack started on 15 December, just as a particularly fierce winter storm began to blanket the region with a thick layer of snow. For the first week the offensive went as planned, with the Republicans managing to capture the surrounding towns of Campillo, San Blas and Muela de Teruel. But after having successfully navigated the harsh weather conditions and rocky terrain around Teruel itself, the Republicans faced stiff resistance from the contingent of Nationalists defending the town. It took nearly two weeks of heavy street fighting, from 22 December to 7 January, before they finally conquered the city. News of their sudden and unexpected victory immediately created a stir in both camps.

On the Nationalist side, the attack on Teruel disturbed Franco so much that he decided to postpone his assault on Madrid and instead launch a counter-offensive aimed at recapturing the town. On 29 December he had ordered Generals Varela and Aranda to relieve the defenders holed up in the city, but the appalling weather conditions prevented them from aiding their besieged comrades. No less significant were the political consequences of the defeat. The fall of Teruel had caused Franco to lose face in front of his fascist allies and, as a result, their confidence in him and the Nationalists' fighting abilities had been shaken. Mussolini in particular was now threatening to cut off aid to the Nationalists if they did not bring a quick end to the conflict (Document 8.13).

Document 8.13 Italian Doubts about Franco's Military Strategy

(a)

As my Italian colleague tells me, Mussolini was very much annoyed with Franco and his manner of conducting the war; he had nevertheless promised him his help once more, but for a limited time only. He does not wish to go along with him for more than 4 to 6 months longer, however. Franco should proceed somewhat more energetically. For this purpose, however, he could have renewed support from the Italians in matériel and perhaps also in troops. To be sure, as General Berti gave Franco plainly to understand, a stricter organization of the army command and a better coordination of the individual units must be assured. At the same time Berti also made it plain that Franco must lend a more willing ear than heretofore to the advice of the Italian military.

Franco replied to these statements, as always, in a calm and friendly tone, stating that in his opinion the war situation was very good; the enemy was throwing more and more of its reserves into the witches' caldron of Teruel (from other reports, however, they are still supposed to have a few more divisions in reserve); in a few days he would launch a sizeable operation near Teruel once more in order to organize his front there better, and possibly even occupy the city again. Then – Franco told General Veith and Admiral Canaris the same thing – he would first undertake occasional small operations in order to shake the enemy's confidence and to train his own men. Then in the spring the big drive would take place.

Source: Documents on German Foreign Policy, Series D, vol. 3 III, p. 576.

(b)

September 22. The Duce has returned to Rome. I conferred with him on the Spanish problem and of course on the Czech situation. The Chief is sceptical about Spain. He believes that Franco, who has now lost his chance of victory, will come to a compromise with the other side. We shall lose our four milliards of credits, and for this reason we must pull out what we can while we can.

Source: Ciano, Count G. (1953) *Ciano's Hidden Diary, 1937–1938*, New York.

For their part, the Republicans heralded their win as a turning point in the war, not least because it demonstrated that the revamped People's Army was capable of defeating the enemy (Document 8.14). Their euphoria, however, was short-lived. Only one week after their victory, the Republicans found themselves in danger of being besieged by the Nationalists, who were resolutely determined to retake the city. For the next two weeks, the Republicans were subjected to heavy shelling from artillery and bombers, the latter of which began flying sorties as soon as weather conditions permitted. Inside Teruel, conditions were rapidly deteriorating for the Republican troops, most of whom were cold and hungry and desperately short of supplies. By 22 February the Republicans faced certain encirclement and were thus forced to abandon the town.

Document 8.14 Aftermath of the Battle of Teruel

(*a*)

The Republic Has Won the Battle of Teruel

On December 15 the Republican army began its successful attack on *Teruel*. For six days the Republican troops advanced undeterred despite the desperate resistance of the enemy and the inclemency of the weather. On the sixth day the town of Teruel, a fortress both natural and artificial, was completely surrounded. The plan of attack which had been worked out in detail had been carried out to perfection. The rebels were compelled to give up further resistance and retreat to the shelter of several buildings serving as citadels in which they made a desperate last stand. But all these buildings have now been taken by the Republicans in a continuous series of attacks . . .

The battle of Teruel, the occupation of the town and the subsequent repulsion of the nationalist counter-offensive constitute what is perhaps the most important military enterprise of the whole war.

Source: International Press Correspondence, vol. 17, no. 1, p. 11, 8 January 1938.

(*b*)

Berlin, January 15, 1938

From the available reports about events in Teruel it appears that the favorable military situation which arose for Nationalist Spain after the mopping up of the Spanish northern front has deteriorated considerably. It is termed serious although not dangerous. As yet none of the observers goes so far as to believe that Franco's final victory is jeopardized . . .

The political consequences of this situation are considerable. While before the events in Teruel the end of the Spanish Civil War seemed to be in sight, today the end of the war seems once again to have moved into the far distant future. While the prospects for a Red victory were hitherto generally considered very poor, the Leftist circles in many countries (compare, for example, the British and French press) have found new hope for a Red victory.

Source: Documents on German Foreign Policy, Series D, vol. 3, Document no. 502, p. 554

The defeat was a major setback for the Republicans: thousands of lives (total casualties are estimated at around sixty thousand) were sacrificed and valuable *matériel* lost in what turned out to be yet another futile effort to turn the tables on their enemy. No less devastating was the toll the loss took on the morale of the troops. After having been buoyed by the early successes of the campaign, Republican soldiers and their military leaders were ill-prepared mentally to confront their staggering losses. To make matters worse, the defeat at Teruel further eroded unity within the army by reviving political rivalries and recriminations. For example, the rough-hewn military leader known as 'El Campesino' later asserted that his efforts to hold on to Teruel were sabotaged by fellow communist commanders Líster and Modesto, allegedly because they wanted to prevent the anti-communist minister of defence, Indalecio Prieto, from claiming a major victory. On the other side, Líster complained of the insubordination of the undisciplined anarchist units and accused El Campesino of abandoning his troops[2] (Document 8.15).

Document 8.15 El Campesino's Fall from Grace

A more significant story is the story of Teruel, and I have to tell it.

At the time of the Fascist rising, this important Aragonese town fell into the hands of the rebels. General Sarabia won it back for the Republic towards the end of 1937. It was a victory of more than military importance. Republican morale had fallen low at this period, and the recapture of Teruel gave the people new faith and new courage.

It also gave renewed prestige to the Socialist leader Indalecio Prieto, under whose orders as minister of defence the action had been carried through. The Communists did not like this. Prieto was no pawn of theirs and stood in their way. While he remained at the head of the Defense Ministry, with his influence undiminished, they could not hope to gain complete control of military affairs. Thus they set out to torpedo Prieto, at the cost of losing Teruel . . .

Gregorovich and Modesto reminded me of the discipline of the Communist movement. And I obeyed. I still had not grasped the full extent of their plans. Because I was not Moscow trained, they did not consider me safe enough to be trusted with them. I knew they were risking Teruel, but thought it was nothing worse than a miscalculation. Only later did I discover that not the endangering but the actual loss of Teruel was a necessary part of their campaign to discredit and discard Prieto.

Their campaign also included my own removal.

It was not that that I had earned the hostility of the Russian Communists by that time. I had not. They were still giving me great publicity as a Communist hero, and continued to do so long after Teruel. But I didn't belong to the inner circle. I was a Spaniard, even if I was a Communist, and never forgot it. I was not devoted to Soviet Russia above everything. I sometimes talked back. They used me while my work served their ends. If ever my death were to serve them better, they would be able to spare me. Now they felt that my death would serve them better.

Source: González, V. and Gorkín, J. (1952) *El Campesino: Life and Death in Soviet Russia*, New York, pp. 25 and 27.

In the meantime, Franco was massing his troops along the entire Aragón front in preparation for a major offensive. Just two weeks after re-conquering Teruel, the Nationalists smashed through Republican lines as part of a large-scale operation along a 60-mile front that involved over a hundred thousand troops, two hundred tanks, and some one thousand aircraft. Meeting only nominal resistance from the other side (disorganized and demoralized Republican forces had not anticipated such a sweeping attack), it took them only six weeks to reach the Mediterranean. Republican Spain was now split in two. For the Nationalists it appeared as though the war would soon be over. But, as events would soon show, their hopes for an imminent victory were premature (Document 8.16).

Document 8.16 The Nationalist Army at the Beginning of 1938

Major de Linde to Sir R. Hogson

Paris, April 26, 1938

To anyone with experience of the Great War, the almost complete absence of warlike activities in all three sectors of the front visited was most striking. Admittedly, of the three sectors, two were static and far from the scene of mobile operations; but the remaining one was at the arrow-head of the present offensive . . .

Another outstanding feature of the Spanish scene is the amazing number of men in uniform to be seen, not only in every town, but in every village, whether it is a hundred miles from the front, like Briviesca, or on the very edge of the forward zone, like Getafe. Although the population seemed contented enough, displayed Nationalist flags in great profusion, wore red Carlist berets or Falangist badges, saluted freely, held 'manifestations' and went through all the motions of good totalitarians, I am persuaded that these countless isolated groups of soldiers are scattered through the country for maintaining what is called – perhaps a little euphemistically – 'public order.' . . .

It is certain that, today, the Nationalist forces have a definite superiority over the Republicans in almost every respect – weapons, ammunition, training, food supplies, transport, foreign assistance. These factors have contributed to their recent successes, but the essential factor has been their ability to concentrate in secrecy a large preponderance of field and medium artillery in the sector selected for the break-through. And now the easy and rapid advance to the sea has added a high morale to their more material advantages. At the same time, it seems that air action has done much correspondingly to lower the enemy's morale . . .

Despite the fact that the Nationalists are now in a situation of manifest superiority to the Republicans, officers in their army are very reluctant to say how much longer they think the war will last. Their disappointments in front of Madrid in 1936 and 1937 have made them very cautious in 1938.

Source: British Documents on Foreign Affairs, series F, Europe, 1919–1939, vol. 27, Document no. 123, pp. 187–9.

Final countdown: Battle of the Ebro

After his troops had reached the Mediterranean, Franco was in a strong position to attack Catalonia, where the seat of the Republican government was located as well as the Republic's last remaining war industry. But instead of moving north – as most observers were expecting – he turned his armies in the opposite direction, towards Valencia. While his critics saw this as a strategic blunder, Franco reasoned that taking Valencia, which appeared to him to be more vulnerable than either Madrid or Catalonia, would so disrupt the enemy's forces that it would bring about a rapid end to the war. Apart from these strategic considerations, Franco's next military move also had to take into account the rapidly changing diplomatic climate at this time. During the opening phase of the Aragón offensive, Franco's loyal ally, Hitler, had captured world attention when he ordered his troops into Austria as the first step towards fulfilling Germany's expansionist goals. The daring feat had generated diplomatic waves throughout Europe and particularly in France, where the consequences of a Franco victory took on new meaning. Since advancing into Catalonia might have provoked the French to come to the aid of the anti-fascist Republicans, Franco decided against a northern offensive. In the event, his decision to turn south was welcomed by the Republican commanders, who desperately needed the time this change of plans bought them for reorganizing and re-equipping their armies. In fact, the respite came at a critical moment. Fresh shipments of arms, aircraft, and equipment (mostly from the Soviet Union) arrived before the French frontier was closed again on 13 June.

As Franco's troops began advancing south-eastwards, General Vicente Rojo and his general staff began laying the groundwork for a massive counter-offensive. Their plan was to draw the Nationalists away from Valencia by mounting a surprise operation on the Catalan front. By mid-July some eighty thousand Republican troops – bolstered by the greater part of the army's remaining aircraft and artillery units – were making final preparations for the Battle of the Ebro, the last great military contest of the war. From the beginning the stakes were high: a Republican triumph might well extend the war until it could become internationalized, while a defeat would spell certain doom for the Republican cause.

On the night of 24–5 July, Republican commandos crossed at the bend of the mighty Ebro river (between Mequinenza and Tortosa). Catching Yagüe's Moroccan army completely unawares, the leading units of Juan Modesto's Army of the Ebro first cut Nationalist communication lines and then proceeded to occupy a wide bridgehead, which they used to drive deeper into Nationalist territory. By the end of the week they had advanced nearly 25 miles and were at the point of taking Gandesa, the centre of an important network of roads and communications. However, it was at this stage of the attack that the offensive began bogging down. Instead of moving forward and exploiting their initial successes, Republican forces became tied down by a small but determined group of Nationalists. The defenders managed to hold on long enough for Yagüe's troops to stabilize their lines. In the following weeks, the battle was transformed into a war of attrition.

The initial phase of the Ebro campaign had achieved its desired goal, namely, to take pressure off Franco's drive towards Valencia. The scale of the Republicans' early successes had also forced the Caudillo to suspend his offensive operations in Estremadura. Furthermore, the offensive had badly shaken the confidence of the Nationalists, who, only a few weeks earlier, were convinced that the end of war was in sight. Now it was the Republicans' turn to be lifted by a surge of optimism. But while Republican propagandists were declaring Ebro to be another turning point in the war, Franco began concentrating his forces for a major counter-attack. As he had done throughout the war, Franco was prepared to abandon his own military objectives in order to prevent the Republicans from gaining ground in Nationalist territory.

From August until the end of October, the two sides were locked in a series of bloody confrontations (Document 8.17). Making the most of the hilly terrain that partially protected their defensive positions, the Republicans stubbornly resisted the Nationalists' repeated efforts to bomb and strafe them into submission. The brutal slogging match – much of it waged in the searing summer heat of the Aragón summer – gradually wore down the Republicans. With their supplies dwindling and lacking adequate air and artillery support, they became increasingly vulnerable to the Nationalists' repeated attacks. The tide of battle finally turned when the Nationalists launched an offensive into the Sierra de Pandols on 30 October. By 16 November, the Republicans had been driven back from all the territory they had conquered since 25 July. The longest and most gruelling contest of the war was finally over.

Document 8.17 The Republican Army's Last Stand: The Battle of Ebro

The Ebro Battle and Its Repercussions at Home and Abroad

The great waters of the River Ebro serve as the dividing line between two historical facts. They divide the two Spains, the Spain of the invaders from the

Spain of free men, who are fighting for the future of their country with their lives.

It is from here that the offensive of the soldiers of the Democratic Republic started. After two years of severe tests and disastrous misfortunes, and after four months heroic and determined resistance which served for the reorganising of the army and the war industry, the Spanish troops crossed the Ebro, and freed the Spaniards subjected to the invaders over an area of 13 miles. They here showed the extraordinary virility of a people who see their most elementary vital rights threatened . . .

By this battle all the plans of the enemy were thrown into disorder. After suffering the severest losses of the whole war (which with the resistance combined with counter-attacks on the Levante amounted to 15–30,000 men, mostly Italians) the enemy was forced to fight on fronts chosen by the Republican General Staff and to abandon his own aims for the time being . . . The recent success of the Ebro army confirms the inexhaustible possibilities on which the Spanish Republic, which is prepared for a long, hard war, may count.

Source: Renau, J., in *World News and Views,* vol. 18, no. 41, Saturday 27 August 1938, pp. 953–4.

Casualties on both sides were high. The Republicans suffered the greatest losses, with over 20,000 men killed and another 55,000 either wounded or captured. By contrast, the Nationalists recorded some 4,000 troops killed, with another 53,000 wounded or missing in action (Document 8.18).

Document 8.18 Military Consequences of the Battle of Ebro

(a)

The military situation has considerably improved for the Nationalists since the last report. Franco has succeeded, by means of an offensive in a direction not expected by the Reds, first in winning back the southeastern part of the bend of the Ebro River which was held by the Reds, and then, turning to the north, in mopping up the rest of the bend. However, he needed almost 3 months to win back the terrain which the Reds occupied in about 2 days by means of the attack across the Ebro. This effort, according to a confidential report from headquarters, cost him 33,000 men. I enclose a clipping of the official Nationalist Army report from the *Unidad* of November 17, in which the enemy's losses in men and equipment are listed. German military sources, however, term the statement that the Reds are supposed to have lost 75,000 men as too high.

Source: Documents on German Foreign Policy, Series D, vol. 3, Document no. 502, p. 554

(b)

Franco's Losses on the Ebro

In Spain, in the course of this week, fascism has in the most despicable manner revenged itself on women and children for the failure of its Ebro offensive. Madrid, Alicante, Taragona, have once more been the scene of particularly barbarous bombardments of civilian populations. Six British ships were damaged during a bombardment of the harbour of Barcelona. Without doubt these latest inhuman aerial attacks testify to the increasing difficulties confronting Franco both at the front and in the hinterland. The fifty-days' unsuccessful counter-offensive on the Ebro has cost Franco 40,000 to 45,000 killed.

Source: World News and Views, vol. 18, no. 46, p. 1064.

In the wake of Ebro, it was apparent that the fighting had exhausted the Republican Army of nearly all its remaining resources. Apart from incurring heavy casualties, the army had depleted its short supply of war *matériel*, much of which had been left behind by retreating soldiers. Equally significant was its devastating impact on morale. The Republicans' collective will to go on fighting was now shattered and most knew that the chances of prolonging the war were rapidly vanishing.

As the battles of Brunete, Teruel, and Ebro had demonstrated, improvements in the military efficiency and discipline of the republican troops had been realized. But, contrary to the optimism expressed by Negrín's government, it was apparent that these changes had not altered the course of the war. Whether this was due more to the government's inability to obtain enough war *matériel* to sustain the army's effectiveness or more to the uninterrupted decline in the morale of the Republican forces, cannot be said with any certainty. In any event, by late 1938 the military outcome of the war was no longer in doubt (Document 8.19).

Document 8.19 Survey of Opposing Forces in 1938

(a)

According to the latest compilation of Special Staff W, Franco has the following forces at his disposal:

At the front	470,000 men
Reserves in the interior	
(a) Ready for action	40,000 men
(b) Incompletely equipped reserves and replacements	35,000 men
In process of organization	12,000 men
Security troops in the interior	25,000 men
	582,000 men

These figures are approximate, since the exact strength is probably not known even in Franco's headquarters itself, in view of the faulty Spanish organization.

According to the latest compilation of Special Staff W. the Red Forces are composed as follows:

At the front and front reserves	342,000 men
Reserves	
(a) Ready for action	75,000 men
(b) In process of organization, at least	45,000 men
Security troops in the interior, at least	30,000 men
	492,000 men

Thus Franco has approximately 90,000 more men at his disposal than the Reds, but it should be kept in mind that among his troops there are probably at least 50,000 to 60,000 Moroccans. In comparing the above figures it is especially noticeable that the Red reserves in the interior and the reserves in process of organization are considerably stronger than Franco's: that is, the Reds are recruiting more, which is evident also from other reports.

Source: Documents on German Foreign Policy, Series D, vol. 3, Document no. 502, p. 556.

(b)

Report to Major Mahoney on the Military Situation in Spain

The Defensive Policy adopted by the Republican High Command.

Defence was the rôle which circumstances imposed on the Republicans at the beginning of the war. As time passed, however, they obtained an equality in man-power and perhaps a superiority in war material. Neither of these increases have enabled them to pass from the defensive to a sustained offensive, during two and a half years of war. Their principal handicap appears to be lack of trained leaders from brigade commanders downwards, and since they have not been able to remedy this they have aimed at exploiting to the utmost the powers of modern defence. The result of this policy is demonstrated by the fact that except for a small operation in western Extremadura in August the Nationalist forces have gained no appreciable amount of ground for some months.

The machine gun and pick and shovel give effect to the Republican defensive policy. The enormous length of the front is a factor in their favour. It compels the dispersion of their enemies, thus imposing upon the latter a defensive rôle also over most of the front. Under these circumstances a liberal supply of automatic weapons, combined with industrious digging, suffice to make the price of attack too high for the other side. Places of strategic importance in Republican territory, such as most of Catalonia, Madrid, and the mines of Almaden are veritable fortresses which could consume a large portion of Nationalist strength in an effort to capture them . . .

The Standard of Training of Nationalist Higher Commanders

Generally speaking, the training and experience of Nationalist senior officers has been based upon the guerrilla type of warfare common in Morocco. Such warfare was parochial in its nature, calling for short advances by small bodies on strictly limited objectives. Valour counted for much more than skill. There was little scope for individual enterprise or need for sustained and agile thought . . .

Divisions are now frequently commanded by lieutenant-colonels who saw active service in Morocco as captains and subalterns. Many of them are of soldierly character, personality, valour and worth, and they are beloved by their men, but more than one has, in the writer's presence, lamented the fact that he had to carry the burden of such a responsible command. The failure of the Nationalists to penetrate into Catalonia after Lerida may be attributed in large part to the inadequate training of their commanders.

Man-power and its Relationship to the Length of the Front

The total length of the combined fronts in Spain is 1,500 kilom. or 937 statute miles. The Nationalist forces, including second-line troops, amount to approximately 80 divisions, or a paper strength of about 800,000 men. A portion of this force has to be detailed for internal security purposes, a portion is under training as recruits and a portion is ineffective through casualties. It is doubtful if the average strength of these divisions available for the front, and still more doubtful if the average strength of these divisions exceeds 7,000 men. What is certain is that large sections of the front are only lightly held by second-line troops, and other sections in the Guadarramas and Extremadura are not held at all.

The above conditions indicate a shortage of man-power. Such a shortage is compatible with a defensive policy like the Republican, and incompatible with an offensive one like the Nationalist. This becomes plainer as time goes on. The Nationalists' will to manoeuvre is rendered sterile for lack of a mass to manoeuvre with. They can only undertake an offensive after a laborious process of cheeseparing all along the line, which does not escape the notice of the enemy. The latter reply with a clever riposte such as Teruel, Brunete, the crossing of the Ebro. Nationalist plans are at first disturbed, then halted, a period of bitter fighting follows on ground chosen by the enemy, it ends indecisively, and the cycle is completed.

Source: British Documents on Foreign Affairs, Series F, Europe, 1919–1939, vol. 27, Document 143, pp. 223–4.

The end comes: The final year of conflict, 1938–39 | **9**

Undermining the Republic from within

On the home front, the last months of the Civil War were marked by declining morale, social disruption and increasingly bitter political conflicts. All of these interrelated conditions were exacerbated not just by Republican defeats on the battlefield but also by the various psychological and material hardships suffered by the civilian population. Particularly problematic for the Republicans throughout the war were the supply and distribution of food. Food shortages were not caused by any single factor. Rather they resulted from a combination of political, social, and economic forces. Political rivalries, for example, often contributed to the breakdown of food production and distribution even when food was available (Document 9.1). Above all, however, the food problem was affected by circumstances largely beyond the control of the local and central governments. This is instanced by the fact that, in contrast to the Nationalist regime, the Republic experienced enormous pressures of population. Throughout the war Republican authorities confronted the enormous task of feeding the people of Spain's most densely populated cities – Madrid, Valencia, and Barcelona – and towns: a problem which grew worse over time as more and more refugees flooded into these urban areas.

Document 9.1 Growing Food Shortages in Republican Spain

(a)

But the communists were no better at organizing food supplies. To live on one's rations was to go hungry; inefficient distribution, moreover, meant that you would eat nothing but broad beans for a fortnight, lentils for the next couple of weeks, chick-peas for the next and so on. Lack of food was one of the major factors in the war-weariness that overtook Catalonia. The republic was unable to solve it.

Source: Fraser, R. (1979) *Blood of Spain*, New York, p. 376.

(b)

Barcelona, January 2, 1937

Sir, . . .

Some disturbances have been reported in the bread queues, and a number of incidents outside Barcelona. The food problem is most acute in Barcelona, where the population is highly concentrated. In the country towns and districts though many articles are short, the situation is by no means as serious. In recent weeks, dwellers in Barcelona have been going into the country to obtain supplies for their households. In some cases they have resorted to violence, robbing gardens and farms, and the country folk have had to defend themselves. A number of municipalities have forbidden the sale of food-stuffs to outsiders, and food is being hidden for fear of requisitions. Persons returning to Barcelona with food obtained in the country have been robbed on entering the outskirts of the city. Recently, members of the C.N.T. confiscated stocks of food accumulated in an Agricultural Co-operative Society warehouse in a town near Barcelona . . .

The food situation is now extremely grave. Catalonia is not self-supporting and has always been dependent upon other parts of Spain, many of which are now cut off, and foreign countries. To maintain sufficient imports she must have foreign exchange, and it seems that without help from the Central Government she will not be able to cope with the situation from her own resources.

G. EDGAR VAUGHAN

Source: British Documents on Foreign Affairs, Series F, Europe, 1919–1939, vol. 27, Document 56, p. 66.

While the central and regional governments adopted emergency economic measures – in the form of rationing and price fixing – which sought to alleviate food shortages and other material hardships suffered in the rearguard, they were unable to address the main structural obstacles to feeding the Republic's citizens. From 1937 on Republican ports were blockaded and commercial links to the outside were severely disrupted. Moreover, the Republican government was, owing to the arms embargo imposed upon it, forced to use more of its limited credit and convertible resources to purchase war *matériel* rather than domestic supplies.[1] The result was that, by late 1938, the food crisis had reached epidemic proportions throughout the remaining Republican territories.

At the same time Republican civilians were enduring food shortages and other debilitating economic hardships, their will to go on fighting was being tested by incessant shelling from artillery and aerial bombings. While it is true that both sides bombed the rearguard, attacks against civilian populations became a one-sided affair when the Nationalists achieved air superiority in 1937. At first these raids, though at times extremely destructive, did not create mass panics or seriously disrupt daily operations. Yet this all changed late in the war, when the Nationalists (assisted by the Italians and Germans) increased both the frequency and severity of their bombing raids. By the spring of 1938 Barcelona and the Mediterranean region of the Republic were being bombed continuously. This time, however, the bombings took a heavy toll on the rearguard, producing heavy casualties and causing a general state of panic among the civilian population (Document 9.2).

Document 9.2 Civilians Under Fire

(a)

The crimes committed by the Fascists, bombing cities in the rear without any military objective, causing irreparable havoc, slaughtering with impunity defenseless citizens, women and children, have deserved the condemnation of the world. But the condemnation of the world is not sufficient to make them stop in their ferocious behaviour, which is a clear demonstration of their impotence. Several times the Minister of National Defense has announced his readiness to renounce any war-like action against the towns of the rear on a basis of a guaranteed reciprocity. Until this is achieved – painful as it may be – the Government declares that it will be compelled to answer enemy aggressions by similar methods. It will answer with appropriate measures to all the crimes of those who, not satisfied with having been traitors to their own country, handing it over to the greed of foreign imperialist powers, prefer in their mad impotence to destroy our country rather than deliver up their banners to the Republic. In this system of reprisals, to which the behaviour of our enemies has led us, the Government is under a two-fold handicap: first, that of humanitarian feeling which it tries to make consistent within the limits of the war, and the grief caused by the ruin of its own national territory, the sacrifice of innocent victims among whom predominate Spaniards faithful to the régime and loyal to the independence of their own country.

Source: Negrín, J. (1937) *Three Speeches of Sr. Juan Negrín*, Paris, Cooperative Etoile.

(b)

In January 1938 the attacks on Barcelona were greatly intensified. Between December 15th and January 20th there were 77 air raids killing 273 people, and wounding 456 . . .

Then in March a new storm burst. The Italian Army with some Spanish support attacked in Aragon after bombardments by a vast fleet, estimated as 700 strong, of German and Italian bombers. It is impossible, and may never be possible, to estimate the casualties caused in the towns behind the Aragon front.

Source: Haldane, J.B.S. (1938) *A.R.P.*, London, pp. 52 and 53.

Possessing limited numbers of aircraft and anti-aircraft weapons, the government was powerless to stop the raids. The Republic's efforts to enlist the support of the international community were also fruitless. Though the Guernica affair had seized the world's attention only a few months earlier, by 1938 the bombings of Republican open cities rarely captured the headlines. This was perhaps partly because the public abroad had become numbed by the numerous horror stories emanating from Spain, and partly because the international spotlight had now shifted to events in central Europe. As we shall see, the fading international interest in Spain's troubles meant that the desperate pleas of Republican politicians failed to compel either Great Britain or France to take action against the fascist powers who were largely responsible for these attacks.

The kinds of physical and mental hardships referred to here naturally had a corrosive effect on the political life in the Republican zone. In the final months of the war, the conflicts among the political parties took centre stage and thereby inevitably hastened the complete collapse of the Republic.

In the shadow of defeat

Ever since he had assumed the premiership in May 1937, Juan Negrín was determined to prosecute the war with the energy and dynamism that was necessary for the republicans to defeat the Nationalists. To this end, he pursued two interrelated strategies. As we have already seen, one was aimed at transforming the Popular Army into a formidable fighting force. The other was to use diplomacy as a means of getting the Western democracies actively involved in searching for a resolution to the Spanish conflict. The two were necessary correlates in Negrín's mind because he insisted that the Republic's diplomatic bargaining power could be measured only in military terms. Thus, at the same time his administration was building the basis for a more efficient and disciplined army, the premier pursued an aggressive diplomatic 'offensive' which was aimed at convincing the Western democracies that a Republican victory was in the best interests of not only Spain but also the rest of democratic Europe.

Up to 1938, the Republicans' foreign policy initiatives had not produced any concrete results. This was not least because their diplomatic moves were blunted by the Non-Intervention Committee based in London. Republican Spain could do little to influence directly a body to which it did not belong. Furthermore, the NIC itself was dominated by Britain and France, both of whom were using the committee as a vehicle for advancing their own foreign policy agendas. Unfortunately for the Republic this meant that, when it came to dealing with the Spanish situation, both countries preferred not to do anything which would undermine their jointly held appeasement strategy towards Germany and Italy. For this reason, the Republic's diplomatic efforts tended to be focused in Geneva, the seat of the League of Nations. Despite the fact that its effectiveness as a diplomatic tool was undermined by the activities of the NIC, the League of Nations provided the Republican government with a pulpit from which they could denounce foreign intervention.

Against the background of Franco's successful drive to cut the Republic in two, Negrín opened a fresh diplomatic offensive on 1 May 1938. In an attempt to gain foreign sympathy for the Republican cause, he enunciated the moderate war and peace aims of the Republic (Document 9.3). Above all, the manifesto sought to dispel the image of a 'red' Republic by identifying the goals of the Negrín government with the values and beliefs of the liberal democratic regimes of Western Europe. For example, the government gave assurances in article six that Catholic religious practices, which had been suppressed in Republican Spain since the outbreak of the Civil War, would no longer be banned. To maximize its impact abroad, Negrín and his communist allies disseminated the 'Thirteen Points' programme far and wide. Reproductions of the text – which was translated into several major languages – appeared in countless left-wing and liberal periodicals and pamphlets published in Europe and the United States. But while these intensive propagandizing efforts helped to create a more favourable public image of the Republic at home and abroad, none of the democratic governments found the Thirteen Points to be compelling.

Document 9.3 Negrín's Thirteen Points

1. The absolute independence and integrity of Spain.
2. The liberation of Spanish territory from foreign occupation and foreign influence.
3. A people's republic.
4. A plebescite on the form of government when the war ended.
5. Respect of regional liberties, compatible with Spanish unity.
6. Full social and civic rights for every Spaniard, including liberty of religious worship and conscience.
7. Protection of private property and the elements of production, but also prevention of such accumulations of wealth as might result in the exploitation of the citizens.
8. Complete agrarian reform.
9. Social legislation guaranteeing rights of workers.
10. The cultural, physical, and moral improvement of the nation.
11. A non-political Army as an instrument for the defense of the people.
12. Renunciation of war as an instrument of national policy and fidelity to the League of Nations.
13. Amnesty for all Spaniards who proved they desired to co-operate in the work of reconstruction – the amnesty to include common soldiers in the Rebel Army.

Source: De la Mora, C. (1939) *In Place of Splendor: The Autobiography of a Spanish Woman*, New York, p. 362.

In the midst of this campaign, the Negrín government stepped up its appeals to the League of Nations to take action against the fascist powers that were violating the sovereignty of the Spanish nation. This message was taken before the League time and again by the Republican representative to the League, Álvarez del Vayo. In May Álvarez del Vayo made an impassioned plea to Britain and other powers to do something to stop the bombing raids being carried out by Italians against Spanish citizens in Barcelona and elsewhere along the Mediterranean. But no matter how egregious the violations of the non-intervention policy may have been in this particular case, they did not provoke even an outcry from the very countries who presumed to be enforcing it.

The prospects for a diplomatic turnaround further dimmed in the autumn of 1938. On the military front, the Republicans were at the point of being defeated in the Battle of Ebro and consequently Negrín lost the leverage he needed to reinforce his foreign policy objectives. Equally damaging to Negrín's diplomatic strategy was the Munich crisis of September. Britain and France indicated through their capitulation to Hitler over the Sudeten question that they were not about to alter their stance on appeasement. As far as the Republic was concerned, this meant that the Negrín government had only a remote chance of inducing either Britain or France to force concessions from Italy and Germany with respect to their participation in the Civil War. In fact, Britain's recent rapprochement with Italy (formalized in the Anglo-Italian accords of April 1938) effectively ruled out any hope that the British would, at this late date, attempt to check Mussolini's actions in Spain.

Though Negrín himself could barely conceal his growing frustration with the latest diplomatic developments, he steadfastly refused to abandon his faith in the policy of resistance.[2] Among other things, this entailed keeping alive his diplomatic 'offensive' at all costs. With this in mind, Negrín announced to the League of Nations at the height of the Munich crisis his decision to withdraw unilaterally the reduced number of foreign troops still fighting for Republican Spain.[3] This was not done purely for dramatic effect, for it was a decision that involved some sacrifice on the part of the Republicans. Even though the combat role of the International Brigades had been greatly reduced by this stage of the war, their continued commitment to the Republican cause was a major source of inspiration for those who wanted to go on fighting.[4] In the event, given that Europe was already caught up in the political drama unfolding in Czechoslovakia, it was scarcely surprising that Negrín's initiative failed to make an impression on the Western powers.

Because Negrín's announcement coincided with the Republicans' general retreat during the Battle of Ebro, it did little to dispel the growing mood of resignation throughout the Republican zone. For many, the foreign volunteers who had come to Spain embodied the international spirit of anti-fascism, and their departure meant that the Republic would lose one of it, last remaining links to the outside world. To soften the blow to public morale, the government made certain to mark the occasion with a great deal of fanfare. In a series of parades held in Barcelona at the end of October, high-ranking government dignitaries presided over these bitter-sweet celebrations at which thousands of ordinary citizens paid homage to the courage and self-sacrificing spirit of the International Brigades (Document 9.4). In sharp contrast to the hero's farewell they received in Spain, those who could return home – the

British and American volunteers, for example – were met with either hostility or icy indifference. Most were seen as 'reds' and not, as they were in Republican Spain, the brave defenders of Western democracy.

Document 9.4 Farewell Address to the International Brigades

Comrades of the International Brigades! Political reasons, reasons of state, the welfare of that same cause for which you offered your blood with boundless generosity, are sending you back, some to your own countries and others to forced exile. You can go proudly. You are history. You are legend. You are the heroic example of democracy's solidarity and universality. We shall not forget you, and when the olive tree of peace puts forth its leaves again, mingled with the laurels of the Spanish republic's victory – come back!

Source: Low, R. (1992) *La Pasionaria: The Spanish Firebrand*, London, p. 110.

Dissension in the Nationalist camp

In spite of the fact that few believed in the spring of 1938 that the Republic would survive another Nationalist offensive, victory continued to elude Franco. As we have seen, his slow and tedious conduct of the war was not popular among his fascist military advisers, who were critical of Franco's slavish commitment to a strategy of attrition. When, after the division of Republican Spain, it appeared to most senior military strategists on both sides as though the Republic could be defeated rapidly by an offensive in Catalonia, Franco once again defied conventional military logic by launching an attack towards Valencia. In this instance, however, his decision provoked dissension among his own commanders (Document 9.5).

Document 9.5 Friction Inside Franco's Army

The speech which General Yagüe, noted and able leader of the Moroccan Corps, made in Burgos on April 19 at the celebration of the anniversary of the establishment of the Unity Party threw an interesting light on these conditions. In his speech, excellent in itself, which only a few newspapers were able to publish (apparently in a milder form), the General expressed his ideas concerning the comprehensive social reforms which he considered necessary, the need for an honest and incorruptible administration of justice, patriotism which is always ready for sacrifices, Christian charity and Spanish chivalry, with a frankness and a critical attitude which were at the very least inconvenient for the present Government. In particular, it was felt that the parts of his speech in which he gave free recognition to the bravery of the Red Spanish opponents, defended the political prisoners – both the Reds and the 'Blues' (Falangists), who were arrested because of too much political zeal – and severely attacked the partiality of the administration of justice, went beyond his authority and represented a lack of discipline; the answer was his recall from his command, at least temporarily . . .

If the antagonism between Franco and the 'Falange's General,' Yagüe, which was brought out once before in the past, has thus entered an acute stage, it is not surprising that there is again talk of disagreements between the Generalissimo and the 'social General,' Queipo de Llano, in Seville. I consider the Yagüe incident and the fundamental differences between Franco and Queipo de Llano, which undoubtedly exist, as by no means serious at the present time; these events, however, do show that the spirit from which the typically Spanish *pronunciamientos* originate has not yet been destroyed, and that in this respect surprises are not impossible if the fortunes of war should prove capricious or if after the war internal political and social antagonisms should clash . . .

Moreover, Franco has undoubtedly succeeded in preserving his authority up to this time. As I brought out in my memorandum on 'The *de facto* and *de jure* relations between Germany and Nationalist Spain' in February, he has very cleverly succeeded, with the advice of his brother-in-law, Minister of the Interior Serrano Suñer, in not making enemies of any of the parties represented in the Unity Party which were previously independent and hostile to one another – particularly the old (original) Falange and the Requetés – but, on the other hand, also in not favoring any one which might thus grow too strong.

Source: Documents on German Foreign Policy (1949), Series D, vol. 3 (Washington), Document no. 586, pp. 658–9.

Franco's questionable military decisions were not the only source of problems developing in the Nationalist camp.[5] Ever since 1937 news of disaffection among Franco's troops – particularly among Carlist, Moorish, and Foreign Legionaries – began making their way into the foreign press reports and diplomatic dispatches emanating from Nationalist Spain (Document 9.6).

Document 9.6 Growing Dissent on the Right

This was evidence of trouble which appears for some time to have been brewing in rebel territory . . .

Early in January it was reported that Moors, and Arabs sent by Signor Mussolini's orders from Libya and Tripoli, were refusing to fight . . .

And disaffection was not confined to Regulars, Moors, Arabs or Foreign Legionaries. It now became open on the part of the two bodies which had done most to pave the way for the military rising, the Falangists and the Requetés. Friction indeed between the General and Falangists was nothing new. Men who had declared that they would not tolerate foreign interference could not be expected to acquiesce in the ever-increasing foreign intervention, accompanied as it was by aggressive assumption of superiority on the part of many Italian and German officers, and the growing control of administrative services behind the lines, more especially on the part of the Germans.

Source: Atholl, K., Duchess of (1938) *Searchlight on Spain*, Harmondsworth, pp. 294 and 295.

After 1937 there were also signs, if not of dissatisfaction, of growing war-weariness among the rank-and-file soldiers. This most likely accounted for the inconsistent performance of Nationalist units on the battlefield. While they were better equipped and fed than their Republican counterparts, the morale of Franco's soldiers was daily being undermined by several factors. The unexpected setbacks they experienced when the Republicans struck an offensive blow was one source of declining morale, were as the high casualty rates that invariably accompanied these bloody slogging matches. While there was no way of knowing how far this particular malaise had advanced among Nationalist troops, there was the ever-present danger that it could spread as long as the war continued.

By the spring of 1938, the generally optimistic mood of the population in the rearguard was increasingly being tested. Ironically, this might have owed something to the triumphal rhetoric underpinning Franco's regime. The accuracy of the regime's indulgent predictions of the imminent demise of the Republic was called into question every time the Republican army forestalled defeat. As a result, disillusionment began to sink in among those who were beginning to believe that the end of the war was not forthcoming.

The mounting number of civilian casualties late in the war also generated rumblings of discontent, particularly among the die-hard nationalists. This was particularly evident in the period when the Nationalists were conducting heavy bombing attacks against the civilian populations on the other side. Though accurate news of these raids was suppressed by Nationalist censors, rumours of the carnage they were causing circulated more freely. The fact that Franco's fascist allies (particularly the Italians) were largely responsible for these bombing missions, caused a certain number of Falangists and Carlists to begin calling for 'Spain for the Spaniards', a subversive refrain that echoed the Republican view that the Germans and Italians were acting like foreign invaders (Document 9.7).

Document 9.7 Carlist Opposition to Foreign Intervention

Requeté Manifesto

Requetés:

With the authority that is ours by virtue of the blood shed by thousands of our brothers, we are going to look this matter straight in the face.

Intent on our struggle, for God and Fatherland, we have overlooked the fact that we were handing our country over to foreigners. Our armed forces, our riches, our land, the Institutions of New Spain, are all in their hands. Their insolence knows no bounds. And if today the indecisiveness of the war forces them to hide somewhat their true intent, what will they do after the victory?

In a long and bloody strife we have tried to keep the Marxist and Masonic Governments from enslaving the Church of Christ; shall we now let the Church be enslaved in a State modeled by the invader? . . .

Down with the anti-Catholic invader! Long live the church of Christ! Let us throw all the foreigners out of Spain!

For God and for the Spanish fatherland!

The Requetés of the 19th of July, 1936.

Source: News of Spain, 8 June 1938, pp. 4–5.

The problems referred to here were serious, but they were not major impediments to Franco's rule. For the most part, the authoritarian state apparatus he was constructing withstood the challenges of dissent and disillusionment. Franco himself managed to weather each crisis with characteristic aplomb – such as his clash with Yagüe over the Caudillo's decision not to advance on Catalonia – and his grip on power remained firm throughout his frustratingly slow and deliberate march to total victory.

The dissolution of Republican politics

Meanwhile, inside Republican Spain, the enormous pressures of war were beginning to dissolve the tenuous political bonds holding together the Popular Front coalition. Following the May disturbances of 1937, prime minister Negrín began cobbling together political alliances that would bring about greater order and stability to the government. At the time he became premier this meant joining forces with three principal groups: (1) the moderate wing of the socialist movement, (2) the middle-class Republican and Nationalist parties, and (3) the communists. Of all these groups, it was the communists who became Negrín's closest and most important ally. As we shall soon see, it was this partnership which became the focus of the political feuding that characterized Republican politics in the last stage of the war.

From the outset of his rule, Negrín promoted the view that the Nationalists could not be defeated until the centrifugal forces – whether it was the revolutionary experimentation of the anarchists or the separatist agenda of the Basques and Catalans – on the Republican side were brought under control. To this end, he undertook to reinvest the state apparatuses of the Republic with the power and authority needed to prosecute the war effort effectively. In pursuing this goal, Negrín tried to maintain good relations with all the non-revolutionary Republican parties. However, of all his political allies, Negrín both recognized and valued the superior organizational and mobilizing strengths of the communists. Because of this and because of the Republic's obvious dependence on the Soviet Union for war supplies, he increasingly turned to them as a source of support in his administration. Whether his relationship with the communists was one in which he was manipulated by them or one in which he managed to maintain his independence remains a matter of historical debate. But what is not in dispute is the fact that Negrín's close ties to the communists eventually forced him into an adversarial relationship with nearly all the anti-communist elements inside and outside his government.

Up to the time of the May Events of 1937, the main rivals of the communists were to be found on the far left. Yet, not long after the government reined in on the revolutionary movement, communist ascendancy throughout the political and military apparatuses was challenged not just by the *caballeristas*, anarchosyndicalists, and *poumistas* but also by high-ranking members of the government itself. For example, as delighted as he was to see the demise of the revolutionary movement, Manuel Azaña, the president of the Spanish Republic, was appalled at the preponderance of Soviet influence in Republican affairs. He was therefore increasingly opposed to Negrín's increasing reliance on the communists. By 1938 Azaña was among the growing number of Republicans who believed that the war had run its course and that it was futile to go on fighting for what would inevitably result in a pyrrhic victory (Document 9.8).

Document 9.8 The President of the Republic Appeals for an End to the Conflict

It is necessary to point out that war does not consist only of military operations, of movements of armies or of battles . . .

Wars undertaken in order to impose universal monarchy have produced liberal uprising, among others that of the Spanish people. Wars undertaken in order to destroy a militarism have left it more alive, have made it appear again more vigorous and have caused a triumph of a social revolution. Our own wars are an example of what I say . . .

After an earthquake it is difficult to recognise the outlines of the land. Imagine a volcano which is extinct, but on whose slopes many peaceful families have lived for generations. One day, the volcano suddenly erupts and causes havoc. When the eruption has ceased and the smoke has cleared away, the survivors look at the mountain and no longer does it seem the same to them . . .

This profound phenomenon, which comes about in all wars, prevents me from speaking of the future of Spain in the moral and political field, because it is a profound mystery, in this country of surprises and unexpected reactions, as to what may happen on the day when Spaniards at peace begin to consider what they have done during the war. I believe that if from this accumulation of evils, the greatest possible good has to emerge, then it will be with this spirit, and unhappy is he who does not so understand it. I have not the optimism of a Pangloss, nor shall I apply to this Spanish drama the very simple doctrine of the proberb, which says 'It is an ill wind that blows nobody any good' . . .

When the war finishes, as we wish it to finish, it is the moral obligation, above all, of those who suffer the war, to draw the greatest good from the lesson and from the muse of chastisement. When the torch passes to other hands, to other men, to other generations, let them remember if they ever feel their blood boil and the Spanish temper is once more infuriated with intolerance, hatred and the appetite for destruction, let them think of the dead and listen to their lesson; the lesson of these men who have bravely fallen in battle, generously fighting for a great ideal, and who now, protected by their maternal soil, feel no hate or rancour, and who send us with the sparkling of their light, tranquil and remote as that of a star, the message of the eternal Fatherland which says to all its sons: Peace, Pity and Pardon.

Source: Speech delivered by Don Manuel Azaña, President of the Spanish Republic, in Barcelona City Hall, on 18 July 1938

Inside Negrín's own cabinet, opposition to communist domination was led by the formidable minister of defence, Indalecio Prieto. Though earlier in the war he had been a willing accomplice in the communists' bid to topple his age-old rival, Largo Caballero, Prieto had regarded his alliance with them as a temporary marriage of convenience. As soon as he took over the reins of his new office, Prieto signalled the breakup of their relationship when he began taking steps to reduce communist influence in the military. One of his first actions as defence minister, for example, was to issue a order calling for an end to 'proselytizing' among the troops, a directive clearly aimed at the communists. During the following weeks Prieto widened the scope of his campaign by dismissing prominent communist or pro-communist commissars and officers from the armed forces. Not surprisingly, Prieto's undisguised hostility towards the communists set the stage for yet another political showdown. This time, however, the lines of conflict were not as well defined as they had been before the May Events. The communists knew that by attacking Prieto they risked splitting the coalition of moderate forces holding together the Popular Front government, above all because several members of the Council of Ministers, including Negrín himself, either belonged or were sympathetic to the *prietista* wing of the socialist movement. Yet communist leaders also believed that allowing Prieto to remain in power posed a far greater threat not only to themselves but also to the future of the Republican war effort. It was undoubtedly for these latter reasons that the communists decided to launch their own offensive against the Minister of Defence (Document 9.9).

Document 9.9 Resistance Versus 'Defeatism'

La Pasionaria on 27 February

Who are these people who spread defeatism and talk about the inefficiency of our army? . . .They are incompetents and cowards, people who burn one candle to God and another to the devil, people who stand with one foot here and the other in the camp of the rebels . . .

We must tell them that our men did not go to the front in order to preserve the privileges of the landlords and bankers; we must tell them that our women did not give their sons in order to return to the old slavery . . .Those who plan to destroy the revolutionary gains of our people won during nineteen months of sacrifice are not qualified to speak of democracy . . .

[When] the general commissariat of war pursues a policy . . .of removing political commissars who are cited for heroism . . .and enjoy the confidence of the soldiers . . ., then we who are inspired solely by the desire to win the war and defeat fascism must say that we will not allow this policy to continue.

Source: Bolloten, B. (1991) *The Spanish Civil War*, Chapel Hill, p. 576.

In their attempt to oust Prieto, the communists exploited the differences that existed between him and his one-time protégé, Juan Negrín. By late 1937 both were sharply divided over a number of fundamental issues, including the conduct of the war effort. While Negrín whole heartedly supported the communist strategy that called for continuing military action at all costs, Prieto believed that, in view of their staggering losses at Brunete, Belchite and Teruel, the outlook for the Republicans was becoming bleaker and bleaker. Prieto's growing despair and disillusionment deepened after the Nationalists recaptured Teruel in early 1938, a defeat which the communists attributed to Prieto's excessive pessimism (Document 9.10). Then, shortly after the Nationalists launched their overpowering spring offensive, Prieto insisted that the Republic should seek a mediated peace as soon as possible. This gave his critics the opportunity to escalate their attacks on the minister of defence, who was now being branded in the communist press as a 'capitulator' and 'defeatist'. Around this time Negrín himself was forced to choose sides in the dispute. Partly because he was convinced that Prieto's inveterate cynicism would undermine his government's resistance policy and partly because he was under immense communist pressure to take a stand against his close friend and colleague, Negrín felt obliged to undertake a complete reorganization of his cabinet. On 5 April, just days before the Nationalists reached the Mediterranean, Negrín dismissed Prieto from his post on the grounds that his defeatist attitude had a demoralizing effect on those around him. Feeling betrayed by his former ally – whom he now accused of being a pawn of the communists – Prieto left the government and soon thereafter withdrew from the republican war effort.[6]

Document 9.10 Reasons for Prieto's Downfall

Next came the Negrin–Prieto Government. The conduct of military affairs was entirely in the hands of Prieto. He began by introducing the principle of 'proportional representation' in the commanding staff of the army, and placed a whole series of incompetents and cowards at the head of the military groups. By refusing to undertake a purge of the military command, and by placing suspicious individuals in responsible posts, he protected wreckers and enemies. Prieto's hatred of the heroic Communists, who had safeguarded the existence of the department of war commissars at the most difficult moments, led to the latter's collapse and conversion into a bureaucratic institution . . .

Prieto's policy, moreover, led to the disruption of the whole eastern front and to the splitting of the republican zone into two parts. His wrecking activities were also to be seen in the way he drew up the military reports, in which he frequently announced the loss of areas, towns and positions before they had actually been captured by the enemy, thereby distorting the true relation of forces in favour of the enemy.

Source: Díaz, J. (1940) *Lessons of the Spanish War 1936–1939*, London, p. 14.

The downfall of Prieto enabled Negrín to shore up the unity of his Popular Front government of resistance, but it did little to stem the rising tide of opposition that was gaining momentum inside the Republican zone. In fact, despite the broad representation of parties in his administration, the political base of Negrín's government was becoming ever more fractured. For example, his efforts to repair relations with anarchosyndicalist leaders – most of whom had supported Prieto in his struggle with the communists – by appointing on 8 May a CNT minister to his cabinet only deepened the internal divisions of the libertarian movement. While some anarchists, such as the reformist secretary-general of the CNT, Mariano Vásquez, argued that Negrín's policy of resistance was the last great hope for the Republicans, others vehemently denounced the collaborationist tendencies of the movement (Document 9.11).

Document 9.11 Anarchist Dissension over Support for Popular Front Policies

National Committee of the CNT

Circular #12

In the Plenary of September, 1937, we agreed to support and defend the principle of elections under the auspices of a Socialist and Federal Republic. In our proposals presented to the UGT and approved by the National Plenary of Regionals, we included a section containing the September agreement. The government declaration . . .spoke of a Popular Republic, which is not opposed to our principles. It is necessary in a declaration of principles to emphasize our respect for religion, especially when we know what an important role it plays abroad, particularly in England and the United States. In both countries the winning over of Catholics to our side would have an enormous importance. We cannot ignore . . .that Britain, France, the United States or any democracy cannot be socialized and will not look favorably on or aid in the triumph of a regime of collectivizations, socialization, or even nationalization controlled by the workers, for fear of setting a precedent . . .

The Peninsular Committee

It is necessary to remove those who belittle our principles. He who is without ideals should not lead our Movement. The 'doctrinal baggage' and the 'hackneyed literature' that have been referred to cannot be disregarded by anyone who still takes pride in being an anarchist. If anyone dislikes our doctrines . . . let him leave. This tendency to justify anything at all is noxious, and puts us in disgraceful positions. We are optimists because we believe in what we have created, and we must overcome our present weaknesses by removing from the leadership of our movement those who either out of ignorance or apostasy no longer believe in the Organization . . .

We are in favour of the CNT–UGT pact, but with guarantees for revolutionary actions that it does not yet have. We do not grant it the virtue of having stopped the collapse of the Eastern Front: our comrades who fought heroically to halt the enemy do not merit such a dismissal. Similarly our entry into the Popular Front solved nothing: we were invited by the Communists. Nor can our entry into the government be considered a success: it came about after we had begged for power. Power is not asked for: it is either taken by force, or handed over because it suits the interests of others. For our movement, ethics is not a luxury item, but rather something essential that distinguishes us from other groups.

Source: Peirats, J. (1974) *Anarchists in the Spanish Revolution*, Toronto, pp. 292–3 and 294.

Negrín also faced the determined opposition of an ever-increasing number of socialists. Months of incessant internecine squabbling had irrevocably divided the movement, and, at this late stage in the war, the boundaries separating the opposing camps had hardened around the issue of resistance. On the one side were those who, because they believed that the fate of the Republic had already been decided, sought to obtain a mediated peace as soon as possible. But peace was not the only issue at stake for this group. For they were also convinced that communists held such a firm stranglehold on the government that a Republican victory would inevitably result in a Soviet-styled dictatorship. Anti-resisters, such as the socialist intellectual Julián Besteiro, therefore increasingly identified themselves as defenders of an anti-communist Republic, and, in so doing, they hoped that Franco would reconsider their demand for an unconditional surrender. For Negrín and his supporters, the 'mediators' were at best naive and at worst traitors to the Republican cause. As regards mediation, Negrín and the resisters insisted that efforts to seek a settlement from the appeasing nations would mean imposing a 'peace of Munich' on Spain (Document 9.12). To avoid the fate of Austria and Czechoslovakia, they maintained that the Republic's only recourse was to prolong the fighting long enough so that the Civil War could be submerged into a larger European conflict. Given the rapidly deteriorating diplomatic climate at the time, they reasoned that war would come sooner rather than later.[7] As to the charge of communist domination, the resisters were adamant that Negrín was not a puppet of the Communist Party and its Soviet advisers. On the contrary, they pointed out that Soviet aid had been indispensable to the war effort, and that a Republican victory would be impossible without the communists' continued support.

Document 9.12 The Policy of Resistance

There is a grim determination among the war leaders of the Government that no intervention by outside nations to impose a 'peace of Munich' on Spain will be tolerated. The Government is quite frank, or its representatives have been in such conversations as I have had with them and in such letters as I have received from them, in its utter lack of faith in the political integrity or the personal honesty of Mr. Chamberlain. They have a feeling of contempt for the weakness of the French Government in constantly yielding to Chamberlain until he has deprived the French of all their allies and reduced France to a second-rate Power . . .

Respectfully yours,
Claude G. Bowers

Source: Cortada, J.W. (ed.) (1985) *A City in War*, Wilmington, p. 172.

No less antagonistic to the Popular Front government were the Basque and autonomous movements based in Catalonia. As we saw earlier, regionalist aspirations had been partially realized during the early phases of the war. In Catalonia, for example, self-rule was so advanced by the spring of 1937 that the Generalitat was able to behave as though it were on a par with the central government. It will be remembered that, not long after it re-emerged as the principal ruling political body of the region, the Generalitat began issuing its own currency, directing its own defence, and conducting its own foreign policy.

The pro-centralist government of Juan Negrín was determined to end this state of affairs, and, as a result, steps were taken to divest Catalonia of its growing 'independence'.[8] Immediately following the May Events, for example, the central government asserted its control over the police forces and army of Catalonia. Shortly thereafter a certain number of the Catalan war industries were also taken over.

Friction between the nationalists and the central government sharpened when Negrín transferred the seat of government to Barcelona in November 1937. While the national government assured the *Esquerra* and other nationalist parties that they would respect regional rights, Catalan and Basque politicians bristled at every measure which curbed their autonomy in the name of the war effort. By the summer of 1938 the Basque (PNV) and Catalan (*Esquerra*) parties refused to co-operate any longer with the government's efforts to centralize its authority (Document 9.13). On 17 August representatives of the Basque and Catalan nationalists, Jaime Ayguadé (minister of labour) and Manuel Irujo (minister without portfolio), resigned from their cabinet posts. Both were angered by the promulgation of recent government decrees which limited the scope of the regional authorities in matters of finance and justice. Following their departure, Negrín vainly sought to smooth over his relations with the nationalists by filling the vacant seats in his ministry with another Basque and Catalan. Significantly, neither Tomas Bilbao, who belonged to the relatively obscure Basque Nationalist Action Party nor Joan Moix, a member of the PSUC, was representative of parties that were identified with the autonomous movements. As a result, Negrín's attempt to patch up the cabinet crisis only exacerbated tensions between him and the Nationalist elements.

Document 9.13 Regionalist Opposition to Negrín's Government of Victory

(a)

Catalunya, both by her will and by her feeling, places her sympathies and her efforts on the side of the lands in which democracy is crushing the doctrine of oppression and the systems of violence.

Together with the Spanish Republic, within our autonomous constitution, one with the Republic of which we are ourselves a part, and which flings out its proud banner upon the bulwarks which defend Liberty and Independence, Catalunya is up in arms. He who was born in this beloved land of ours, land of Peace and well-being, of culture and of Law, and who does not defend her, he is not truly a Catalan nor does he deserve to be free.

Source: Address of President Lluís Companys to the Parliament of Catalunya, 1 March 1938.

(b)

The question about Irujo (Basque, minister of justice). Basque nationalist. Catholic. A fine Jesuit, a worthy disciple of Ignatius Loyola. Compromised in the Salamanca-France banking affair. Acts like a real fascist. Especially devotes himself to hunting down and persecuting people from the masses and the antifascists who last year in August, September, October, and November treated imprisoned fascists brutally. He wanted to arrest Carrillo, the general secretary of the United Socialist Youth because, at the time when the fascists were nearing Madrid, Carrillo, who was then a governor, gave the order to shoot several arrested officers of the fascists. In the name of the law, this fascist Irujo, a minister of justice in the Republican government, is organizing a system of searches of Communists, Socialists, and anarchists, who brutally treated imprisoned fascists. In the name of the law, this minister of justice freed hundreds upon hundreds of arrested fascist agents or disguised fascists. Together with Zugazagoitia, Irujo does everything possible and impossible to save the Trotskyists and to sabotage trials against them. And he will do everything possible to acquit them. This same Irujo was in Catalonia the last few days and with his boss Aguirre, the famous president of the famous Basque republic. They arranged secret meetings with Companys to prepare a separation of Catalonia from Spain. They are intriguing in Catalonia, declaring: the fate of the Basque nation awaits you. The Republican government sacrificed the Basque nation. They will also sacrifice Catalonia.

Source: Radosh, R., Habek, M.R. and Sevastianov, G. (eds) (2001) *Spain Betrayed*, New Haven, pp. 223–4.

With pressing international, cabinet and military issues demanding the attention of Negrín's administration in the autumn of 1938, there can be no doubt that the POUM trial which began on 11 October was held for purely political reasons. Negrín himself wanted more than just to exorcize a political ghost that still haunted the Republic. He most likely regarded the trial as a public medium for showcasing the government's efforts to prosecute groups that were guilty of undermining the Republican war effort by fomenting discord and disorder in the rearguard. Secondly, if it could be shown that the POUM was guilty of treason, the government's harsh persecution of the party (and by extension all others who were responsible for conducting espionage and treasonable contacts with the enemy in the rearguard) could be legally justified. For the communists the trial had an even greater purpose. As we have seen, in the months following the May disturbances, they had campaigned vigorously to repress the POUM, which they identified in their propaganda as a 'Trotskyite' Fifth Column party. Putting the POUM on trial would therefore serve the same function as the Moscow trials that had just ended, namely, to prove that the threat of 'Trotskyism' was not just a Soviet phenomenon. No less important to the communists was the opportunity the trial afforded them to uphold their own credibility by publicly unmasking the POUM. This was necessary not least because they feared that the POUM might continue to be a rallying point for the anti-communist factions.

Once the trial got under way, the communists quickly discovered that, notwithstanding their energetic efforts to whip up public hatred towards the POUM outside the courtroom, they could not re-enact the Soviet-style show trials in Spain. What was particularly frustrating for them was the fact that much of the evidence they provided to the prosecutor was so obviously fabricated – the clumsily forged correspondence between Andreu Nin and Franco, for example – that it ultimately cast doubt on the charge that the POUM was acting in collusion with the Nationalists (Document 9.14). When a verdict was finally reached on the 20th it fell short of fulfilling the communists' expectations. The judge rejected the accusations that the POUM was a treasonous organization and that its leaders were agents of Franco. While managing to salvage its revolutionary reputation, the POUM was none the less to be sacrificed in the name of 'internal order'. The party was found guilty of playing a seditious role in the May Day disturbances of 1937, and, as a result, both Negrín and the communists won their legal battle to have the POUM dismantled. The court ordered that the POUM and its youth organization (JCI) be officially dissolved, and its entire leadership, including Julián Gorkín, Pere Bonet, and Juan Andrade, were imprisoned for the remainder of the war.

Document 9.14 The Fruits of a False Conspiracy

(a)

The Trial of the P.O.U.M. [October 1938]

By Gonzales

On October 11 began the trial of the Spanish Trotskyists, members of the so-called *P.O.U.M.*

The task of the agents of the 'Fifth Column' in Spain was to disrupt the national unity of the Spanish people in the struggle against the German–Italian interventionists, to bring about a split in the People's Front. In their paper, *Batalla*, they attempted to incite the parties of the People's Front against one another. Day by day their gutter press slandered the Communist Party, saying that the Communists wished to seize power for themselves, that they were conspiring against the Socialist Party behind Caballero's back, that they were preparing to assassinate officials of the C.N.T., and that they were organising a St. Bartholomew's eve against the Anarchists. The heroic fighters of the International Brigades, who had come to Spain from various countries, they called 'Pretorians,' whom the Communist International had allegedly sent to Spain in order to organise a 'Communist revolution.' At the same time they accused the Socialist Party, which was co-operating loyally in the work of the People's Front, of pursuing an 'ambiguous policy of impotent compromise, a policy designed to bring about the rebirth of the bourgeoisie. At the same time they incited Caballero to take violent measures against the Communist Party. The Trotskyist agents of fascism endeavoured to cause a split between the Catalonian Government and the Government of all Spain, in Valencia; they attempted to stir up the Anarchist workers to rebellion and provoke the soldiers into leaving the front.

Source: World News and Views, p. 1165

(b)

Republican Justice

POUM Trial

Spain's most important treason trial of the war came to an end last week, brought freedom to some, prison sentences to others and high praise to the Spanish Government from newspaper correspondents and other impartial observers for the fairness of Republican justice.

The nine defendants were members of the ill-famed POUM – Partido Obrero de Unificación Marxista (Marxist Unification Party) – and were charged with responsibility for the uprising in Barcelona in May, 1937, which resulted in the deaths of 950 and the wounding of many more. Despite the seriousness of the charges against them, the defendants were not tried by court martial but were given a public trial under the old Spanish code, described by the United Press 'as more favorable to defendants than any other in Europe.'

Observations

Commentators at the two trials made the following observations: (1) The conduct of the trials gave adequate proof of the fairness of Republican justice and (2) the evidence brought forth contributed to an understanding of the almost insuperable difficulties overcome by the Republic in the first year of the war when it was faced with the tasks of building a loyal army (the old army had in large part deserted to the Rebels) and with restoring order behind the lines (most of the national police force, the Guardia Civil, had also sided with the Rebels).

Source: News of Spain (New York), 2 November 1938, p. 4.

(c)

P.O.U.M. frame-up fails

I have been in courts a great many times in my life. I therefore expected to find the same harshness, vindictiveness, and lack of fairness at the trial of the P.O.U.M. as I have known in America in the past. I was therefore considerably surprised with the tone maintained during the eleven days. The prosecuting attorney was obviously either a communist or strongly in sympathy with the Stalin followers. He was vindictive, hard, and did his utmost to incriminate the prisoners. At the close of his summing up, he demanded no less than fifteen and thirty years imprisonment for them. The very fact that he did not dare to call for the death penalty was in itself a proof that the whole fabricated charges had collapsed . . .

The readers of *Vanguard* may well ask how it comes that five of the indicated members of the P.O.U.M. were given eleven and fifteen years imprisonment respectively. The reason for the sentence is twofold. First the judges had to do something to appease the insatiable appetite on the part of Stalin's representatives. The second, to prevent the disappearance of Gorkin and his comrades as Nin and others disappeared. This is not only my impression, but also the impression of a number of people who attended the trial.

Source: Goldman, E. (1 February 1939) *Vanguard*, New York.

Fall of Catalonia

As he had done following the battle of Teruel, Franco used his victory at Ebro as a springboard for another major offensive. With over two hundred thousand troops already concentrated on the Catalan front, Franco wasted no time in launching what turned out to be his last significant offensive. On 23 December large-scale aerial and artillery bombardments were unleashed against enemy positions along the Republic's eastern zone. Given the enormous weight of the Nationalist forces, who were reinforced by the Condor Legion and well-armed Italian units, the outcome of the assault was never in doubt. By the middle of January, Franco's army had pushed into the heart of Catalonia, capturing thousands of Republican soldiers and draining the Popular Army of the remainder of its reserves of war supplies. It was a cruel irony that, at a time when the Republican army was down to its last pieces of artillery and hand weapons, a large shipment of war supplies from the Soviet Union was being held up on the French border. Much of the equipment – which included badly needed aeroplanes and torpedo-boats – had been in sitting in French ports since September.[9] But, despite the entreaties of the Spanish government, Daladier's government steadfastly refused to allow these supplies to cross the frontier until Franco's troops were already at the point of overrunning Catalonia.

As the Nationalists pushed closer to Barcelona, more and more Republican troops and civilians began trekking towards the French–Spanish frontier. With each passing day resistance to the advancing Nationalist troops was crumbling. By the time they reached the outskirts of Barcelona on 25 January, they were met with virtually no opposition (Document 9.15). Inside the city, the civilian population of some two million was so demoralized from food shortages, incessant bombings, and endless political feuding that very few were willing to go on fighting to the end. For many the time had come to flee rather than take a stand, and as long as an escape route to France remained opened, they chose to make the long and arduous journey towards the border. In the following days tens of thousands of civilians and soldiers clogged the roads and footpaths leading out of Spain (Document 9.16).

Document 9.15 The Fall of Barcelona

(a)

On January 26, Barcelona fell to the enemy. The feared event occurred like a natural phenomenon. Resistance was scarce, not to say null. The enemy succeeded in entering the city and was able to continue its movement westward with the same ease it had used in the days preceding . . .One cannot help but note a tremendous contrast. The situation of Madrid in November 1936 was very similar to the one we have described in Barcelona. But what a different atmosphere! What enthusiasm then! What a feverish desire to fight, two years before, and what discouragement now! 48 hours before the enemy's entry, Barcelona was a dead city. It had been killed by the demoralization of those who fled to France, and those who remained in hiding, without even the courage to go out into the streets, or end those last hours of bitterness destined for the city. For this reason, it is no exaggeration to say that Barcelona was lost simply because there was no will to resist, either among the populace or among certain troops that had been contaminated by the atmosphere. Morale was crushed.

Source: Rojo, V., *¡Alerta los pueblos!*, translated in Ranzato, G. (1999) *The Spanish Civil War*, New York, p. 114.

(b)

The fascists had passed the last ring of fortifications protecting Barcelona. Now we planned to tear up the city pavement and build barricades within the city limits. Women were to be supplied with oil – to be lighted and poured on the heads of the fascist invaders. We would sell our lives dearly.

But the conference was heavy-spirited and the plans for the fortification of the city limits seemed fanciful even to those of us who made them. Nine times during the evening we had to suspend our meeting during a fresh bombardment and nine times we stood alone while the bombs crashed, each of us reflecting on what none of us would say aloud.

For Barcelona, in all truth, was untenable, and we knew it, but we could not say it – the words stuck in our throats.

The city lies in a beautiful natural hollow, surrounded by hills, and easily accessible from the south where the river Llobregat flows. The enemy was advancing and once they held the heights, Barcelona would be completely cut off from the rest of the world. The fascists could make short work of it by sea, air, and land.

Source: De la Mora, C. (1939) *In Place of Splendor*, New York, p. 379.

Document 9.16 Exodus from Nationalist Spain

I heard in Paris of the fall of Barcelona, and was filled with rage and despair . . .

We drove to the frontier. It was as though we had arrived too late at a vast public meeting which was just breaking up. We threaded our way through the crowd hurrying homewards. The landscape was a tragic one. Beneath a flowering shrub a man lay dying, his face yellow, his eyes staring up at the blossoms. Men lay huddled together, drinking at a stream. A shaggy-haired man with a donkey, which had apparently refused to go any farther, was seated on the ground, waiting.

The frontier, when we reached it, was like a medieval picture of the Crucifixion. Groups of men in civilian clothes were streaming down from the hills. They bore themselves with dignity, advancing with evident trust towards the fate that awaited them on the guarded plain teeming with soldiers.

Some still had earth clutched in their hands which they had snatched up as they left their villages. When I saw one of the *gardes mobiles* forcibly open one of these clenched hands and scatter the soil in disdain I knew that the soldiers of France did not understand the meaning of the word 'home,' and I wished that one day they might pay for it. It was an impermissible wish, a meaningless one, but at that moment rage at defeat, not reason, filled my heart.

Source: Regler, G. (1959) *The Owl of Minerva: The Autobiography of Gustav Regler*, London, p. 321.

When Yagüe's troops marched into Barcelona on 26 January, they found a subdued and half-starved population awaiting them. Fifth Columnists came out of hiding and thronged the streets alongside war-weary citizens who were relieved that the war was finally over for them (Document 9.17). In the following days, the conquering army carried out reprisals against resisters and began eradicating all traces of Republican rule. Catalan independence, which had been compromised under the Republic's wartime regimes, was now wholly extinguished. Under the new regime, the authorities made it clear that everyone was regarded as Spanish and that everyone was required to speak Castilian.

Document 9.17 Occupying Barcelona

Friday, 27 January. What a crazy day! We had a hurried cup of coffee and at 9 o'clock the lorries were loaded and I set off in my car to Barcelona. Except for a few dreadful patches the road was good, but due to blown up bridges we had to go a long way round and finally arrived at 10.30. Barcelona is a lovely big spacious town and quite unharmed though very dirty. We drove madly all round it. The port is a shambles due to the hard work of the aviation. The streets were crowded with people showing considerable enthusiasm. Everyone shouting and cheering, and all the girls parading up the street with flags. The troops marching through were surrounded by cheering crowds, and everyone was in splendid form. And yet as soon as one was out of the main streets, where all the fun was going on, the people looked surly, and as though there had never been a war.

Source: Scott-Ellis, P. (1995) *The Chances of Death: A Diary of the Spanish Civil War*, Norwich, p. 183.

Meanwhile, the Republican government accompanied the tattered remnants of the Army of Catalonia as they made their retreat towards the frontier. Before crossing into France, however, government leaders paused briefly in the border town of Figueras. On 1 February Negrín announced to a rump session of the Cortes a simple three-point plan for peace. In addition to calling for the evacuation of all foreign troops and the right of the Spanish people to decide their own political future, his resolution insisted that there should be no persecution of those who had opposed the July Rebellion. Yet, in view of the fact that a Nationalist victory was close at hand, there was little reason to believe that any of these conditions would be met (Document 9.18).

Document 9.18 The Republican Government in Disarray

Both from the military and political point of view, the war was long since lost, and if we had been governed by a Spaniard, who would learn and interpret the will of the people, it would have ended in 1937. The unjustifiable collapse of the Catalonian fronts, the consequent loss of that region in which were all the most important industries, made our defeat perfectly clear . . .

All that remained of our Government was a group of men who called themselves the legitimate Government of the Nation, but who were outside the country. These practically constituted a Dictatorship, since for some time past they had suppressed the rights of the Head of the State, followed a war policy which was fatal as well as un-Spanish, and coerced certain Ministers, who seemed to be the slaves of their own timidity.

Source: Casado, S. (1939) *The Last Days of Madrid: The End of the Second Spanish Republic*, London, pp. 100–1.

By this time, the institutional framework of the Republic itself was falling apart. On 6 February the President of the Republic, Manuel Azaña, went into exile. When he resigned his post at the end of the month, his designated successor, Martínez Barrio, refused to return to Spain. In this same period, another near-fatal blow was delivered to the integrity of the regime. On 27 February, both Britain and France recognized Franco as the legitimate head of the Spanish government.

In spite of the growing state of political dissolution, Negrín and his supporters clung to the hope that all was not lost. They were convinced that a European war was imminent, and that the Republic would be saved if it could hold out against the Nationalists a little longer. Moreover, Negrín maintained that the Republic had no choice but to resist until there were guarantees that the vanquished would not be subjected to the merciless reprisals of a vindictive regime.

To continue waging war, Negrín relied on the nearly half million troops that remained in the Republican zone, whose borders extended from Madrid to Valencia and south to Almería. From a political standpoint, Negrín faced an even more Herculean task. Apart from a few cabinet ministers and the communists, it was well known that few military and political leaders supported his stand on resistance. Thus, when the premier and his communist entourage returned from France on 10 February, their first task was to re-establish the authority of government. To determine the prevailing state of political and military affairs in the central-southern zone, Negrín travelled on 12 February to Madrid, where he met with Colonel Segismundo Casado, the head of the Army of the Centre. In their conversation, Casado described what he saw as a hopeless situation. According to him, months of food shortages, physical privations, and acute mental fatigue brought on by the strains of war had brought the Madrid population to its knees. The only recourse left, Casado contended, was to surrender. In fact, Casado had no intention of supporting Negrín's plans for continued resistance. As he was one of the leaders of a broadly based anti-communist (and by extension anti-Negrínista) coalition that had taken shape in the period immediately following the collapse of Catalonia, Casado himself had already been in contact with Nationalist agents in Madrid (members of the SIPM, Information Service and Military Police) with a view to sounding out a peace settlement. In so doing, he and his fellow plotters had set the scene for the final act of the Republican drama.

Any hopes Negrín may have still entertained regarding the Republic's capacity for forestalling defeat were exploded only a few days after he left Madrid on 28 February. On 5–6 March 1939 anti-government conspirators seized control of Madrid's central radio exchange and made the stunning announcement that they had established an anti-communist junta called the National Defence Council (Document 9.19). Joining Casado in the coup were several politicians and military leaders, the most notable of whom were the socialist intellectual Julián Besteiro, General Miaja, the commander-in-chief of the armed forces, and the anarchist military commander, Cipriano Mera. The men justified their rebellion on several counts. First and foremost was the fact that they did not recognize the legitimacy of Negrín's communist-dominated government. (This was a reference to the legal limbo to which the government had been consigned following the resignation of Azaña.) Nor did it, in their eyes, reflect the true interests of the vast majority of Republicans who wanted to end the war. Finally, they maintained that an honourable and conciliatory peace could be now be achieved as the Nationalists would be more likely to negotiate with an anti-communist authority (Document 9.20).

Document 9.19 An Anti-Communist Manifesto

Spanish Workers, People of Anti-Fascist Spain –

The moment has come in which we must proclaim to the four winds the truth of the situation in which we find ourselves. As revolutionaries, as proletarians, as Spaniards, and as anti-Fascists, we cannot continue passively to accept any longer the improvidence, the lack of foresight and organisation, and the absurd lethargy shown by the Government of Dr. Negrin. These critical times through which we are passing, and the climax which is approaching, impel us to end the silence and uncertainty which have increased our mistrust in that handful of men who still claim the title of government, but in whom nobody believes and nobody trusts . . .

We cannot tolerate that while the people are expected to keep up mortal resistance, their leaders should be preparing for a comfortable and lucrative flight. We cannot permit that while the people struggle, fight and die, a few privileged persons should continue their life abroad.

To prevent this, to remove the memory of that shame, to avoid desertion at the gravest moments, the National Council of Defence has been formed, and today, taking full responsibility for the importance of our mission, with absolute certainty of our past, present and future loyalty, in the name of the National Council of Defence which has picked up authority from where Dr. Negrin's Government threw it away . . .

Constitutionally, the authority of Dr. Negrin's Government is without any lawful basis; in practice it lacks also any sort of confidence or good sense, and the spirit of sacrifice which should be required of those who want to rule the destinies of a people as heroic and self-denying as the Spanish people . . .

We oppose the policy of resistance, to save our cause from ending in mockery or vengeance. For this, we ask for the support of all Spaniards and for this we give our assurance that nobody, absolutely nobody, shall escape the fulfilment of his duties.

Source: Casado, S. (1939) *The Last Days of Madrid: The End of the Second Spanish Republic*, London, pp. 140–1 and p. 142.

Document 9.20 Casado Outlines Steps Needed for a Conditional Surrender

1. A categorical and final declaration of national sovereignty and integrity. We believe that the Nationalist Government will be as interested as we are in the confirmation of this principle, but we think a guarantee from them is necessary, for the spirits of everybody at home and abroad will be raised when they feel the certainty and reality of this.

2. The security that all civilians and soldiers who have taken part honourably and cleanly, through their enthusiasm or through their ideals, in this hard and lengthy struggle, shall be treated with the greatest respect, both as persons and in the matter of their interests.

3. A guarantee that there will be no reprisals and no sentences except those passed by competent tribunals for which every kind of proof will be necessary, including witnesses. To avoid mistakes it would be best to define and limit in a clear and final manner political and public crimes.

4. Respect for the lives and liberty of soldiers in the Militia, and of political Commissars who are not guilty of any criminal offence.

5. Respect for the life, liberty and employment of professional soldiers who have not been guilty of crime.

6. Respect for the life, liberty and interests of public officials on the same conditions.

7. A concession of twenty-five days for the expatriation of all persons who wish to leave the country.

8. That in the zone under litigation there shall be no Italian or Moorish troops.

9. If this should be accepted by the Council, the Councillor for Defence and the General in Command of Aggroupment shall be chosen to present it to the enemy.

Madrid, March 11th, 1939.

Source: Casado, S. (1939) *The Last Days of Madrid: The End of the Second Spanish Republic*, London, pp. 200–2.

Upon hearing the news of the demise of his government, Negrín realized that the war was now over for him (Document 9.21). As he made final preparations to leave Spain for good, a mini-civil-war broke out in different parts of Republican Spain.

Military forces still under communist command took up arms against the units supporting the Council of Defence. For the next several days, street fighting raged in Madrid and wherever else the communists refused to surrender (Document 9.22). Throughout this time, the Council itself was desperately trying to cobble together a peace agreement with Franco. But it soon became apparent that Franco was in no mood to make any concessions. His quest for a total victory was now within his grasp and he therefore felt no need to reach an understanding with the anti-communist representatives of the Defence Council. A few days after the fighting between the communists and their leftist enemies ended, Franco gave the order for his troops to occupy Madrid. On 27 March, Nationalist troops began slowly marching into the capital, and four days later Franco declared that the war was over.

Document 9. 21 Confronting Prime Minister Negrín

(a)

Prime Minister: General, I have just heard the manifesto which you have given out to the country, and I think what you have done is madness . . . I must tell you that what has been done has the support of the whole people, whose rightful representatives are with me, and who are very pleased, because, like me, they are convinced that they have given Spain real service.

Prime Minister: I hope that you will reflect, because I understand that there is still time for us to make some arrangement.

Colonel Casado: I do not understand what you mean. I believe that everything is arranged as the people wish.

Prime Minister: At least, I must ask you to send a representative so that I may hand over the powers of Government, or I will send one to Madrid with these powers.

Colonel Casado: Don't worry about that. You can't hand over what you haven't got. Actually, I am taking up the powers which you and your Government have abandoned.

Prime Minister: Then you will not accede to that request?

Colonel Casado: No.

Source: Casado, S. (1940) *The Last Days of Madrid: The End of the Second Spanish Republic*, London, pp. 149–50.

(b)

The Prime Minister telephoned to Casado. 'What is going on in Madrid, General?' he asked. 'What is going on is that I have rebelled,' was the reply. 'That you have rebelled! Against whom? Against me?' 'Yes, against you.' 'Very well, you can consider yourself relieved of your command,' answered Dr.

Negrín quietly. After all, he was still Prime Minister of Spain and Commander-in-Chief of the armies. Very soon he was to discover that the steps he could take to assert his authority were few.

Source: Alvarez del Vayo, J. (1940) *Freedom's Battle*, New York, p. 312.

Document 9.22 The Defeat of Communism

(a)

The establishment of the junta and the flight of N. [Negrín] and his government (this flight, in my view, was a tragic mistake and quite inexplicable; I end up suspecting N. of complicity with Casado: your relations with N. outside the country, your statements concerning him, etc. will have to be very careful) have created an extremely serious situation in the country, of confusion, disorder and something resembling 18 July – with the aggravating difference of a brutal repression unleashed against our p. This repression was ordered by the junta from above, with the manifest intention of thus making an agreement with Franco possible, and was fed at the base by an explosion of all the hatred for our party and spirit of revenge of anarchists, provocateurs, etc., etc. The plan was to shatter our p. and in effect suppress it. The p. was surprised by this wave of repression, which moreover highlighted our weaknesses, especially in relation to our links with the masses. There is no organization of the p. – so far as I know – that had the capacity to defend itself by posing the problem of defence of the p. as a mass problem. The majority took the course of utilizing 'positions' of the p. within the army and the civilian apparatus of the State, but a considerable proportion of the men holding such 'positions' failed us (the airmen, for example, accepted Casado's orders to bomb the lines occupied by our comrades in Madrid). So far as the masses are concerned, in the first days at least the anti-communist campaign chalked up some successes, thanks to the profound weariness of the masses themselves, who desired peace above all else . . . In Madrid the comrades were provoked to armed struggle by the junta's measures, the arrests and summary executions of our command staff and commissars, etc. etc. Moreover, they thought the government was resisting elsewhere in the country. I do not yet know all the details, but it seems to me that once the decision was taken to defend ourselves by every means, our comrades lacked decision. Their sense of responsibility, undoubtedly, prevented them from calling extra forces into the capital, with the risk of breaching the fronts . . .

Source: Carr, E.H. (1984) *The Comintern and the Spanish Civil War*, New York, pp. 99–100.

(b)

Spain's Final Tragedy

Paris, March 13, by Cable

It is all very sad. This bloodshed in Madrid is senseless. The very officers and soldiers who saw Communists die in thousands at their side are shooting down the Communist executives. The few remaining Loyalist planes, tanks, and cannon rain explosives on Loyalists.

Now, of course, many people will say, 'I told you so. I always knew the Loyalists were reds.' But it seems to me that this last and ugly phase of the Spanish struggle proves the very opposite. Casado, Besteiro, Miaja, and their friends in the defense junta are all prominent Loyalists; yet they are bloody anti-Communists. Moreover, if Republican Spain were Communist, could Casado in three days have turned a large part of the army against the Communists? Before the Socialist Negrin and Del Vayo, together with many Communist leaders, left Spain last week, Negrin rang up all the important cities and army centers. Casado told Negrin over the telephone, 'I've rebelled.' Valencia, Murcia, Albacete, and Estremadura answered in much the same way. In the little village where Negrin and Del Vayo stayed, a handful of militiamen volunteered to make a last stand, but several companies of the Casadist troops were already en route to arrest the Negrin government. Where, then, was that Communist Spain which Mussolini, Hitler, and some sincere anti-fascists had summoned up in their imagination? Part of it never existed; part of it lies in unmarked graves.

The Communists are putting up a swell fight. According to the last report published by the Paris *Temps* civilians are joining the Communist soldiers, and private information suggests that non-Communists are supporting the Communists against the junta; but whoever wins, Franco wins. It is clever of him to wait. The longer the intra-Loyalist war goes on, the less resistance he will encounter when he advances.

The Casadist revolt diminishes the possibility of obtaining terms from Franco. Why should Burgos negotiate even an unopposed Loyalist surrender? The fascists want a complete victory, achieved by force of arms. Italy and Germany will reject any peace parleys chiefly because France and England have favored them. Apparently both foreign partnerships feel that the manner of ending the war will help determine their rival positions in Spain after the war.

Source: Fischer, L. 'Hitler's New Threat', *The Nation*, 30 March 1939, 312.

Legacy of civil war

In the aftermath of war, Spaniards on both the winning and losing sides faced an uncertain future. First and foremost, they needed to recover from the emotional and psychological traumas brought on by a conflict which had claimed the lives of over

350,000 people and had caused the flight of close to half a million more citizens. Added to this was the fact that nearly everyone had to endure the many hardships of day-to-day living. Food shortages, inadequate housing (especially in the urban areas that had been subjected to continuous bombings), and widespread unemployment were not least of the obstacles they had to overcome.

Precisely how Spain was to rise from the ashes of war would be determined in large part by two major factors. One was the outbreak of the Second World War. Just five months after the civil war ended Europe was plunged into another general war that would last for the next six years. As a result, Spain could not expect economic or any other form of material assistance from abroad since it was the fate of Europe as a whole and not Spain itself which became the overriding concern of most countries.

At home, Spain's recovery was placed in the hands of General Francisco Franco, who was to rule his country as a dictator for the next thirty-six years. The peace and stability that Franco and his Nationalist allies had brought to Spain came at a high price. The fighting on the battlefields may have ended but Franco's efforts to repress those who resisted his rule continued for the next several decades. Reprisals against his former enemies on the left were exceedingly harsh, particularly in the decade after the war when thousands of Republicans were imprisoned and between 10,000 and 28,000 were executed (Document 9.23).

Document 9.23 The Victors and the Vanquished

(a)

Order Restricting Meetings, Manifestations, and Public Activities (20 July 1939)

1. The holding of meetings and manifestations shall require authorization from the Minister of the Government. This must be requested in ample time, through the Civil Governor of the province, and must set forth the purpose of the action, the names of speakers who are supposed to speak, and the themes they are to discuss. The Civil Governors will forward these petitions to the Ministry with due information.

2. Exempted from the requirement of ministerial authorization are:

(a) Meetings held by legitimately established associations in accordance with their statutes, but this shall not prejudice the government's right to restrict the exercise of this right of association.

(b) Processions of the Catholic faith.

3. Such public acts as commemorations, inaugurations, dedications, homages, and analogous things also require ministerial authorization . . .

Source: Delzell, C. F. (ed.) (1970) *Mediterranean Fascism, 1919–1945*, London, p. 315.

(b)

Conversation With Generalissimo Franco

19th July, 1939–XVII

Instinctively Generalissimo Franco tends to shift the conversation from the political to the military plane. He is still more head of an army than head of a State. Political problems, which, in the course of his life and of his military career, he has touched on only superficially, now – together with the new responsibilities of Caudillo of a revolution and of a nation – present themselves to his mind with the imperious urgency of a duty, but still present themselves in a confused manner; and he himself does not conceal his difficulty. To deal with, Generalissimo Franco is the same man as one has learned to know from his achievements, his words and his very photographs. There are no surprises and no disappointments. A man, simple in his bearing and his thought, calm in his examination of questions and in his judgment, he limits his conversation to a lucid account of events and of the situations arising from them without ever venturing beyond them . . .

The problems which face the new regime are many and serious; first of all there is the so-called question of the Reds. Of them there are already 200,000 under arrest in the various Spanish prisons. Trials are going on every day at a speed which I would almost describe as summary . . .

I myself saw numerous squads of prisoners busily engaged in repairing bridges and roads; the treatment given to them is good, which is proved by the fact that there are only very few attempts to escape. The sons of Reds executed or killed in the war are treated with a spirit of great humanity; they are mixed with the sons of Nationalists in the youth organisations of the Falange. It would be useless to deny that all this still causes a gloomy air of tragedy to hang over Spain. There are still a great number of shootings. In Madrid alone between 200 and 250 a day, in Barcelona 150; in Seville, a town which was never in the hands of the Reds, 80. But this must be judged in terms of the Spanish mentality and one must add that even in the face of these events, the populace maintains an impressive spirit of calm coolness. During my stay in Spain, while more than ten thousand men already condemned to death awaited in the prisons the inevitable moment of their execution, only two, I repeat two, appeals for pardon were addressed to me by families. I may add that the Caudillo granted them forthwith.

Source: Ciano, Count G. (1948) *Ciano's Diplomatic Papers*, London, pp. 290 and 294.

The authoritarian state that Franco controlled between 1939 and 1975 passed through several stages. In the first one, the fascist model of government, such as those found in Hitler's Germany and Mussolini's Italy, were greatly admired and emulated. And while Franco's rule depended to a large extent on the support of non-fascist institutions – the Catholic Church, for example – he none the less set himself the task of transforming the social, political, and economic structures of Spain so that they conformed to the 'fascist' Europe that was envisaged by the Axis powers. The Allied victory in 1945, however, forced Franco to downplay if not entirely abandon many of the fascist features of his dictatorship. Even so, the Caudillo steadfastly refused to bring Spain into the liberal-democratic order that emerged in Western Europe in the era following the Second World War. By doing so he effectively consigned Spain to a state of isolation for the next several years.

Barriers between Spain and the West began to break down with the onset of the Cold War (1946–89), not least because of Franco's well-established anti-communist credentials. A defence treaty signed with the United States in 1953 and a concordat with the Holy See that same year paved the way for Spain's gradual reintroduction into the international community. Above all, these ties to the outside world compelled Franco and his ministers to make further modifications to his dictatorship. Perhaps the most significant of these was Franco's decision in 1959 to loosen the reins of state control over the economy. In so doing, Franco unintentionally set in motion modernizing forces that would transform much of Spanish society in the following decade.

By the time Franco died in November 1975, the vast majority of Spaniards no longer wanted to identify themselves with a regime that had for nearly forty years looked more to the past rather than to the future. In the course of the next two years, the foundations were laid for a democratic government, which came into being in 1978. Since then Spain has become one of Europe's most dynamic countries, demonstrating, among other things, that the deep wounds inflicted by the Civil War (1936–39) were finally healing.

Glossary

Important political groups and working-class organizations

AMA Agupación de Mujeres Antifascistas (Antifascist Women's Organization) – communist-led women's organization founded in 1934. Branches included the Catalan women's group, Unió de Dones de Catalunya (UDC).

BOC Bloc Obrer i Camperol (Workers' and Peasants' Bloc) – independent Marxist organization founded in 1931 by the Marxist intellectual Joaquín Maurín.

CEDA/JAP Confederación Español de Derechas Autónomas/Juventudes de Acción Popular (Spanish Confederation of Autonomous Right-wing parties/Popular Action Youth) – composite political organization of the legalist right founded in 1933 and its ultra-rightist youth movement (Youth of Popular Action).

CNT/FIJL Confederación Nacional del Trabajo/Federación Ibérica de Juventudes Libertarias (National Confederation of Labour/Iberian Federation of Libertarian Youth) – anarchosyndicalist trade union organization established in late 1910 and its independent youth federation, founded in 1932.

ERC Esquerra Republicana de Catalunya (Left-Republican Party of Catalonia) – fusion in 1931 of various Catalan republican parties, including Acció Catalana, Partit Republicà Català and the separatist Estat Català.

FAI Federación Anarquista Ibérica (Iberian Anarchist Federation) – the insurrectionary vanguard organization of the anarchist movement, founded in 1927.

FE/JONS Falange Española/Juntas de Ofensiva Nacional Sindicalista (Spanish Phalange/Leagues of National Syndicalist Offensive) – Spanish fascist party and revolutionary syndicalist organizations which merged in early 1934.

FNTT Federación Nacional de Trabajadores de la Tierra (National Federation of Land Workers) – the militant agrarian land workers' section of the UGT.

FSPOUM Secretariado Femenino del POUM (Women's Bureau of the POUM) – Women's bureau of the dissident Marxist party.

HISMA/ROWAK Compañía Hispano-Marroquí de Transportes/ Rohstoff- und Waren-Einkaufsgesellschaft – import/export agencies set up in Spain (July 1936) and Germany (October 1936) during the war in order to co-ordinate economic relations between Hitler's Germany and Nationalist Spain.

ML Mujeres Libres (Anarchist Free Women) – independent anarchist women's organization formed in the spring of 1936.

NKVD Nardonyi Komissariat Vnutrennikh Del (People's Commissariat of Internal Affairs) – Soviet secret police, formerly known as GPU/OGPU.

PCE Partido Comunista de España (Spanish Communist Party) – the Moscow-orientated communist party, founded in 1921.

PNV Partido Nacionalista Vasco (Basque Nationalist Party) – the Christian Democrat Basque Nationalist Party, created in 1895.

POUM Partido Obrero de Unificación Marxista (Workers' Party of Marxist Unity) – Leninist-style revolutionary vanguard party created in 1935, which united left communist dissidents from the BOC and former Trotskyists from the ICE.

PSOE Partido Socialista Obrero Español (Spanish Socialist Workers' Party) – the Spanish Socialist Workers' Party, established in Madrid in 1879.

PSUC Partit Socialista Unificat de Catalunya (Socialist Party of Catalonia) – merger of several Catalan socialist and communist parties (Unió Socialista de Catalunya, Partit Comunista de Catalunya, and Partit Català Proletari). Led by Joan Comorera (USC), it functioned during the war as the Catalan branch of the Spanish Communist Party.

SF Sección Femenina (Women's Section of Spanish Fascists) – Women's section of the Spanish fascist movement, founded by Pilar de Primo de Rivera in 1934.

SIM Servicio de Investigación Militar (Military Intelligence Service) – Republican secret police which was dominated by the communists during the last phases of the Civil War.

UGT Unión General de Trabajadores (General Workers' Union) – the trade-union branch of the socialist movement, established in Barcelona in 1888.

UME Unión Militar Español (Spanish Military Union) – clandestine right-wing army officers' society founded in 1933.

UMRA Unión de Militares Republicanos Antifascistas (Military Union of Republican Anti-fascists) – liberal union of anti-fascist officers formed in opposition to the UME.

Notes

Introduction

1 The fact that an unscrupulous Spanish publisher managed to bring out an unauthorized expurgated edition of *The Grand Camouflage* that was put to propagandistic use inside of Franco's Spain further reinforced the false notion that Bolloten was a Cold War ideologue.

2 See, for example, Helen Graham's 'War, Modernity, and Reform: The Premiership of Juan Negrín, 1937–1939', in Anne MacKenzie and Paul Preston (eds) *The Republic Besieged* (Edinburgh, 1996), pp. 163–96.

3 Already a controversial figure for his contributions to the debates on the McCarthy era (Amerasian case and the Rosenbergs), Radosh has also become identified with one of the most divisive issues surrounding the role of foreign intervention during the Civil War. Since the mid-1980s Radosh has become an outspoken critic of the role that the communists played on the Republican side. He has devoted himself not only to exploding the so-called myth of the International Brigades as the defenders of an Abraham Lincoln style of democracy but also to proving beyond doubt that the communists were aiming not to pluck a democratic state from the jaws of fascism but to transform the Republic into a satellite state of the Soviet Union. See *Spain Betrayed* (Yale University Press, Annals of Communism series, 2001). Other volumes in this series that are relevant to the activities of the communists in Spain during the interwar era are: *Dimitrov and Stalin, 1934–1943: Letters From the Soviet Archives*, edited by Alexander Dallin and F.I. Firsov (Yale, 2000) and *Enemies Within the Gates: The Comintern and the Stalinist Repression, 1934–1939*, edited by William J. Chase (Yale, 2001).

4 A recent example of this can be found in Helen Graham's article on the Barcelona May Events of 1937. In this study the vast majority of the numerous documents relating to the ideological and political dimensions of this episode are ignored because they suggest an interpretation of this pivotal episode which conflicts with the theoretical orientation of the author. According to Graham, it was the longstanding class struggle between the workers and middle classes in Catalonia that lay at the heart of this uprising and not the political machinations of the communists and

their moderate allies. See her chapter on the May Events in *The Spanish Republic at War* (Cambridge, 2002).

5 This criticism is taken up by the author of the only social history of the war published to date, Michael Seidman, *Republic of Egos* (Madison, 2002).

6 Michael Seidman, *Republic of Egos* (Madison, 2002), p. 236.

7 Cultural approaches to the study of the Second Republic and Civil War can be found in Pamela Beth Radcliff's *From Mobilization to Civil War* (Cambridge, 1996) and Sandie Holguín's *Culture of the Second Republic* (Madison, 2002).

Chapter 1

1 Article 26 of the document, which would be invoked time and again in the coming years by the opponents of the regime, was a particularly controversial section of the Constitution, above all because of the discretionary powers it granted to the state in religious matters. Among other things it called for the dissolution of all orders constituting a threat to the government, as well as to those orders – such as the Jesuits – requiring a special oath in addition to the normal canonical work.

2 Occupying the right wing of the socialist movement was an orthodox Marxist faction headed by Julián Besteiro. His refusal to commit to either the reformist (centrist) or radical wings of the movement left Besteiro without a substantial following. During the war he mostly retired to the background.

3 Pieced together from contemporary press reports some thirty-five years later, these figures represent the most complete and accurate rendering of the election results. As such, they differ from the electoral totals listed in Document 1.2. See Javier Tusell, *Las elecciones del frente popular en España*, Madrid: Edicusa, 1974.

4 Among other things, municipal councils were suspended, press censorship was introduced, and, in 1935, the Catalan Statute of Self-Government was suspended.

5 Stanley G. Payne, *Spain's First Democracy* (Madison, 1994), p. 356.

Chapter 2

1 Gerald Howson, *Arms for Spain* (Washington, DC, 1991), p. 137.

2 *Spain Illustrated* (London, n.d.).

3 Antonio Barea, *The Forging of a Rebel* (New York, 1946), p. 642.

Chapter 3

1 With few exceptions, general histories of Spain and the Civil War pay little attention to this aspect of the war. See, for example, the chapter devoted to the Civil War in Francisco Romero Salvadó, *Twentieth-century Spain* (New York, 1999) and the scattered references to the revolution in Michael Seidman's *Republic of Egos* (Madison, 2002).
2 Most of our first-hand knowledge of rural collectives comes from the eyewitness accounts of anarchists such as Gaston Leval and Agustin Souchy. Non-libertarians – Franz Borkenau (*The Spanish Cockpit*, 1937) and H. Kaminski (*Ceux de Barcelone*, 1937), for example – have also surveyed the collectivist experiments, although with a more critical eye than their occasionally zealous anarchist counterparts.
3 Levante: 900-plus collectives (Federación Regional de Campesinos de Levante, FRCL). Aragón: 400, and another 340. Altogether there were around three thousand collectives established in the different regions of Republican Spain (R. Alexander, *The Anarchists in the Spanish Civil War* (London, 1999), vol. I, p. 325).
4 Partly because forced collectivization ran counter to anarchist ideals and partly because pro-collectivist groups were not always powerful enough to impose their will on the local population, a mixed form of collectivization existed in some parts of Republican Spain. In these circumstances, the CNT alone or in conjunction with another left-wing organization (usually the UGT) supervised the collectivization projects of a locality, while those who refused to join the collectives (often referred to as 'individualists') were allowed to run their own enterprises.
5 The executions, which were provoked by the Nationalists' rapid advance towards the capital in early November, took place in the villages of Parcuellos del Jarama and Torrejón de Ardoz.
6 Ronald Fraser, *Blood of Spain* (New York, 1978), p. 52.
7 Still other stories were spun from whole cloth. See, for example, the fabled executions of Nationalist supporters in the town of Ronda, Andalusia. J.R. Corbin, 'Truth and Myth in History: An Example from the Spanish Civil War', *Journal of Interdisciplinary History*, vol. XXV, no. 4 (Spring 1995), 609–25.

Chapter 4

1 In addition to dominating significant segments of the economy, the anarchosyndicalists exercised considerable power through their control of numerous anti-fascist committees.
2 Before the fall of Asturias seven Basque battalions were sent to assist other Republican troops there.
3 For Franco's rise to power in this period see Paul Preston, *Franco* (London, 1993), pp. 184ff.

4   See the account given by Franco's brother-in-law and *éminence grise*, Ramón Serrano Súñer, *Entre Hendaya y Gibraltar* (Madrid, 1947).

5   At the time it was founded in September 1935, the POUM claimed around 7,000 members, approximately 6,500 coming from the independent communist Bloque Obrero y Campesino (BOC), and 500 from the Trotskyist Izquierda Comunista (IC). By the time the war broke out, the POUM itself had some ten thousand members, while its trade-union affiliate, Federación Obrera de Unidad Sindical (FOUS) had an estimated membership of approximately sixty thousand.

6   It was because of their former association with the left opposition movement that both Gorkin and Nin entreated Generalitat president Lluis Companys to grant Trotsky asylum in Catalonia during the summer of 1937.

7   In addition to the fact that Joan Comorera, the PSUC's general secretary, and Rafael Vidella belonged the PCE's central committee, the PSUC was subject to the discipline of Comintern officials. During the war the Hungarian communist Ernö Gerö exercised a guiding influence over the PSUC.

Chapter 5

1   Claude Bowers, *My Mission to Spain* (New York, Simon and Schuster, 1954), p. 363.

2   Richard Veatch, 'The League of Nations and the Spanish Civil War, 1936–1939', *European History Quarterly* (London, Newbury Park, and New Delhi), vol. 20 (1990), 181–207.

3   Michael Alpert, *A New International History of the Spanish Civil War* (New York, 1994), p. 113.

4   See Robert H. Whealey, *Hitler and Spain: The Nazi Role in the Spanish Civil War, 1936–1939.* (University of Kentucky: Lexington, 1989).

5   On this aspect of German/Nationalist relations see Christian Leitz, *Economic Relations between Nazi Germany and Franco's Spain: 1936–1945* (New York: Oxford University Press, 1996).

6   For a discussion of the military importance Spain's war held for the Germans see especially Raymond Proctor, *Hitler's Luftwaffe in the Spanish Civil War* (Westport, Conn., 1983).

7   See, Brian R. Sullivan, 'Fascist Italy's Military Involvement in the Spanish Civil War', *The Journal of Modern History* (Chicago), vol. 59 (October 1995), 697–727.

8   On Portuguese involvement see, especially, Alejandro Raya-Rivas, 'An Iberian Alliance: Portuguese Intervention in the Spanish Civil War (1936–1939)', *Portuguese Studies Review*, vol. VIII, no. 1 (fall–winter 1999–2000), 109–25.

Chapter 6

1 María Rosa de Madariaga, 'The Intervention of Moroccan Troops in the Spanish Civil War: A Reconsideration', *European History Quarterly* (London, Newbury Park, and New Delhi), vol. 22 (1992), 82–4. On the Moroccan question before the Civil War see Sebastian Balfour, *Deadly Embrace* (Oxford, 2002).
2 Quoted in A. Guttman, *Wound in the Heart* (New York, 1962), p. 100.
3 Anti-Semitism on the Nationalist's side derived largely from their insistence on picturing the war as a Christian crusade against 'Jewish-Bolshevism'.
4 P. Preston, *Franco*, pp. 184–5.
5 For Spain's relations with the Vatican during the Civil War see, especially, Peter C. Kent, 'The Vatican and the Spanish Civil War', *European History Quarterly* (London, Beverly Hills, Newbury Park, and New Delhi), vol. 16 (1986), 441–61.
6 Mary Nash, 'Political Culture, Catalan Nationalism, and the Women's Movement in Early Twentieth-Century Spain', *Women's Studies International Forum*, vol. 19, nos 1/2 (1996), 45–54.
7 See Mary Vincent, 'The Martyrs and the Saints: Masculinity and the Construction of the Francoist Crusade', *History Workshop Journal*, issue 47 (1999), 72–97.
8 A. Morcillo, *True Catholic Womanhood* (De Kalb, 2000), p. 25.
9 M. Nash (Denver, 1995), *Defying Male Civilization*, pp. 105–97.
10 See Mary Nash, '"Milicianas" and Homefront Heroines: Images of Women in Revolutionary Spain (1936–1939)', *History of European Ideas*, vol. 11 (1989), 235–44.
11 See Gaston Leval's article in S. Dolgoff (ed.), *The Anarchist Collectives* (Montreal, 1974), p. 167.
12 Michael Seidman, 'Women's Subversive Individualism in Barcelona during the 1930s', *International Review of Social History*, vol. XXXI/ii (1992), 161–76.
13 See Aurora Morcillo, *True Catholic Womanhood*, (DeKalb, 2000).

Chapter 7

1 See Burnett Bolloten, *The Spanish Revolution* (North Carolina, 1979).
2 For a critical view of Orwell's testimony see the relevant sections in Robert Stradling, *History and Legend: Writing the International Brigades* (Cardiff, 2003).
3 Souchy, A., *The Tragic Week in May* (Barcelona, 1937), p. 17.
4 For various estimates see *La Vanguardia*, Barcelona, 5 May 1937. Perhaps the most accurate accounting of those killed can be found in J. M. Solé and J. Villaroya, 'Les Víctimes dels Fets de Maig', *Recerques*, no. 12 (Barcelona, 1982), 218.

5 Of far greater importance to the future of the Republic were the political consequences that flowed from them. The first and visibly most jolting one precipitated a government crisis which led to the downfall of the premier, Largo Caballero. Another direct consequence of the May crisis was the dramatic and irrevocable shift of power in Catalonia. Not only had the revolutionaries lost for ever their commanding position in the region, but, as we have seen, the middle-class regionalist parties had been compelled by the pressure of circumstances to surrender their autonomy to the central government.

6 *The Tragic Week in May* (Barcelona, 1937), p. 43.

7 Caballero's refusal early on in the war to embrace the revolution had cost the left dearly, but, despite his lack of resolve, he was still widely seen as the principal leader of the left socialists.

8 Given that Negrín and the ruling parties did not rely on an electorate to hold office, the near-collapse of the PSOE's popular base did not weaken the leadership's control of the levers of government. Rather they exercised power because of the support they received from the PCE and foreign communists, who had become by this point the most powerful single political force in Republican Spain.

9 Carrillo, the secretary of the JSU, did not officially join the PCE until 1936. Álvarez del Vayo, the Foreign Minister under Caballero and head of the Commissariat system, never became a member, while Amaro del Rosal, a member of the socialist executive, joined the party years after the Civil War.

10 For a detailed accounting of how this process worked see Burnett Bolloten's *The Spanish Civil War* (Chapel Hill, 1991), especially pp. 124–44.

11 Fenner Brockway, *Towards Tomorrow* (London, 1977), p. 126.

Chapter 8

1 How this and other bombing missions contributed to the development of German air tactics and strategy is discussed in Christopher C. Locksley, 'Condor over Spain: The Civil War, Combat Experience and the Development of Luftwaffe Airpower Doctrine', *Civil Wars* (London), vol. 2, no. 1 (spring 1999), 69–99.

2 Enrique Líster, *Nuestra guerra* (Paris, 1966), p. 182.

Chapter 9

1 Despite the government's efforts to secure credit from abroad, no such aid was forthcoming. Even the Soviet Union, the only country willing to supply essential materials, was growing increasingly reluctant to extend any further credit to the ailing Republic.

2 Referring to the fact that it was well known that Italian planes were responsible for bombing Barcelona and other open cities, Negrín complained that 'Almost every non-Fascist nation condemns air bombardment of civilian populations, but nobody will sell us [Republicans] anti-aircraft guns. Commissions come and go, but nothing happens afterwards' (*News of Spain*, 28 September 1938).

3 At the time there were only some six thousand foreign volunteers still fighting in the International Brigades.

4 Negrín's decision was also calculated to thwart efforts by outside nations to grant belligerent rights to Franco. By removing the communist-dominated International Brigades, it was hoped that the Republic could prove that it was not being manipulated by the Soviet Union.

5 In the course of the war, Franco had successfully decapitated the leadership of the civilian movements that could rival his authority. The head of the Falange, Manuel Hedilla, was placed under arrest and the independent-minded Carlist leader, Manuel Fal Conde, had been sent into exile in Portugal.

6 Dissension on the left: Prieto's ambitious efforts to revamp the military met with some success. But when he attempted to curb communist influence in the command structure – as evidenced by his dismissal of the key pro-communist commissar Álvarez del Vayo – he fell foul of Negrín and the pro-communist elements in his government. Prieto was also widely regarded as a 'defeatist', that is, someone who believed that the war was costing too many lives and that the Republican government should therefore concentrate on negotiating peace with the Nationalists. On both counts, he was increasingly at odds with his close friend and erstwhile colleague, Negrín, the premier.

7 In fact, Negrín did seek mediation in the wake of the Munich crisis. However, his efforts to hammer out a peace settlement that did not call for unconditional surrender with the Duke of Alba came to nothing.

8 The belief that the nationalists were pushing their autonomy too far was shared by Republican politicians such as Manuel Azaña. An ardent defender of regional autonomy before the war, Azaña complained during the war that the Catalans in particular were placing their own interests above those of the Republic.

9 Only a portion of these supplies had found their way into Catalonia.

Select bibliography

Archives and Library Collections consulted

Archivo Histórico Nacional. Sección Guerra Civil. (Salamanca)
Brandeis University. Special Collections Library. Veterans of the Abraham Lincoln Brigade Archives (Waltham, Massachusetts). Now housed at the Tamiment Library & Robert F. Wagner Labor Archives at New York University under the title 'The Abraham Lincoln Brigade Archives'
—— American Bureau to Aid Spanish Democracy (New York). Archive
—— Edward Barsky. Papers
—— Fredericka Martin. Papers
British Library. (London)
Cambridge University Library and Archives. (Cambridge)
Centre d'Estudis Històrics Contemporánis, Fundació Figueras. (Barcelona)
Hoover Institution Library and Archives. (Stanford, California)
—— Alice Beer. Papers
—— Blodgett Collection of Spanish Civil War Pamphlets (microfiche)
—— Burnett and Gladys Bolloten Collection of Spanish Civil War materials
—— Milly Bennett. Papers
—— International Brigade Association Collection, Marx Memorial Library, London (microfilm)
——Joaquín Maurín Juliá. Papers
—— Bertram Wolfe. Papers
London School of Economics. Library and Archives. (London)
New York Public Library. Special Collections Department. (New York)
Tamiment Institute, New York University. (New York)
University of California at San Diego (La Jolla, California). Library. Special Collections Department. Herbert Southworth Collection

Primary Sources: English/Spanish

Abad de Santillán, Diego. *After the Revolution: Economic Reconstruction in Spain Today.* New York: Greenberg Publisher, 1937.
——. *Por qué perdimos la Guerra.* Buenos Aires: Editorial Inmán, 1940.
Academy of Sciences of the USSR, *International Solidarity with the Spanish Republic.* Moscow: Progress Publishers, 1975.

Acier, Marcel, editor, *From Spanish Trenches*. New York: Modern Age Books, 1937.

Aguirre, H.E. José A. de. *An Address by His Excellency the President of the Government of Euzkadi, H.E. José A. de Aguirre*. Broadcast from Radio Euzkadi, 22 December 1936.

Aguirre Prado, Luis. *The Church and the Spanish War*. Madrid: Servicio Informativo Español, 1965.

Álvarez del Vayo, Julio. *Freedom's Battle*. New York: Alfred A. Knopf, 1940.

——. *The Last Optimist: A Spanish Democrat Tells His Story*. New York: The Viking Press, 1950.

——. 'Speech delivered before the League of Nations on the 25 September 1936.'

American Friends of Spanish Democracy. *The Persecution of Protestants in Fascist Spain*. New York, 1936.

Amorós, Miquel. *La revolución traicionada: La verdadera historia de Balius y los Amigos de Durruti*. Barcelona: VIRUS Editorial, 2003.

Antipode: A Radical Journal of Geography. Vol. 10, no. 3/vol. 11, no. 1, 1979.

'Appeal by the Spanish Government: White Book', *League of Nations Official Journal*. Geneva, 1937.

Arrarás, Joaquín. *Francisco Franco: The Times and the Man*. London: Geoffrey Bles, 1938.

Atholl, Katherine, Duchess of. *Searchlight on Spain*. Harmondsworth: Penguin, 1938.

Azaña, Manuel. *Madrid*. London, 1937.

——. *Speech by His Excellency the President of the Spanish Republic (Valencia, 21 January, 1937)*. London: Victoria House, 1937.

Barea, Arturo. *The Forging of a Rebel*. New York, 1946, and London: Granta, 2001.

Bates, Ralph. 'Castilian Drama: An Army Is Born', *The New Republic*, 20 October 1937.

Bedford-Jones, Nancy. *Students Under Arms: Education in Republican Spain*. New York: Medical Bureau and North American Committee to Aid Spanish Democracy, 1938.

Blázquez, José Martín. *I Helped to Build an Army: Civil Memoirs of a Spanish Staff Officer*. Translated by F. Borkenau and Eric Mosbacher. London: Secker and Warburg, 1939.

Boletín de Información: CNT/AIT/FAI, Barcelona, 1937.

Bolín, Luís. *Spain: The Vital Years*. London: Cassell, 1967.

Borkenau, Franz. *The Spanish Cockpit: An Eye-witness Account of the Political and Social Conflicts of the Spanish Civil War*. Ann Arbor, Michigan: University of Michigan Press, 1963, 1974.

Brandt, Willy. *In Exile: Essays, Reflections and Letter, 1933–1947*. Translated by R.W. Last, London: Oswald Wolff, 1971.

British Documents on Foreign Affairs: Reports and Papers from the Foreign Office. Confidential Report, Part II: From the First to the Second World War, Series F Europe, 1919–1939, Volume 27: Spain, July 1936–January 1940. Edited by Anthony Adamthwaite. Frederick, MD: University Publications of America, 1990.

Brockway, Fenner. *The Truth About Barcelona.* London: Independent Labour Party, 1937.

Cardozo, Harold, G. *The March of a Nation: My Year of Spain's Civil War.* London: The Right Book Club, 1937.

Casado, Segismundo. *The Last Days of Madrid: The End of the Second Spanish Republic.* Translated by Rupert Croft-Cooke. London: Peter Davies, 1939.

Catholics and the Civil War in Spain. London: National Council of Labour, 1936.

Catholics Speak for Spain. New York: North American Committee to Aid Spanish Democracy, 1937.

Chase, William J., editor, *Enemies Within the Gates: The Comintern and the Stalinist Repression, 1934–1939.* New Haven and London: Yale University Press, 2001.

Ciano, Count Galeazzo, *Ciano's Diplomatic Papers.* Edited by Malcolm Muggeridge. London: Odhams Press, 1948.

——. *Ciano's Hidden Diary, 1937–1938.* Translated by Andreas Mayor. New York: E.P. Dutton & Co., Inc., 1953.

Collum, Danny Duncan, editor, *African Americans in the Spanish Civil War: 'This Ain't Ethiopia, But It'll Do.'* New York: G.K. Hall, 1992.

Comorera, Juan. 'Catalonia and Communism.' *The Labour Monthly*, vol. 19 (9 September 1937)

Companys, Lluís. *Address of Lluís Companys to the Parliament of Catalunya March 1, 1938.* London, 1938.

Controversy: The Monthly Forum for Socialist Discussion. (London), 1936–39.

Controversy on Spain: Between H.A. Gwynne, C.H. and A. Ramos Oliveira. London: United Editorial Ltd., 1937.

Corkhill, David, and Rawnsley, Stuart J., editors, *The Road to Spain: Anti-Fascists at War, 1936–1939.* Dunfermline: Borderline Press, 1981.

Cortada, James W., editor, *A City in War: American Views on Barcelona and the Spanish Civil War, 1936–1939.* Wilmington, Delaware: Scholarly Resources Inc., 1985.

Costa, Luis, et al., editors, *German and International Perspectives on the Spanish Civil War: The Aesthetics of Partisanship.* London: Camden House, 1992.

Costello, John, and Tsarev, Oleg, *Deadly Illusions: The KGB Orlov Dossier Reveals Stalin's Master Spy.* New York: Crown Publishers, 1993.

Cox, Geoffrey. *Defence of Madrid.* London: Victor Gollancz, Ltd, 1937.

Cunningham, Valentine, editor, *Spanish Front: Writers on the Civil War.* Oxford and London: Oxford University Press, 1986.

Cusick, Lois. *The Anarchist Millenium: Memories of the Spanish Revolution, 1936–37.* Gainesville, Florida, 1978. Unpublished manuscript.

Dallin, Alexander, and Firsov, F.I., editors, Dimitrov and *Stalin: Letters from the Soviet Archives, 1934–1934.* New Haven and London: Yale University Press, 2000.

A Day Mournful and Overcast . . . , 1937. Reprinted London: Anarchist Black Cross, 1993.

Degras, Jane, editor, *The Communist International, 1919–1943. Documents.* Vol. III: 1929–1943. Oxford/London/N.Y.: Oxford University Press, 1965.

Delzell, Charles F., editor, *Mediterranean Fascism 1919–1945.* London: Macmillan, 1970.

Díaz, José. *Lessons of the Spanish War 1936–1939.* London: Modern Books, 1940.

Díaz-Plaja, Fernando. *La guerra en España en sus documentos.* Barcelona: Ediciones GP, 1969.

Dimitrov, George. *The United Front. The Struggle Against Fascism and War.* New York: International Publishers, 1938.

Documents on British Foreign Policy. Volume 17, British Foreign Office. Edited by E.L. Woodward and Rohan Butler. London: HMSO, 1949.

Documents on German Foreign Policy. Series D, volume 3. Washington, DC: US Government Printing Office, 1949–.

Dolgoff, Sam, editor, *The Anarchist Collectives: Workers' Self-management in the Spanish Revolution, 1936–1939.* Montreal: Black Rose Books, 1974.

Domingo, Marcelino, et al., editors, *The Spanish People's Struggle: The Facts and their Significance.* London: Modern Books, 1936.

Ehrenburg, Ilya. Eve of War, 1933–1941. Translated by Tatiana Shebunina. London: MacGibbon & Kee, 1963.

Elliot, John. 'With the Rebels', *The Atlantic Monthly*, vol. 158, issue 5, November 1936.

Emanuel, W.V. *The Naval Side of the Spanish War.* London: The Fortnightly Review, 1938.

Ercoli, M. (aka Palmiro Togliatti). *The Spanish Revolution.* New York: Workers Library Publishers, 1936.

Farmborough, Florence. *Life and People in National Spain.* London: Sheed & Ward, Ltd, 1938.

Fischer, Louis. 'Hitler's New Threat', *The Nation* (New York), 30 March 1939.

——. *Men and Politics: Europe Between the Two World Wars.* New York: Harper & Row, 1966.

——. *Why Spain Fights On.* Foreword by C.R. Atlee. London: The Union of Democratic Control, 1938.

Foss, William and Gerahty, Cecil. *The Spanish Arena.* London: The Right Book Club, 1938.

Franco's Rule: A Survey. London: United Editorial Ltd, 1938.

The French Yellow Book: Diplomatic Documents, 1938–1939. London: Hutchinson and Co., 1939.

Friends of Durruti Group. *Towards a Fresh Revolution.* Sanday: Cienfuegos Press, 1978.

Gadant, Monique, editor, *Women of the Mediterranean.* Translated by A.M. Berrett. London and New Jersey: Zed Books, Ltd, 1986.

Gallegos Rocafull, José Manuel. *Crusade or Class War?* Washington, DC: American Friends of Spanish Democracy, 1937.

Gellhorn, Martha. *The Face of War.* New York: Atlantic Monthly Press, 1988.

Godden, G.M. *Conflict in Spain, 1920–1937.* London: Burns, Oates & Washbourne, 1938.

Goebbels, Joseph. *The Truth About Spain: Speech Delivered at the National Socialist Party Congress, Nürnberg, 1937.* Berlin: M. Müller und Sohn, 1937.

Goldman, Emma. 'P.O.U.M. Frame-up Fails', *Vanguard*, 1 February 1939.

——. *Vision on Fire.* New Paltz, NY: Commonground Press, 1983.

——. 'Where I Stand', *Spain and the World* (London), 2 July 1937.

González, Valentín and Julian Gorkin. *El Campesino: Life and Death in Soviet Russia.* New York: G.P. Putnam's Sons, 1952.

Gorkín, Julián. *'We Conquer or Die.'* London: Independent Labour Party, 1937.

Graham, Marcus, editor, *Man! An Anthology of Anarchist Ideas, Poetry and Commentaries.* London: Cienfuegos Press, 1974.

Guernica: Being the Official Report of a Commission Appointed by the Spanish National Government to Investigate the Causes of the Destruction of Guernica on April 26–28, 1937. London: Eyre & Spottiswoode, 1938.

Gurney, Jason. *Crusade in Spain.* London: Faber and Faber, 1974.

Haldane, J.B.S. *A.R.P.* London: Victor Gollancz, 1938.

Harrison, Joseph. *An Economic History of Modern Spain.* New York: Holmes & Meier, 1978.

How the German Fleet Shelled Almeria. London: Union of Democratic Control, n.d.

Ibárruri, Dolores. *They Shall Not Pass: The Autobiography of* La Pasionaria. New York: International Publishers, 1966.

——. *Speeches and Articles, 1936–1938.* London: Lawrence and Wishart, 1938.

International Committee for the Application of the Agreement Regarding Non-Intervention in Spain. Spain No. 2 (1936). London: HMSO, 1936.

International Press Correspondence, 1936–1938 (Inprecorr). English Edition of ECCI (Executive Committee of the Communist International). From 1938 continued as *World News and Views.*

International Workingmen's Association/Anarchosyndicalists. *IWMA Bulletin of Information* (Barcelona), 1 June 1937.

Justicia en Guerra: Jornadas sobre la administración de justicia durante la Guerra Civil Española: Instituciones y fuentes documentales. Organized by the Archivo Histórico Nacional Sección 'Guerra Civil.' Madrid: Ministerio de Cultura, 1990.

Kaminski, H.E. 'A Peasant Experiment in Anarchist Communism', *Anarchy*, no. 5, 'Spain: The Revolution of 1936', London: Freedom Press, July 1961.

Kemp, Peter. *Mine Were of Trouble.* London: Cassell & Co., 1957.

Kenwood, Alun, editor, *The Spanish Civil War: A Cultural and Historical Reader.* Providence and Oxford: Berg, 1993.

Knoblaugh, Edward. *Correspondent in Spain.* New York: Sheed & Ward, 1937.

Koestler, Arthur. *The Invisible Writing.* London: Hamish Hamilton, 1954.

Krivitsky, W.G. *I Was Stalin's Agent.* London: Hamish Hamilton, 1939.

Labour Research: The Monthly Circular of the Labour Research Department. (London), 1936–39.

Lambda. *The Truth about the Barcelona Events.* New York: Workers' Age Publishers, 1937.

Langdon-Davies, John. *Behind the Spanish Barricades.* New York: National Travel Club, 1936.

——. 'The Struggle for Anti-Fascist Unity in Spain', *The Labour Monthly* (London), vol. 19, no. 10 (October 1937), 609–20.

Larios, José, *Combat Over Spain: Memoirs of a Nationalist Fighter Pilot, 1936–1939.* London: Neville Spearman, 1966.

Leval, Gaston. *Collectives in the Spanish Revolution.* London: Freedom Press, 1975.

Línea de fuego: Portavoz de la columna de hierro en el frente de Teruel. Pueblo de Valverde, 1936.

Loveday, Arthur F. *World War in Spain.* London: John Murray, 1939.

Low, Mary and Breá, Juan. *The Red Spanish Notebook: The First Six Months of the Revolution and Civil War.* San Francisco: City Lights Books, 1979.

Lunn, Arnold. *Spanish Rehearsal for World War: An Eyewitness Account of the Spanish Civil War (1936–1939).* Old Greenwich: Devin-Adair Company, 1974.

McConnell, Dorothy. 'As to Women: Gibraltar to Málaga, The 'Real' Spanish women and the women of the people.' In *The Fight*, New York: (August 1937), 24.

MacDonald, Nancy. *Homage to the Spanish Exiles: Voices from the Spanish Civil War.* New York: Human Sciences Press, 1987.

MacKee, Seumas. *I Was a Franco Soldier.* London: United Editorial Limited, 1938.

McNair, John. *Spanish Diary.* Edited and with a commentary by Don Bateman. Manchester: ILP Publications, 1973.

Maisky, Ivan. *Spanish Notebooks*. London: Hutchinson, 1966.

Manning, Leah. *What I Saw in Spain*. London: Victor Gollancz, 1935.

Manuilsky, D.Z. The Work of the Seventh Congress of the *Communist International*. New York: Workers Library Publishers, 1937.

Martin, J.G. *Political and Social Changes in Catalonia during the Revolution (July 19th–December 31st 1936)*. Ed. Generalitat de Catalunya. Barcelona: Generalitat de Catalunya, 1936.

Marty, André. *Heroic Spain*. New York: Workers' Library Inc., 1937.

Matthews, Herbert L. *The Education of a Correspondent*. New York: Harcourt, Brace, and Company, 1946.

Maurín, Joaquín. 'Perspectives for Spanish Revolution', *The International Class Struggle*, vol. I, no. 2 (Winter 1936).

Ministerio de Defensa Nacional. *Un ejercito popular y democrático al servicio del pueblo*. Barcelona: Ediciones Españoles, 1936.

Modern Monthly: An Independent Journal of Radical Opinion (New York), vol. X, no. 8 (September 1937).

Monks, Noel. *Eyewitness*. London: Frederick Muller Ltd., 1955.

Mora, De la Constancia. *In Place of Splendor: The Autobiography of a Spanish Woman*. New York: Harcourt, Brace & Co., 1939.

Moss, Geoffrey. *The Epic of the Alcazar: A History of the Siege of the Toledo Alcazar, 1936*. London: Rich and Cowan, Ltd., 1937.

Mujeres Libres: Luchadoras Libertarias. Madrid: Fundación de Estudios Libertarios de Anselmo Lorenzo, 1999.

'Nationalist women, "Spanish Woman" issued by the Catholic Union of Women of Seville', in R. Abella, La vida cotidiana *durante la guerra civil*. Barcelona: Planeta, 1973.

The Nazi Conspiracy in Spain. London: Victor Gollancz, 1937.

Negrín, Juan. *Three Speeches of Sr. Juan Negrín*. Paris: Cooperative Etoile, 1937.

A Negro Nurse in Republican Spain. New York: The Negro Committee to Aid Spain / Medical Bureau and North American Committee to Aid Spanish Democracy, 1937.

Nelson, Cary, and Hendricks, Jefferson, editors, *Madrid 1937: Letters of the Abraham Lincoln Brigade from the Spanish Civil War*. New York and London: Routledge, 1996.

Nelson, Steve. *The Volunteers*. New York: Masses & Mainstream, 1953.

The New Statesman and Nation. (London), 1936–39.

News of Spain. New York: The Spanish Information Bureau, 1938–39.

O'Duffy, Eoin. *Crusade in Spain*. Clonskeagh: Browne and Nolan Limited, 1938.

Oehler, Hugo. *Barricades in Barcelona: The First Revolt of the Proletariat against the Capitalist People's Front*. New York: Demos Press, 1937.

Oltra Pico, J. *Socialización de las fincas urbanas y municipalización de los servicios*, Barcelona: Editorial Marxista, 1937.

One Year of War 1936–1937. New York: The Paulist Press, 1937.

O'Neill, Carlota. *Trapped in Spain.* Toronto: Solidarity Books, 1978.

Orlov, Alexander. *The Secret History of Stalin's Crimes.* New York: Random House, 1955.

Orwell, George. *Homage to Catalonia.* Introduced by Lionel Trilling. Boston: The Beacon Press, 1964.

——. The Collected Essays, Journalism and Letters of *George Orwell (Volume I): An Age Like This, 1920–1940.* Edited by Sonia Orwell and Ian Angus. New York and London: Harcourt Brace Jovanovich, 1968.

Palencia, Isabel de. *Smouldering Freedom: The Story of the Spanish Republicans in Exile.* New York and Toronto: Longmans, Green, and Co., 1945.

Payne, Robert, editor, *The Civil War in Spain, 1936–1939.* New York: G.P. Putnam's and Son, 1962.

Peirats, José. *Anarchists in The Spanish Revolution.* Toronto: Solidarity Books, 1974.

A Preliminary Official Report on the Atrocities Committed in Southern Spain in July and August, 1936, by the Communist Forces of the Madrid Government. (Issued by the authority of the Committee of Investigation Appointed by the National Government at Burgos.) London: Eyre and Spottiswoode, 1936.

Puente, Isaac. *Libertarian Communism.* Sydney: Monty Miller Press, 1982.

Radosh, Ronald, Habeck, Mary R., and Sevostianov, Grigory, editors, *Spain Betrayed: The Soviet Union in the Spanish Civil War.* New Haven: Yale University Press, 2001.

Regler, Gustav. *The Owl of Minerva: The Autobiography of Gustav Regler.* Translated by Norman Denny. London: Rupert Hart-Davis, 1959.

Ries, Karl and Hans Ring. *The Legion Condor.* Translated by David Johnson. West Chester, PA: Schiffer Military History, 1992.

Rios, Fernando de. *Spain: Front Line of Democracy.* Washington, DC: Spanish Embassy 1937.

——. *What Is Happening in Spain?* London: Spanish Embassy, 1937.

Robeson, Paul. *Paul Robeson Speaks: Writings, Speeches, Interviews 1918–1974.* Edited by Philip S. Foner. New York: Bruner/Mazel, 1978.

Rocker, Rudolf. *The Tragedy of Spain.* New York: Freie Arbeiter Stimme, 1937.

Ruíz Vilaplana, Antonio. *Burgos Justice: A Year's Experience of Nationalist Spain.* New York: Knopf, 1938.

Rust, William. *Spain Fights for Victory.* London: Marston Printing Co., 1938.

Schneider, Luis Mario, editor, *Inteligencia y Guerra Civil Española: II Congreso Internacional de Escritores Antifascistas (1937), Vols 1–3.* Barcelona: Editorial Laia, 1978.

Scott-Ellis, Priscilla. *The Chances of Death: A Diary of the Spanish Civil War.* Edited by Raymond Carr. Norwich: Michael Russell, 1995.

Sencourt, Robert. *Spain's Ordeal: A Documented Survey of Recent Events.* London, New York, and Toronto: Longmans, Green and Co., 1938.

Sender, Ramón. *The War in Spain.* London: Faber and Faber, 1937.

Serge, Victor. *Memoirs of a Revolutionary, 1901–1941.* Translated and edited by Peter Sedgwick. Oxford: Oxford University Press, 1975.

Soria, Georges. *Trotskyism in the Service of Franco.* London: Lawrence and Wishart, 1938.

Souchy, Augustín. *The Tragic Week in May.* Barcelona: Oficina de Información Exterior de la CNT y FAI, 1937.

——. *With the Peasants of Aragon: Libertarian Communism in the Liberated Areas.* Translated by Abe Bluestein. Minneapolis: Soil of Liberty, 1982.

Soviet Documents on Foreign Policy. Edited by Jane Degras. New York: Oxford University Press, 1951.

Spain at War. London, 1938.

Spain 1936–1939: Social Revolution and Counter-revolution: Selections from the Anarchist Fortnightly Spain & The World. London: Freedom Press, 1990.

Spain. Tribunal Supremo, Ministerio Fiscal. *The Red Domination in Spain: The General Cause (Causa General).* Fourth edition. Madrid: n.p., 1961.

Spain's War of Independence (Public Addresses by President Azaña, Juan Negrín, Indalecio Prieto, Martínez Bande, Alvarez del Vayo, and Portella Valladares). Washington, DC: Spanish Embassy, 1937.

Spanish Embassy, Bureau of Information. *The Agrarian Reform.* Washington, DC: Spanish Embassy, 1936.

Spanish Institute for Agrarian Reform, *Agrarian Reform in Spain.* London: United Editorial Ltd, 1937.

The Spanish News Bulletin: Issued by the United Socialist Party of Catalonia. Barcelona, 1937.

Spanish Revolution: A Bulletin Published by the United Libertarian Organizations. Introduced by Russell Blackwell. Volumes 1–2, 1936–38. New York: Greenwood, 1968.

The Spanish Revolution: Weekly Bulletin of the Workers' Party of Marxist Unification of Spain (POUM) (Barcelona), vols I–II, 1936–37. Introduced by Russell Blackwell. New York: Greenwood Press, 1968.

Spender, Stephen. 'Hitch-hiking in Republican Spain.' Unpublished manuscript. Milly Bennett Collection, Hoover Institution Archives, Stanford University.

The Story of the Abraham Lincoln Brigade: Written in the Trenches of Spain. New York: Friends of the Abraham Lincoln Brigade, 1937.

Strong, Anna Louise. *Spain in Arms.* New York: Henry Holt and Company, 1937.

Tarradellas, Josep. *The Financial Work of the Generalitat of Catalunya.* Barcelona, 1938.

Tennant, Eleonora. *Spanish Journey: Personal Experiences of the Civil War.* London: Eyre and Spottiswoode, 1936.

Thomas, Frank. *Brother Against Brother: Experiences of a British Volunteer in the Spanish Civil War.* Edited by Robert Stradling. Phoenix Hill: Sutton Publishing, 1998.

Thomson, Charles A. 'Spain: Issues Behind the Conflict', *Foreign Policy Reports* (New York), 1 January 1937.

Tisa, John. *Recalling the Good Fight: An Autobiography of the Spanish Civil War.* Boston: Bergin and Garvey, 1985.

Trotsky, Leon. *The Spanish Revolution, 1931–1939.* New York: Pathfinder Press, 1973.

Voice of Spain. (London), 1939.

The Volunteer for Liberty. (New York), 1937.

Wolfe, Bertram D. *Civil War in Spain.* New York: Workers Age Publishers, 1937.

Woolsey, Gamel. *Málaga Burning.* Paris: Pythia Press, 1998.

World News and Views, 1938–. English Edition of ECCI (Executive Committee of the Communist International).

Yates, James. *Mississippi to Madrid.* New York: Shamal Books, 1986.

Secondary sources: English/Spanish/French/German

Ackelsberg, Martha. *Free Women of Spain: Anarchism and the Struggle for Female Emancipation.* Bloomington and Indianapolis: University of Indiana Press, 1991.

Alba, Victor and Schwartz, Stephen. *Spanish Marxism Versus Soviet Communism: A History of the POUM.* New Brunswick and Oxford: Transaction Books, 1988.

Alexander, Robert J. *The Anarchists in the Spanish Civil War*, 2 vols. London: Janus, 1999.

Alpert, Michael. *A New International History of the Spanish Civil War.* New York: St. Martin's, 1994.

——. 'The Clash of Spanish Armies: Contrasting Ways of War in Spain, 1936–1939', *War in History*, vol. 6, no. 3 (1999), 331–51.

Arenillas, José María. *The Basque Country, Euzkadi: The National Question and the Socialist Revolution.* Leeds: ILP Square One Publications, 1970.

Balcells, Albert. *Catalan Nationalism: Past and Present.* Edited and introduced by Geoffrey J. Walker. Basingstoke: Macmillan, 1996.

Balfour, Sebastian. *Deadly Embrace: Morocco and the Road to the Spanish Civil War.* Oxford and New York: Oxford University Press, 2002.

Balfour, Sebastian, and Preston, Paul, editors, *Spain and the Great Powers.* London: Routledge, 1999.

Baquer, Miguel Alsonso, editor, *La Guerra Civil Española (Sesenta años después).* Madrid: Actas, 1999.

Beevor, Antony. *The Spanish Civil War*. Harmondsworth: Penguin, 1982.

Bernecker, Walther. *Colectividades y revolución social: El anarquismo en la guerra civil Española, 1936–1939*. Barcelona: Crítica, 1982.

Blinkhorn, Martin. *Carlism and Crisis in Spain, 1931–1939*. Cambridge: Cambridge University Press, 1975.

Bolloten, Burnett. *The Spanish Civil War: Revolution and Counter-revolution*. Chapel Hill: University of North Carolina Press, 1991.

Bosworth, R.J.B., and Dogliana, Patrizia, editors, *Italian Fascism: History, Memory and Representation*. London and New York: Macmillan and St. Martin's Press, 1999.

Boyd, Carolyn P. *Historia Patria: Politics, History, and National Identity in Spain, 1875–1975*. Princeton: Princeton University Press, 1997.

Brademas, John. *Anarcosindicalismo y revolución en España (1930–1937)*. Barcelona: Ariel, 1974.

Brenan, Gerald. *The Spanish Labyrinth: An Account of the Social and Political Background of the Spanish Civil War*. Cambridge: Cambridge University Press, 1971.

Broué, Pierre and Emile Témime. *The Revolution and the Civil War in Spain*. Cambridge, MA: The MIT Press, 1970.

Buchanan, Tom. *Britain and the Spanish Civil War*. Cambridge: Cambridge University Press, 1997.

Carr, E.H. *The Comintern and the Spanish Civil War*. New York: Pantheon Books, 1984.

Carr, Raymond. *The Civil War in Spain, 1936–1939*. London: Weidenfeld and Nicolson, 1986.

——, editor, *The Republic and the Civil War in Spain*. Basingstoke: Macmillan, 1971.

Carroll, Peter N. *The Odyssey of the Abraham Lincoln Brigade: Americans in the Spanish Civil War*. Stanford, CA: Stanford University Press, 1994.

Casanova, Julián. *De la calle al frente: El anarcosindicalismo en España (1931–1939)*. Barcelona: Crítica, 1997.

——. 'Anarchism and Revolution in the Spanish Civil War: The Case of Aragon', *European History Quarterly*, vol. 17 (1987), 423–51.

Castells Duran, Antoni. *El proceso estatizador en la experiencia colectivista catalana (1936–1939)*. Madrid: Nossa y Jara, 1996.

——. *Las transformaciones colectivistas en la industria y los servicios de Barcelona (1936–1939)*. Madrid: Fundación Salvador Seguí, 1991.

Cattell, David, T. *Communism and the Spanish Civil War*. New York: Russell & Russell, 1965.

——. *Soviet Diplomacy and the Spanish Civil War*. Berkeley: University of California Press, 1957.

Cierva, Ricardo de la, 'Propaganda and Information in the Spanish Civil War.' Translated by Alfonso de Bertodano Stourton. Unpublished paper.

Coca Hernando, Rosario. 'Towards a New Image of Women under Franco: The Role of Sección Femenina', *Intellect*, vol. 11, no. 1 (1998), 5–13.

Corbin, J.R. *The Anarchist Passion: Class Conflict in Southern Spain, 1810–1965*. Aldershot: Avebury, 1993.

——. 'Truth and Myth in History: An Example from the Spanish Civil War', *Journal of Interdisciplinary History*, vol. xxv, no. 4 (Spring 1995), 609–25.

Costa, Luis, et al., editors, *German and International Perspectives on the Spanish Civil War: The Aesthetics of Partisanship*. London: Camden House, 1992.

Courtois, Stephane, et al., editors, *Black Book of Communism: Crimes, Terror, Repression*. Translated by Jonathan Murphy and Mark Kramer. Cambridge, MA: Harvard University Press, 1999.

Coverdale, John F., *Italian Intervention in the Spanish Civil War*. Princeton: Princeton University Press, 1975.

Edwards, Jill. *The British Government and the Spanish Civil War*. London: Macmillan, 1979.

Elorza, Antonio, and Bizcarrondo, Marta, editors, *Queridos camaradas: La internacional comunista y España, 1919–1939*. Barcelona: Planeta, 1999.

Enders, Victoria L., and Radcliff, Pamela Beth, editors, *Constructing Spanish Womanhood: Female Identity in Modern Spain*. Albany: State University of New York Press, 1999.

Esenwein, George and Shubert, Adrian. *Spain at War: The Spanish Civil War in Context, 1931–1939*. London and New York: Longman, 1995.

Falcoff, M., and Pike, F., editors, *The Spanish Civil War. American Hemispheric Perspectives*. Lincoln: University of Nebraska, 1982.

Fraser, Ronald. *Blood of Spain: An Oral History of the Spanish Civil War*. New York: Pantheon, 1989.

——. 'Reconsidering the Spanish Civil War', *New Left Review*, no. 129 (September–October 1981), 35–50.

Gibson, Ian. *The Assassination of Federico García Lorca*. Harmondsworth: Penguin, 1979.

Gies, David F., editor, *Modern Spanish Culture*. Cambridge: Cambridge University Press, 1999.

Graham, Helen. *Socialism and War: The Spanish Socialist Party in Power and Crisis, 1936–1939*. Cambridge: Cambridge University Press, 1991.

——. *The Spanish Republic at War, 1936–1939*. Cambridge: Cambridge University Press, 2002.

Guttman, A., *Wound in the Heart: America and the Spanish Civil War*. New York: Free Press of Glencoe, 1962.

Haslam, Jonathan. *The Soviet Union and the Struggle for Collective Security in Europe, 1933–1939*. London: Macmillan, 1984.

Historia y memoria de la Guerra Civil. Vols 1–3. Julio Aróstegui, Coordinator. Madrid: Junta de Castilla y León, 1988.

Hofmann, Bert, i Tous, Pere Joan, and Tietz, Manfred, editors, *El anarquismo español y sus tradiciones culturales*. Frankfurt am Main: Vervuert, 1995.

Holguín, Sandie. *Creating Spaniards: Culture and National Identity in Republican Spain*. Madison: University of Wisconsin Press, 2002.

Hopkins, James K. *Into the Heart: The British in the Spanish Civil War*. Stanford: Stanford University Press, 1998.

Howson, Gerald. *Aircraft of the Spanish Civil War, 1936–1939*. Washington DC: Smithsonian Institution Press, 1991.

——. *Arms for Spain: The Untold Story of the Spanish Civil War*. London: John Murray, 1998.

Jackson, Michael. *Fallen Sparrows: The International Brigades in the Spanish Civil War*. Philadelphia: The American Philosophical Society, 1994.

Johnston, Verle B. *Legions of Babel: The International Brigades in the Spanish Civil War*. University Park and London: The Pennsylvania State University Press, 1967.

Keene, Judith. *Fighting for Franco: International Volunteers in Nationalist Spain During the Spanish Civil War, 1936–1939*. London and New York: Leicester University Press, 2001.

Kelsey, Graham. *Anarchosyndicalism, Libertarian Communism and the State: The CNT in Zaragoza and Aragon, 1930–1937*. Boston and London: Kluwer Academic Publishers, 1991.

Kent, Peter C. 'The Vatican and the Spanish Civil War', *European History Quarterly* (SAGE, London/Beverly Hills), vol. 16 (1986), 441–64.

Krasikov, Anatoly. *From Dictatorship to Democracy: Spanish Reportage*. New York: Pergamon Press, 1984.

Landis, Arthur. *The Abraham Lincoln Brigade*. New York: The Citadel Press, 1967.

Lannon, Frances. *Privilege, Persecution, and Prophecy: The Catholic Church in Spain, 1875–1975*. Oxford: Clarendon Press, 1987.

Lannon, Frances, and Preston, Paul, editors, *Elites and Power in 20th Century Spain: Essays in Honour of Sir Raymond Carr*. London and Oxford: Clarendon Press, 1990.

Leitz, Christian, and Dunthorn, David J., editors, *Spain in an International Context*. New York/Oxford: Berghahn Books, 1999.

Líster, Enrique, *Nuestra guerra: Aportaciones para una historia de la guerra revolucionaria del pueblo español, 1936–1939*. Paris: Librarie du Globe, 1966.

Little, Douglas. *Malevolent Neutrality: The United States, Great Britain, and the Origins of the Spanish Civil War*. Ithaca and London: Cornell University Press, 1985.

Locksley, Christopher C. 'Condor over Spain: The Civil War, Combat Experience and the Development of the Luftwaffe Airpower Doctrine', *Civil Wars* (Frank Cass, London), vol. 2, no. 1 (Spring 1999), 69–99.

Low, Robert. *La Pasionaria: The Spanish Firebrand*. London: Hutchinson, 1992.

Luis de Mesa, José. *Los otros Internacionales: Voluntarios extranjeros desconocidos en el Bando Nacional durante la Guerra Civil (1936–1939)*. Madrid: Ediciones Barbarroja, 1998.

Mangilli-Climpson, Massimo. *Men of Heart of Red, White, and Green: Italian Antifascists in the Spanish Civil War*. New York, Washington, Atlanta, Los Angeles and Chicago: Vantage Press, 1985.

Mangini, Shirley. *Memories of Resistance: Women's Voices from the Spanish Civil War*. New Haven and London: Yale University Press, 1995.

Manuel, Frank E. *The Politics of Modern Spain*. New York and London: McGraw Hill, 1938.

Martínez Bande, José Manuel. *La batalla del Ebro*. Madrid: San Martín, 1978.

——. *La batalla de Teruel*. Madrid: Servicio Histórico Militar, 1974.

——. *La campaña de Andalucía*. Madrid: Servicio Histórico Militar, 1969.

——. *El final de la guerra civil*. Madrid: San Martín, 1985.

Miralles, Ricardo. *Juan Negrín: La República en Guerra*. Madrid: Temas de Hoy, 2003.

Momryk, Myron. 'Hungarian Volunteers from Canada in the Spanish Civil War, 1936–39', *Hungarian Studies Review*, (Toronto), vol. xxiv, nos 1–2 (1997), 3–13.

Monds, Jean (aka Jon Amsden). 'Krivitsky & Stalinism in the Spanish Civil War', *Critique* (London), Spring/Summer, 1978.

Monteath, Peter. *Writing the 'Good Fight': Political Commitment in the International Literature of the Spanish Civil War*. Westport and London: Greenwood Press, 1994.

Morcillo, Aurora G. *True Catholic Womanhood: Gender Ideology in Franco's Spain*. DeKalb: Northern Illinois University Press, 2000.

Nash, Mary. *Defying Male Civilization: Women in the Spanish Civil War*. Denver: Arden Press, 1995.

Payne, Stanley G. *Politics and the Military in Modern Spain*. Stanford: Stanford University Press, 1967.

——. *Spain's First Democracy: The Second Republic, 1931–1936*. Madison: The University of Wisconsin Press, 1994.

——. *The Spanish Civil War, The Soviet Union, and Communism*. New Haven and London: Yale University Press, 2004.

Payne, Stanley G., and Tusell, Javier, editors, *La Guerra Civil: Una nueva vision del conflicto que dividio España*. Madrid: Temas de Hoy, 1996.

Paz, Abel. *Durruti: The People Armed*. New York: Free Life Editions, 1977.

Peers, E. Allison. *Catalonia Infelix*. Westport: Greenwood Press, 1970.

Powell, T.G. *Mexico and the Spanish Civil War*, Albuquerque: University of New Mexico Press, 1981.

Preston, Paul. ¡Comrades!: *Portraits from the Spanish Civil War*. New York: Harper Collins, 1999.

——. *Franco: A Biography.* New York and London: Basic Books and HarperCollins, 1994, 1993.

Proctor, Raymond L. *Hitler's Luftwaffe in the Spanish Civil War.* Westport and London: Greenwood Press, 1983.

Pugliese, Stanislao G. *Carlo Rosselli: Socialist Heretic and Antifascist Exile.* Cambridge, MA: Harvard University Press, 1999.

Ranzato, Gabriele. *The Spanish Civil War.* Translated by Janet Sethre Paxia. New York: Interlink Books, 1999.

Raya-Rivas, Alejandro. 'An Iberian Alliance: Portuguese Intervention in the Spanish Civil War (1936–1939)', *Portuguese Studies Review* (Durham, New Hampshire), vol. VIII, no. 1 (Fall–Winter 1999–2000), 109–25.

Rees, Tim, and Thorpe, Andrew, editors, *International Communism and the Communist International, 1919–1943.* Manchester and New York: Manchester University Press, 1998.

Reig Tapia, Alberto. *Violencia y terror: Estudios sobre la guerra civil Española.* Madrid: Akal, 1990.

Rein, Raanan, editor, *Spain and the Mediterranean Since 1898.* London: Frank Cass, 1999.

Richardson, Dan R. *Comintern Army: The International Brigades and the Spanish Civil War.* Lexington: University of Kentucky Press, 1985.

Rivas Cherif, Cipriano de. *Portrait of an Unknown Man: Manuel Azaña and Modern Spain.* Translated and edited by Paul Stewart. Madison and Teaneck: Fairleigh Dickinson University Press, 1995.

Rosa de Madariaga, Maria. 'The Intervention of Moroccan Troops in the Spanish Civil War: A Reconsideration', *European History Quarterly* (Sage, London, Newbury Park, New Delhi), vol. 22 (1992), 67–97.

Salas Larrazábal, Jesús. *Air War over Spain.* London: Ian Allan, 1969.

Salas Larrazábal, Ramón. *Los datos exactos de la guerra civil.* Madrid: Dracena, 1980.

——. *Historia del ejército popular de la republica.* Vols I–IV. Madrid: Editora Nacional, 1973.

Sánchez, José M. *The Spanish Civil War as a Religious Tragedy.* Notre Dame: University of Notre Dame Press, 1987.

Santos Juliá, et al., editors, *Víctimas de la guerra civil.* Madrid: Temas de Hoy, 1999.

Seidman, Michael. *Republic of Egos: A Social History of the Spanish Civil War.* Madison: University of Wisconsin Press, 2002.

Singerman, Robert. 'American-Jewish Reactions to the Spanish Civil War', *Journal of Church and State*, vol. 19, no. 2 (1977): 261–78.

Southworth, Herbert Rutledge. *Guernica! Guernica!* Berkeley: University of California, 1977.

Stradling, Robert A. *History and Legend: Writing the International Brigades.* Cardiff: University of Wales Press, 2003.

——. *The Irish and the Spanish Civil War.* Manchester: Mandolin Press, 1999.

Sullivan, Brian R. 'Fascist Italy's Military Involvement in the Spanish Civil War', *The Journal of Modern History* (Chicago), vol. 59 (October 1995), 697–727.

Taylor, F. Jay. *The United States and the Spanish Civil War*. New York: Bookman Associates, 1956.

Thomas, Martin. *Britain, France and Appeasement: Anglo-French Relations in the Popular Front Era*. Oxford: Berg, 1997.

Tosstorff, Reiner. *Die POUM im Spanischen Bürgerkrieg, 1936–1939*. Frankfurt am Main: isp Verlag, 1987.

Townson, Nigel. *The Crisis of Democracy in Spain: Centrist Politics Under the Second Republic, 1931–1936*. Brighton and Portland: Sussex Academic Press, 2000.

Toynbee, Philip, editor, *The Distant Drum*. London: Sidgwick and Jackson, 1976.

Tusell, Javier. *Las electiones del frente popular en España*. Madrid: Edicusa, 1974.

Vincent, Mary. 'The Martyrs and the Saints: Masculinity and the Construction of the Francoist Crusade', *History Workshop Journal*, issue 47 (1999), 72–97.

Whealey, Robert H. *Hitler and Spain: The Nazi Role in the Spanish Civil War*. Lexington: University of Kentucky Press, 1989.

Index